Early Buddhist Meditati

This book offers a new interpretation of the relationship between 'insight practice' (*satipaṭṭhāna*) and the attainment of the four *jhānas* (i.e., *right samādhi*), a key problem in the study of Buddhist meditation. The author challenges the traditional Buddhist understanding of the four *jhānas* as states of absorption, and shows how these states are the actualization and embodiment of insight (*vipassanā*). It proposes that the four *jhānas* and what we call '*vipassanā*' are integral dimensions of a single process that leads to awakening.

Current literature on the phenomenology of the four *jhānas* and their relationship with the 'practice of insight' has mostly repeated traditional Theravāda interpretations. No one to date has offered a comprehensive analysis of the fourfold *jhāna* model independently from traditional interpretations. This book offers such an analysis. It presents a model which speaks in the Nikāyas' distinct voice. It demonstrates that the distinction between the 'practice of serenity' (*samatha-bhāvanā*) and the 'practice of insight' (*vipassanā-bhāvanā*) – a fundamental distinction in Buddhist meditation theory – is not applicable to early Buddhist understanding of the meditative path. It seeks to show that the common interpretation of the *jhānas* as 'altered states of consciousness', absorptions that do not reveal anything about the nature of phenomena, is incompatible with the teachings of the Pāli Nikāyas.

By carefully analyzing the descriptions of the four *jhānas* in the early Buddhist texts in Pāli, their contexts, associations and meanings within the conceptual framework of early Buddhism, the relationship between this central element in the Buddhist path and 'insight meditation' becomes revealed in all its power.

Early Buddhist Meditation will be of interest to scholars of Buddhist studies and Asian philosophies and religions, as well as Buddhist practitioners with a serious interest in the process of insight meditation.

Keren Arbel holds a PhD in Buddhist Studies and teaches at the Department of East Asian Studies in Tel Aviv University, Israel. Her research interests include early Buddhism, Buddhist Meditation, Indian contemplative traditions and South Asian Buddhism.

Routledge Critical Studies in Buddhism

Edited by Stephen C. Berkwitz
Missouri State University, USA

Founding Editors: Charles S. Prebish and Damien Keown
Utah State University, USA and Goldsmith's College, London University, UK

Routledge Critical Studies in Buddhism is a comprehensive study of the Buddhist tradition. The series explores this complex and extensive tradition from a variety of perspectives, using a range of different methodologies.

The series is diverse in its focus, including historical, philological, cultural and sociological investigations into the manifold features and expressions of Buddhism worldwide. It also presents works of constructive and reflective analysis, including the role of Buddhist thought and scholarship in a contemporary, critical context and in the light of current social issues. The series is expansive and imaginative in scope, spanning more than two and a half millennia of Buddhist history. It is receptive to all research works that are of significance and interest to the broader field of Buddhist Studies.

Editorial advisory board

Tibetan Buddhism in Diaspora
Ana Cristina Lopes

Engendering the Buddhist State
Reconstructions of Cambodian History
Ashley Thompson

Oxford Centre for Buddhist Studies
a project of The Society for the Wider Understanding of the Buddhist Tradition

Ethical Practice and Religious Reform in Nepal
The Buddhist Art of Living
Lauren Leve

Early Buddhist Meditation
The Four Jhânas as the Actualization of Insight
Keren Arbel

Birth in Buddhism
The Suffering Fetus and Female Freedom
Amy Paris Langenberg

Early Buddhist Meditation

The Four *Jhānas* as the Actualization of Insight

Keren Arbel

Routledge
Taylor & Francis Group
LONDON AND NEW YORK

First published 2016 by Routledge

2 Park Square, Milton Park, Abingdon, Oxfordshire OX14 4RN
52 Vanderbilt Avenue, New York, NY 10017

Routledge is an imprint of the Taylor & Francis Group, an informa business

First issued in paperback 2018

British Library Cataloguing-in-Publication Data
A catalogue record for this book is available from the British Library

Library of Congress Cataloging-in-Publication Data
A catalog record for this book has been requested

ISBN: 978-1-138-93792-5 (hbk)
ISBN: 978-0-367-11137-3 (pbk)

Typeset in Times New Roman
by Apex CoVantage, LLC

To the most important people in my life:
my father and my mother
my brother
my soul mate, Yossi
With love and deep gratitude

Contents

Acknowledgements

Writing this research was an adventure involving all aspects of life. It is the result of many years of study and contemplations. Completing this project holds the joy of remembering all those who have helped and supported me along this long but fulfilling journey. I would like to take this opportunity to express my sincere gratitude to all those who assisted me on this path and inspired my study, both directly and indirectly. These pages reflect my relationships with many generous and inspiring people, some of whom I met personally and some who inspired me by their writings. I cherish each of their contributions and feel deep appreciation.

First to Jacob Raz, my thesis supervisor at Tel Aviv University. I am deeply grateful for his support, illuminating discussions and precious comments; I also appreciate the profound impact he has had over the years on my thinking about Buddhist practice and philosophy. I am grateful for his allowing me to enjoy the freedom of study while supporting me at every step.

I would like to express my heartfelt gratitude to Menachem Lorberbaum and Ornan Rotem. Without their encouragement and support in the early stages of my academic life, I would not have continued to graduate studies. I owe them a great debt for their unlimited kindness when we barely knew each other. I will forever be grateful to my MA supervisor, Rupert Gethin, whose writing on early Buddhism initiated me into the field of Buddhist Studies, inspired my thinking and motivated my academic path. I am profoundly grateful to Meir Shahar for his generosity, encouragement, friendship and unselfish help. I would also like to extend deep thanks to Dr. Pushpa Kale, with whom I had the good fortune to read Pāli in her home when I lived in Pune. I thank Professor P.D. Premasiri and Professor G.A. Somaratne, for their kindness and willingness to share with me their knowledge of Pāli and Buddhism, when I came to study in Sri Lanka. I want to thank Professor Stanley Insler, who deepened my knowledge of Pāli when he took the time to read Pāli texts with me when I visited Yale as a Fulbright fellow.

This work benefited from the inspired studies of scholars around the world such as Tilmann Vetter, Sue Hamilton, Andrew Olendzki, Stuart Ray Sarbacker, Richard Gombrich, Johanness Bronkhorst, Lance Cousins, K.R. Norman, Bhikkhu Anālayo and Bhikkhu Bodhi. Without the research of all of these scholars, my project would have been made much more difficult. I would like to express a special gratitude to Peter Harvey, who generously converse with me and offered perceptive comments which illuminated aspects I had not seen without his insights.

A major portion of Chapter 2 was published under the title "Joy (*pīti*) and Pleasure (*sukha*) in the Early Buddhist Path to Awakening" in *Buddhist Studies Review* 32, no. 2 (2015). Thanks to the publisher for permission to reprint this material.

I would like to thank the Routledge Critical Studies in Buddhism Series Editor, Stephen Berkwitz, for his interest in the manuscript and the editorial team at Routledge Press who guided me through the many publication logistics. I thank, too, Cynthia Col for copyediting the manuscript and for compiling the index. Thank you to the Israel Science Foundation, which supported the publication of this book.

To my invaluable network of supportive and loving friends: Vered Lam, Shiri Shoham, Dana Merzel, Orit Kahana, Erez Joskovich and Iris Toister. A deep gratitude to Shlomo Shantideva Springer, with whom I have had many deep and productive discussions over the years about the Buddhist path. I would like to express my gratitude to Daniel Stambler for his patience, kindness and helpful comments when editing the PhD. Many other friends and colleagues gave me strength along the way. I apologize for not mentioning all of them by name.

I am deeply grateful to my Dharma teachers, Rob Burbea, Shaila Catherine, Kittisaro, Thanissara, Stephen Batchelor and Joseph Goldstein, who inspired my practice, deepened my understanding and enriched my scholastic writing.

No acknowledgements would be complete without appreciating wholeheartedly my parents, who have supported me in all my pursuits. Without their unconditional love, unfailing support and encouragement, I would never have been able to choose this path and follow it through. With all my heart, I wish to thank them and my loving and supporting brother, Avri, for their complete confidence in me and utter understanding during the long years of research which took me all over the world. I have been blessed with the most supportive and loving family; thank you.

Last, but certainly not least, I wish to express my eternal gratefulness to my loving partner, Yossi, my *kalyāṇa-mitta*. Thank you for your limitless encouragement, love and support, which has allowed me to delve deeply into this experience without worrying where it will take me. Thank you for always being there and for being a full-fledged partner in this journey. Thank you from the bottom of my heart.

Abbreviations

AA	Aṅguttara Nikāya Aṭṭhakathā
AN	Aṅguttara Nikāya
Bṛh	Bṛhadāranyaka Upaniṣad
Chānd	Chāndogya Upaniṣad
DA	Dīgha Nikāya Aṭṭhakathā
DDB	Digital Dictionariy of Buddhism
DN	Dīgha Nikāya
Kauṣ	Kausītaki Upaniṣad
Kaṭha	Kaṭha Upaniṣad
Kv	Kathāvatthu
MA	Majjhima Nikāya Aṭṭhakathā
MMW	Monier Monier-Williams, a Sanskrit-English dictionary (2008)
MN	Majjhima Nikāya
Paṭis	Paṭisambhidāmagga
PED	Pāli English Dictionary
SA	Saṃyutta Nikāya Aṭṭhakathā
SN	Saṃyutta Nikāya
Sn	Sutta Nipāta
Śvet	Śvetāsvatara Upaniṣad
Tait	Taittirīya Upaniṣad
Ud	Udāna
Vibh-a	Vibhaṅgaṭṭhakathā (= Sammohavindanī)
Vin	Vinaya
Vism	Visuddhimagga
YS	Patañjali's *Yoga Sūtra*

Introduction

> Bhikkhus, just as the river Ganges slants, slopes, and inclines towards the east, similarly, a bhikkhu, who develops and cultivates the four *jhānas* slants, slopes, and inclines towards Nibbāna.[1]

This book is about the four *jhānas* in the early Buddhist meditative path. It is about the way the early Buddhist texts in Pāli conceived and described the progression of the meditative path culminating in complete liberation. It is about the relation between the deepening of liberating insight (*paññā*) and the attainment of the four *jhānas*. It seeks to offer a fresh look at how these path-factors interrelate and integrate into a coherent model of the path to awakening in the Pāli Nikāyas.

First and foremost, this study critically examines the traditional Buddhist distinction between the 'practice of serenity' (*samatha-bhāvanā*) and the 'practice of insight' (*vipassanā-bhāvanā*); doing so challenges the traditional positioning of the four *jhānas* under the category of 'serenity (or concentration) meditation' and the premise regarding their secondary and superfluous role in the path to liberation. It seeks to show that the common interpretation of the *jhānas* as absorption concentration or 'altered states of consciousness' that do not reveal anything about the nature of phenomena[2] is incompatible with the teachings of the Pāli Nikāyas. It will become clear that a close reading of the early Pāli texts suggests a different interpretation of the nature of and liberating role of the four *jhānas* in the Nikāyas' teaching of awakening.

The interrelation between *samatha-bhāvanā* and *vipassanā-bhāvanā* is a controversial issue in the study of early Buddhism. According to the Theravāda tradition,[3] the practice of *samatha*, namely, the *jhānas* and the *arūpa samāpattis,* is not necessary for the attainment of liberation. A common supposition shared by modern Theravāda meditation teachers[4] and some Buddhologists is that the *jhānas* (conjointly with the 'formless attainments') are a borrowed element from Indian contemplative traditions; in contrast, *vipassanā-bhāvanā*, namely, the practice of *satipaṭṭhāna*, is the only Buddhist innovation.[5] Thus, my primary task throughout these pages is to offer a new interpretation of the four *jhānas*, shedding a new light on their nature, their liberative importance in the early Buddhist path and their relation to other path-factors such as the practice of *satipaṭṭhāna* and the perfection of *sīla*, *paññā* and the 'seven factors of awakening' (*bojjhaṅga*).

In contrast to previous studies that analyzed the four *jhānas* by heavily relying on the Theravāda commentarial literature, the focus of this study is the fourfold *jhāna* model as it is depicted in the Pāli Nikāyas. It aims at offering a model which speaks in the Nikāyas' distinct voice. Hopefully this work will not only offer some new understanding of this central and debated theme but also an opportunity to rethink some of the fundamental views we might have on the nature of the early Buddhist path of liberation.

By phenomenologically examining the various descriptions of the four *jhānas* in the suttas (not relying exclusively on the formulaic description) and by analyzing the combination of mental and physical factors in each *jhāna*-state, I will demonstrate the significance of the *jhānic* process for liberating the mind from clinging, aversion and ignorance, thereby clarifying the abstruse and enigmatic process, by which the mind becomes purified (*visuddhi*) and awakened (*bodhi*) according to the Nikāyas. Further, by re-thinking traditional interpretations of key terms, it will become clear that the structure of the meditative path as it is presented in the Nikāyas is different from the common hierarchical-polarized model of the path, in which the development of the *jhānas* is preliminary, at best, to the practice of *satipaṭṭhāna*. I will show how the *jhānas* are intrinsic and essential in the Nikāyas' theory of developing liberating wisdom; moreover, I argue that the fourfold *jhāna* model embodies a distinct Buddhist view of mental cultivation. My argument is that the *jhānas* are the outcome of both calming the mind and developing insight into the nature of experience. The *jhānas* are psychosomatic states that allow the practitioner to further deepen insight into the nature of phenomena and de-condition misconceived perceptions and unwholesome tendencies based on ignorance. In other words, the four *jhānas*, and what we call *vipassanā*, are integral dimensions of a single process that leads to awakening. They exemplify a gradual development of an awakened awareness of experience. They are not just specific experiences, but actually modes of apprehension, modes of perceiving, that fabricate less.

Although the *jhānas* were the subject of quite a few scholarly and Buddhist publications that discussed the nature of *samatha-bhāvanā* in comparison to *vipassanā-bhāvanā*,[6] I agree with Cousins's observation that 'the topic is difficult and much remains to be understood.'[7] This is especially true since none of the studies that have discussed the four *jhānas* offer an in-depth and critical phenomenological analysis of this meditative model in the Nikāyas, independent from traditional explications. To date, all theories involving the relationship between *samatha-bhāvanā* and *vipassanā-bhāvanā* assume the phenomenological sameness of the *jhānas* and of the *arūpa samāpattis*. The common supposition in the study of Buddhist meditation is that the *jhānas* and the *arūpa samāpattis* belong to the same 'meditation vehicle' called *samatha-bhāvanā*: the first part of a 'meditation vehicle' called *samatha-yāna*, that is, deep *samatha* (peace) prior to the practice of *vipassanā*. This view sees the *jhānas* as arising from a meditative technique that aims at increased mental absorption by means of maximal one-pointed concentration, possibly on a synthetic object (*kaṣina*), that is, on a mentally created object.[8] According to the Theravāda tradition and also many

Buddhologists, the only difference between the *jhānas* and the *arūpa samāpattis* is the intensity of concentration and abstraction attained. This view is exemplified by the Theravāda epithet *arūpa jhānas*; however, this designation does not appear even once in the Pāli Nikāyas (while it is widely used by contemporary Buddhist meditation teachers and scholars of Buddhism). The implication of this view is significant. It has resulted in the characterization of the four *jhānas* as 'absorption concentration' (*appaṇā samādhi*):[9] a meditative technique that is separated and distinguished from the practice of *satipaṭṭhāna*. Most importantly, the four *jhānas* are almost unanimously perceived in the Buddhist tradition, and subsequently by most scholars of Buddhism, as meditative states that can be attained without the development of liberating wisdom (*paññā*) in the sense of insight into the three characteristics of experience.[10] That is, they are seen as attainments not relevant to the process of de-conditioning misconceived perceptions.[11]

The problem

In the study of Buddhist meditation and in many translations of the early Buddhist texts into English, the word *jhāna* (*dhyāna* in Sanskrit) was mainly translated as 'trance', 'absorption' and 'meditation'. However, it will become clear that the denotation of the *jhānas* as 'trance' or 'absorption' is problematic. Likewise, the fourfold *jhāna* model does not have the vague meaning of meditation; rather it is a technical term for specific psychosomatic experiences.[12] In modern scholarship, the *jhānas* are also referred to as 'altered states of consciousness'. In my view, using this idiom for describing the four *jhānas* is insufficient for understanding their transformative power. Many people experience various 'altered states of consciousness' during life. Still, not every altered state of consciousness transforms the mind and loosens attachments.[13] Furthermore, Buddhist theories of meditation claim that one should not produce or desire specific experiences or meditative attainments since all experiences have the same nature: they are impermanent, not-self and *dukkha*. However, in many Buddhist texts, some experiences are more conducive to liberation than others. The obvious questions are: why are certain psychosomatic states conducive to liberation? Can we consider the four *jhānas* as such states? And, if so, why is this so? In other words, what is the special virtue of the *jhānas* – all four of them – that can bring about the realization of the unconstructed and unconditioned (*asaṅkhata*)?[14]

This last question is philosophically problematic since *nibbāna*, the 'unconditioned', cannot have any causal connection with any meditational process. Yet, there must be some relation between *nibbāna* and the attainment of the *jhānas* (and other path-factors) as indicated in the quote that opened the introduction.

The relation between the four *jhānas* and *nibbāna* also raises other important questions about Buddhist notions of awakening: are we to understand the end of the Buddhist spiritual path as having a specific conceptual content or are we to see liberation as non-discursive in nature? In other words, is *paññā* some kind of discursive knowledge of certain 'Buddhist metaphysical categories', as argued by Griffiths,[15] possibly the Four Nobles' Truths, or is it an 'unspecified and un-specifiable kind of insight' as suggested by Johannes Bronkhorst?[16] Moreover, is there *any* cognitive content that can transform and liberate the mind?

Furthermore, the polarized model of the meditative path into *samatha-bhāvanā* and *vipassanā-bhāvanā* has aroused tension surrounding the manner in which the *jhānas* can be combined and integrated with the practice of *satipaṭṭhāna*. Since there is unanimous agreement in Buddhist scholarship and within the Buddhist tradition that the *arūpa samāpattis* are not necessary for liberation, the issue of the four *jhānas* is much more challenging. This is because *sammā-samādhi* – one of the factors of the Eightfold Path – is another designation for the attainment of the four *jhānas*. Thus, the traditional interpretation of the *jhānas* as a narrow field of awareness – an absorption into one object of perception – evoked a difficulty in understanding the relationship between this path-factor (i.e., *sammā-samādhi*) and the practice of *satipaṭṭhāna* (i.e., *sammā-sati*). In a crude way, the practice of *satipaṭṭhāna* is regarded as the observation of the changing phenomenal field, conceptualized in the Nikāyas, into four categories of experience: body, feeling, mind-states and mental phenomena. The *jhānas*, on the other hand, have been depicted as meditative techniques that yield various spiritual powers but which are not necessary for liberation. The assumption has been that since the *jhānas* cannot involve 'liberating insight' – the insight into the nature of experience – they are not required for the attainment of *nibbāna*. This view has resulted in the Theravādic idea that one can 'bypass' the attainment of the *jhānas* on the path to liberation. Those who attain Arahantship without attaining the fourfold *jhāna* model are called in the Pāli commentaries 'dry insight' (*sukkha-vipassaka*) arahants: a type of arahants who are classified under the category of 'liberated by wisdom' (*paññā-vimutti*).[17]

Research questions

The classical interpretation of the *jhānas* raises several obvious questions: if the *jhānas* are a meditative procedure leading to one-pointed absorption that is disconnected from the experience of the five senses, how can they be combined and integrated with a meditative technique that aims at seeing (*vipassanā*) the true nature of phenomena? In other words, how can we integrate *sammā-samādhi* with *sammā-sati* if these two path-factors are seen as two different types of meditation techniques, directed at two different perceptual aims?[18] Second, if the *jhānas* are extrinsic to the Buddhist path – a borrowed element from Indian contemplative traditions – how can we explain their central position in the Nikāyas' liberation scheme while having a key role in the Buddha's own awakening story? If, as argued by Walpola Rāhula, 'all these mystic states, according to the Buddha, have nothing to do with Reality, Truth, Nirvana,'[19] why are they described in eighty-six different places in the Nikāyas[20] and mainly in the context of awakening?

However, if we assume that the fourfold *jhāna* model is a 'Buddhist' innovation, that is to say, only the term itself was adopted from non-Buddhist sources, in what way are they actually Buddhist? What is the psychological and liberative value of the *jhānas* in the path of awakening? How do they express phenomenologically the unique Buddhist understanding of the path to liberation and the notion of an awakened mind? Is it plausible to argue against the claim of Paul Griffiths that the fourfold *jhāna* model 'does not itself have soteriological effect'?[21] That is, how do the *jhānas* benefit the practitioner, and if they do so, how do these attainments incline the practitioner's mind towards *nibbāna*? With these questions in mind I ventured into this study.

Motivation

My research was initially motivated by the questions already outlined that emphasize the tension between the representation of the four *jhānas* in the Nikāyas and their depiction in the Theravāda commentarial literature and by most modern Theravāda teachers. Initially this seemed a worn-out subject of exploration. However, when I delved into this research I realized that previous studies that treated the *jhānas* in the early Buddhist texts portrayed them mostly in general terms. Much less attention has been given to the emotive, cognitive and physical aspects that the *jhānic* process exemplifies in the Nikāyas theory of mental development, independently from commentarial perception, and within the Nikāyas' mind-set. Several pivotal issues around their usual interpretation kept drawing my attention. I slowly began to notice that there is a lack of precision in the way key concepts such as *samādhi, sukha, pīti, vitakka, ekodibhāvaṃ, upekkhā, vipassanā, samatha* and so on are interpreted in the context of the Nikāyas' theory of meditation. It became clear that many studies on this subject merely recapitulate the accounts given in the *Visuddhimagga*, but they do not advance our understanding of the Nikāyas' teaching on this issue.

Commentaries are an important contribution to any tradition. They clarify difficult issues and many times deepen our understanding of the root texts. However, every commentary is a product of a certain historical, spiritual and intellectual context; as such, each commentary expresses specific understanding and views. That is, every commentator is rooted in a specific milieu and expresses different interests. The Theravāda commentarial tradition is no exception. It was written in a different context and milieu than the Nikāyas and expresses views and concerns relevant to that point of time and specific understanding of Buddhist practice. When we look at the commentary understanding of the *jhānas*, I believe that it actually is problematizing rather than clarifying. Furthermore, I think that ideas of what constitute liberation in the Nikāyas – and what are the means necessary for attaining this liberation – were sometimes tainted by later conceptualizations.

Although I do not think that conceptual reframing of the Nikāyas teaching is necessarily a distortion of the first 'most genuine' teachings, as pointed out correctly by Noa Ronkin,[22] in the case of the fourfold *jhāna* model, later conceptualizations do seem to diverge significantly from the Nikāyas' understanding. I have come to believe that a fresh look at this model, as it is presented in the earliest strata of the Buddhist tradition, can offer a new perspective on the way the Pāli Nikāyas envision the unfolding of the spiritual path and provide different categories of thinking on the nature of the meditative process and its relation to the awakening event.

What I have set out to do here became less attractive in the current state of Buddhist Studies in the West. Nevertheless, I believe it is an important enterprise that I hope will benefit both scholars of Buddhism and Buddhist practitioners. The Nikāyas are part of the normative literature of Buddhism, and they have an important role in shaping the way many Buddhists conceive their spiritual path. In the past few decades, the study of the Pāli suttas became relevant for many Buddhist practitioners in Asia and in the West. More and more people approach these texts directly and thus are motivated and guided by the practices and spiritual ideas they envision in ways that seem to have been long forgotten in the Buddhist tradition. For that reason, I believe critical textual study of these texts – an analysis that re-evaluates common presuppositions – might be a valuable enterprise for many people who are not part of academia. This study is offered to them as well.

It should be noted that this study does not explore contemporary *jhāna* practices or the experiences of contemporary practitioners of *samatha* meditation. It is also not a practical guide for attaining the *jhānas*. It might be that some of the material presented here will overlap with what contemporary meditators of *samatha* meditation experience in their practice, while some will probably not. My aim is not to argue that experiences and instructions depicted in the *Visuddhimagga* (and other meditation manuals based on this text) are wrong, or that reports of practitioners who follow these instructions are not true or genuine. What this study does challenge, however, is the assumption that Theravāda commentarial literature refers to the same *jhānas* as the Nikāyas. The question is, can we look at the *jhānas*, as they are described in the Nikāyas, with fresh eyes, not conditioned by later interpretations?[23]

Having this last question in mind, what will be suggested here is that what the Nikāyas call *jhānas* seems to be different type of experiences; experiences that are the fruit of insight and what allow the meditator to perceive more and more clearly the nature of phenomena. This interpretation by no means negates the existence of the type of experiences the Theravāda tradition calls *jhānas*. Absorptions are part of the human experience and the contemplative life. Yet, what I am suggesting is that we should be open to the possibility that these two textual corpuses – the Nikāyas and the Theravāda commentarial tradition – might be talking about two different types of experiences brought about by two different types of practices.

Having said that, the intention underlying this study is not to argue that only the Pāli Nikāyas represent 'real' or 'pure' Buddhism. This study is not concerned with Buddhism as a religious phenomenon or with what Buddhists really did 'on the ground'. The main aim of this study is to try to understand the Nikāyas' view of the path to awakening and the liberative role and interdependence of the various qualities, experiences and attainments that this textual corpus is presenting.

Furthermore, I am less interested in the unresolved question whether the Pāli suttas were actually taught by the Buddha. Yet, I do believe that there is sufficient evidence for arguing that the four primary Nikāyas (along with the Sutta Nipāta, the Āgamas and some Sanskrit sources) are the earliest stratum of the Buddhist tradition, dated before the origination of the early schools. This argument has been presented in various studies and I will not repeat them here;[24] yet, a few words are in order.

Comparisons between the Pāli Nikāyas, the Chinese Āgamas and the fragments of the Saṃyukta Āgamas preserved in the Senior Collection provide an important source for the antiquity of the Pāli Nikāyas; such comparisons also support the view that the Nikāyas do represent early Buddhist practices and ideas.

Bhikṣu Thich Minh Chau, who has studied the Madhyama Āgama of the Sarvāstivāda in its Chinese translation, has concluded that

> [T]he high percentage of similarities between the Chinese and the Pāli versions, and the presence of many literally identical passages show that there existed a basic stock, not only of doctrines, but also of texts, agreeing in all essentials with both the Chinese and the Pāli versions.[25]

He has pointed out that the fundamental doctrines, such as the *satipaṭṭhāna*, the *jhānas*, the *rūpa* and *arūpa* worlds, the Eightfold Path and the Four Noble Truths are similar, and the wording is identical.[26]

Andrew Glass has studied the relationships between the Saṃyuktāgama type sūtras preserved in the Senior Collection and the other extant versions of the Saṃyuktāgama/Saṃyutta Nikāyas preserved in the Pāli, Chinese and Tibetan.[27] After comparing these versions, Glass has concluded that the Gāndhārī text is not identical with any other tradition; nevertheless, in almost all cases, the Pāli provides the closest match.[28] Although he points out that the Gāndhārī collection has a stronger connection to the arrangement of the Chinese Saṃyuktāgama, the contents of the four sūtras on Scroll 5 have a closer match to the Pāli. He states that if this is typical of the Gāndhārī collection, and not limited to the texts on this manuscript, we must come to one of the following conclusions:

> The three traditions, Gāndhārī (Dharmaguptaka), Pāli (Tāmraśāṭīya), and Chinese (Sarvāstivāda), stem from a common source. The Gāndhārī and Chinese collections split from Pāli. Some rearrangement in the sequence of the Connected Discourses took place in either or both traditions. The Gāndhārī and Pāli texts preserve separate witnesses to this post-rearrangement phase. The tradition preserved in Chinese underwent textual developments (some of which are also seen in the Pāli Majjhima-Nikāyas), up to the end of the fourth century A.D. when the text transported to China.[29]

Bhikkhu Anālayo, who studies the Chinese Āgamas and the Pāli Nikāyas, has stated recently that

> [T]he most important finding so far is the close resemblance of the parallel versions as far as essential aspects of the teachings are concerned. This makes core teachings found in the Pāli discourses the common heritage of all Buddhist traditions and an important reference point for the follower of any Buddhist school.[30]

To conclude, if we put aside the marginal differences noted by these various studies, we find that the Pāli Nikāyas, the Chinese Āgamas and the parallel fragments of the Saṃyukta Āgama are almost completely identical in doctrinal issues and that they most probably were preserved the Buddhist teachings prior to the first schism. Even though the different collections are not in the same exact layout, the existence of the same texts in the different schools suggests they were the common heritage of the various early Buddhist schools.[31] It seems, then, that Thich Minh Chau's hypothesis, that none of the existing versions have anteriority but all of them are manifestations of the earliest Buddhist canon, might be a valid hypothesis.[32] However, since we do not have any concrete evidence for this hypothesis, the Pāli Nikāyas, the Chinese Āgamas and the Saṃyukta Āgama are quite enough for demarcating the early Buddhist textual tradition (i.e., mainstream Buddhism), without the need for an earlier common canon. They can be viewed, however, as versions of an earlier nucleus,[33] while the minor differences reflect the different environments in which these versions were preserved and eventually arranged and closed.

The *Jhānas* in Theravāda Meditation Theory: Pivotal Discrepancies with the Nikāyas

Much has already been written on the subject of the *jhānas* in the commentarial literature and in the *Visuddhimagga*. A thorough summary of Buddhaghosa's account of the *jhānas*, and the practice leading to their attainment, has already been conducted by Roderick Bucknell.[34] Hence a simple summary is sufficient for our purposes.[35]

Bucknell's summary shows quite clearly that for Buddhaghosa the *jhānas* are the absorption into a specific object of meditation. According to Buddhaghosa, after gazing upon the chosen object (or, for example, by observing the breath), the object becomes a clear mental representation; this is an image in the mind as a vivid reality (this is the *uggaha nimitta*). This stage is termed 'preliminary concentration' (*parikamma samādhi*). When the image is turned into a concept (*paññatti*) or an 'after-image', it can no longer be imagined concretely; it is now termed the 'counterpart sign' (*paṭibhāga nimitta*).[36] At this stage, the meditator extends the sign in two stages: first, for attaining 'access concentration' (*upacāra samādhi*), in which the mind is unified upon its object, and then for attaining 'absorption concentration' (*appaṇā samādhi*), in which the mind sinks into the object. With the perfection of the latter, the meditator enters into the first *jhāna*.[37] Buddhaghosa identifies the attainment of the *jhānas* as the absorption into a meditation object. Appropriately, he entitles these states 'absorption *samādhi*' (*appaṇā samādhi*).[38] The same series of sub-stages of concentrating on a chosen object is practiced for entering the other *jhānas* and *arūpa samāpattis*[39] (which the commentaries identify as *arūpa jhānas*).

This clear-cut identification of the *jhānas* with specific concentration exercises on a chosen object, which does not require the development of wisdom, is completely absent from the Nikāyas' accounts, as pointed out rightly by Bucknell.[40] Moreover, the *arūpa samāpattis*[41] were considered by the commentarial tradition, and consequently by Buddhaghosa, as a type of *jhāna* attainment; that is, as similar in nature. In spite of this similarity, the *arūpa samāpattis* are never referred to in the Nikāyas as *jhānas*. Although they sometimes appear as states attained after the fourth *jhāna*, they also appear as part of a meditation model that is separated from the four *jhānas*.[42] In light of all this, Bucknell's main argument seems valid when he observes that Buddhaghosa's account is not 'merely a more detailed and precise formulation of the account found through the Nikāyas, rather, it is fundamentally different version which is in serious conflict with the Nikāya account'.[43]

Another problem with Buddhaghosa's presentation of Buddhist meditation theory is his systematization of the path (*magga*) under the headings *sīla*, *samādhi* and *paññā*.[44] According to Rupert Gethin, we should not rely too heavily on Buddhaghosa's systematization of the path under these headings. Gethin has observed that this division can be misleading, since it

> [C]an make it appear that much of the account of the development of *samatha* given under the heading 'purification of consciousness' (*citta-visuddhi*) has rather little bearing on the remaining five 'purifications', which are therefore to be understood more or less exclusively in terms of wisdom and insight.[45]

Note also, that this classification means that the development of *samatha* or *samādhi* is separated from the development of insight and is not dependent on it. In other words, this classification led to the assumption that the *jhānas* can be developed before one possesses *paññā*.[46]

Further, according to Buddhaghosa, the development of *samādhi* has different levels, and not all of them are required for attaining *nibbāna*. Some practitioners develop deep states of concentration, such as the *rūpa jhānas* and the *arūpa samāpattis*; others develop only 'access concentration' – a level of concentration before the attainment of the first *jhāna*. Buddhaghosa states that this preliminary *samādhi* is enough for the practice of *vipassanā* and the attainment of *nibbāna* (e.g., Vism XI.212). The concept of 'momentary concentration' (*khaṇika-samādhi*) appears rarely in the *Visuddhimagga*. Nevertheless, it became central in certain lineages of contemporary *vipassanā* meditation;[47] indeed, these lineages consider this type of *samādhi* as necessary and sufficient for insight practice and the attainment of liberation.[48] Cousins has also observed that in the Theravāda view, direct knowledge (*abhiññā*) can occur on the basis of access concentration alone, and hence, one can embark on insight practice from that stage without entering the *jhānas* at all.[49] According to Cousins, the path was divided between the vehicle (*yāna*) of *samatha* or *samādhi* and the vehicle of insight (*vipassanā-yāna*). In the former, the practitioner develops the *jhānas*, and optionally the four formless attainments and the various special powers (*iddhi*); only then does the practitioner embark on the development of insight (*paññā*). Alternatively, one can choose to pursue the vehicle of insight alone, by developing a minimal degree of concentration (either 'access concentration' or 'momentary concentration'), which is less than the *samādhi* of the *jhānas*.[50] According to the commentaries, an arahant who attains liberation without the *jhānas* is called 'liberated by wisdom' (*paññā-vimutti*). The commentaries explain that *paññā-vimutti* arahants includes 'those who attain Arahantship either as a dry insight meditator (*sukkha-vipassaka*)[51] or after emerging from one or another of the four *jhānas*'.[52]

Thus, according to these commentaries, the *jhānas* can be attained without the development of *paññā*, while *paññā* (a specific liberating knowledge) can be developed without the attainment of the *jhānas*, or only with the first *jhāna* as a basis.[53] In other words, the *jhānas* were perceived as a meditation technique for attaining certain higher states of mind that might be used as a basis for insight practice, but only if one wishes or is able to attain these higher states. If the *jhānas* are viewed as attainments in which the mind is absorbed into one object of perception, while *vipassanā* and *paññā* as insight arisen from observing the changing phenomenal field, it is difficult to integrate these two factors into one coherent path-structure.[54]

It should be noted that nowhere in the Nikāyas is there any mention of the possibility that *paññā-vimutti* arahants, or any other arahants for that matter, achieve liberation without the four *jhānas*.[55] This discrepancy with the Nikāyas' account is supplemented not only by the commentaries' dubious linkage of the *jhānas* with the *kasiṇa* practice, as a key exemplar method for attaining them, but also by their view that the *jhānas* are mere concentration exercises that do not involve insight.[56] This understanding has resulted in the misleading interpretation of the *jhānas* as twofold: *lokiya-jhānas* (ordinary *jhāna*) and *lokuttara-jjhānas* (supramundane *jhāna*). According to the Abhidhamma and the commentaries, *lokiya-jhānas* are what we discussed earlier: the four *jhānas* and the four 'formless attainments' that can be achieved by the practice of concentration on particular objects. This type of *jhānas* (*rūpa* and *arūpa*), according to the Abhidhamma and the commentaries, is not a necessary component in the path to liberation. However, the Abhidhamma created another 'type' of *jhāna*: *lokuttara jhāna,* which is different from the 'ordinary' *jhāna*. For the Abhidhamma, the *lokuttara-jjhānas* are a label for the moment one attains one of the four stages of awakening. According to the Abhidhamma, the path-moment (*magga*) and the fruit moments (*phala*) are moments of consciousness which are experienced together with a particular set of *jhāna* factors that correspond to each of the four *jhānas*, respectively.[57]

While the *jhānas* in the Nikāyas are quite clearly a part of the *path* to liberation (before one attains *nibbāna*) – for the Abhidhamma and the commentaries – the *lokuttara jhāna* are actually seen as occurring in the moment the mind experiences *nibbāna* at the time of becoming a stream-enterer, once-returner, non-returner or arahant.[58] That is, the *jhānas*, according to this view, have no liberative value since they are only the fruit of liberation (or a concentration state which can be developed, if wished, for special powers).

Bhikkhu Brahmāli, in his article 'Jhāna and Lokuttara-jjhāna', has convincingly shown that the *jhānas* do not have this twofold meaning in the Nikāyas, that is they do not sometimes refer to ordinary *jhāna* and sometimes to *lokuttara jhāna*. According to Bhikkhu Brahmāli:

> There appear to be only one possible solution to this problem and that is to assume that *jhānas* and *samādhi* in the *suttas* always refer to 'ordinary' *jhāna* and *samādhi*, even if this goes directly against the commentarial view.[59]

He further states that 'when *jhāna* or *samādhi* occur in the suttas, the commentaries decide whether "ordinary" *jhāna* is meant or *lokuttara-jjhāna*.'[60] In other words, when the *jhānas* are described as necessary in the suttas, the commentator seems to decide that this particular sutta refers to *lokuttara-jjhāna* and not to 'ordinary' *jhāna* (and vice versa). Bhikkhu Brahmāli ends his article with a noteworthy conclusion:

> [T]he commentaries' redefinition of *jhāna/samādhi* in terms of *lokuttara-jjhāna* has the effect of shifting the reality of *jhāna* from being a factor of the path to becoming a result of the practice of the path. Thus, the suttas' insistence on the centrality of *jhāna/samādhi* as a path-factor is undermined, an undermining which only serves to seriously distort the timeless message of the Buddha.[61]

As for the identification of the *jhānas* with the *kaṣina* practice (which is connected to the view that the *jhānas* are mere states of one-pointed concentration aimed at gaining special powers and good rebirth), there is no textual evidence in the Nikāyas for such identification. For example, DN III.268 describes the 'ten bases for wholeness' (*dasa kaṣināyatanāni*), as states brought about by perceiving different *kaṣinas* (earth, water, fire, wind, blue etc.) 'above, below, on all sides, undivided, unbounded'.[62] Here we can see a specific reference to absorption by the practice of perceiving a chosen *kaṣina*, in such a way that the meditator is completely absorbed in it. However, this sutta, or any other sutta in the Nikāyas, does not link the *kaṣinas* with the attainment of the *jhānas*. On the contrary, Alexander Wynne has convincingly shown that the *kaṣinas*, the element meditation and the *arūpa samāpattis* are connected, but not with the *jhānas*. He has argued that the *kaṣinas*, the element meditation, and the *arūpa samāpattis* were borrowed from Brahminic thought,[63] as a form of meditation that aims to reverse the process of cosmic creation through inner concentration.[64]

In light of all this, there are four obvious and significant discrepancies between the Theravāda commentarial interpretation of the fourfold *jhāna* model and the way they are conceived and expounded in the Nikāyas. First, in the Nikāyas, there is never any mention of the possibility that *paññā-vimutti* arahants – or any other arahant – achieves liberation without the four *jhānas*. Second, while the Nikāyas clearly state that the formless attainments do not lead to *nibbāna*,[65] there are various affirmations in the Nikāyas that the four *jhānas* are conducive to awakening[66] and that they are the unique teaching of the Buddha.[67] Third, the Nikāyas never identify the practice of one-pointed concentration on the *kaṣinas* with the attainment of the four *jhānas*[68] nor do they refer to the *jhānas* as mere concentration exercises that do not involve insight into the nature of reality. Further, we cannot find in the Nikāyas any statement that the *jhānas* are trance-like experiences in which one is completely cut off from the five sense stimuli.[69] On the contrary, the Cūḷavedalla Sutta, for example, states clearly that the 'signs' (*nimitta*) of *samādhi* are the four *satipaṭṭhānas*[70] – not the *kaṣinas* or the *brahma-vihāras* – and the Dantabhūmi Sutta, to give another example, clearly correlates the deepening of the practice of *satipaṭṭhāna* with the attainment of the four *jhānas*.[71] Fourth, the commonly used idioms *samatha-bhāvanā* and *vipassanā-bhāvanā* – which express the idea that the Buddha actually taught in the Pāli Nikāyas two distinct meditative procedures – cannot be found in the Nikāyas. More than that, there is no clear correlation in the Nikāyas, to the best of my knowledge, between the term *samatha* and the attainment of the *jhānas*, while the term *vipassanā* is never defined as the practice of *satipaṭṭhāna* or associated with the term *sammā-sati*.

In light of these discrepancies my primary task in this study is to challenge four widespread assumptions:

1. The assumption that the jhānas have no liberative value, as they are taken to be an adopted element from non-Buddhist sources.
2. The perception that the four *jhānas* belong to the 'path of serenity' (*samatha-bhāvanā*) and can be attained separately from the practice of *satipaṭṭhāna* (i.e., *vipassanā-bhāvanā*).
3. The related notion that the four *jhānas* cannot involve 'liberating insight' (*paññā*) as they are a narrow field of awareness, an absorption in which the mind is fixed on an unchanging object of perception, and therefore, cannot reveal anything about the nature of experience.
4. The view that one can 'bypass' the attainment of the four *jhānas* and attain Arahantship as a dry insight (*sukkha-vipassaka*) arahant.

Methodology

Up until now the study of the *jhānas* has been primarily based on a research method that examined superficially only formulaic descriptions, without giving much attention to other accounts that illuminate the nature of each *jhāna* separately, or to the *jhānic* process as a whole. In order to rectify this lacuna, my research began by using the Chaṭṭha Saṅgāyana CD-ROM,[72] for examining depictions of the various *jhānic* factors and for considering the contexts within which the fourfold *jhāna* model is described. I decided on this course of action since it seems the most comprehensive way of obtaining a fuller sense of the different ways the Nikāyas delineate the liberative value of each of the *jhānas* and construe the nature and role of the fourfold *jhāna* model as a whole in the spiritual path.

This study has phenomenological, philosophical, psychological and historical facets, and it is grounded in close textual analysis of the Pāli Nikāyas in the original Pāli. In using the term 'phenomenology', I do not refer to the modern philosophical school by that name, but have in mind its root meaning – the study of *phenomena*:[73] a systematic reflection of the structures of consciousness in the *jhānic* process as they are depicted in the Nikāyas, and of the phenomena that appear in these acts of consciousness. The aim of this type of investigation is to carefully define the quality and nature of the *jhānic* experience and its psychological and philosophical meaning from the perspective of the Nikāyas' theory of spiritual development. I also have used critical and philological analysis but have gone beyond mere textual analysis in order to take on some philosophical reconstruction.

The history and philosophy of a distant past and ancient texts is a narrative in which the scholar moulds meaning into the different elements he or she finds. Many times, it discloses more about the scholar's perspective, views and intellectual and emotional tendencies than about 'real' past events and ideas. This is an 'obstacle' that we cannot totally escape. The past will always be tinged by our current perceptions and our historical and cultural situated-ness. Only an acute awareness of the differences between the way people thought in the past and the way we think and perceive reality in the present can partially bypass the tendency to project current conceptual ways of thinking onto the subject matter. Acute sensitivity to the original setting, the author(s) and the audience of the studied texts is necessary in the endeavour for a meaningful interpretation. However, it cannot be perfected due to the obvious reason that we cannot be completely detached from our own personal biases and historical conditions. That is, there is no neutral vantage point from which we can reveal the 'real' meaning of a text; there is no way to arrive at an objective reading of a text or at the 'original meaning'.

Thus, I find Gadamer's hermeneutic methodology a valuable perspective for the present study. Gadamer suggests approaching a text with the presumption that the text forms a unity, an internally consistent whole, and this regulative ideal of unity can assist in assessing the adequacy of one's interpretation of its various parts. This method starts with a specific presumption and is approached with the criterion of unity, but can be revised after rereading:

> The text must be approached as an internally consistent whole because it is this assumption of self-consistency that provides a standard for keeping or discarding individual interpretations of the text's parts. Conversely, if one denies that a given text is internally coherent from the start, one has no way of knowing whether its inconsistency is the fault of the text or one's understanding of it.[74]

In this study I have approached the Pāli Nikāyas from this hermeneutic perspective. Gadamer has also maintained that the presumption of unity is not sufficient to resolve the problem of misunderstanding; in other words, one can still distort the meaning of a text. I hope this study will be sensitive enough not to fall into this pitfall. I am taking Gadamer's suggestion to be open to the otherness and distinctiveness of the text and to the challenges the text presents to one's own views. For Gadamer, an illuminating interpretation depends on openness to the possible truth of the study object. This assumes that the text says something new that is truer and more complete than what I previously believed about it and the subject matter. Bearing this in mind is a way to avoid confirming the original views and assumptions of the interpreter.[75]

When I started to write on the topic of Buddhist meditation theory in my master's dissertation,[76] I approached this object of study from the assumption that the Pāli Nikāyas present two different types of meditative procedures: *samatha* and *vipassanā*. I had also accepted the traditional view that the four *jhānas* and the four formless attainments are similar in nature and belong to the same meditation process. This conjecture was based on many publications on this issue both from the Buddhist tradition and from Western scholars. In my master's dissertation I accepted this common premise but suggested that these two meditative procedures should be understood as interrelated systems of meditations. However, as I progressed in the present study, I have challenged my own original interpretation. Putting aside categories of thinking and interpretations that were embedded in the way I read these texts before has opened the way for a fresher and illuminating reading. It exposed a different interpretation and meaning that found internal coherence where I did not see it before, clarity that I could not have imagined. Thus, because my starting point is quite different than my ending point, I feel confident that I did not simply project what I was looking for onto these texts.

While I think it is not possible to claim without any reservations that the whole Pāli Nikāyas proffer an entirely a consistent picture, I suggest that when one reads the early texts closely, one can observe an unanticipated overall consistency with regard to the role of the *jhānas* in the path to liberation.[77] I am well aware of deconstructionists' criticism that has been advocated by certain scholars of Buddhism regarding tensions, contradictions, editorial motivation and so forth which, according to their view, are reflected in the Pāli Nikāyas. This perspective is a plausible perspective; however, this is not the perspective adopted in this study. My aim – first and foremost as a research method – has been to find coherence and accord among the various elements, descriptions and prescriptions found in the Nikāyas. My research methodology set out to look for the wholeness and integrity of the four primary Nikāyas, to grasp interconnections, correspondences and resemblances among the various contemplative and meditative prescriptions and path-descriptions expounded in these texts. This was an intentional point of departure. The choice of this hermeneutic perspective is due to the apparent reality that, at times, deconstruction as a research method leaves us with nothing except from the deconstructing process itself. Many times I have found that discovering inconsistencies and conflicting views is more a matter of interpretation and hermeneutic orientation than the 'truth' of the matter. In this regard I believe Gombrich was perceptive when he wrote that 'an obscurity or difficulty is not necessarily a discrepancy'.[78] An examination of numerous and sometimes surprising occurrences of the four *jhānas* – and descriptions of what seem to portray the *jhānas* in a different formulation – aroused my inspiration and led me to propose a new theory regarding the phenomenology of the four *jhānas* according to the Nikāyas framework and mind-set.

Having said that, I do not wish to claim that there are no passages in the Nikāyas that present somewhat a different picture, perhaps more in accordance with the traditional interpretation. Yet, I do wish to claim that there is ample evidence which suggests a different understanding of the phenomenology of the four *jhānas* and their role in the path of awakening. This book is based on these numerous references. Readers are left to decide for themselves whether this is indeed the case. I adhere to Jonathan Silk's statement that 'a theory is nothing more than a structure or construct within which to organize data.'[79] I hope readers will find my theory of the *jhānas* to be a coherent construct of the Nikāyas' data.

It is my hope this study will offer readers, many of whom are well versed in these issues, a new and meaningful interpretation of the various path-factors and their relation to each other in the early Buddhist path to awakening. I also hope that this study will offer insights into issues that were obscure or problematic before, that it will produce a new appreciation for the role of the four *jhānas* in the path of liberation, and that it will rekindle an interest in these attainments as part of the practice of insight.

An outline of the chapters

Chapter 1 offers some historical discussions. It traces and examines the term *jhāna/dhyāna* in early non-Buddhist texts – texts that are the immediate historical and cultural context of the Pāli Nikāyas. It draws out several conclusions about the term *jhāna/dhyāna* in the early Upaniṣads and Jain texts and discusses the occurrences of the term *jhāna* in the Pāli Nikāyas in contexts of which non-Buddhist practices are described.

Chapters 2 to 6 offer an in-depth analysis of the four *jhānas* and educe the philosophical implication that derives from this analysis. Each chapter presents a theory regarding the liberative value of a specific *jhāna* but also considers each of the *jhānic* states as part of a gradual and linked spiritual ascension, fruition and realization. These chapters demonstrate that the fourfold *jhāna* model designates a gradual spiritual ascent in which each step signifies a more clarified perception of experience.

Chapter 2 offers an analysis of the first *jhāna* and opens with the question of whether entering into the first *jhāna* is brought about by the practice of one-pointed absorption. The chapter then offers an in-depth investigation of the nature of *jhānic* joy (*pīti*) and pleasure (*sukha*) and their liberative role. The chapter concludes with reflections on the nature of *vitakka* and *vicāra* in the first *jhāna*.

Chapter 3 analyzes the second *jhāna* and demonstrates that by progressing from one *jhāna* to the next one further purifies the mind from what obstructs 'clear seeing' (*vipassanā*). This chapter explores in detail the notion of *samādhi* of the second *jhāna* and offers a new interpretation of this type of *samādhi* and the associated term *ekodibhāvaṃ*.

For the purpose of calling attention to the noticeable parallelism between the fulfilment of the seven factors of awakening as 'awakening factors' (*bojjhaṅgas*) and the attainment of the *jhānas*, Chapter 4 takes a slight divergence. This chapter outlines the essential connection and interdependency between the arousal of the seven factors of awakening, as 'awakening factors', and the attainment of the first three *jhānas*. This is done by using a close textual analysis of what Rupert Gethin has entitled 'the *bojjhaṅga* process formula'.

Having established in the previous chapter that the entrance into the third *jhāna* is brought about by developing the seven *bojjhaṅgas*, Chapter 5 offers further analysis of the nature of the third *jhāna* and its liberative significance. In this chapter I suggest that in the third *jhāna* a specialized form of awareness is beginning to be established: a mind which is not conditioned by habitual reaction-patterns of likes and dislikes, conscious or latent. I argue that the third *jhāna* signifies another step in the deconstruction of the fabricated sense of self.

Chapter 6 concludes this section by offering a detailed examination of the fourth and final *jhāna*. Through an analysis of the formulaic description and passages that seem to refer to the fourth *jhāna* and its mental and physical factors, Chapter 6 argues that *upekkhā* in the fourth *jhāna* denotes a profoundly wise relation to experience, not tainted by any kind of wrong perception and mental reactivity rooted in craving (*taṇhā*). In this chapter I further show that *sati* is a multidimensional and versatile concept and that *sati's* mode of function in a wholesome, non-discursive and non-reactive field of awareness, that is, the fourth-*jhāna* awareness, is different from its mode of function in an ordinary cognitive process. The chapter suggests that the fourth *jhāna*, although conditioned and impermanent (as all experiences and insights are), is nonetheless further ameliorating the connection between the conditioned and unconditioned by familiarizing the practitioner with an awakened awareness of reality.

The next part of the book includes two chapters that consider the fourfold *jhāna* model in the context of the Nikāyas' path to liberation. Having developed a theory regarding the nature of the four *jhānas*, Chapter 7 will offer further reflections on the interrelation between the attainment of the *jhānas* and the perfection of *sīla* (morality) and *paññā* (liberating wisdom). It suggests that the *jhānas* – particularly the fourth and final *jhāna* – exemplify in the Nikāyas' theory of spiritual development the ideal mind. It expresses what I will call 'wisdom-awareness'.

Chapter 8 challenges some assumptions that are rooted in classical Buddhist phenomenology of meditation. It discusses two important questions: can we consider the *arūpa samāpattis* to be a type of *jhāna*, as the later Buddhist tradition has maintained, and can we find in the Pāli Nikāyas concrete references to the view that one can attain *nibbāna* without the attainment of the four *jhānas*?

Notes

1 SN V.308: *Seyyathā'pi bhikkhave, gaṅgā nadī pācīnanintā pācīnapoṇā pācīnapabbhārā, evameva kho bhikkhave bhikkhu cattāro jhāne bhāvento cattāro jhāne bahulīkaronto nibbānaninno hoti nibbānapoṇo nibbānapabbhāro.*
2 See, for example, Rahula 1978, 68.
3 I recognize that the term 'Theravāda' is problematic as Peter Skilling has shown (Peter Skilling 2009, 72). I use the term 'Theravāda', nonetheless, since it became a standard term for the form of Buddhism in Southeast Asia. I use it as referring to the form of Buddhism which is based upon the fifth-century commentaries (*Visuddhimagga* and *Āṭṭhakathā*) and the later sub-commentaries (*ṭīkā*) and manuals. It is now also evident that before modern times no lay person would have called themselves a 'Theravādin'. As pointed out by Juliane Schober and Steven Collins in a recent review article, '"Theravāda" is a term for a socio-religious tradition involving laity as well as monks, which is now known to be a modern, nineteenth century western invention. It has become widespread among Buddhists within Southeast Asia since a decision by the international World Fellowship of Buddhists in the early 1950s to use the term as an

alternative to the pejorative "Hīnayāna" ("Lesser Vehicle") and to the imprecise "Southern Buddhism", which were at that time widely used' (Schober and Collins 2012, 158).

4 From Kornfield's reviews of important contemporary Theravāda meditation teachers, it is evident that *vipassanā* meditation is central and salient while the *jhānas* are mostly absent from their teachings (Kornfield 1977, 288). The view that one can be liberated without the *jhānas* is also clear in Ledi Sayadaw's teaching. In a book on Ledi, Erik Braun cited from Ledi's *Manual on Insight Meditation* in which he stated that 'those whose perfection of knowledge is ripened (*pāramī ñāṇm̆ nu sū myā*) need not cultivate concentration' (Braun 2013, 138–9, 141). Buddhadāsa Bhikkhu has claimed that 'it must not be forgotten that there exist another way of practice which leads to intuitive insight directly. This is the way of emancipation through Insight, which by-passes the Jhānas' (Buddhadāsa and Thepwisutthimethi 1989, 319–20). Furthermore, Buddhadāsa also considered the possibility of 'dry insight' (the one who by-passes the *jhānas*) to be more universally applicable (Ibid., 61). In a book dedicated to explaining Pa-Auk Sayadaw's teaching of the *jhānas*, the authors explains that one can attain awakening without the *jhānas* but the *jhānas* nonetheless were part of the Buddha's own path (Houtman 1990, 181; Snyder and Rasmussen 2009, 32). For a discussion on the *vipassanā*-concentration dispute in Burma, see Houtman 1990, 185–9. According to Sarbacker in Tibetan Buddhism, for example, *samatha* is still regarded as an important part of the path, but *vipasyanā* is the key to liberation: '[T]hus it is said that they are complementary, but not equal in importance, with the process of liberation' (Sarbacker 2005, 24).

5 See, for example, La Vallée Poussin 1916, 163; Rahula 1978, 68; Katz 1982, 82; King 1992, viii; Crangle 1994, 272; Gunaratana 1999, 78; Solé-Leris 1999, 73.

6 See Cousins 1974, 115–31; Griffiths 1981, 605–24; Cousins 1984, 56–68; King 1992; Solé-Leris 1999.

7 Cousins 1974, 115.

8 The *kasiṇa* is a meditation object that can come in four colours: blue/black, yellow, red and white and as light *kasiṇa*, water *kasiṇa*, earth *kasiṇa*, fire *kasiṇa*, air *kasiṇa* and limited space *kasiṇa* (Vism III.105). According to Buddhaghosa, all types of *kasiṇa* can be used for attaining the four *jhānas*. This is contrary to the four-element meditation that brings only access concentration (Vism III.106 and XI.44). At Vism XVIII.5 Buddhaghosa explains that the discernment of the four elements is the way to achieve 'purification of view' for 'one whose vehicle is pure insight'. For a clear presentation of this practice by a contemporary Theravāda meditation teacher, see Pa-Auk Sayadaw 2003, 73–9.

9 E.g., Vism III.106.

10 See Cousins's statement that 'if *jhāna* practice is undertaken, it will be necessary to return therefrom in order to develop insight' (Cousins 1974, 123). Note however, that there is a concept called *vipassanā-jhānas* in the modern Theravāda meditation tradition; a term seemed to be coined by Sayadaw U Pandita (U Pandita 1991, 180–1). *Vipassanā-jhānas* is a concept that describes the development of *vipassanā* in relation to the *jhānas*, as part of the model of the sixteen *vipassanā-ñāṇas*. The sixteen *vipassanā-ñāṇas* are a gradual model of insight that is outlined in the Visuddhimagga (for a detailed description see Mahāsi 2016, 303–466). The *vipassanā-jhāna* concept is committed to this insight model, although in this context, the various insights are not described in detail. The map of the sixteen *ñāṇas* is central to the Burmese meditation traditions (contrary to the Thai forest tradition), and hence, the *vipassana-jhāna* model is an endeavour to place the four *jhānas* into the elaborated model of the sixteen *ñāṇas*. *Vipassana-jhāna* is an interesting concept, but unfortunately, the material I could find on it is scarce and quite short (see U Pandita 1991, 195–205). It should be noted, however, that the sixteen *ñāṇas* cannot be found, as such, in the Nikāyas (the Rathavīnita Sutta is the basis for the seven purifications outlined in the Visuddhimagga). Thus, although my interpretation of the *jhānas* can be designated as *vipassanā jhānas*, it is different in the sense that it is not committed to the model of the sixteen *ñāṇas* and the

seven purifications. The present study attempts to understand and interpret the four *jhānas*, as part of the practice of insight, from the perspective of the Nikāyas' teachings alone.

11 See, for example, Ajahn Dhammadaro's statement about absorption concentration that 'there is additionally a danger of this fixed concentration. Since it does not generate wisdom it can lead to clinging to bliss or even misuse of the powers of concentration, thereby actually increasing defilements' (Kornfield 1977, 266). See also Ajahn Chah 2002, 149 and Buddhadāsa Bhikkhu's statement that 'a deeply concentrated mind [which clearly refers to the *jhānas*] is in no position to investigate anything. It cannot practice introspection at all; it is in a state of unawareness and is of no use for insight' (Bucknell and Kang 1997, 107). He further emphasizes that 'deep concentration *is a major obstacle to insight practice*' (Bucknell and Kang 1997, 107; italics in the original).

12 PED: 286.

13 Robert Gimello has stated that the *jhānas* have a powerful delusive potential. However, this notion is not found in the Nikāyas. Gimello 1978, 193.

14 E.g., SN V.308.

15 Griffiths 1981, 618.

16 See Bronkhorst 1993, 108. This issue will be addressed in detail in the next section.

17 SA II.127: *paññāvimuttā kho mayaṃ, āvusoti āvuso, mayaṃ nijjhānakā sukkhavipassakā paññāmetteneva vimuttāti dasseti.*

18 One possible answer to that dilemma is to say that in the process of trying to calm and still the mind, a meditator can have various insights, such as about *anicca anttā* and *dukkha*. Furthermore, on emerging the a *jhānas*, or close to it, one is also very sensitive to small changes, and subtle *dukkha*, However, these insights can be said to be a by-product, as one does not direct the mind to this type of investigation. Mahāsi Sayadaw, for example, stated that the breath can be used for both tranquillity (i.e., the *jhānas*) and for insight. However, 'the only difference is that observation of the conceptual form of the breath produces tranquillity, while attention to its touch and movement produces insight' (Mahāsi Sayadaw 2016, 130). Hence, when a meditator's aim is to achieve one-pointed concentration on a chosen object, whether insights regarding the nature of experience will register or be transformative, really depends on the practitioner intention and inclination of mind. It is quite possible that if the intention is to attain one-pointed concentration, and if there is no interest in other aspects of the nature of the mind and the body, a meditator can just not 'see' these insights in a meaningful way.

19 Rahula 1978, 68.

20 Griffiths 1983, 57.

21 Griffiths 1981, 615.

22 Ronkin 2005, 6.

23 I suggest a thought experiment at this point. Imagine knowing only the descriptions of the four *jhānas* in the Nikāyas: would you perceive the four *jhānas* as absorptions in a particular object of meditation, just from reading their description in the Nikāyas, without knowing the Theravāda prescription? Would you think that they are a separate meditation technique, diametrically opposed to the practice of observing experience (the practice of *satipaṭṭhāna*)? And lastly, would you think that the Nikāyas express the view that they are an optional element in the path?

24 See, for example, Norman, who has stated that some Pāli text can be dated with great probability to pre-Aśoka time, while the rest can be dated from his time (Norman 1993, 111). This hypothesis is strengthened by the fact that canonical Pāli texts (not commentarial or post-canonical texts) do not mention or refer to Aśoka. This suggests that the Pāli canonical texts predate Aśoka. Alexander Wynne has pointed out that it seems probable that the Pāli Canon being was closed to materials from other sects at an early date. He states that 'whereas some of the other sects periodically shared literature and changed their canonical material in the sectarian period, the Theravādins of Sri Lanka

did not – they confined the received material to non-canonical books'. He suggests that 'the Pāli canon was relatively closed after its reduction at an early date' and can even be 'pushed back' depending upon 'the date when the Pāli texts reached Sri Lanka, i.e. the date at which the sectarian period begun' (Wynne 2003, 8, 11). He further suggests that the Pāli texts arrived in Sri Lanka in the middle of the third century BC, and states that 'much of what is found in the Suttapiṭaka is earlier than 250 B.C., perhaps even more than 100 years older than this' (Ibid., 22). Venerable Sujato also maintains that since Sinhalese is a completely different language than Pāli, 'it is inconceivable that the Sinhalese would have deliberately composed a canon in a foreign language, so they must have brought their scriptures from the mainland, where they were already relatively fixed in a canonical language. The persistence of the scriptures in a non-native tongue is further evidence of an early date for the Pali canon' (Sujato, 'A Higher Criticism of Archaeology'). See also Bond, who points out that the internal evidence of the Pāli canon suggests it did not evolve in Sri Lanka, since it also contains no references to people or events in Sri Lanka, something that we would expect if it had evolved there. He further asserts that 'the indications are that the Pāli Canon was complete or largely complete when it reached Śri Lanka from India' (Bond 1980, 54).

25 Bhikṣu Thich Minh Chau 1991, 14.

26 Ibid.

27 His research investigated in detail one manuscript from this collection, the Senior Kharoṣṭhī Fragment 5, which contains four of the twenty-four texts, associated with the Connected Discourses.

28 Glass Andrew 2006, 63–5. The most extensive differences between these two come in the Sāña-sūtra, yet this *sūtra*, appears to be unique to the Gandhārī tradition. The differences in the next three *sūtras* from their parallels in the Saṃyutta Nikāyas are in all cases rather minor.

29 Glass 2006, 65.

30 Bhikkhu Anālayo stated this in an interview to the *Insight Journal of the Barre Center for Buddhist Studies*; http://www.bcbsdharma.org/2012-08-31a-insight-journal/

31 Bhikkhu Anālayo has pointed out that variations found appear to be simply the kind of errors that are natural to material preserved over a longer period by oral means (Bhikkhu Anālayo 2010b, 17).

In an e-learning course, in the Centre of Buddhist Studies, University of Hamburg, Anālayo has also concluded more generally in one of his lectures, that there are many variations between the Pāli and Chinese versions, but only rarely, it is in terms of content or way of presentations (e-learning course, 'Purification, Ethics and Karma in Early Buddhist Discourse – Studies in the *Madhyama āgama*,' lecture 2, the 21st of April 2011, 0:13: 27–8).

32 Pande has also stated that the materials of both the Nikāyas and the Āgamas are pretty much the same, except from the order of arrangements (p. 4). Pande has commented that the 'general similarity in content appears to be as clear as that of difference in grouping and arrangement. That both sets of collections go back to a common original is apparent (Pande [1957]1999, 6).

33 In his *History of Indian Buddhism*, Étienne Lamotte has concluded that 'the doctrinal basis common to the Āgamas and Nikāyas is remarkably uniform. Preserved and transmitted by the schools, the sūtras do not however constitute scholastic documents, but are the common heritage of all the sects . . . any attempt to reconstruct a "pre-canonical" Buddhism deviating from the consensus between the Āgamas and Nikāyas can only end in subjective hypotheses' (Étienne Lamotte 1988, 156). See also Wynne 2003, 15.

34 Bucknell 1993, 387–95.

35 The Theravāda commentarial interpretation of the *jhānas* is a comprehensive issue by itself that is not the aim of this study.

36 See *Abhidhammatthasaṅgaha* (Shwe Zan Aung trans. 1995, 54); Gunaratana 1999, 79. According to Buddhaghosa, *vitakka* and *vicāra* indicate that for entering the first *jhāna*, the mind is directed to the meditation object. E.g., Vism IV.27–33; IV.88–91.

37 In Vism III.2; IV.33 Buddhaghosa explains that the difference between access concentration and *jhānas* is that in access concentration the factors are not strong and the mind holds the object of meditation only for a short time. According to Pa-Auk Sayadaw, a contemporary Burmese monk who is one of the leading *jhāna* teachers, both access concentration and absorption concentration (i.e., the *jhānas*) have the same *paṭibhāga nimitta*. The difference, according to Pa-Auk Sayadaw is that in access concentration the *jhāna* factors are not fully developed and therefore the *bhavaṅga* still occurs (Sayadaw 2003, 49). Furthermore, it seems that as soon as the mind drops the particular meditation object that was chosen for entering the *jhānas*, happiness and tranquillity disappear and the mind is again beset by the flow of defilements. In other words, the *jhānas* are dependent on the particular object one has chosen and cannot be sustained when the awareness moves to another object

38 Shwe Zan Aung 1995, 56. Note that for Buddhaghosa, and contemporary Theravāda thinkers and meditation teachers, the *jhānas* are not merely one-pointed concentration, but one-pointed absorption. See, for example, Buddhadāsa Bhikkhu 1980, 156.

39 Bucknell 199, 387–8. Note that some objects can lead up to the fourth *jhāna*, while others do not.

40 Bucknell 1993, 403. See a detailed treatment of the *kaṣina* and its relation to the *arūpa attainments* in Wynne 2007, 28–30.

41 The *arūpa samāpattis* are four meditational states. Each is referred to by the name of its respective objective sphere. The first *arūpa* attainment transcends all perception of objects of the five senses and it is called the 'sphere of infinite space' (*ākāsānañcāyatana*). From there, one proceeds to the 'sphere of infinite consciousness' (*viññāṇañcāyatana*). The next two *arūpa* attainments are the 'sphere of nothingness' (*ākiñcaññāyatana*) and the sphere of 'neither-perception-nor-non-perception' (*nevasaññānāsaññāyatana*). Thus, this meditative process is completely detached from external stimuli; it increases abstraction and produces quietude of all mental events in the mind (e.g., SN IV 263–8). It should be noted here that Bronkhorst has demonstrated that Jaina meditation has features that are similar to the four *arūpa samāpattis* and also that this list of meditational states agrees well with what he calls 'main stream meditation' viz. a process that aims to stop mental activity. He also has inferred that these meditational states entered Buddhism from Jainistic or related circles (Bronkhorst 1993, 88). For a full discussion, see Bronkhorst 1993, 30–67.

42 The last two *arūpa samāpatti* are described as attainments attained through the teachings of Uddaka Rāmaputta and Āḷara Kalama, while the *jhānas* were taught only by the Buddha.

43 Bucknell 1993, 403.

44 The model of the *Visuddhimagga* is based on the seven purifications. However, this model, though it appears in the Rathavinīta Sutta of the MN, is not common in other suttas. Also, the complete path structure that Buddhaghosa presents in the *Visuddhimagga*, has no parallel in any of the suttas of the Pāli Canon.

45 Gethin 2001, 350.

46 Cousins 1974, 123. Buddhaghosa states that to attain *jhāna* one must balance the five faculties (Vism IV 45–9) and the seven *bojjhaṅgas* (IV 51–64). However, it is not clear what kind of wisdom he is referring to. Perhaps the wisdom (*paññā*) in this regard is not insight into the three characteristic but an understanding of how to train the mind to attain the *jhāna*s (that is, how to still the mind) and also how to re-attain the *jhāna*s easily, when they are lost (Vism IV 120–2). That is, "learning one's consciousness sign" (Vism IV 122). Nevertheless, as pointed out to me correctly by Peter Harvey, with regard to the *jhāna*s, even though the wisdom Buddhaghosa refers to was not about *vipassanā* into the three characteristics, one does see the ever-changing nature of the mind naturally when trying to still it. Furthermore, the mind that emerges from the *jhāna*s is also very sensitive to small changes and subtle *dukkha*. Even if this is so, it seems that for Buddhaghosa, the *jhāna*s are states of absorption that can aid the process

of wisdom when stilling the mind and also when emerging from them; however, one cannot develop insight into the nature of experience while dwelling in them.

47 In most occasions, Buddhaghosa refers to only two kinds of *samādhi*: 'access *samādhi*' (*upacāra samādhi*) and 'absorption *samādhi*' (*appaṇā samādhi/jhāna*) (Cousins 1994–6, 46). In his notes, Cousins gives the reference to this twofold division of *samādhi*: Vism III.5ff. However, Buddhaghosa mentions a threefold *samādhi*: momentary, access and absorption in Vism IV.99.

48 See Vism I.6 and the commentary note (n.3) that explains that what can be excluded from the path is *samatha*, in the sense of the *jhānas*. This is because some degree of concentration is needed, but not the *jhānic* concentration). It seems that for Pa-Auk Sayadaw, the most renowned teacher of *samatha* meditation in contemporary Theravāda, just as for Buddhaghosa, it is preferable that a yogi will attain the *jhānas* and the *arūpa samāpattis* as a basis for insight practice as it facilitates it (and according the Mahāsi, who cites the MN Aṭṭhakathā, the *jhānas* are a way to find ease from the practice of insight (Mahāsi Sayadaw 2016, 33). However, as pointed by two of Pa-Auk Sayadaw's disciples in a book dedicated to his meditation system, 'the venerable Pa-Auk Sayadaw indicates that if someone finds, after exhaustive effort, that she or he cannot progress through the *jhānas* beginning with *ānāpāna-sati* meditation, the student may be directed to try the four element meditation . . . These practitioners would be considered "vipassanā yogis" or "dry-insight yogis," as they are proceeding directly to the vipassanā practice.' It is important to bear in mind that for Pa-Auk Sayadaw, one cannot attain the *jhānas* using the four elements, as they are objects of momentary concentration. Yet this meditation can lead to access concentration (see also Vism XI.44) and liberation (see Vism XI.117) (Snyder and Rasmussen 2009, 120). This view is also presented by Buddhaghosa in Vism XVIII.5 in which he instructs the discernment of the four elements as the way to achieve 'purification of view' for 'one whose vehicle is pure insight'.

49 Cousins 1974, 123.

50 Cousins 1974, 116; Vism XVIII.5.

51 See chapters 8 and 9 for more detailed discussion.

52 SA II.127.

53 Cousins has pointed out that in the Abhidhamma, the transcendent path (*lokuttaramagga*) must be at least the degree of the first *jhāna* (Dhs, 60; 69ff) (Cousins 1994–6, 48). This view is also presented in the Aṭṭhakanāgara Sutta (MN I.350). Interestingly, this view is not presented in this suttas as a statement made by the Buddha, but by Ānanda, who was not an Arahant. Furthermore, the sutta does not mention that the Buddha confirmed or approved of Ananda's teaching.

54 Griffiths has claimed that the attempt to integrate *samatha* and *vipassanā* into a single process of liberation is particularly difficult (Griffiths 1999, 19).

55 E.g., AN IV.451–6, which describes various types of liberated persons. Interestingly, none of them is envisioned without the attainment of the *jhānas*.

56 In MA III.256 the commentator identifies the eight liberations with the *jhānas* and the *kaṣina* practice.

57 Brahmāli Bhikkhu 2007, 77.

58 Note that even the interpretation of the four stages of awakening, as a path-moment and fruit moments, cannot be found in the Nikāyas.

59 Brahmāli Bhikkhu 2007, 84–5.

60 Brahmāli Bhikkhu 2007, 81. See, for example, the commentary to MN II.28 [MA III.270].

61 Brahmāli Bhikkhu 2007, 90.

62 DN III.268: *pathavīkasiṇameko sañjānāti uddhaṃ adho tiriyaṃ advayaṃ appamāṇaṃ.*

63 Wynne 2007, 30–7.

64 Wynne 2007, 111. According to Wynne, 'the goal of Āḷāra Kālāma (*ākiñcañña*) corresponds to the Brahminic notion that the unmanifest *brahman* is a state of 'non-existence' . . . the goal of Uddaka Rāmaputta (*nevasaññānāsaññā*) corresponds to the description of the

unmanifest state the cosmos in the Nāsadīvasūkta . . . and the ultimate state of self in the Māṇḍūkya Upanṣas' (Ibid.).

65 MN I 166: 'This Dhamma does not lead to disenchantment, to dispassion, to cessation, to peace, to direct knowledge, to awakening, to Nibbāna, but only to reappearance in the base of neither-perception-nor-non-perception' (*nāyaṃ dhammo nibbidāya na virāgāya na nirodhāya na nibbānāya saṃvattati, yāvadeva nevasaññānāsaññāyatanūp apattiyāti*). The same was said by the bodhisatta with regard to the teaching and attainment of Āḷāra Kālāma (MN I 165).

66 E.g., DN III.132, SN V.308.

67 MN I.246–7 and SN I.48.

68 In MA III.256 the commentator identifies the eight liberations with the *jhānas* and the *kaṣina* practice.

69 E.g., Vism VI.67 and Sayalay 2005, 133.

70 MN I.301.

71 MN III.136.

72 Chaṭṭha Saṅgāyana CD-ROM Version 3 of the Vipassanā Research Institute.

73 I use the term 'phenomena' to refer what occurs in the mind: mental phenomena are acts of consciousness (or their contents), and physical phenomena are objects of external perception. Phenomena are things *as* they are given to our consciousness, whether in perception, imagination, thought or volition.

74 Warnke 1987, 83.

75 Warnke 1987, 87.

76 Arbel 2004.

77 Schmithausen has divided the different approaches to this matter into two groups. One is the British Buddhologists (not exclusively), who 'stress the fundamental *homogeneity* and substantial authenticity of at least a considerable part of the Nikāyic material' (Ruegg and Schmithausen (ed.) 1990, 1). Another group, in which Schmithausen includes himself, applies the method of higher criticism to canonical texts, 'in order to isolate accretions, different strata or heterogeneous components' (Ibid., 2). Other scholars also support the first group. See L. S. Cousins 1984, 67 note 2; Govind Chandra 2000, 4. For a discussion of the problem of employing a method of higher criticism to the canonical texts, see Hinṃber 1994, 73.

78 Gombrich 1998, 5.

79 Silk 2002, 383.

1 The Fourfold *Jhāna* Model

Buddhist or not?

Prior to his awakening, the unawakened Bodhisatta was an ascetic wanderer (*samaṇa*).[1] He was one among others in ancient India who decided to leave home for homelessness in search of liberation (*mokṣa*) from *dukkha* (*duḥkha*) and the round of *saṃsāra*. These ascetic wanderers were part of a spiritual milieu that we now define as the 'forest traditions': spiritual seekers who left society for the life of mendicants, formulating various metaphysical theories and practicing different types of ascetic and contemplative practices.[2] The spiritual journey of the young Siddhattha Gotama within this setting appears in various places in the Pāli Nikāyas. According to these texts, he had practiced diverse practices with other *samaṇas* and under recognized teachers of his time.[3] However, after his awakening, the 'awakened one' (Buddha), formulated a unique path (*Dhamma*) denouncing various theories,[4] perceptions and practices prevalent among other *samaṇas*[5] and *brāhmaṇas*.[6] The language of the Buddha's teaching as presented in the Nikāyas was not foreign to his spiritual companions as evidenced by his use of known terms and accepted theoretical framework. However, by virtue of its conceptual content and practical instructions, in many cases innovative, it did herald a different approach to the spiritual quest.

This setting, in which the Buddha's teaching was formulated and taught, has prompted scholars to try and determine what elements derive from innovations in the Buddha's teaching and what elements were borrowed from non-Buddhist traditions.[7] The interpretation of various concepts and practices in the Pāli Nikāyas was often influenced by these preconceptions about what is 'really' Buddhist and what is not. This was done especially with reference to Buddhist meditation theory. In particular, the existence of two ostensible types of meditation, namely, *samatha* (i.e., the *jhānas*, the *arūpa samāpattis* and *saññāvedayitanirodha*) and *vipassanā* (the practice of *satipaṭṭhāna*) evoked an apparent difficulty in their interpretation in the Buddhist path of awakening. As a result, in the Theravāda commentarial tradition,[8] in the study of early Buddhism,[9] and in modern Theravāda meditational circles, the supposition that the *jhānas* are a borrowed element from Indian contemplative traditions,[10] while *vipassanā* is the only unique liberating technique which is distinctively Buddhist, became a predominant view. In other words, the *jhānas* were perceived as attainments which do not lead to liberation, on the assumption that they are not part of the unique teaching of the Buddha.[11]

Writing on the subject of the *jhānas*, Walpola Rāhula gives a clear presentation of modern Theravāda perception on this issue: '[A]ll these mystic states, according to the Buddha have nothing to do with Reality, Truth, Nirvana.' Rāhula further proclaimed that *samatha* meditation existed before the Buddha, and that it should not be considered as a practice leading to liberation.[12] Robert Gimello, for example, has also stated in his article 'Mysticism and Meditation' that 'it is especially to be emphasized that *samādhi* and its associated experiences are not themselves revelatory of the truth of things, nor are they sufficient unto liberation from suffering'.[13] As Sarbacker has correctly pointed out in his book *Samādhi: The Numinous and the Cessative in Indo-Tibetan Yoga*, *vipassanā* and *samatha* have been a subject of considerable controversy in Buddhist studies, 'where there has been difficulty understanding why such an important part of Buddhist meditation theory (*samatha*) has become not only a marginal practice but one that might even receive ridicule by some practitioners'.[14]

This issue has been approached in various ways by different scholars. Paul Griffiths, for example, presented a theory that attempts to resolve the difficulty, in his view, of integrating *vipassanā* and *samatha* meditation. Griffiths claimed that *samatha* meditation has a different aim from that of *vipassanā* meditation.[15] According to Griffiths, the attempt to reconcile the two methods of meditation and to integrate them into a single process of liberation is particularly difficult.[16] La Valleé Poussin has maintained that trance (*dhyāna*) in Brahmanism 'is the necessary path to the merging of the individual self into the universal self',[17] and that 'Buddhist trances were practiced by non-Buddhists, and scholars agree that Buddhists did actually borrow from the common store of mystical devises'.[18] La Valleé Poussin does distinguish between trance that does not have the right aim and trance that does, and he reminds that 'Śākyamuni obtained "enlightenment" by the practice of trance'.[19] However, La Valleé Poussin also states that 'trance, like asceticism, is not an essential part of the Path'.[20]

In his book *Tranquillity & Insight: An Introduction to the Oldest Form of Buddhist Meditation*, Amadeo Solé-Leris presents a common view in modern Theravāda regarding the role of *samatha* meditation in the Buddhist path. He states that tranquillity meditation

> [I]s not essentially different from the techniques used in other meditative traditions . . . These were the techniques (except, of course, for the attainment of cessation) to which Gotama the prince turned after abandoning his royal home. He tried them out and found them incapable of producing the definitive enlightenment he sought . . . This is why he left the two Yoga teachers with whom he had been practising and struck out on his own. The result of his endeavours was *vipassanā*, insight meditation, which, as I said before is distinctively Buddhist Meditation.[21]

The preceding references are only a few examples of the view concerning the secondary and superfluous role of the *jhānas* in the path of liberation. I will not pursue this here since the interpretation of how the *jhānas* can be seen as an integral and intrinsic part of the Buddhist path to awakening will be addressed in subsequent chapters. Rather, I attempt to rethink the premise that the *jhānas* are a borrowed element from non-Buddhist sources. This will be done by searching for the origin of the fourfold *jhāna* model in early non-Buddhist texts (i.e., the model of four successive states that are referred to in the Pāli Nikāyas as the first, second, third and fourth *jhānas*).[22] I will first show that the *jhānas* – as a distinct model of four successive states – cannot be found in any known early non-Buddhist texts. Second, I will trace references of the term *jhāna*/*dhyāna* in earlier non-Buddhist sources and examine their meaning and use. Third, I will argue that even though the term *dhyāna* appears in early Jain texts, it alludes to a different attainment when compared to depictions of the *jhānas* in the Pāli Nikāyas. Finally, I will discuss the occurrences of the term *jhāna* in the Pāli Nikāyas in contexts of which non-Buddhist practices are described. This will illustrate that the fourfold *jhāna* model is never associated in the Nikāyas with non-Buddhist practices as opposed to many other practices and attainments.

I Searching for the origin of the *jhānas*

It is evident that the search for 'origin' faces serious difficulties. First, we do not have evidence from all the relevant sources from which the Buddha might have borrowed his 'spiritual techniques'. It is reasonable to assume that early Indian contemplative settings were richer and more varied than textual evidence reveals. It is certain that some early Indian oral meditation traditions were lost in the course of time. However, this should not detract from exploring this issue, using the sources available, both within and without the Buddhist tradition. There are quite a few textual sources that record rich contemplative environments. Though not without limitations, I believe this endeavour is important and significant given that it refers to a central and recurrent element in early Buddhist awakening vision. This element has evoked much debate. Moreover, in many ways, it has determined the way Theravāda Buddhists perceived the practice and goal of the spiritual path.

A second obstacle in the search for the origin of the *jhānas* is the existence of non-Buddhist texts that depict similar states, or better put, describe what looks similar; such examples are found in Jaina materials, the *Yoga Sūtra* of Patañjali and some later Upaniṣads (e.g., Maitrī Upaniṣad). This poses the question of who borrowed from whom. It is almost certain that bilateral influence was at play in the early Indian contemplative scene. While the exact mode this reciprocal influence operated remains speculative, I hope to show that it is reasonable to argue that the fourfold *jhāna* model was originally Buddhist, despite the fact that the term itself was borrowed from earlier traditions. In other words, I wish to make clear that the theory which considers the fourfold *jhāna* model to be an adopted element from non-Buddhist traditions cannot be based on firm ground. This chapter will therefore complement the research of Tilmann Vetter,[23] Johannes Bronkhorst,[24] and

Alexander Wynne,[25] by taking into account additional historical considerations and by offering some new reflections on the way the term *dhyāna/jhāna* was used in early Indian contemplative texts. My main aim is to elicit, develop, and analyze issues that were only pointed out briefly or have never been discussed before. In this manner, I hope to establish the hypothesis that the fourfold *jhāna* model was originally conceived by the Buddha (or the early compliers of the Pāli Nikāyas); hence, it should be understood as an intrinsic and indispensable element in the Buddhist path to liberation.

As previously mentioned, some early non-Buddhist texts contain instances of the term *dhyāna/jhāṇa* in their meditation systems. However, these non-Buddhist texts cannot be dated before the beginning of the Christian era.[26] Although the dating of the Pāli Nikāyas is a moot issue, it is reasonable to date the four primary Nikāyas before the origination of the various early Buddhist schools. Locating the teaching presented in the four primary Nikāyas before the third century BCE (and possibly from the Buddha's own time), makes these texts a very early record of an elaborate and structured meditational system. From the available early Indian texts, it is quite clear that Buddhism was the first recorded spiritual tradition in ancient India that presented a systematic meditational structure; a methodical exposition of the spiritual path and the liberation process. While it is possible to posit that lost pre-Buddhist oral meditation traditions had an influence on the Buddha and his early community, from the available source materials, it is only possible to detect specific influences. That is, there are ideas and practices that appear in the Nikāyas that quite obviously originated from non-Buddhist traditions. Some of these practices are associated with the teachings of specific teachers, probably historical figures,[27] and some seem to have been prevalent in the general ascetic-contemplative traditions. These practices are usually denounced by the awakened Gotama as unbeneficial to the spiritual quest (although not without exceptions)[28] or as practices that are not necessary for liberation.[29] Since the Buddha was part of a spiritual environment, there are central theoretical and practical elements in the Pāli Nikāyas that are embedded in earlier non-Buddhist sources (such as the notion of *karma*, *brahmacariya* and *mokṣa*). Although these ideas are not uniquely Buddhist, many of them were developed, revised and adjusted by the Buddha. Furthermore, terms and contemplative elements that appear in the Vedas and early Upaniṣads in a vague and rudimentary manner became fully developed, explicated and modified in the Pāli Nikāyas to fit the Buddhist conceptual framework and spiritual scheme.[30]

The question with which we must start our search for the source of the fourfold *jhāna* model concerns methodology. What will be the appropriate method for determining if the *jhānas* were a Buddhist novelty or a borrowed element from a 'common store of mystical devises'?[31]

A heuristic method that can be employed in exploring this problematic issue is source criticism, a method developed in Biblical Studies. Source criticism presupposes that a literary work carries the imprint of the historical environment from which it has originated, and that the interpretation of a text is best served by situating it within its historical context. The main aim of this historical approach in

Biblical Studies is to detect and study sources that are not mentioned directly in the Bible (and in our case, in the Pāli Nikāyas). Source criticism assumes that the authors of a certain text might have incorporated, written and interpreted traditional materials, such as stories that were already in circulation within their communities.[32] In Buddhist Studies, this approach became dominant, even though it is not formulated and theorized as explicitly as in Biblical Studies.

The study of the Pāli Nikāyas, which can be considered part of the earliest Buddhist strata, presupposes that these texts carry imprints and influences of earlier sources of the Indian subcontinent which were circulating in the area the Buddha supposedly lived and taught. It is quite obvious from the vocabulary of the Nikāyas that the Buddha or the compilers of these texts used known words and concepts drawn from previous and contemporary spiritual traditions in texts transmitted in vernacular languages and Sanskrit. Yet, it is also clear that there are pivotal terms that do not occur in texts preceding the Nikāyas (e.g., *nirvana/nibbāna*).[33] When we do find central Buddhist terms in earlier non-Buddhist sources, there are (1) some that have the same meaning and pre-eminence (e.g., terms derived from *vi+muc/vimutti*; *manas/mano*; *sukha*); (2) some that have a different meaning but still a central role (e.g., *Dhamma/Dharma*); and (3) some that have a different meaning, while at the same time, occur rarely in earlier sources. The latter option coincides with the position of the term *jhāna/dhyāna* in earlier non-Buddhist sources.[34]

Thus, an exploration for sources that might have been possible ancestors of the fourfold *jhānas* model should start with textual materials that can be dated before the third century BCE at the latest. Although, as pointed out earlier, we do not have access to all possible influences on early Buddhism, we do have three valuable textual sources: the Vedas, the older Upaniṣads and references to practices exercised by other *samaṇas* and *brāhmaṇas* that are recorded in the Nikāyas themselves.[35] While this type of analysis is not without limitations, it has an evident heuristic value.

In his study of practices in early Indian contemplative texts, Edward Crangle has used contextual analysis for exploring important terms belonging to Indian contemplative practices.[36] He chooses three terms that are the most common: *upāsanā*, *dhyāna* and *yoga* and their derivatives. He had two aims: first, to evaluate if there is a foundation for meditative practices in pre-Buddhist Upaniṣads, 'which may have made their way into the Pāli suttas', and second, to evaluate the possibility 'of cross-fertilization of ideas and practices from early Buddhism and other heterodox systems to the post-Buddhist Upaniṣads'.[37]

A number of his observations are particularly pertinent for our purposes. He maintains that in the Ṛg Veda, only the *muni-sūkta* reflects the same type of practices as later contemplative traditions, such as those in the Upaniṣads and Buddhism. He observes that 'their designation as *munayo* (connoting ecstatic and ascetic practices) implies contemplation rather than worship of gods as their main absorption'. He further remarks that the 'naked *munis*' (*vātarasana*) might be a description of early yogis that influenced Vedic ritual.[38] Furthermore, he suggests that yogic disciplines were practiced initially as a separate method from those documented in the Vedic hymns,[39] and that this hymn seems to be the work of an outsider.[40] Werner has also distinguished between Vedic hymns that represent conceptual thinking and hymns that are like the *Keśin* hymn, which was probably written by an observer of the yogic practice of the *muni* 'who was not quite congenial to them'.[41]

Whatever the source of these hymns is, the Ṛg Veda generally speaking, presents only rudiments of contemplative practices. Neither the Ṛg Veda nor the later Vedas give any indication of the doctrine of *karma/kamma* or offer praxis for liberation from the cycle of death and rebirth[42] – the epitome of the various contemplative-ascetic traditions in early India. Thus, themes that became the focal point of yogic praxis and world view cannot be found in early Vedic texts.

In light of this, Crangle's suggestion that the themes connected to yoga practices might have non-Vedic origin and must be found beyond the Vedic/Aryan context,[43] might stand as a hypothesis.[44] However, even if non-Vedic oral traditions are the origin of various yogic ideas and practices, we have no available sources for predicating such a hypothesis or determining what these practices were.[45] Fortunately, we do have a few relevant sources that record non-Buddhist contemplative practices, such as the early Upaniṣads. Earlier texts such as the Āraṇyakas and Brāhmaṇas represent only an initial understanding of the efficacy of mind and contemplation, by associating the performance of the mental sacrifice with the external rite.[46] Only in the Upaniṣads can we find the idea that meditation can replace the external sacrifice by way of visualization and, thereby, become a form of worship/meditation (*upāsanā*).[47] Thus, the search for meditation techniques and contemplative instructions, with specific references to the term *dhyāna/jhāna*, starts with the early Upaniṣads.

At this point, a few words concerning the chronology of the Upaniṣads are in order. The principle Upaniṣads were divided by Arthur Macdonell into four classes on the basis of internal evidence.[48] For the purpose of this study, the first two classes are important: the oldest group, which contains the Bṛhadāranyaka, Chāndogya, Taittirīya, Aitareya, Kausītaki (around eighth century BCE) and the Kena, which forms a transition to a decidedly later class; and the second group, which contains the Katha, Iśa, Śvetāsvatara, Mundaka and Mahānārāyana Upaniṣads (composed around fourth century BCE).[49]

In his survey for the term *dhyāna* in the Upaniṣads, Edward Crangle has observed that terms stemming from the root *dhyai*[50] (e.g., *dhyāna/jhāna*) occur only twenty-six times in total in the oldest Upaniṣads.[51] On the other hand, terms derived from *upa* + *ās* (e.g., *upāsanā*) occur 188 times in total. Crangle's study has showed that terms derived from *upa* + *ās* represent pivotal contemplative practices in the oldest Upaniṣads, while *dhyāna* played a minor role. Since *dhyāna* occurs rarely in the older Upaniṣads, it is difficult to ascertain its meaning; therefore, it was translated in various ways, such as 'contemplation',[52] 'thought'[53] and 'meditation'.[54] This problem arises from the fact that the term *dhyāna* is not explicated in the older Upaniṣads in terms of its meaning or use. In Chānd VII.6.1–2, for example, *dhyāna* is one of a series of mental faculties and external objects[55] that should be meditated upon (*upāste*) as Brahman. In this context, it is not clear what *dhyāna* actually means, but it is obvious that it is an object of meditation among other objects. In Kauṣ III.2–4, 6 and Bṛh IV.3.7,[56] *dhyāna* seems to mean simply 'a thought' or 'to think' (*dhyāyatīva*).

Upāsanā, on the contrary, occurs many times. It is beyond the scope of this study to discuss this term extensively; however, a very brief summery is in order. *Upāsanā* literally means the 'act of sitting or being near an object at hand' and is also associated with adoration and worship. It is translated as both 'worship' and 'meditation'.[57] Crangle has observed that 'the objects of *upāsanā* are mainly verbal symbols and abstract ideas',[58] for example, the worship/meditation on one's self (*ātman*).[59] He asserts that

> [T]erms formed from '*upa* + *ās*' indicate that *upāsanā* is, on the whole, a contemplative process wherein the object of worship is an object of concentration . . . various tangible objects, in addition to abstract images located internally, are the focus of constant meditation as the means to realize *Brahman*.[60]

Crangle further maintains that 'inclusion of specific yoga techniques into the overall process of *upāsanā* is not obvious or recognized'.[61] Interestingly, Bhikkhu Sujato has pointed out the similarity between *upāsanā* – the most important term for contemplative practice in pre-Buddhist texts – and the term *upaṭṭhāna* from the Pāli and concluded that

> [T]he major contemplative practice of the pre-Buddhist period is *upāsanā*, and this practice finds its closest Buddhist connection, surprisingly enough, not with *jhāna* or *samādhi* but with *satipaṭṭhāna*.[62]

Two additional contemplative terms/methods apart from *upāsanā* are prominent in the older Upaniṣads as means for realizing Brahman – the goal of the Upaniṣadic sage. The first does not occur in the Nikāyas at all while the other functions only in an ordinary sense. The former is the uttering of the syllable *Aum* (and *udgītha*),[63] and the latter is the term *prāṇa*, the 'vital breath' (which is also recurrent in the *saṃhitās*).[64] *Aum* appears in the older Upaniṣads many times and is often associated with the derivative of the root *upa+ās* (e.g., Chānd I.1.7–8; Chānd I.4.1). *Aum* is identified with Brahman (Tait I.8.1; Bṛh V.1.1) and understood as omnipotent, omnipresent and omniscient: 'as such, *Aum* is the bringer of immortality and the fulfiller of desires'[65] (Chānd I.1.6–8; I.4.4–5). The uttering of this verbal symbol was considered to have great power in the Upaniṣads since 'this syllable is, verily, the everlasting spirit. This syllable, indeed, is the highest end; knowing this very syllable, whatever anyone desires will, indeed, be his' (Kaṭha I.2.16).

Prāṇa is also a recurrent theme in the early Upaniṣads, and it is also coupled many times with the root *upa+ās* (e.g., Kauṣ III.2). Indra explains: 'I am *prāṇa*, meditate on me (*upāsva*) as *prajñātma*, as immortality . . . for indeed with *prāṇa* one obtains immortality in this world.'[66] Another verse states that with *prāṇa* one obtains immortality in this world, or leaves this body, goes to where the devas are, and becomes immortal there (Kauṣ II.14).

Given the preceding studies and references, it seems that contemplative practices mentioned in the Upaniṣads centre mainly on the term *upāsanā*, the uttering of a sacred syllable and the concentration on the *ātman* or the 'vital breath' (*prāṇa*) as immortal objects. Interestingly, the notion that specific sounds have the power to transform the reciter, thus helping him to achieve immortality and transcendence, was not used or taught by the Buddha. On the contrary, such a practice was criticized by the Buddha, especially when used for worldly gain.[67] Yet, what about the role of *prāṇa/pāṇa* in the early Buddhist practice: is it different from the way it is conceptualized in Vedic texts?

Prāṇa had a ritual role in the recitation of mantras in Vedic texts, a role that involved breath control and rhythmic breathing.[68] This type of utilizing the breath is opposite to the way the Buddha instructs his disciple. In the Nikāyas, one has to first observe the breath, without manipulating or controlling it, and then use it for tranquilizing the breath itself and the body.[69] As for the notion of the 'vital breath' – as a superior object of meditation[70] – there is only an apparent resemblance with the Nikāyas' teachings. A small survey of the use of the Pāli term *pāṇa* (Skt *prāṇa*) in the Nikāyas shows that it usually refers to a 'living being' or 'life' in general. The term for 'breath' as an object of meditation is *ānāpāna*, 'inhaled and exhaled breath', and not *pāṇa*. This may have been because the Buddha wanted to avoid an association that the term *pāṇa* had with *ātman*, or it could have been because *ānāpāna* designates a process rather than a 'thing'.

In the 'sutta on the mindfulness with breathing' (*Anāpānasati Sutta*), the use of the breath as an object of observation might be compared to the treatment of the 'vital breath' in the Upaniṣads. In the Nikāyas, the 'in-and-out breath' is an object that helps the meditator to cultivate and develop the seven factors of awakening (*bojjhaṅga*); when these factors are fully developed, they lead to liberation. While the in-and-out breath is a useful object of meditation, it is not only a preliminary object according to this sutta; rather, in-and-out breath mainly serves as an aid to actually observing the four *satipaṭṭhānas*[71] and impermanence. In other words, after an initial observation of the in-and-out breath, it is substituted by more subtle objects; that is, first by the three *satipaṭṭhānas* (*vedanā*, *citta* and *dhamma*) and finally by the *bojjhaṅgas*, as part of the observation of *dhammas*.

In the Upaniṣads, on the contrary, *prāṇa* was conceived as the ultimate object of meditation since it was perceived as the closest physical manifestation of the unchanging principle in each person – the embodiment of Brahman, namely, the *ātman*. However, the Upaniṣads are not clear as to how one meditates (*upāsva*) on *prāṇa* as '*prajñātma*' (Kauṣ III.2). Kenneth Zysk has pointed out various practices associated with *prāṇa* in the Upaniṣads, such as fasting, washing the mouth with water (the mouth is where *prāṇa* is),[72] the offering of oblations to each of the five bodily winds, eating the remaining offering, washing the mouth again and meditating on *ātman* with a mantra (e.g., Maitri Upaniṣad 6.9).[73] He further explains that one has to practice rhythmic breathing for attaining divine *prāṇa*.[74]

Thus, as far as I can observe, the instructions in the early Upaniṣads of how one uses *prāṇa* to attain divine *prāṇa* are quite vague. It is also not clear whether *prāṇa* in the early Upaniṣads is (1) the actual breath; (2) the sensation of breath in a specific organ (the heart or the nose, for example); or (3) an abstract notion of breath as the 'life principle'. This is contrary to specific instructions given by the Buddha in the *Anāpānasati Sutta* and the *Satipaṭṭhāna Sutta*. In these texts, the practitioner has to observe the actual process of breathing in and out; that is, as the process of breathing is manifest in each moment.

It would seem to me that the early Upaniṣads share similar intentions and vision with the various 'forest traditions', namely, the search for liberation from rebirth and the attainment of immortality. However, the overall impression is that, rather than prescribing a practical path to liberation, the Upaniṣadic sages were more engaged in speculating about metaphysical theories; that is, the nature of the self, the realization of Brahman and the state of immortality. What I am suggesting is that there is very little evidence that early Upaniṣads were the product of practitioners who were part of the ascetic-meditative traditions.

The apparent lack of a detailed and precise contemplative praxis in the Upaniṣads suggests that those practices that do occur in these texts might have been the product of philosophical speculation or borrowed from non-Vedic contemplative traditions. Bronkhorst has come up with an interesting hypothesis concerning this issue. He suggests that the early Upaniṣads bear witness to two religious currents: (1) the Vedic emphasis on knowledge and the goal of reaching Brahma, and (2) the non-Vedic idea of liberation from rebirth. The details of Bronkhorst's research are available in his book.[75] Here, it will suffice to review one of his examples for supporting this hypothesis. He quotes a passage from the Chāndogya Upaniṣad:

> [T]hose who know this (i.e., the identification of various objects with aspects of the sacrificial fire), and those who worship in the forest with the thought 'tapas is faith' . . . will reach Brahma. This is the path leading to the gods.[76]

According to Bronkhorst, this Chāndogya passage 'borrows the non-Vedic aim of liberation from rebirth, puts it in a Vedic garb, and offers it as reward for typically Vedic type of knowledge' (i.e., reaching Brahma).[77] Bronkhorst concludes his chapter on the early Upaniṣads by saying that the real interest of the early Upaniṣads

> [I]s the non-Vedic search for the true nature of the self. The ideal of the non-Vedic ascetic who, through cessation of activity, aspired to become freed from the effect of activity did not find much resonance in these Upaniṣads, though, and is not obviously present in them.[78]

If one accepts this line of reasoning, it can be surmised that while the Buddha was aware of the various speculative ideas the Brahmins had been theorizing,[79] his contemplative techniques could not have been borrowed from the Upaniṣadic type of spiritual quest. If this is so, it can also be postulated that references to yogic practices in later Upaniṣads might very well have expressed Buddhist (and Jain) influences, and not vice versa.

Relatedly, Crangle has also pointed out that in later Upaniṣads, explicit and detailed references to yoga techniques suddenly appear.[80] This is particularly evident in the second Upaniṣadic group (Katha, Iśa, Śvetāsvatara, Mundaka and Mahānārāyana Upaniṣads). The greatest number of terms derived from the root *dhyai* (twenty) occurs in the Śvetāsvatara and Maitrī Upaniṣads.[81] However, both the Śvetāsvatara and Maitrī Upaniṣads are dated after the rise of Buddhism[82] and seem to demonstrate the influence of Buddhism on later Upaniṣadic thought.

For instance, in Śvet I.11, the *kleśas* and the destruction of suffering are connected to the practice of *dhyāna*, a terminology that is distinctively Buddhist in nature.[83] The Maitrī Upaniṣad also seems to show a clear Buddhist influence, which exhibits a dialogue with the Buddhist tradition. This indicates that by the time the Maitrī Upaniṣad was composed, the Buddhist tradition was already a well-known religious tradition in India. Maitrī 7.8, for example, seems to refer to the Buddhists by accusing those who advocate a doctrine that 'denies the self by false comparisons and proof, [and] does not discern between wisdom and knowledge'.[84]

Given that, it appears obvious that Buddhist doctrine and praxis were already well known to the authors of this Upaniṣad, since they explicitly refer to a notion that is absent from the oldest group and hints to Buddhist doctrine. The use of *mithyā dṛṣṭānta* to refer to the denial of the doctrine of self (*nairātmya-vāda*)[85] seems to allude to the Buddhist use of *micchā diṭṭhi* as a description of non-Buddhist views. Furthermore, the reference to 'thieves unworthy for heaven' who deny the doctrine of self and do not discern between wisdom and knowledge (*na janāti veda-vidyāntarantu yat*) points to the intention of the Maitrī Upaniṣad to give superiority to the term *veda* over the term *vidyā* (Pāli *vijjā*) that was central in Buddhist thought. It looks as though the authors of the Maitrī Upaniṣad see themselves as part of the Brahmanic-Vedic tradition while excoriating heterodox traditions that do not see the Veda as authoritative.[86] Two such traditions can be Buddhism or Jainism. Therefore, I tend to agree with Crangle's assertion:

> The evidence suggests that the ideas and fundamental techniques of yoga have been appropriated by the Upaniṣads from heterodox sources. Buddhism is the most probable source. This conclusion further undermines the theory of a purely linear development. The sudden appearance of explicit, detailed reference to yoga in the post-Buddhist Upaniṣads lends support to the theory of a synthesis of indigenous, yogic practices with the Aryan methods and ideas.[87]

II The fourfold *jhāna* model in the Jain tradition

In the previous sections I discussed the likelihood that Brahmanism was the source for the fourfold *jhāna* model. This hypothesis seems quite doubtful at this point. Having said that, I would like to make few reflections regarding the possible influence of Jainism on Buddhist meditation theory. One very interesting fact is that the practice of the *jhānas* is never associated in the Nikāyas with either Nigaṇṭha Nātaputta[88] or with the Ājīvikas.[89] SN IV.298–302, for example, depicts both Nigaṇṭha Nātaputta and the naked ascetic Kassapa as two persons who do not believe the *jhānas* are even possible, never mind having experienced them. Furthermore, as a complete series of meditative states, the practice of the *jhānas* appears in the Nikāyas only as a teaching given by the Buddha and his disciples. This is contrary to depictions of ascetic and meditative practices that were practiced by the unawakened Bodhisatta before his awakening and proclaimed by him to be unbeneficial to the spiritual quest.[90] Yet, the Buddha never made such declarations with regard to the four *jhānas*.[91]

Interestingly, Jain texts provide little information on the details of *dhyāna* practice.[92] According to Bronkhorst, there are only a few occurrences of *jhāṇa* and its derivatives in the *Āyāraṃga Sutta/Ācārāṅga Sūtra*, one of the oldest Jain texts.[93] In addition, all these occurrences are found, according to Bronkhorst, in the ninth or eighth chapter; therefore, they may be a later addition.[94] A more elaborate description of the term *dhyāna* occurs in the *Tattvārtha Sūtra*, an early Jain Sanskrit text from the second century CE. This text was accepted as authoritative by all Jain sects.[95] It summarizes 'in aphoristic form the basics of Jaina epistemology, metaphysics, cosmography and practice'.[96]

In this sūtra, *dhyāna* is divided into four types: mournful,[97] wrathful,[98] analytic and pure *dhyāna*.[99] The first two are one-pointed concentrations which may occur spontaneously by focusing upon objects unsuitable for spiritual progress.[100] Therefore, they are mediations that are connected to unwholesome states.[101] Only the last two kinds of *dhyāna* – analytic *dhyāna* (*dhammam*) and pure *dhyāna* (*śukla*) – lead to liberation.[102] According to the *Tattvārtha Sūtra*, analytic *dhyāna* is the investigation of the scriptural commandments, the nature of physical and mental suffering, the effects of *karma* and the shape of the universe and its content.[103] Note that this type of *dhyāna* seems quite similar both to the Buddha's instruction to learn his teaching and reflect upon them[104] and to the Buddhist practice of contemplating experience in terms of the three characteristics. There is no resemblance to the description of the fourfold *jhāna* model in the Nikāyas. The Jain version seems to refer to broad contemplative praxis and not to specific states, such as the Nikāyic fourfold *jhāna* model.

The highest *dhyāna*, according to the *Tattvārtha Sūtra*, is 'pure *dhyāna*' (*śukla dhyāna*) and it is divided into four varieties: (1) multiple contemplation, (2) unitary contemplation, (3) subtle infallible physical activity and (4) the irreversible, motionless state of the soul.[105] In the first two kinds, the activities of body, speech and mind still operate; the third kind is attained by the omniscient person a moment before final liberation, when all gross and subtle activities of speech and mind and body stop altogether. According to Jain commentary, there is no fall from this state. When the third *dhyāna* variety is over, the omniscient person continues to the last variety – the irreversible, motionless state of the soul. This last attainment is where the soul becomes still as a rock and the omniscient person immediately attains disembodied liberation.[106]

The similarity between the *Tattvārtha Sūtra* account of 'pure *dhyāna*' (and the other types of the lower *dhyānas*) and the description of the *jhānas* in the Pāli Nikāyas is not evident. The only apparent resemblance between the two is the reference to *vitarka* and *vicāra*[107] in the first two varieties of 'pure *dhyāna*'. The *Tattvārtha Sūtra* describes a process in which the meditator contemplates the multiplicity of objects (this is when both *vitarka* and *vicāra* operate) and then contemplates the oneness with no change of object (at this stage *vicāra* is absent). It is noteworthy that although these two terms appear in the first *jhāna*, the *Tattvārtha Sūtra* account resembles more closely the Buddhist practice of observation (*anupassana*) and investigation of phenomena (*dhamma-vicaya*). Lastly, according to the *Tattvārtha Sūtra* and its commentaries, the omniscient person who attains the third variety of *śukla dhyāna* does not return to active life, since the attainment of this meditation ends with disembodied liberation (*ayoga kevalī*) of the fourth variety.

In contrast to this depiction, other attainments occur when a person is still alive and still allow such a realized person to return to normal activity. These are the attainment of the *jhānas* and even the attainment of cessation (*nirodha-samapatti*), which might be compared to the attainment of complete stillness. Bronkhorst has offered an interesting observation regarding the last two stages of 'pure *dhyāna*'. He points out that these two stages are described in physical terms rather than mental terms.[108] This is contrary to the fourth *jhāna* (and the 'attainment of cessation'), which is characterized in terms of mental qualities – the purification of *sati* and *upekkhā* (and the cessation of perception and feeling in the case of the attainment of cessation).

What I would like to suggest in light of the preceding is that the identification of the *jhānas* with Jain *dhyānas* is problematic; the suggestion that the Jains are the originators of the fourfold model in the Nikāyas is even more problematic. In other words, when we consider the preceding, the identification of the *jhānas* with Jain *dhyānas* has no firm basis; moreover, all Jain accounts of *dhyāna* practice are later than the Pāli Nikāyas (and never associated in the Pāli suttas with the type of spiritual praxis presented by the Jains).

It is interesting to mention in this regard Jaini's observation that the correlation between the *śukla dhyāna* and the precise mechanism whereby the passions are negated (the *summum Bonum* of the Jain spiritual path) is not fully explained by Jain texts.[109] In light of this, it is possible that Jain thinkers, who had contact with Buddhist ideas from the origination of Buddhism, were influenced by these ideas and practices and thereby incorporated a terminology that was central to early Buddhist texts for polemical purposes. The word 'influence' in this regard should be understood as referring to the idea that central and innovative ideas (and terms) of a rival religious system might stimulate various reactions by its opponents. One reaction can be to create a philosophical negation of the opponent's idea. This reaction is exemplified by what the Buddha did with regard to the idea of purification by water.[110] Another reaction is to consciously ignore it. This tactic can cause rival religious systems to remodel their opponent's idea to fit their own understanding of the spiritual path, even at the expense of generating some ambiguities. A good example of the latter in Buddhist thought is the use of the term *āsava*. The term *āsava* is a central Jain term that occurs frequently in the Nikāyas[111] even though it seems incompatible with Buddhist understanding of the nature of the impure mind. The term *āsava* derives from the verb *ā+srū* and means 'flowing in' or 'flowing out'. In Jain philosophy it is used to describe the karmic matter that 'flows in' when one performs actions; as a result, it sticks to the soul and prevents the soul to be pure and liberated. Somaratne has pointed out that it is quite probable that the arahant's depiction as *āsava's* free, represents the Jain notion of a liberated person. This is contrary to the term *saṃyojana*, which is purely a Buddhist categorization and is compatible with Buddhist understanding of bondage and liberation.

The preceding example shows how remodelling the opponent's idea to fit another religious system can be seen as a tactic for responding to an adversary's challenges. This can be done by adopting central terms from other religious traditions, moulding them into a different conceptual system and thereby giving them a new meaning.[112] I would suggest that the term *dhyāna*, which was central in early Buddhist awakening scheme, was adopted and re-moulded by the Jains and later on by other yogic traditions.

III Some historical considerations

I would like to address one further historical consideration to support the theory that the fourfold *jhāna* model is a Buddhist innovation. It is most likely that Buddhism wielded great influence in pre-Common Era India. This would account for the term *jhāna*, a central term in early Buddhist texts, having become prominent in other yogic systems. I will propose that the lack of early evidence for the existence of the fourfold *jhāna* model in non-Buddhist traditions that suddenly became central in later yogic texts (in various adaptations) is due to the influence of Buddhist meditation theory. As every inquiry has its limits, I shall confine mine to some reflections and provisional suggestions.

After the rapid growth of Buddhism in early India, and up to the revival of Hinduism during the Gupta dynasty (fourth to sixth centuries CE) and the decline of Buddhism in India (from the twelfth century CE), it is reasonable to assume that Buddhism became dominant enough to affect other religious traditions. When Aśoka became the propagator of Buddhism (269–232 BCE), it seems likely that the Buddhist community already had reached a considerable size and was influential. Indeed, it would be hard to imagine why an emperor would have chosen as his personal religious belief an unknown and un-influential religious tradition, to propagate to his people. It has been suggested by Romila Thapar that Aśoka's choice of propagating the Dhamma was the result of looking for unifying principles that could be accepted by any religious sect.[113] Although Aśoka did not intend to force Buddhism as his state religion, it seems dubious to ignore the political significance of choosing publicly one religious tradition over others, including the use of distinct Buddhist ideas and formulations in public monuments.[114] Note Romila Thapar's observation that at the time of Aśoka:

> Buddhism in the context of society as it was then, was not just another religion. It was the result of a widespread movement towards change which affected many aspects of life from personal beliefs to social ideas. Any statesman with an understanding of the period would have had to come to terms with such an important new development.[115]

Thapar also asserts three reasons that Buddhism was an appealing religious movement in early India: (1) Buddhists demanded relaxation of the social rigidity, a position that had a tremendous appeal among lower sections of the caste system; (2) the conception of the 'middle way' that 'propagated a code of ethics which took into consideration the practical necessities of daily life' made it accessible to those who could not become ascetics; and (3) there was an element of democracy in the organization of Buddhist monasticism.[116] Thus, Aśoka's choice to become a Buddhist,[117] apart from emulating his father and grandfather who chose non-Brahamanic traditions as their personal beliefs,[118] seems to exemplify his political shrewdness. If Thapar is correct, and Buddhism was already a well-known and influential tradition at the time of his accession, Aśoka must have been quite astute in his political observation, using the power of the new religious movement for his own agendas.

It is most likely that Aśoka acted as patron of the Buddhist tradition. Royal patronage meant substantial constitutional support, which must have helped the Buddhist tradition to become even more widespread. The Aśokan Schism Edict from Allahabad, Sañci and Sarnath exemplifies this active participation of Aśoka with issues concerning the Buddhist saṅgha. This edict was the subject of considerable debate, a debate whether it describes Aśoka's active part against a schism in the saṅgha (that, according to the Theravāda sources, led to the origination of the Theravada School) or, as suggested by Bechert and reinforced recently by Herman Tieken, represents his concern with divisions within local individual saṅghas.[119] In either case, it shows that the emperor had an interest in regulating the Buddhist saṅgha. Herman Tieken has argued in his article that Aśoka's concern with the possibility of a split of local saṅghas into two separate communities shows that he feared the saṅgha's split would interfere with the smooth flow of trade.[120] This conclusion supports the assumption that by the time of Aśoka's reign, the Buddhist communities around India (monastics and lay) had been important and influential enough to cause the emperor concern regarding splits within local Buddhist communities. If the Buddhist tradition was not widespread and influential, it would be hard to imagine why Aśoka was actively engaged with the saṅgha's internal affairs.[121]

If this hypothesis is correct, it can be assumed that the new religious movement had an impact on other ascetics and contemplative traditions as well, especially since it presented systematic meditational praxis and a new vision of the spiritual path.

Further, the growth of Buddhism meant more monastics and lay support. Monks and nuns who lived in monasteries most likely travelled from one place to the other. Wandering in various places, they would have encountered other contemplatives and ascetics, sharing their teachings and practices. It is reasonable to suggest that Buddhist practices and ideas were spread increasingly in various contemplative and philosophical environments, especially since they were not confined to a geographical area, specific language or social class. Spreading all around North India, it very well would have been adopted and adapted or created objection and reaction.

What I am suggesting is that, to a greater extent than has been previously assumed, Buddhist contemplative practices had a greater impact on other meditation traditions, though not exclusively or unilaterally.[122] This seems especially true when referring to elements that have an important and recurrent role in the Nikāyas' (and the Āgamas') awakening scheme such as the fourfold *jhāna* model. It may be deduced that this model was adopted and adapted by other contemplative traditions, as a reaction to the innovative Buddhist vision of the spiritual path. Bronkhorst has correctly observed that certain elements in Buddhist *jhāna* 'could only be made to fit clumsily' in non-Buddhist systems.[123] Not only did this term presented a unique Buddhist view on the path to liberation, it also was a revolutionary notion on the nature of awakening. However, after the rise of Buddhism, the wide usage of the term *dhyāna* indicates that Buddhist meditation theory was an important reference point to early Indian contemplative traditions.

The principle I am trying to illustrate is that the centrality and importance of the term *dhyāna* in the teaching of the growing Buddhist tradition brought about its recurrent usage by other contemplative traditions; that is, competing traditions needed to respond to the challenges presented by Buddhism. This was done by using Buddhist language, while moulding it to fit into their various conceptual and contemplative systems (just as the Buddha did). I disagree with Bronkhorst's assertion that 'the main stream of ancient meditation largely lived a life of its own, showing developments both theoretical and practical which could be explained without reference to Buddhism'.[124] Although Bronkhorst is correct when he noted that the influence of Buddhist meditation was terminological, I believe that it was not 'merely terminological'.[125] The adaptation of a pivotal and central Buddhist term by non-Buddhist traditions meant that these traditions found Buddhist praxis and conceptual framework challenging and perhaps even threatening; this was especially the case since Buddhism was spreading all over the Indian subcontinent.

Thus, although the relationship between Buddhism and other contemplative traditions was reciprocal, it might have been different than usually envisioned. For example, it might be, as pointed out by Bronkhorst, that the notion of 'liberating insight' (*paññā*) as a specific content was not originally Buddhist but an adaptation of the non-Buddhist idea, specifically the idea that 'liberation in life is always accompanied by an explicit liberating "insight"'.[126] According to Bronkhorst, explicit descriptions of the content of liberating insight (such as the Four Noble Truths and the twelve links of dependent origination) were added by Buddhists later on under the influence of mainstream meditation.[127] Thus, the notion of liberation as the realization of specific 'knowledge' (*paññā*) might have been a non-Buddhist idea initially, while the original Buddhist vision of liberation included the attainment of the *jhānas*. These stood as attainments that have no specific content. *Paññā*, in this vision of liberation, could have been something quite different than the realization of some specific conceptual insight, especially at the completion of the spiritual path. This issue will be further elaborated in subsequent chapters.

IV 'unworthy *jhāna*' in the Pāli Nikāyas

Turning to the Pāli Nikāyas, I wish to examine closely the occurrences of the term *jhāna* in a context which refers to practices undertaken by the unawakened Bodhisatta and in reference of what is designated as 'unworthy *jhāna*'.

In the *Mahāsaccaka Sutta* of the MN, the Buddha describes his ascetic practices before his awakening. Several of these practices include 'meditating a meditation without breathing' (*appāṇakaṃ-yeva jhānaṃ jhāyeyyaṃ*). This practice, of actively stopping the in-and-out breath, is something that the Buddha mentions only in reference to his unfruitful practices before his awakening. What is interesting for us in this depiction is the occurrence of the term *jhāna*. One might claim that this proves that *jhānas* are non-Buddhist practices that were first declared as unbeneficial, and thus, they were incorporated later on by the Buddha or compilers of these texts who advocated this practice. This would mean they cannot be considered as a necessary practice for attaining liberation. Yet, note that in this context, the term *jhāna* is associated with a specific practice, namely, the 'stopping of in-and-out breath' (*assāsa-passāse uparundhiṃ*). Here the Buddha names this practice specifically as *appāṇakaṃ jhānaṃ*.

Apart from the *Mahāsaccaka Sutta*, the term *jhāna* appears in its singular form also in MN III.13–4. There, Ānanda explains to the brahmin Vassakāra that 'the Blessed One did not praise all [types] of *jhānas*' (*so bhagavā sabbaṃ jhānaṃ na vaṇṇesi*). He explains that *jhāna* in which the mind has the hindrances (*nīvaraṇa*) and is without understanding as to the escape from theses hindrances are a type of *jhāna* that the Blessed One did not praise. In these misdirected states, 'one meditates, premeditates, out-meditates and mis-meditates' (*jhāyati, pajjhāyati, nijjhāyati, apajjhāyati*).

It is unclear what kind of *jhāna* the Blessed One did not praise, and there is no specific description of the practice. What is evident, though, is that this type of *jhāna* is a state that contains the *nīvaraṇas* – the hindrances that are specifically declared absent in the description of the fourfold *jhāna* model. It could be that the use of the term *jhāna* in the singular, in this context, refers to the practice of *appāṇakaṃ jhānaṃ* which is mentioned above. Thus, it seems that the Buddha used the word *jhāna* generically only rarely, and in cases where the audience probably was familiar with it as a technical term for some kind of meditative practice.

However, it should be noted that the fourfold *jhāna* model, contrary to the occurrences of the term *jhāna* in singular, does not appear with the verb from the same root (i.e., *jhāyeyyaṃ/jhāyati, pajjhāyati, nijjhāyati, apajjhāyati*). I would like to suggest that the use of the verb from the same root, in connection to the term *jhāna* in these occurrences, indicates an active meditative practice of some kind. However, in the description of the fourfold *jhāna* model, the depiction is almost always the same and quite different than the above: one just 'enters and abides' (*upasampajja viharati*) in the *jhānas*. In other words, the fourfold *jhāna* model is a description of an attainment – the fruit of a previous practice – and not a specific practice by itself.

Given the preceding we can conclude that apart from the aforementioned occurrences, the *jhānas* are mostly associated with depictions of awakening (especially those of the Buddha's awakening) and always as a model of four gradual states. They (1) are never referred to as *appāṇakaṃ jhānaṃ*; (2) always occur with adjectives that indicate their number in the fourfold model, that is, *paṭhamaṃ, dutiyaṃ, tatiyaṃ* and *catutthaṃ*; and (3) are never associated with a verb from the same root.

V Conclusion

One common feature of the Buddha's teaching was his use of known terms from the Vedic/Upaniṣadic/Śramaṇic traditions, while changing their meaning to suit his own teaching. There are many examples of this technique, and I will not elaborate here. Suffice it to mention terms such as *kamma*,[128] *brahmacariya*[129] and *Brahmā*,[130] which express these practices in the Nikāyas. It seems odd that this obvious feature of the Buddha's teaching technique was completely overlooked with regard to the use of the term *jhāna*. Even if this term was used widely in non-Buddhist traditions with whatever meaning (something which seems doubtful in light of the available textual evidence), it is very reasonable to assume that the Buddha did the same thing that he did with other pivotal terms: he gave it a different meaning.[131]

It might appear implausible to assert that any new spiritual tradition has not borrowed, revised and improved spiritual 'techniques' and religious concepts that already existed and circulated in some form or another in previous and contemporary religious traditions. However, we have seen that (1) the term *dhyāna* rarely appears in pre-Buddhist texts; (2) when it does appear, it has a very vague meaning while having a marginal role compared to other techniques/terms; (3) while it seems that non-Buddhist texts present a similar *jhānic* model to that of the Pāli Nikāyas, in a closer analysis, it is only an apparent resemblance. Thus, these points suggest that the *jhānas*, in the format of a fourfold model, are uniquely Buddhist, even though the term itself was adopted from the Indian 'pool' of contemplative terms. In other words, after adopting a term that had little importance in other contemplative traditions, the Buddha redefined and used it in accordance with his own understanding of the spiritual path.

Notes

1 The term *śramaṇa* from the root *śram*, 'to exert', occurs once in the Upaniṣads. It occurs in the Bṛhadāraṇyaka Upaniṣad IV.3.22, where it is coupled with the term *tāpasa* from the root *tap*, 'to warm'; this term can be translated as 'an ascetic' or as '[a religious practitioner who] practices austerities'. For a detailed examination of the term *śramana* in early Indian materials, see Olivelle 1993, 11–15.

2 E.g., MN I.242–3; MN I.77–82.

3 E.g., MN I.163–6.

4 DN I.65–95 gives a description of six views of other *śramaṇa* traditions at the time of the Buddha.

5 E.g., MN I.92.

6 A good example is the *Brahmajāla Sutta* of the DN and MN I.39; MN I.242ff; MN I.514–21; DN I.282; DN I.238; SN I.29; SN IV.118; SN V.230; AN II.200–1.

7 Pratap Chandra has mapped the views of scholars about ancient Indian philosophies to those who considered the Buddha's teaching to have been influenced by the Upaniṣads, and those who 'appear keen to establish the "supremacy" of the Upaniṣads' (Pratap 1971, 319).

8 See, for example, MA III.188 and DA II.511 where it is said that one can be liberated without attaining the *jhānas*, as a *paññā-vimutti* arahant. There are five types of *paññā-vimutti* Arahants according to this commentary – four types are those who reach Arahantship on the basis of any one of the four *jhānas*, and the fifth one is the 'dry insight' (*sukkha-vipassaka*), who attains Arahantship without attaining the *jhānas* at all. See also Paṭisambhidāmagga (Paṭis II, 92–103).

9 Gimello 1978, 181, 184; Griffiths 1981, 614; King 1992, viii; Crangle 1994, 272; Premasiri 2003, 164.

10 See La Vallée Poussin 1936/7, 230. He however, sees the four *arūpa* states as demonstrating Buddhist originality in meditative techniques, since they do not appear in non-Buddhist sources (La Vallée Poussin 1936/7, 225).

11 Gunaratana 1999, 78. However, in more recent article Gunaratana's view seems to have changed. In this essay he advocates practicing *vipassanā* in the *jhānas*. His presentation on the *jhānas* in this essay does not rely on the *Visuddhimagga* as in his other publications on this subject (Gunaratana 2012).

12 Rahula 1978, 68.

13 Gimello 1978, 184.

14 Sarbacker 2005, 90.

15 Griffiths 1999, 156 n55.

16 Griffiths 1999, 19.

17 La Vallée Poussin 1916, 160.

18 La Vallée Poussin 1916, 163.

19 La Vallée Poussin 1916, 162.

20 La Vallée Poussin 1916, 161.

21 Solé-Leris 1999, 73.

22 *Paṭhamaṃ, dutiyaṃ, tatiyaṃ* and *catutthaṃ jhānaṃ*.

23 Vetter 1988.

24 Bronkhorst 1993.

25 Wynne 2007.

26 See Dundas 1985, 164; Jaini 1990, 52–3; Basham 1996, 289; Bhattacharyya 1999, 37–8. As for the *Yoga Sūtra* of Patañjali, most scholars believe that there were several 'Patañjalis' in the history of Indian thought; most agree that the one who wrote the *Yoga Sūtra* (YS) lived around the second or third century CE (Whicher 1998, 1). However, there are scholars who date the YS earlier. Radhakrishnan and Moore, for example, have dated Patañjali at the second century BCE, and Flood has dated Patañjali between 100 BCE and 500 CE (Radhakrishnan and Moore 1957, 453; Flood 1998, 96). For a detailed discussion, see Puri 1990, 3–11. See also Cousins, who has maintained that there were many influences from Buddhist sources on the *Yoga Sūtra*

(Cousins1992, 137). The Maitrī Upaniṣad, which exhibits similar elements, is dated by Macdonell, Winternitz and Deussen to be around the first century CE (Deussen 1966, 271; Macdonell 1971, 197; Winternitz 1981, 218–20).

27 Wynne has offered a very convincing argument for the historicity of Uddaka Rāmaputta and Āḷāra Kālāma. Wynne 2003, 23–8.

28 In MN II.225, the Buddha permits the practice of asceticism for a certain purpose. But when this purpose is achieved, one should not continue to exert himself in what is painful.

29 E.g., MN I.30–1; III.41–2.

30 Note, for example, that terms such as *mukti* and *bodhi* are not prevalent in the older Upaniṣads (E.g., BṛhU IV.2.1, IV.3.36, IV 4.7–8; KaṭhaU I.11, III.15; ChaṇḍU VI.14.2). Andrew Fort has also pointed out that derivatives of the verb *muc* are surprisingly rare in the early Upaniṣads (Fort 1994, 37–90).

31 La Vallée Poussin 1916, 163.

32 McKenzie and Haynes 1999, 36.

33 The concordance to the *Principle Upaniṣads and Bhagavadgītā*, gives only five entries: in Yogatattva, Muktikā, Kshurikā and Āruṇeya (Jacob 1999, 501). Staal also points out that the term *nirvāṇa* does not occur in the early Upaniṣad (Staal 2008, 310).

34 Note that the terms derived from *yuj* (e.g., *yoga*) occur only seven times in total in the earliest Upaniṣads. Furthermore, while in later Buddhist and non-Buddhist texts, the term 'Yoga' referred to a spiritual practice, in the Pāli Nikāyas, the term *yoga* refers to 'bonds' that prevent us from becoming liberated. The four *yogas* in the Nikāyas are the bond (1) of sensuality, (2) of existence, (3) of view and (4) of ignorance (SN V.59, AN II.10; DN III.230). What is more, a recurrent idiom concerning *nibbāna* in the Nikāyas is *yoga-kkhema* (peace from bondage), namely, Arahantship (e.g., DN III.123)

35 We should be extra cautious when we consider the Nikāyas' descriptions of practices exercised by other *samaṇas* as a reliable historical record, mainly because they might be biased; nevertheless, I do believe these descriptions provide valuable information. This is especially true when what they describe does not contradict information we have from other sources.

36 Crangle 1994, 13.

37 Crangle 1994, 79.

38 Werner 1975, 181–3 cited by Crangle 1994, 35.

39 Crangle 1994, 269.

40 See also the Keśin hymn, Ṛg Veda 10.136.

41 Werner 1975, 182.

42 Crangle has observed that even in the Upaniṣads, terms such as, *mokṣa* and *mukti* occur minimally. Crangle 1994, 70.

43 Crangle 1994, 35; Lindtner 1999, 6. Conversely, there are those who support the theory of a synthesis of non-Aryan practices (maybe from the Indus civilization) with Aryan methods. See Crangle 1994, 1. This debate regarding the origin and development of early Indian contemplative practices has no clear resolution; rather, it points to the fact that these practices were not developed in a simple linear fashion or as a result of a single synthesis.

44 See also Bronkhorst 1998, 60–1.

45 The only non-Vedic source for such a claim is the Harappan seal that shows a figure in a yogic posture. This seal is the earliest indication of the possible existence of Yoga practice in pre-Vedic India. This one seal is not enough for a final and solid conclusion of yogic practice in pre-Vedic culture. Werner 1975, 180.

46 Bronkhorst has also maintained that the Brāhmaṇas and especially the Atharva Veda show no link to ideas about rebirth, liberation and the true nature of self (Bronkhorst 1998, 57).

47 Kaelber 1989, 96–7; Crangle 1994, 268.

48 Crangle 1994, 68. Crangle has also pointed out that both Winternitz and Deussen accepted Macdonell's division (Deussen 1966, 271; Macdonell 1971, 197; Werner 1975, 186).

49 Macdonell 1971, 191; Crangle 1994, 65.

50 Interestingly, Frits Staal mentioned in his book *Exploring Mysticism*, Gonda's observation in the book *The Vision of the Vedic Poet* that the noun *dhī* in the Vedas denotes a 'vision' or 'to have an inspiration' (Staal 1975, 79).

51 That is, the Bṛhadāranyaka, Chāndogya, Taittirīya, Aitareya and Kausītaki (Crangle 1994, 68). Note that the fourfold *jhāna* model occurs eighty-six times in the Pāli Nikāyas (Griffiths 1983, 57).

52 Chānd VII.6.1–2 in Radhakrishnan (1994).

53 E.g., Kauṣ III.2, where *dhyāna* is the faculty of *manas*, just like a sound (is heard by the ear): ' . . . *cakṣuṣā rūpam, śrotena śabdam, manasā dhyānam*'. See also kauṣ III.6 and Kauṣ III.4. Ibid.

54 E.g. Chānd VII.7.1. There the word *dhyāna* was translated by Radhakrishnan as 'contemplation'. In this passage, the exact meaning of the word *dhyāna* is not clear, but it is surely different from what we see in the Pāli Nikāyas. In Chānd VII.26.1, *dhyānam* occurs as one of the physical and mental elements that originate from the self (*ātmā*). It includes *prāṇa*, *smaraḥ* (memory), *ākāśaḥ* (ether), *vijñānam* (understanding), *dhyānam*, *cittam* and so on. In Chānd I.4.12 *kāmam dhyāyann* is translated as meditation on *kāma*. Yet, again, it has a vague meaning. Ibid.

55 Chānd VII.2.1ff. The list contains objects such as *cittam, vijñānam, balam, āpo, ākāśo* etc.

56 Bṛh IV.3.7: '*katama ātmeti. yo'yam vijñānamayaḥ prāṅeṣu, hṛdyantarjyotiḥ puruṣaḥ, sa samānaḥ sann ubhau lokāu anusañcarati, dhyāyatīva lelāyatīva, sa hi svapno bhūtvā, imam lokam atikarāmati, mṛtyo rūpāṅi*'. Here, again, the term from the root *dhyai* refers to the mental capacity of thinking. In this passage the person who is asleep seems to be thinking and moving (as a usual person), while he is actually in a sleep state.

57 Crangle 1994, 72.

58 Crangle 1994, 73.

59 Brh 1.4.1, 5, 7. See also Chand VIII.14.1, where the meditation is on 'hope' (*āśā*).

60 Crangle 1994, 74–5. Crnagle also cites Neela Velkar, who wrote her PhD dissertation on *upāsanā* (Neela A. Velkar, *Upāsanā in the Upaniṣads* [unpublished PhD thesis], University of Bombay, June, 1969). According to Crangle Velkar concluded 'that *upāsanā* evolves out of the concept of sacrifice in the pre-Upaniṣadic period where the worshipper invokes and seeks communion with the deity by means of external offerings' (cited in Crangle 1994, 87). At the Upaniṣadic time the sacrifice became symbolic and shifted to meditative worship.

61 Crangle 1994, 89.

62 Sujato 2005, 92–3.

63 Note Staal's observation that the Chāndogya Upaniṣad that 'deals very largely with typically Sāmavedic topics such as the syllable Om, which refers to the *udgītha*, probably was composed further west from the area in which the Buddha lived'. This might explain the absence of this praxis in the Pāli Nikāyas (Staal 2008, 311).

64 For a full discussion of *prāṇa* in the Saṃhitās and the early Upaniṣads, see Zysk 1993, 198–206.

65 Crangle 1994, 81.

66 Kauṣ III.2: *prāṇena hu evāsmim loke'mṛtatvam āpnoti*. See also Chand I.6.3; II.3.5.

67 SN IV.118 and DN I.238.

68 Zysk 1993, 204.

69 MN I.56.

70 E.g., Chānd V.1.1; V.1.12.

71 MN III.85: *evaṃ bhāvitā kho, bhikkhave, ānāpānassati evaṃ bahulīkatā cattāro satipaṭṭhāne paripūreti*.

72 Zysk 1993, 201.

73 Zysk 1993, 204.

74 Zysk 1993, 205.

75 Bronkhorst 1998.

76 Chānd Upaniṣad V.10.1–2: *tad ya ittham viduḥ, ye ceme'raṇye śraddhā tapa ity upāste . . . sa enān brahma gamayati*. See also DN I.235.

77 Bronkhorst 1998, 57.
78 Bronkhorst 1998, 63.
79 The *Tevijja Sutta* [DN I.235–52] seems to be a good source for the knowledge the Buddha had about the Upaniṣads.
80 Crangle 1994, 89.
81 Crangle 1994, 66, 90.
82 Deussen 1966, 271; Macdonell 1971, 19; Winternitz 1981, 218–20; Crangle 1994, 66. See also the introduction in Radhakrishnan's translation of the principle Upaniṣads. Radhakrishnan does not consider the Maitrī Upaniṣad to be one of the oldest pre-Buddhist Upaniṣad (Radhakrishnan 1994, 22).
83 See also Śvet 2.15.
84 Radhakrishnan 1994, 855.
85 Note that one of the four types of clinging (*upādāna*) in the suttas is the 'clinging to a doctrine of self' (*attāvāda-upādānaṃ*) (e.g., SN II.3).
86 Maitrī 7.9–10. Radhakrishnan 1994, 856.
87 Crangle 1994, 270.
88 Johannes Bronkhorst has suggested that Nātaputta and Mahāvīra were not the same person (Bronkhorst 2000, 517).
89 The Nigaṇṭhas are usually depicted as ascetics who hold certain views concerning the consequences of doing evil (*pāpa*) action/rod (*kamma*/*daṇḍa*), while advocating that the bodily rod (*kāya-daṇḍaṃ*) as the most reprehensible. See, for example, MN I.372–4; SN IV.318; AN I.220. In MN II.214, the Nigaṇṭhas are depicted as holding the view that 'by destroying with asceticism (*tapasā*) past actions, and by not doing fresh actions, there will be no consequences in the future' (*purāṇānaṃ kammānaṃ tapasā byantībhāvā, navānaṃ kammānaṃ acarian, āyatiṃ anavassavo*). In MN I.92, the Buddha refers to the Nigaṇṭhas' practice and describes it as a practice of asceticism that causes pain (*opakkamikā dukkha tibbā kharā kaṭukā vedanā vedayanti*) – a practice quite far from the experience of the *jhānas*, which is far from being painful.
90 E.g., MN I.242ff.
91 It should be noted that there are no such declarations with regard to the complete scheme of the *jhānas*, the *arūpa samāpatti* and *saññāvedayitanirodha*, or regarding the 'eight liberations' (*aṭṭha vimokkha*). To the best of my knowledge, these various schemes do not appear in non-Buddhist traditions. The 'eight liberations' are described in DN II 111–2; DN III 261; DN III 288; AN IV 306; AN IV 349; MN II 13; MN III 222.
92 Jaini 1990, 251.
93 Bronkhorst 1993, 39.
94 Bronkhorst 1993, 39.
95 The *Tattvārtha Sūtra*, which means 'A Manual for Understanding All That Is', was written by the philosopher-monk Umāsvāti, and on which the great Jain thinkers wrote their commentaries. See *Tattvārtha Sūtra* (1994, xvii).
96 Dundas 1985, 168.
97 *Tattvārtha Sūtra* 9.31–5.
98 *Tattvārtha Sūtra* 9.36.
99 *Tattvārtha Sūtra* 9.29: *ārta-raudra-dharma śuklāni*. Bronkhorst has concluded that this division is not reliable and was probably made by early systemizers (Bronkhorst 1993, 44).
100 Jaini 1990, 252.
101 Note that the association of these two types of *dhyāna* with unwholesome objects makes them quite different from the description of the Buddhist *jhānas*, which can be attained when one has been detached from *akusala dhammas*.
102 *Tattvārtha Sūtra* 9.30: *pare mokṣahetū*.
103 *Tattvārtha Sūtra* 9.37. In medieval times, some Jain authors recommended four types of *dhyāna* as useful preliminaries to attaining the 'bright (pure) meditation' (*śukla*). These techniques, which involve concentration on an imaginary object, display tantric and even Mahāyāna forms of meditation. They include concentration on chants, on the form of the Jīna, and on that which transcends form – the nature of the siddha. See Jaini 1990, 254–6.

104 E.g., MN I.480.
105 *Tattvārtha Sūtra* 9.39–43.
106 Ibid.
107 *Tattvārtha Sūtra* 9.44–6. The sūtra explains that *vitarka* is the pondering over the content of the scripture [*Tattvārtha Sūtra* 9.45] while *vicāra* is explained as the movement between various object of meditation: substance/object (*dravya*), words, which are linguistic symbols that signify the object, and activities of body, speech and mind (for a detailed explanation of substances, see *Tattvārtha Sūtra* 5.2 and 5.37).
108 Bronkhorst 1993, 40.
109 Jaini 1990, 258.
110 MN I.39; SN IV.312.
111 Interestingly, it became less common in later Theravāda works and works produced by other Buddhist schools; in contrast, these works started to use the term *kilesa*/*kleśa* more frequently.
112 Somaratne 1999, 131.
113 Thapar 1960, 49.
114 See, for example, the 'minor rock edict': 'Piyadasi, King of Magadha, saluting the Sangha and wishing them good health and happiness, speaks thus: You know, reverend sirs, how great my faith in the Buddha, the Dhamma and Sangha is. Whatever, reverend sirs, has been spoken by Lord Buddha, all that is well-spoken. I consider it proper, reverend sirs, to advise on how the good Dhamma should last long. These Dhamma texts – extracts from the Discipline, the Noble Way of Life, the Fears to Come, the Poem on the Silent Sage, the Discourse on the Pure Life, Upatisa's Questions, and the Advice to Rahula that was spoken by the Buddha concerning false speech – these Dhamma texts, reverend sirs, I desire that all the monks and nuns may constantly listen to and remember. Likewise, the laymen and laywomen. I have had this written that you may know my intentions'.
115 Thapar 1960, 44.
116 Thapar 1960, 46–7.
117 See Thapar who maintained that 'it is clear from Aśoka's edicts that he was a Buddhist' (Thapar 1960, 44). Also, it is clear from the epigraphic materials, that Aśoka used a collection extracted from the Buddhavacana.
118 Thapar 1960, 45–6.
119 Bechert 1982, 61–8; Tieken 2000, 2.
120 Tieken 2000, 27.
121 Thapar has also observed that the 'Buddha had greater success among the cities of the monarchical kingdoms. The kṣatriya oligarchies were not so forthcoming in their support and some were more partial to the Nirgranthas' (Thapar 1960, 71).
122 See also Cousins 1992, 137.
123 Bronkhorst 1993, 70.
124 Bronkhorst 1993, 78.
125 Bronkhorst 1993, 77.
126 Bronkhorst 1993, 111.
127 Bronkhorst 1993, 99–100.
128 E.g., AN III.414: 'I say, monks, *kamma* is volition (*cetanāhaṃ, bhikkhave, kammaṃ vadāmi*)'.
129 E.g., AN II.211 and SN V.26–7. See, for example, the Buddha's explanation that Brahminhood (*brahmaññaṃ*) is the eightfold path and the fruit of Brahminhood is the attainment of the states of the four noble persons and the destruction of lust, hatred, and delusion. SN V.25–6.
130 E.g., AN II.208; DN III.233; MN I.349; DN III.84.
131 See, for example, the term *brāhmacariya*: SN V.26; AN IV.13 and the term *brāhmaṇa* Sn 618–47, 655–6.

2 The First *Jhāna*

A turning point in the spiritual path

> Separated from the desire for sensual pleasures, separated from [other] unwholesome states, a bhikkhu enters upon and abides in the first *jhāna*, which is [mental] joy and [bodily] pleasure born of *viveka*, accompanied by thought and reflection.[1]

This is the formulaic description of the first *jhāna*. At first glance, this description (as with the descriptions of the other three *jhānas*) seems straightforward. Due to its apparent simplicity, this description has received little attention from modern Buddhist scholarship; no one has endeavoured to understand the exact nature of this state and its liberating value. As I have observed in the introduction, a common perception in the Theravāda tradition understands this description as referring to one-pointed absorption that is brought about by the practice of concentration. However, I think this state is much more intricate and interesting than it appears to be at first and that it reveals quite a lot about the nature of the Buddhist path to liberation and its psychological and phenomenological aspects.

The attainment of the first *jhāna* has a momentous place in the Buddha's own awakening story. The spontaneous attainment of the first *jhāna* marked a turning point in the Buddha-to-be's spiritual path:

> After the Bodhisatta had practiced severe asceticism, [he thought to himself], 'Even with this severe and hard practice, I have not attained states beyond [ordinary] human [condition], and any distinction in insight and knowledge which fits the noble ones. Could there be a different path to awakening?' Then it occurred to me: 'I realized that when my father the Sakyan was working, while I was sitting under the cool shade of the rose-apple tree, separated from the desire for sensual pleasures, separated from [other] unwholesome states, I entered and abided in the first *jhāna*, which is [mental] joy and [bodily] pleasure born of *viveka*, accompanied by thought and reflection. Could that be the path to awakening?' Then, following that memory, I realized: 'this is the path to awakening.'[2]

This record from the *Mahāsaccaka Sutta* of the MN is well known in the Buddhist tradition. Although it seems to depict an important experience and realization, one that steered the unawakened Bodhisatta into the correct path to awakening, after years of unfruitful meditative and ascetic practices, there are several interesting questions which are unanswered: what was so special in this reflective memory and the following re-attainment of this state that enabled the unawakened Gotama to discover the correct path to awakening? Does this attainment have liberative value to the Buddha's disciples as well? Since there are no apparent techniques through which the Bodhisatta attained this state, how can one retrace the Buddha's own path and attain it? If absorption into one object of meditation is not the way to achieve this state, what is? In other words, are there any other prescribed techniques in the Nikāyas for entering the first *jhāna*?

Other questions are also unclear: is this state really cut off from the five sense stimuli as the Theravāda (and Sarvāstivāda) traditions have claimed? What kind of joy (*pīti*) and pleasure (*sukha*) is this attainment referring to (i.e., born of *viveka*)? How should we understand the term *viveka* in this context? And lastly, why are *vitakka* and *vicāra* present in this state but absent from the rest of the three *jhānas*?

To find some valid answers to these questions, this chapter will analyze the factors of the first *jhāna* according to their treatment in various suttas. It will also critically examine diverse descriptions and references that can shed light on the nature of this state, its phenomenology and liberative value.

I Entering the first *jhāna*

As observed before, there is no support in the Nikāyas for the view that entering the first *jhāna* is the outcome of one-pointed concentration and absorption into a specific meditation object, and even more so, by an absorption into a certain *kaṣina*. There is also no textual evidence for arguing that this attainment is not originally Buddhist. Interestingly, although the Nikāyas do not offer specific techniques through which one can enter into the first *jhāna*, many suttas describe gradual training (*sikkha*) and development (*bhāvanā*) that lead to the attainment of the *jhānas* and consequently to liberation.

These common descriptions depict a unique vision of the spiritual path and a structured model that places the *jhānas* as the last phase before one attains liberation. This model describes a series of practices that enable the practitioner to possess the qualities that comprise the Buddhist path. These practices are (1) the training in morality (*sīla-khandha*); (2) the practice of guarding and restraining the impressions brought about by sense experience (*indriya-saṃvara*); and (3) the practice of full awareness (*sampajāna*). Numerous suttas state that, after following these practices, a person possesses (*samannāgato*) three qualities: (1) the aggregate of noble virtue, (2) noble restraint of the faculties and (3) noble mindfulness and full awareness (*sati-sampajāna*).[3] At this point of the spiritual path, one can advance to the last stage, namely, resorting to a secluded place, where the instruction is very clear: to 'sit down, folding the legs crosswise, setting the body erect and establishing mindfulness in front',[4] the famous opening practice prescribed by the Buddha in the beginning of the *Satipaṭṭhāna Sutta* (and other suttas which describe the establishing of *sati*). When this is achieved, the practitioner abandons the five hindrances (*nīvaraṇa*) and enters into the first *jhāna*, after which, one attains the other three *jhānas* and the three types of knowledge.[5] The last type of knowledge is the knowledge of the destruction of the *āsavas* and the attainment of liberation.

This is a well-known path-structure in the Pāli Nikāyas, and it clearly points to the obvious fact that one can enter into the first *jhāna* only after one possess qualities such as *sīla*, *sampajāna* and *sati* and also has abandoned the five hindrances that obstruct wisdom (*paññā*).[6] In other words, the cultivation of these path-factors is a prerequisite for entering the first *jhāna*. What is more, from this path-structure, it can be inferred that wisdom (*paññā*) arises when one enters the *jhānas*, a point I will discuss later on.

The formulaic description of the first *jhāna* does not, however, specify how exactly the practitioner abandons the hindrances and enters into the first *jhāna*. For an interesting and illuminating description of the process by which one enters the first *jhāna*, I turn to SN V.198. This sutta explains that having made relinquishment (or letting go) his basis (*vossagga ārammaṇam karitvā*), one enters into the first *jhāna*.[7] The term *vossaga* ('relinquishment' or 'letting go')[8] appears repeatedly in the Nikāyas as the result (*pariṇāmiṃ*) of cultivating the seven factors of awakening (*bojjhaṅgas*); on other occasions, *vossaga* also occurs in relation to cultivating the five powers (*bala*).[9] The cultivation of these qualities is 'supported by discernment (*viveka*), dispassion, and cessation, and resulting in *vossagga*'.[10] In other words, when the seven factors of awakening are developed to a certain extent, the result is relinquishment (*vossagga*). But what is being relinquished?

A possible answer is the clear and recurrent statement that for entering the first *jhāna* one must be separated from the hindrances and [other] unwholesome (*akusalehi dhammehi*). That is, one has to relinquish, or let go of, any unwholesomeness for entering the first *jhāna*.[11] This is the proximate cause, and it is done by developing the other path-factors. Further, MN III.95 states that Māra (as the personification of unwholesomeness) can find support only in one who does not cultivate (*bhāvita*) and intensify (*bahulīkato*) mindfulness referring to the body (*kāyagatā-sati*), which is developed and intensified by the attainment of the four *jhānas*.[12] The sutta explains that when one enters the *jhānas*, one has included within himself whatever wholesome states there are that partake of true knowledge (*vijjābhāgiyā*).[13] In other words, for entering the first *jhāna* – a completely wholesome state – all other unwholesome states must cease.[14]

Note that this is very different from the common perception that for entering the *jhānas* one has to focus the mind on a particular object (such as the *kaṣinas*).[15] In SN V.198 the Buddha stated that it is not by focusing the mind or being absorbed into a meditation object that one attains the first *jhāna*; rather, it is by releasing and letting go of the foothold of unwholesome mind. This seems to be achieved by the cultivation of the seven factors of awakening to some extent[16] and by the practice of morality, sense restraint and observation of phenomena, as prescribed in the Satipaṭṭhāna Sutta, which allow one to 'be endowed with' noble mindfulness and full awareness.

Given the preceding, it is no surprise that the Buddha's memory of the first *jhāna*, and the consequent re-entering into this state just before his awakening, enabled him to re-discover its power and significance in the spiritual path. While his asceticism and meditative practice up to that moment of remembrance did not take him 'beyond [ordinary] human [condition] or granted him any distinction in insight and knowledge that fits the noble ones', this attainment did. It allowed him to abandon exactly the thing that he was aiming for – the unwholesome states of mind.[17]

II Abandoning the *nīvaraṇas*

I have already pointed out that according to numerous suttas the first *jhāna* is attained when the mind is purified from the hindrances (*nīvaraṇas*). This is a pre-requisite for entering the first *jhāna*.[18] These hindrances are specifically referred to in various suttas as the 'five hindrances, imperfection of mind that weakens wisdom'.[19] While Buddhaghosa considers the hindrances to be specifically obstructive to the *jhānas*, given that they do not allow the mind to concentrate on the meditation object,[20] I would argue that the five *nīvaraṇas* are obstructive to seeing things as they are[21] and for perfecting and consummating the seven factors of awakening. In other words, a mind that is not purified from these obstructions cannot see clearly; therefore, it does not have the ability to eradicate the *āsavas* for attaining complete liberation. SN V.92 clearly states this. It has the Buddha compare the purified mind to refined gold, while the five hindrances are likened to impurities that corrupt gold from being malleable, wieldy and radiant:

> So too bhikkhus, there are there five corruptions of the mindcorrupted by which the mind is neither malleable nor wieldy nor radiant, but brittle and not rightly calmed for destruction of the *āsavas*. What five? Sense desire . . . ill will . . . sloth and torpor . . . restlessness and remorse . . . doubt are corruptions of the mind.[22]

The *nīvaraṇas* do not just obstruct strong concentration, they actually obstruct liberation. Although it is quite clear that liberation is possible only when the *nīvaraṇas* are absent, the actual way to purify the mind from these five corruptions is not explicated in detail in the Nikāyas. The *Satipaṭṭhāna Sutta* instructs the practitioner to observe not only whatever is present and absent at each moment but also the causes for the arising of the various phenomena (wholesome and unwholesome). We can say that the *Satipaṭṭhāna Sutta* presents a theory of meditation in which 'desire-less observation' is the key (but not the only method the sutta presents) to weakening and eliminating the various unwholesome states. Yet, the Nikāyas also offer a more precise depiction of the mental process (and not a technique) by which the mind is actually purified from the hindrances (presumably by first recognizing them as prescribed in the *Satipaṭṭhāna Sutta*).[23] This depiction reveals the mechanism by which the five *nīvaraṇas* can be abandoned (and not only observed and weakened). It starts with the instruction of sitting down while establishing mindfulness in front of the meditator. This instruction of placing 'mindfulness in front' occurs both in the *Satipaṭṭhāna Sutta* and in the *Ānāpānasati Sutta* (and in suttas that depicts the gradual path). I believe that this phrase alludes to the necessity of developing the four foundations of mindfulness as prescribed in the *Satipaṭṭhāna Sutta* and the *Ānāpānasati Sutta* to some extent, and implies the preliminary development of the seven factors of awakening as a prerequisite for abandoning the *nīvaraṇas*. Hence, establishing mindfulness (*sati*), which is done by following the instructions of the *Satipaṭṭhāna Sutta* (and alternatively the *Ānāpānasati Sutta*), enables the meditator to develop the seven factors of awakening to some degree. This can then be seen as the basis for abandoning the five hindrances.[24] When mindfulness is established, the Buddha explains that:

1 Abandoning covetousness for the world, he abides with a mind free from covetousness. [Thus] he causes the mind to become pure from covetousness.
2 Abandoning ill will and hatred, he abides with a mind free from ill will, compassionate for the welfare of all living beings. [Thus] he causes the mind to become pure from ill will and hatred.
3 Abandoning sloth and torpor, he abides free from sloth and torpor. Thus, he has clear perception; he is mindful and fully aware. [Thus] he causes the mind to become pure from sloth and torpor.
4 Abandoning restlessness and remorse, he abides un-agitated with a mind inwardly peaceful. [Thus] he causes the mind to become pure from restlessness and remorse.
5 Abandoning doubt, he abides having gone beyond doubt, un-perplexed about wholesome states. [Thus] he causes the mind to become pure from doubt.[25]

From this account it is quite clear that a mind in which these obstructions are not present is a mind where wholesome qualities are present, such as compassion, clear perception, mindfulness, full awareness, peacefulness and confidence regarding what is wholesome (i.e., discernment of what wholesome and unwholesome). What is more interesting in these accounts is the repeated description that one dwells (*viharati*) with a mind free from the five hindrances (presumably when one enters the first *jhāna* and during the attainments of the other three *jhānas*); by this 'dwelling' (*viharati*) the practitioner 'causes the mind to become pure' (*cittaṃ parisodheti*).[26]

From the way the clauses are constructed in Pāli, it seems that the actual abiding (*viharati*) when the mind is free from the various hindrances is the mechanism by which the mind actually becomes purified. This, I would suggest, is reflected by the last sentence of each clause, since it uses the verb *parisudh* in the causative form (*parisodheti*). Here we find the notion that what causes the mind to become purified from the hindrances is the actual abiding – for a period of time – in a state of mind that is free from these hindrances.

SN V.95 also points out that 'when the five *nīvaraṇas* are not present in the mind, on that occasion, the seven factors of awakening progress to fulfilment by development'.[27] In other words, one can start to develop the seven factors of awakening while the mind is not purified from the hindrances. Yet, until the five *nīvaraṇas* are not completely absent from the mind, these wholesome factors cannot be perfected and matured.[28] As we will see in Chapter 4, the entrance into the first *jhāna* opens the way to the complete perfection of the seven factors of awakening by way of *jhāna*. And only when the seven factors of awakening are fully developed and matured can one realize the fruit of true knowledge and liberation.[29]

Interestingly, SN V.97 states that 'these five hindrances are causing blindness, causing lack of vision, causing lack of knowledge, impeding wisdom, tending to vexation, leading away from *nibbāna*'.[30] MN I.276 further states that when these hindrances are abandoned, the practitioners sees (*samanupassti*) that there is a situation akin to 'freedom from debt (*ānaṇyaṃ*), healthiness (*ārogyaṃ*), release from prison (*bandhanāmokkhaṃ*), freedom from slavery (*bhujissaṃ*) and a land of safety (*khemantabhūmiṃ*)'.[31] In other words, only when the five hindrances are absent, presumably when one is dwelling in the *jhānas*, the final stages of liberation can occur by perfecting and fulfilling the seven factors and by eradicating the *āsavas*.[32] Note that although the *nīvaraṇas* impede wisdom (*paññā*), there is nowhere an explanation of what kind of 'wisdom' (*paññā*) they impede. A possible understanding is that when the mind is free from the various obstructions (*nīvaraṇas*) and unwholesome states (*akusala dhammas*), and contains only wholesome factors, experience is perceived without any distorted perception and mental impediments.[33] In other words, when the mind is wholesome and pure, it is a 'state of wisdom' – a state in which no *akusala dhammas* exist. What I am trying to suggest is that the absence of one thing (i.e., *nīvaraṇas*) does not necessarily point to the presence of something else (i.e., some conceptual wisdom or specific cognitive content). Thus, it is quite justified to suggest that the *jhānas* are states where wisdom is strong since the mind is not hindered by mental obstructions and experience can be seen more clearly that is, it is less fabricated by unwholesome states and conceptual overlays.

III Viveka

The Pāli English Dictionary, and consequently most translators, translates *viveka* as 'detachment', 'separation' and 'seclusion'.[34] Buddhaghosa explains that *viveka* means either the disappearance of the hindrances, or that the *jhāna* factors are secluded from the hindrances.[35] However, according to the Sanskrit dictionary, the first meaning of *viveka* is 'discrimination'.[36] The Sanskrit dictionary further describes *viveka* as '(1) true knowledge, (2) discretion, (3) right judgement, and (4) the faculty of distinguishing and classifying things according to their real properties'. These meanings of the term *viveka* seem to assist in interpreting this term in the Buddhist context as well, since *viveka* has no clear definition in the Nikāyas and it seems to be used in different ways. I suggest that the use of *vivicca* and *viveka*, in the description of the first *jhāna* (both from the verb *vi+vic*), plays with both meanings of the verb; namely, its meaning as discernment and the consequent 'seclusion' and letting go. Although there are times that the Buddha changes the meaning of a Sanskrit term completely, sometimes he does not; for example, he retains the meanings of terms such as *dukkha*, *sukha* and so on. I believe that the term *viveka* retained in the Nikāyas also its Sanskrit meaning as 'discernment'.

This interpretation is supported by a description from SN V 301. In this *sutta*, the quality of *viveka* is developed by the practice of the four *satipaṭṭhānas*. Anuruddha declares that

> [i]ndeed friends, when that bhikkhu is developing and cultivating the four establishings of mindfulness, it is impossible that he will give up the training and return to the lower life. For what reason? Because for a long time his mind has slanted, sloped, and inclined towards *viveka*.[37]

Here Anuruddha clearly states that by seeing clearly (*anupassati*) body, feeling, mind and *dhammas* (the four focuses of mindfulness) the practitioner develops the quality of *viveka*. In this context, it seems that *viveka* is a quality connected to clear seeing, to discernment of the nature of experience.[38] We also see here that the *jhānas* follow the development of the four *satipaṭṭhānas* and not some practice of one-pointed concentration.[39] The preceding also indicates that the development of the four *satipaṭṭhānas* inclines the mind towards discerning the true nature of phenomena; discernment that allows the mind to see the disadvantage of sense pleasures and, hence, let go of the desire for them and other unwholesome states (such as clinging and aversion, for example).That is, the cultivation of the four *satipaṭṭhānas* develops the ability to recognize and discern the mechanism of mind and body for seeing clearly into the nature of the various physical and mental phenomena. I would suggest that this discernment of phenomena (*dhammas*), and the consequent detachment (*vivicca*) is indicated by the term *viveka*, the same *viveka* from which *pīti* and *sukha* of the first *jhāna* are born.[40] Discerning the nature of phenomena enables the mind to change its inclinations; that is, it allows us to let go of our basic unwholesome tendencies and desires, which are based on a mistaken perception of reality. This letting go (*vossagga*) is the proximate cause for entering the first *jhāna*.

IV Detachment from sensual pleasures *(kāma)*

One common understanding of the nature of the *jhāna* attainments is that these states are trance-like experiences in which one is completely cut off from sense experience.[41] According to the Kathāvatthu, for example, the five senses and related classes of consciousness (eye-consciousness etc.) do not operate in the *jhānas*.[42] However, the description of the first *jhāna* implies something quite different and it seems that the Kathāvatthu and subsequent commentators missed the point. What the description of the first *jhāna* indicates is that one is separated from two things upon entering the first *jhāna*: *kāma* and unwholesome states (*akusalehi dhammehi*). For our present enquiry, *kāma* is the pivotal term.

If the first *jhāna* is a state in which the practitioner is cut off from objects of the five senses, it would be reasonable to expect a clear statement in the text that the meditator is cut off from either the five faculties (*indriya*), which refer to the five sense organs,[43] or those of the twelve *āyatanas*, which designate the senses and their corresponding objects (i.e., the fields of perception). Further, a statement that one is cut off from 'the five strings of sensual desires' (*pañca-kāma-guṇā*) – namely, forms, sounds, odours, flavours and tangibles – would clearly point to the cutting off of sensory experience while in the *jhānas*.[44] In other words, while the term *pañca-kāma-guṇā* describes sense experience (excluding the sixth sense, *mano-viññāṇa*), the term *kāma* refers quite straightforwardly to the attachment and clinging to the five *guṇas* together with attachment to the various mental objects (*mano-viññāṇa*).

AN III.411 explicitly clarifies the difference between the 'five strings of sensual desire; (*pañca-kāma-guṇā*) and *kāma*'. In this sutta, the Buddha unequivocally states that *pañca-kāma-guṇā* are desirable objects of the five sense objects. He further states that the 'five stings of sensual desire' that are 'agreeable, pleasing, charming, endearing, fostering desire, enticing'[45] are not *kāma* in the Buddha's teaching.[46] *Kāma*, on the contrary, is the 'thought of desire' (*saṅkapparāga*). The Buddha explains this point in a beautiful verse

> The thought of desire in a person is *kāma*,
> not the wonderful sense pleasures [found] in the world.
> The thought of desire in a person is *kāma*.
> The wonderful [things] remain as they are in the world,
> while the wise men remove the impulse [for them].[47]

It is safe to say that since the description of the first *jhāna* does not mention that one is separated from the *indriyas*, the five sense-related *āyatanas* or the *kāma-guṇas*, the assumption that one is cut off from sense experience while in the *jhānas* is a misunderstanding.[48] In light of this, I would suggest that what is *not* present in the experience of the *jhānas* is the movement of desire – the internal movement in which sense objects capture and captivate the mind. Furthermore, according to the description of the first *jhāna*, one is not separated from all mental phenomena, that is, from all objects of the sixth sense (*mano-viññāṇa*), but only from *akusala dhammas* – those mental factors that are not conducive to liberation.

In summary, this discussion shows that when the practitioner enters and abides in the first *jhāna*, he or she is in fact separated from the attachment and desire for sensual pleasures – the basic tendency of an ordinary cognition[49] – and not from sense experience.[50] This conclusion corresponds with the earlier interpretation of *viveka*. Being separated from desire and attachment to sensual pleasures (and other unwholesome states of mind) must originate from insight into the nature of the world of the senses. Desire for sense pleasures is a basic tendency of an un-liberated mind that considers sense pleasure as gratifying and worth seeking. Being separated from this basic tendency, and from other unwholesome states, is quite an advanced realization. It points to the strong insight into the impermanence of the various objects of cognition and to the understanding of the futility in holding on to them. Thus, the *jhānas* are an experience quite different from ordinary experience but at the same time, not separated from it. They are psychosomatic states in which one has a different experience of being an embodied being in the midst of experience. I will return to this point later on.

V Seeking pain for attaining pleasure

While trying to understand the significance of the first *jhāna* to the Buddhist path, I have come to think that *jhānic pīti* (mental joy and ease) and *sukha* (bodily pleasure)[51] are the key elements for deciphering this state. In the following investigation, we will see that these two factors (*nīrāmisa pīti* and *nīrāmisa sukha*), which characterize the first and second *jhānas* (*sukha* is also one of the factors of the third *jhāna*), are pleasure and joy that do not involve desire and attachment. On the contrary, they can only arise when one encounters the world of phenomena without clinging. When one discerns (*viveka*) the true nature of phenomena, that is, the unreliability, impermanence and lack of substantiality of all phenomena, *jhānic pīti* and *sukha* are born.[52] Furthermore, it is the very attainment of *jhānic pīti* and *sukha* which allows the mind to abandon completely the desire for sense pleasures (*kāma*) and the latent tendency (*anusaya*) to seek this type of pleasure.

Let us backtrack for a moment and go into a deeper investigation of the term *kāma*, which is pivotal for understanding the liberative value of the first *jhāna*. In Buddhist thought, *kāma* – the desire for sense pleasures – is a fundamental impediment to liberation. This is clearly stated by the Buddha in MN II.261–2:

> Bhikkhus, [the objects of] sensual pleasures are impermanent, hollow, false, deceptive; they are illusory, the prattle of fools. The desire for sensual pleasure here and now and the desire for sensual pleasures in lives to come, sensual perceptions here and now and sensual perceptions in lives to come – both alike are Māra's realm, Māra's domain, Māra's bait, Māra's hunting ground. On account of them, these evil unwholesome mental states such as covetousness, ill will, and presumption arise. And they constitute and obstruction to a noble disciple in training here.[53]

It is no surprise that sense-based pleasures were considered an impediment to the spiritual life. We can even say that most ascetic-contemplative traditions fear sensual pleasures[54] and conceive these pleasures as the foremost thing to be renounced by a true seeker of spiritual liberation.[55] In fact, ascetic practices are a means to transcend sensual pleasures that are conceived as mundane.[56] Some ascetic worldviews connect sensual pleasures with the body, which is viewed in its entirety as impure. A passage from the Nāradaparivrājaka Upaniṣad exemplifies this view:

> Let him abandon this impermanent dwelling place of the elements. It has beams of bones tied with tendons. It is plastered with flesh and blood and thatched skin. It is a foul-smelling, filled with feces and urine, and infested with old age and grief. Covered with dust and harassed by pain, it is the abode of disease.
>
> If a man finds joy in the body – a heap of flesh, blood, pus, feces, urine, tendons, marrow, and bones – that fool will find joy even in hell.[57]

The desire for sensual pleasures and the body as the vehicle for enjoying these pleasures was regarded as the primary distraction to the spiritual seeker. In the

Indian context, an underlying assumption was that painful feelings[58] caused by *tapas* are the antidote to the desire for these pleasures. In this ascetic context, sense pleasures in general, no matter how subtle, were conceived as inappropriate to the spiritual life.[59] A good example of this attitude was the disgust felt by the five ascetic companions of the unawakened Bodhisatta upon seeing him eat some rice porridge. This incident followed his realization that his severe ascetic practices did not lead him to awakening. That simple meal, indisputably not a feast, was interpreted by the five ascetics as the abandonment of the holy life and return to luxury by their companion.[60]

In his book *Tapta Mārga: Asceticism and Initiation in Vedic India*, Walter O. Kaelber has pointed out that one of the connotations of the root *tap*, which can be translated as asceticism,[61] is to suffer or feel pain.[62] Some forms of *tapas*[63] such as hunger, jealousy or anguish were not desirable in the Vedas since they are involuntary and are not self-generated for the purpose of knowledge or other religious aims. However, 'pain' (*tapas*) can also refer to self-generated pain.[64] Self-imposed pain was considered in early Indian texts to 'burn out', 'consume' and 'destroy' evil forces and thereby purify. Kaelber asserts that the prevalent meaning of the word *tapas* in the Brāhmaṇas is self-imposed austerities:

> Just as Prajāpati exerted himself to become pure and cleanse himself of impurities, so at the Dīkṣā the sacrificer exerts himself through asceticism, through *tapas*, to become pure. Further, the dīkṣita, through his self-imposed 'mortification', his self-imposed suffering and pain, generates an inner heat, which is also referred to as *tapas*.[65]

Kaelber further points out that the early meaning of *tapas*, as pain experienced within the body, once undesirable, became religiously significant and necessary.[66] The physical pain was viewed in the Brāhmaṇas and later on, as a way to be liberate – as pain that destroys evil, sin and impurities (e.g., Vasiṣṭha Dharma Śāstra 20, 47).[67] The Jains understood *karma* as a physical matter that sticks to the soul and prevents it from being liberated.[68] This notion led to the view that physical asceticism is the way to eliminate bad *karma*. In Jain philosophy, penance is the way to achieve the spiritual goal understood as (1) the elimination of *karma*, (2) the non-production of new *karma*[69] and (3) omniscience and freedom of the soul after death. Enduring hardship was conceived of as a way to 'prevent deviation from the spiritual path and wears of bound *karma*'.[70] There are, according to the *Tattvārtha Sūtra*, twenty-two hardships such as hunger, thirst, cold heat, seat and posture for practicing austerities.[71] There are six external austerities and six internal ones,[72] which are aimed at eliminating *karma*. The difference between a hardship and austerities is that hardship is random while austerities are created by the soul to purify itself from impurities.[73]

In the Buddha's teaching, desire for sensual pleasures (*kāma*), or better put, desire for sense gratification (together with the pleasure attained dependent on this gratification) is also considered as a central impediment to attaining liberation.[74] *Kāma* is enumerated in all the different lists of hindrances and obstacles. It is the first in the list of *āsavas*, the *nīvaraṇas*, the *ogha* ('the floods'), the *yoga* ('the bond') and the *anusayas* ('the latent tendencies'):

> Udāyin, the pleasure and joy that arises dependent on these five cords of sensual pleasure are called, sensual pleasure – a filthy pleasure, a coarse pleasure, an ignoble pleasure. I say of this kind of pleasure that it should not be pursued, that it should not be developed, that it should not be cultivated, that it should be feared.[75]

We know from Gotama's own spiritual quest that asceticism, with its severe bodily pain, did not lead him to awakening. Although the young Siddhattha Gotama practiced severe asceticism, his desire was not eradicated and liberation was not achieved. In light of this, we may ask, compared with other ascetic worldviews of his time, what was different about the Buddha's notion of *kāma* and the way he prescribed to eradicate the basic tendency of mind to cling to sense pleasures? This, I believe, is answered quite directly in the famous story about how he suddenly remembered his attainment of the first *jhāna* when he was younger. This reflective memory, of a unique body-mind attainment, was a pivotal turning point in his spiritual quest. At this important moment, he realized what the path to awakening is (and what it is not):

> After the Bodhisatta had practiced severe asceticism, [he thought to himself], 'Even with this severe and hard practice, I have not attained states beyond [ordinary] human [condition], and any distinction in insight and knowledge which fits the noble ones. Could there be a different path of awakening?' Then this occurred to me: I realized that when my father the Sakyan was working, while I was sitting under the cool shade of the rose-apple tree, separated from sensual pleasures and unwholesome states, I entered and abided in the first *jhāna*, which is happiness and [bodily] pleasure born from *viveka*, accompanied with applied and sustained thought. Could that be the path of awakening? Then, following that memory, I realized, 'This is the path of awakening.' Then it occurred to me, 'Why am I afraid of that pleasure, which is apart from sensual pleasures and unwholesome states?' Then in occurred to me, 'I am not afraid of that pleasure, which is apart from sensual pleasures and unwholesome states.'[76]

This passage describes how Gotama realized that he should not fear all types of pleasure, as he did when he practiced *tapas*. He understood that there are pleasures (*sukha*) and joys (*pīti*) that lead one to awakening and do not perpetuate desire.[77] Although the Buddha was quite adamant in explaining that *kāma* should be feared,[78] since it is 'the first army of Māra',[79] he has also stated time and again that another type of pleasure should not be feared. On the contrary, it should be cultivated: 'I say of this kind of pleasure that it should be pursued, that it should be developed, that it should be cultivated, and that it should not be feared.'[80]

In this statement, the Buddha makes an important distinction: there are various types of pleasure; some pleasures should be renounced and feared and some should be cultivated and seen as aids to purify the mind. This distinction points out that different types of pleasures (mental and physical) impact the mind in different ways. The path to awakening, according to the Buddha's own spiritual journey, goes through these types of physical and mental pleasures, presumably having the power to transform and liberate the mind. This was Gotama's breakthrough when he realized that the first *jhāna* leads the way to awakening (*bodhi*).[81]

According to DN III.131–2, this unique understanding – that specific types of pleasure and joy lead to liberation – incited accusations that the followers of Gotama are addicted to a life of devotion to pleasure.[82] However, the Buddha did not hesitate to announce that the end of the spiritual path will be gained through pleasure, not pain, meaning a specific kind of (bodily) pleasure and (mental) joy. The statement that the end of the spiritual path will be gained through pleasure, not pain, needs to be further clarified and put into context. It is clear from the Buddha's own story that his memory of the nature of the first *jhāna* was a reflective moment in which he understood what is the right path to liberation (contrary to his practices up to that point). In the context of Indian ascetic practices, this was no trivial realization. Other ascetic traditions considered any kind of pleasure as something that should be avoided, yet while performing painful practices (*tapas*),[83] the Buddha discovered that pleasure – a specific kind of pleasure – is an important mental and physical factor for purifying and liberating the mind from attachment and clinging. There are pleasures and joys that operate as tools for purification. This, however, is not the 'bliss of liberation' (*ānanda*) described in various Indian spiritual texts (i.e., the fruit of liberation) but pleasure attained while one is still 'walking the path.' This realization was a counter understanding to ascetic worldviews about pleasure and pain in the spiritual path.

In the *Kandaraka Sutta* of the MN, the Buddha enumerates four types of persons:

1 A person who torments himself and pursues the practice of torturing himself.
2 A person who torments others and pursues the practice of torturing others.
3 A person who torments himself and pursues the practice of torturing himself and torments others and pursues the practice of torturing others.[84]
4 A person who does not torment himself or pursue the practice of torturing himself and does not torment others or pursue the practice of torturing others.

Only the first and fourth types are relevant to our discussion. The first refers to various types of ascetics, such as those who reject conventions, practice restriction on food and so on, while the fourth describes the one who practices the Buddhist path. The Buddha explains in regard to the fourth type that by the practice of *sīla*, restraining the impressions brought about by sense experience, the development of mindfulness and the abandonment of the hindrances, one attains the *jhānas* and liberation (the gradual path discussed above). The result is that

> [s]ince he torments neither himself nor others, he is here and now hunger-less, extinguished, and cooled, and he abides experiencing pleasure (*sukha*) having himself become holy.[85]

While the fourth type is the one the Buddha extols, the first type can be identified mainly with the practice of the Nigaṇṭhas (and perhaps also the Ājīvikas). In the Nikāyas, the view of the Nigaṇṭhas is presented as that which advocated 'severe, painful, racking, piercing feeling' (*opakkamikā dukkha tibbā kharā kaṭukā vedanā vedayanti*) as the way to achieve liberation. The *Cūḷadukkhakkhandha Sutta* describes an encounter between the Buddha and a number of Nigaṇṭhas. To the Buddha's question why they practice such painful practices, they reply with the teaching they were given by their teacher, Nigaṇṭha Nātaputta, probably a Jain teacher:

> Nigaṇṭhas, evil action was done by you in the past. Annihilate this by severe and hard practice. If you are restrained here and now in body, speech and mind, then, there is no formation of evil action in the future. That is, by annihilation of past actions by asceticism (*tapasā*), [and] by refraining from doing any new karma, there is no effect in the future. With no effect in the future, there is the destruction of karma. With the destruction of karma, there is the destruction of suffering . . .[86]

The Buddha first criticizes the Nigaṇṭha's blind acceptance of a doctrine which relies on information that cannot be verified by them, that is, information about their evil actions in previous existences and the misleading way to annihilate it. The Nigaṇṭhas reply to his criticism by explicating the rationale behind their view:

> Pleasure is not to be gained by pleasure; pleasure is to be gained by pain. For were pleasure to be gained through pleasure, then King Seniya Bimbisāra of Magadha would gain pleasure, since he abides in greater pleasure than the Venerable Gotama.[87]

This statement indicates that the Nigaṇṭhas classified 'pleasure' (*sukha*) into only two types: first, the pleasure of the senses (*kāma*), which is the kind of pleasure that a wealthy king experiences quite frequently. This type of pleasure should be feared and avoided. The second type of pleasure is pleasure gained at the end of the spiritual path, the pleasure that the Buddha himself described as one of the characteristics of *nibbāna*.[88] For the Nigaṇṭhas, the only acceptable pleasure is the 'ultimate pleasure', the pleasure experienced at the end of the spiritual path. This is the only pleasure that is worthy of seeking, since in their view, there is no pleasure that can be conducive (or necessary) for attaining liberation. Moreover, for attaining this 'ultimate pleasure' – the pleasure of liberation – one must practice painful asceticism (*tapas*) as their statement indicates: 'pleasure is to be gained by pain'. Thus, according to the doctrine of Nigaṇṭha Nātaputta, pain, brought about by *tapas*, is the way to annihilate past *karma*, which leads to the cessation of suffering.

Interestingly, the same question about *kamma* and its ending is explained by Ānanda in a way that coincides with Buddhist understanding and differs from the aforementioned Nigaṇṭhas' view. Ānanda explicates in AN I.220: (1) how to stop producing fresh *kamma*; (2) how to put an end to former *kamma*; and (3) how to realize *nibbāna*. He explains that the Buddha taught this can be done by training in morality, by attaining the four *jhānas*[89] and by the destruction of the *āsavas*. From this explanation it appears that *sīla* is the way to stop producing fresh *kamma*. In other words, one can stop producing unwholesome *kamma* by acting wholesomely in body, speech and mind through the training in *sīla*. Note, however, that in Buddhist philosophy, the complete stopping of *kamma* is the domain of only awakened beings. That is, only Arahants and Buddhas do not produce *kamma*. Those on the path train and make an effort to produce only wholesome *kamma* (and stop producing unwholesome *kamma*). As to the four *jhānas*, it seems from Ānanda's explanation, that one can make an end to former *kamma* by attaining these states.

Former *kamma*, in the Buddhist context, means the underlying tendencies (*anusaya*). It seems that the *jhānas* are the way to eliminate these tendencies, which are impressions of former actions and intentions imbedded in the mind. These latent impressions condition future actions of body, speech and mind. Here, the Nikāyas imply a connection between the attainment of the *jhānas* and the uprooting of the underlying tendencies.[90] While this is only implied in this context, it is stated explicitly elsewhere; I will return to this issue later on.

Having made these observations, we are still left with two important questions. The first one is what kind of pleasure and happiness is conducive to *nibbāna*; the second is how does it work? The later will be address shortly, but the former has a straightforward answer given in the *Pāsādika Sutta*. In this sutta, the Buddha states that if wanderers of other sects say that the followers of Gotama are addicted to life of devotion to pleasure, one should answer them that there are four kinds of pleasure which are conducive to *nibbāna*. These are the four *jhānas*:[91]

> These [four *jhānas*] are the four kinds of life devoted to pleasure that are entirely conducive to disenchantment, to dispassion, to cessation, to tranquillity, to special knowledge, to full awakening, to *nibbāna*.[92]

Most importantly, however, is the Buddha's statement that one needs 'to know how to define pleasure and knowing that, one should pursue pleasure within oneself'.[93] In this statement, there is a hidden criticism against other traditions that were not able to discern the differences among types of pleasure and joy correctly, with their different qualities and effects on the mind.[94] *Jhānic pīti* and *sukha* are states of (mental) joy and (bodily) pleasure which aid the process of purification and liberation.[95]

VI *Jhānic sukha* and *pīti*

The Nikāyas enumerates three types of *sukha* and *pīti*:[96] (1) carnal (*sāmisa*) *sukha* and *pīti*, which are pleasure and happiness that arise in dependence of the five cords of sensual pleasures (*kāma*); (2) spiritual (*nirāmisa*) *sukha* and *pīti*, which are the pleasure and happiness experienced in the *jhānas*; and (3) *sukha* and *pīti*, which are more spiritual than the spiritual (*nirāmisā nirāmisataraṃ*). The latter is explained in this way:

> When a bhikkhu whose taints are destroyed reviews his mind liberated from lust (*rāga*), hatred (*dosa*) and delusion (*moha*), there arises happiness. This is called happiness more spiritual than the spiritual.[97]

This last type of joy and pleasure seems to refer to the same type of pleasure the Nigaṇṭhas accept as worthy. However, it is not relevant to our discussion, since it describes the happiness attained *after* liberation, when the liberated person reviews his mind and realizes that his mind is now liberated.[98] What is relevant here are spiritual (*nirāmisa*) *sukha* and *pīti*, which are the pleasure and joy experienced in the *jhānas* and before one attains liberation.

According to the *Visuddhimagga*, *sukha* is included in the *vedanā khandha* while *pīti* is included in the *saṅkhāra khandha*.[99] This interpretation is compatible with the Nikāyas, especially since 'spiritual' (*nirāmisa*) *sukha* is characterized in the third *jhāna* as 'happiness experienced with the body' (*sukhañca kāyena paṭisaṃvedeti*). This suggests that *sukha* is a physical pleasure while *pīti* is a mental one.

In MN II.203–4 the Buddha uses a simile of a fire for describing two types of *pīti*. He asks the brahmin student Subha:

> Which of these two fires would have a better flame, colour and radiance – a fire that might burn in dependence on fuel, such as grass and woods, or a fire that might burn independent of fuel such as grass and wood?[100]

Subha, of course, answers that the one which burns independent of fuel such as grass and wood is better. The Buddha then explains that *pīti* of the first two *jhānas* is like a fire that does not depend on fuel to burn, while *pīti* that depends on the five cords of sensual pleasures is like a fire that depends on fuel to burn (it seems reasonable to assume that this characterization applies to the two types of *sukha* as well). But what does it mean that *jhānic pīti* (and *sukha*) are not dependent on the five cords of sensual pleasures? What does it mean to not be dependent on sense experiences, while not being cut off from them? I believe that the preceding paragraph from the same sutta can elucidate this point. In this paragraph, the Buddha explains how the brahmin Pokkharasāti relates to the five cords of sensual pleasures (which produce the unwholesome *pīti*). According to the Buddha,

> the brahmin Pokkharasāti is enslaved by these five cords of sensual pleasures, having desire for them, being infatuated with them, and being utterly committed to them, since he enjoys them without seeing the danger in them or understanding the escape from them.[101]

The problem, according to the Buddha, is ignorance regarding the dangers of desiring sense pleasures. Since an ignorant person does not understand the true nature of sensual pleasures, he or she superimposes qualities onto these experiences that are not true; thus, the happiness that arises in dependence on these experiences is not 'noble' or conducive to liberation. According to Buddhist theory, it creates more desire and perpetuates delusion. However, *jhānic pīti* (and *sukha*) are independent of the five cords of sensual pleasures (but not cut off from sense experience) since they arise due to clear seeing of the danger of sense gratification. When one sees the danger and true nature of sense pleasures, one can enjoy experience without any unwholesome mental states such as clinging, aversion and so forth.[102]

This line of reasoning is strengthened by what we discussed previously concerning *kāma*, *viveka* and the process of entering into the first *jhāna*. By developing insight into the nature of phenomena, one is separated from the desire for sense gratification (*kāma*). One understands that true and abiding pleasure and happiness do not depend on the arising of gratifying sense experiences or the passing away of unpleasant and painful experiences. This insight inclines the mind to renunciation (*nekkhamma*), which is a mental standpoint in which infatuation with sense pleasures is absent:

> Bhikkhus, desire and lust for the eye is a corruption of the mind. Desire and lust for the ear . . . for the nose . . . for the tongue . . . for the body . . . for the mind is a corruption of the mind. When a bhikkhu has abandoned the corruptions of mind in these six cases, his mind inclines to renunciation. A mind fortified by renunciation becomes wieldy in regard to those things that are to be realized by direct knowledge.[103]

It may be deduced that sense contact can occur without desire, lust, and aversion, even before the attainment of awakening, and for prolonged period of time (that is, not a momentary experience). I would contend that this occurs during the experience of the *jhāna*-states. Experiencing phenomena without these corruptions of mind allows the mind to find delight, not in sense pleasures, but from seeing the true nature of phenomena.[104]

Leading on from this, the next question is whether *jhānic pīti* and *sukha* have a certain purpose in the path to liberation, or whether they are, in a manner of speaking, only the fruit of clear seeing. In our attempt to understand the *jhānas* as a vital and necessary path-factor,[105] the next section will explore this question and offer a hypothesis regarding the transformative and liberative value of *jhānic pīti* and *sukha*.

VII The first *jhāna* as a middle path

In the *Cūḷadukkhakkhandha Sutta* of the MN, the lay disciple Mahānāma asks the Buddha why – even though he understood the Dhamma taught by the Blessed One that greed, hatred and delusion are imperfections that defile the mind – at times these unwholesome states still invade his mind and remain. Mahānāma further wonders what (mental) state (*dhamma*) is still un-abandoned by him internally (*ajjhattaṃ*), owing to which these defilements still invade his mind.[106] The Buddha explains that since he had not abandoned one thing internally, he still enjoys the home life and the gratification born from sensual experiences. He explains that

> [E]ven though a noble disciple has clearly seen, as it is, with proper wisdom, how sensual pleasures provide little gratification, much suffering and much despair, and how great is the danger in them, he is (still) not un-enticed by sensual pleasure. As long as he does not attain [mental] joy and [bodily] pleasure other than sensual pleasures, other than unwholesome states, or to something more peaceful than that,[107] he may still be enticed by sensual pleasures.[108]

This explanation is interesting and its implication important. First, it is clear from this answer that the internal mental state Mahānāma did not abandon is *kāma*. In other words, the Buddha points out that the source for Mahānāma's moments of greed, hatred and delusion is attraction, aversion and confusion regarding sense pleasures. This is not surprising. Desire arises due to sense gratification while aversion arises due to its passing away or absence.[109] A second important point is that the Buddha's answer refers specifically to an advanced disciple (*ariyasāvakassa*). We can assume quite confidently from this sutta that Mahānama was not a beginner in the spiritual path (although a lay person), but an advanced disciple, possibly even a 'once-returner' (*sakadāgāmi*). Otherwise the Buddha would not have opened his answer to Mahānama with the designation *ariyasāvaka*.[110] This seems a reasonable assumption since Mahānama indicates that greed, hatred and delusion invade his mind and remain only 'at times' (*ekadā*). The use of the adverb *ekadā* in this context shows the rarity of which these unwholesome states take hold of his mind. That is to say, they have limited power. Thus this sutta gives us an interesting account of a question posed by an advanced disciple to the Buddha, and explicates the process of how desire and involvement with sense pleasures (i.e., *kāma*) – a basic tendency of the human mind – can be uprooted completely.[111]

Mahānāma's question, together with the Buddha's answer, is significant because it touches upon the relationship between insight and liberation: between the ability to 'see clearly as it is with proper wisdom' (*yathābhūtaṃ sammappaññāya sudiṭṭhaṃ hoti*) and the purification of mind from the defilements. Though he is an advanced practitioner who understood that greed, hatred and delusion are imperfections of the mind (and if we assume that he is a 'once-returner,' it means that he had some kind of direct insight about it), Mahānāma wonders why this insight into the Dhamma did not eradicate these defilements? This time, the Buddha's answer is surprising: even though a noble disciple has insight into the true nature of sensual pleasures, this insight is not enough for the mind to become disillusioned and disenchanted with sense gratification (and abandon aversion to their passing away or absence). This is a surprising statement. A common perception of Buddhist theory of liberation is that knowing how things really are is enough for attaining liberation.[112] However, it seems that even though the cause for our attachments is partly cognitive and associated with our distorted perception, according to this sutta (and other suttas that will be discussed later), this cognitive capacity is not enough for uprooting the tendencies of desire (or for attaining complete liberation). That is, 'wisdom' (*paññā*) and 'clear seeing' (*sudiṭṭhaṃ*) of 'things as they are' (*yathābhūtaṃ)*[113] cannot transform the mind completely. Something else is required for abandoning the attraction and desire for sense pleasures.

A similar point of view is presented in SN II.117–118 regarding the attainment of *nibbāna*. In this sutta, the venerable Saviṭṭha asks the venerable Nārada if 'other than faith, other than personal preference, other than oral tradition, other than reasoned reflection, other than acceptance of view after pondering it, does the venerable Nārada have personal knowledge'[114] of the twelve links of dependent origination in their arising and cessation modes. Nārada answers that apart from all of those things, he knows and sees (*ahametaṃ jānāmi ahametaṃ passāmi*) the twelve links of dependent origination in their arising and cessation modes. Note that Nārada not only accepts a view after hearing or reflecting upon it; he also declares that he knows and sees this reality directly. After Saviṭṭha's investigation regarding the twelve links of dependent origination, he also asks Nārada if he has personal knowledge (*paccattameva ñāṇaṃ*) that '*nibbāna* is the cessation of existence' (*bhavanirodho nibbānaṃ*). Nārada answers that he does know and see *nibbāna* as the cessation of existence. At this point of the investigation, Saviṭṭha concludes that Nārada must be 'an arahant whose taints are destroyed' (*nārado arahaṃ khīṇāsavo*). However, Nārada's response is quite unexpected. He says that even though he has clearly seen (*sudiṭṭhaṃ*) as it is (*yathābhūtaṃ*) with correct wisdom (*sammppaññāya*) (similar phrasing to the *Cūḷadukkhakkhandha Sutta*) that *nibbāna* is the cessation of existence, he is not an arahant whose taints are destroyed (*na camhi khīṇāsavo*). He explains his statement in terms of a simile about a thirsty traveller. This thirsty person can see water in a well, but because no rope or a bucket is available, he is unable to quench his thirst; that is, he 'was not able to dwell having touched [the water] with the body' (*na ca kāyena phusitvā vihareyya*). Nārada continues by saying,

> So too, friend, though I have clearly seen as it is with correct wisdom: '*nibbāna* is the cessation of existence', I am not an arahant, one whose taints are destroyed.[115]

The *Sekha Sutta* of the SN is another sutta that presents this notion. It explains the difference between a *sekha* ('a trainee') – one of the first three noble persons – and an *asekha* ('one who is beyond training', an arahant). The Buddha explains that a *sekha* knows the Four Noble Truths and the five spiritual faculties (trust, effort, mindfulness, *samādhi* and wisdom) but:

> He does not yet dwell having touched with the body, their destination, their culmination, their fruit, and their final goal; but having pierced it through with wisdom, he sees. This too is a method by means of which a bhikkhu who is a trainee, standing on the plane of a trainee, knows: 'I am a trainee.'[116]

That is, a 'stream-enterer', a 'once-returner' and a 'non-returner' have seen the nature of experience as it is and have penetrated with wisdom *(paññā)* the Four Noble Truths. However, since they did not yet 'dwell having touched with the body' in the final goal (*kāyena phusitvā viharati*), they are not fully liberated; thus, they are still trainees.

These two suttas from the Saṃyutta Nikāya elucidate the difference between 'seeing clearly with proper wisdom', that is, the cognitive insight that arises through seeing things as they are (which a *sekha* has achieved), and the actual experience of full freedom (which only arahants attain). According to SN II.118, seeing clearly that *nibbāna* is the cessation of existence does not make a person liberated. Similarly, according to SN V.229–30, understanding the Four Noble Truths is not enough for becoming an arahant; nevertheless, it is the turning point where one becomes a *sekha*. Although the Saṃyutta Nikāya suttas discuss the nature of *nibbāna* while the *Cūḷadukkhakkhandha Sutta* discusses the eradication of *kāma*, the principle is the same: cognitive understanding cannot transform the mind completely, although it is an important step in the transformation.[117]

Here we find the notion that while *paññā*, as a specific cognitive understanding, is an initial and important quality in the process of awakening, it is not enough for liberating the mind. To quench a thirst, just as to become an arahant, one needs more than seeing the way out clearly; one has to experience this quenching reality directly. These two suttas describe this direct experience as 'touching with the body'. In the very same way, only by experiencing a different type of bodily and mental pleasure can one actually let go of the rooted desire for sensual pleasures. The cognitive understanding that these pleasures are impermanent can be the impetus for the spiritual path, but cannot transform rooted tendencies. For a deeper change – for the transformation of ordinary, recurrent patterns – a different *embodied* reality must be experienced.[118]

The *Māgandiya Sutta* of the MN presents a similar view to that of the *Cūḷadukkhakkhandha Sutta* and elucidates further the liberative role of *jhānic pīti* and *sukha*. The *Māgandiya Sutta* describes a conversation between the Buddha and the wanderer Māgandiya about the dangers of the desire for sensual pleasures and the way to abandon this desire. The Buddha explains to Māgandiya how one can become free from the desire and lust for sense pleasures. The Buddha describes a twofold process: first, one develops insight into the true nature of sense experience (the cognitive wisdom aspect) and then one 'abides without thirst with a mind inwardly at peace.'[119] The latter statement makes more sense when the Buddha explains this process by describing his own experience:

> On a later occasion, having understood as they actually are, the origin, the disappearance, the gratification, the danger and the escape in the case of sensual pleasures, I abandoned craving for sensual pleasures . . . I see other beings who are not free from lust for sensual pleasures, being devoured by craving for sensual pleasures, burning with fever for sensual pleasures, indulging in sensual pleasures, and I do not envy them, nor do I delight in that. Why is that? Because there is, Māgandiya, a delight other than sensual

pleasures and unwholesome states, which surpasses divine pleasure. Since I take delight in that, I do not desire what is inferior, nor do I indulge [myself] therein.[120]

It is justified to assume that in this context the term *rati* ('delight') can be read as synonymous to *jhānic sukha* and *pīti*. Perhaps the term *rati* was more familiar to the Buddha's interlocutor, who was not a disciple of the Buddha. Thus, this passage points at several important issues. Above all, the Buddha states that pleasure, other than sensual and divine pleasures (*dibbaṃ sukhaṃ*), is pleasure that allows the mind to let go of coarser pleasures, such as the desire for sensual and divine pleasures. The Buddha clearly states that he was able to abandon desire for sensual and divine pleasures (the pleasure attained in the heavenly worlds, either by meditation or by being reborn there),[121] and remove burning for these pleasures, by abiding in that delight which is apart from sensual pleasures and unwholesome states. Such a state is achieved presumably by abiding in the first two *jhānas*.[122]

This statement is similar to the one made in the *Cūḷadukkhakkhandha Sutta*. The Buddha clarifies his statement about the importance of *jhānic pīti* and *sukha* by giving a simile. He describes a householder who is reborn in a heavenly world, enjoying 'divine sensual pleasures' (*dibbehi pañcahi kāmaguṇehi*). Since he experiences this type of divine pleasure, he could no longer envy a householder who experiences only 'ordinary human sensual pleasure' (*kāma*). The principle is that through the direct and intimate experience of a loftier pleasure, one can let go of attachment to pleasures which were perceived as desirable and attractive before.[123]

This account also points at the important distinction between 'divine pleasure' (*dibbaṃ sukhaṃ*) – the pleasure attained in heavenly worlds of the *kāma-dhātu*, the *rūpa-dhātu* and the *arūpa-dhātu* –[124] and the pleasure of the *jhānas*. This is significant, since it can be argued that the Buddha surpassed only 'divine sensual pleasures' (*dibba-pañca-kāmaguna*) when he attained the first *jhāna*. This argument is based on a problematic identification of *jhānic* pleasure with the pleasures of the *rūpa* realms. I will discuss this issue later on, but here I would just like to point out that the Buddha clearly states that he was able to abandon *kāma*, because he experienced pleasure which 'surpasses divine pleasure', and not only 'divine sensual pleasures' (*dibba-pañca-kāmaguna*). We can take this to mean that the pleasure of the first *jhāna* surpasses all types of divine pleasures, including those experienced in the *kāma, rūpa* and *arūpa* realms.[125]

At this point, I would like to make a few observations concerning the Chinese version of the *Cūḷadukkhakkhandha Sutta*. The earlier account from the *Cūḷadukkhakkhandha Sutta*, in which the Buddha states that the experience of *jhānic pīti* and *sukha* allows the mind to abandon *kāma* [MN I.91–2], has no parallel in the Chinese version.[126] At first glance, it seems as though the Chinese version is quite similar to the Pāli one, apart from the aforementioned missing part; this parallel might be an argument against the authenticity of the passage. However, in a closer look, the two versions have a different 'flavour'. I would suggest that the Chinese version primarily deals with the external state of the spiritual seeker, while the Pāli version is more concerned with the internal mental state, that is, with elucidating the mental process of purification and liberation.

Both versions open with Mahānama's question about greed, hate and delusion. In the Chinese version, Mahānama asks the Buddha why these three things do not cease in him permanently, even though he is mindful. In this version, the Buddha states, quite differently than in the Pāli version, that Mahānama still lives with his wife and children, which shows that he has lust (*lobha*/*raga*), and this lust causes him to remain a householder. The Buddha adds that a *bhadra* [賢] (a practitioner who is advanced beyond the level of a worldling 凡夫)[127] knows that although separation from family life is difficult, the happiness (*sukha*) from renouncing lay life is greater; this is because happiness from being a householder is impermanent. Here it is quite clear that the external choice of Mahānama to stay a householder, rather than becoming a monk, is the main issue. That is, renunciation in the Chinese version refers quite explicitly to the external renunciation of family life. After this statement, the Buddha continues to describe the lower happiness of the five strands of sensual pleasures connected to the householder life (these are also described in the Pāli version). The end of this version is also different from the Pāli one. The Chinese version ends with a remark to the monks about the importance of giving back to parents; this is something that is absent from the Pāli and seems to be more Chinese in nature. It also points to social and external conditions of the monks' choice and their behaviour and relationship with their families. As I have noted, it seems that the Chinese version was mainly directed to monks (even though the main character is a lay person), and its concern was to reinforce the choice of becoming a monastic. In other words, this version was more concerned with the external condition that might sustain greed, hatred and delusion; according to this version, these three poisons belong to the life of a householder. At the same time, this version advocates for the choice of becoming a monastic as the external condition most conducive to eradicating the three poisons. In the Pāli version, however, Mahānama asks the Buddha specifically what state (*dhammo*) is still un-abandoned by him internally (*ajjhattaṃ*), by which these unwholesome states still invade his mind.[128] Neither Mahānama nor the Buddha is discussing his situation as a householder. Thus, the Pāli version is concerned explicitly with the internal state that impedes the mind from being free, and with the internal mental process of abandoning *kāma*. The Buddha points out clearly that Mahānama's situation as a householder has no significant bearing on his spiritual progress; rather, the problem is internal mental attachment and not his life as a lay person. As previously pointed out, although this internal state (*dhammo ajjhattaṃ*) is not specified, it is quite clear that the Buddha refers to the desire for sensual pleasures (*kāma*) – desire that arises in both lay persons and monastics.

Given these differences between the two versions, I do not think that it is possible to determine which version is more 'authentic' or early. Although one criterion for determining if a text is early or late is the fact that later versions usually contain additional material, in our case, the versions are not identical in their concerns, and hence, it might be misleading to compare them in terms of antiquity. Furthermore, an important presupposition in textual criticism is that, rather than add problematic elements, editors and scribes would tend to extract odd words and difficult passages and replace them with more familiar terms and less controversial ones. Thus, it is hard to imagine why the Theravāda tradition would add the description of the first *jhāna* as an explanation for eradicating *kāma*, when this path-element (i.e., the *jhānas*) was considered non-essential for liberation quite early in the history of this tradition. The view that one can bypass the *jhānas* in the path of awakening is evident already in the Paṭisambhidāmagga (Paṭis II, 92–103),[129] which was dated by A. K. Warder to the third century and early second century BCE. The notion that the *jhānas* are not necessary to the attainment of awakening is well established also in the Aṭṭhakathā literature.[130] Therefore, it is not very plausible to contend that the earliest version of the *Cūḷadukkhakkhandha Sutta* did not contain a description of the first *jhāna*, meaning that it was added later by the Theravāda tradition.

In this regard, it is also interesting to note that other sūtras in the Chinese Āgamas lack descriptions of the *jhānas*. The *Ariyapariyesanā Sutta* contains a section in which the Buddha describes the *jhānas*, the *samapattis* and the attainment of cessation as a way to escape Māra. These descriptions are also absent in the parallel version in the Chinese Āgama.[131] The same absence occurs in the Chinese parallel to the *Mahāvedalla Sutta* of the MN. The Pāli version describes eight questions that deal with the first *jhāna* and the signless liberation of mind. However, the Chinese version makes no reference to these questions. Therefore, it seems more reasonable to hypothesize that the Chinese version (or the source of the Chinese version) omitted these references, than to argue that the Pāli version added them later. It is quite obvious that the *jhānas* are not a later addition to the Buddha's teachings.[132] It may be deduced that even though the Chinese version of the *Cūḷadukkhakkhandha Sutta* lacks the reference to the first *jhāna*, this passage might be a remnant of an early understanding of the spiritual process. It might be that the Pāli suttas represent an old stratum of Buddhist teaching about the *jhānas*, which perceived these attainments as an essential component of the path to awakening.

We concluded the last section with a question: do *jhānic pīti* and *sukha* have certain purpose in the path to liberation or are they only the fruit of clear seeing? We find that the *Cūḷadukkhakkhandha Sutta* and the *Māgandiya Sutt*a provide an answer: *jhānic pīti* and *sukha*, the result of clear seeing, also have a significant liberative role in the path of purification (as *sammā-samādhi*). By experiencing *jhānic pīti* and *sukha*, the practitioner can let go of 'coarse' attachments, such as the desire for sensual and divine pleasures. Furthermore, I would also observe that *jhānic sukha* – as a pleasurable wholesome physical factor – is important for the mind to relax, let go and see experience clearly. When one does not experience bodily pain, bodily pleasure arises and allows the mind to become steady for seeing phenomena as it is:

> Which nine things greatly help? Nine conditions rooted in wise attention: when a monk practices wise attention, gladness arises in him; being glad, joy arises. From his feeling joy, his body is calmed; as a result of his calming the

> body he feels pleasure. From his feeling pleasure, his mind becomes steadied; with his mind thus steadied, he knows and sees [things] as they really are. With his thus knowing and seeing [things] as they really are he becomes disenchanted; with disenchantment he becomes dispassionate, and by dispassion he is liberated.[133]

Having said that, I would like to offer the following reflection. We all experience moments of 'spiritual' pleasure and joy, that is, happiness independent of sense gratification, which may be similar to *jhānic pīti* and *sukha*.[134] However, these moments are usually brief and therefore not able to loosen our attachment to sense pleasures. In other words, since this 'spiritual' pleasure is so brief, the ordinary mind cannot become familiar enough with it to abandon desire for sense gratification; it is a deep tendency of the human mind. What I would like to suggest is that the power of the *jhānas* and the experience of *jhānic pīti* and *sukha* lie in the description of the *jhānas* as attainments that one 'enters into and abides in' (*upasampajja viharati*).[135] The verb *viharati* indicates that the practitioner dwells in – or better put, experiences 'being in' – this attainment for a period of time. This abiding enables one to be soaked by this spiritual joy and pleasure.[136] Such a comprehensive experience allows the mind to experience fully and intimately a different mode of being, very different from ordinary experience. Knowing closely that there is a different type of pleasure – one which does not rely on pleasant sense experience – is the way to uproot our deep tendency to consider sense pleasures (*kāma*), as the most gratifying experiences.

We can safely say it takes more than intellectual understanding that sense pleasures are impermanent and not worth grasping before we are able to get beyond our enchantment for and attachment to them. When we familiarize ourselves deeply with another type of pleasure and joy, the mind is able to transform its basic inclination to seek delight in sense gratification, especially when unpleasant and painful feelings are experienced. According to SN IV.209, each time a noble disciple does not seek delight in sense pleasure, through his close experience with a different type of pleasure and joy (in all probability the first two *jhānas*), the mind becomes pure. According to SN IV.209, this is how a noble disciple does not create any new unwholesome underlying tendencies.[137] This is further strengthened by the *Cūḷavedalla Sutta* from the MN, where the nun Dhammadinnā explains to Visākha that entering the *jhānas* is the way to abandon the underlying tendencies (*anusaya*).[138] Dhammadinnā explains that in the first *jhāna* one abandons the underlying tendency to lust. She further states that in the next two *jhānas* one will abandon aversion and the underlying tendency to aversion, and when one abides in the fourth *jhāna*, ignorance and the underlying tendency to ignorance are abandoned. In other words, the *jhānas* cannot originate from lust, aversion and ignorance and do not create any new tendencies. They seem to spontaneously arise from the development of renunciation and insight. Thus, it is plausible to argue that these attainments are the actual fulfilment of the path of purification, and as such, they exemplify a mind which is wholesome and have clear perception of reality.

VIII *Vitakka* and *vicāra*

To conclude our discussion on the first *jhāna*, we turn our attention to *vitakka* and *vicāra*, which are said to accompany (*savitakka savicāra*) the two key factors: *pīti* and *sukha*. *Vitakka* and *vicāra* were translated in various ways, such as 'applied and sustained thought', 'initial cognition and reasoned examination' or 'thinking and reflecting'.[139] Note that all these translations point at the cognitive, discursive, conceptual and dualistic nature of *vitakka* and *vicāra*. In the Abhidhamma, *vitakka* and *vicāra* received a more meditative meaning in the context of the first *jhāna*. *Vitakka* was interpreted as the ability to apply the mind to a meditation object, while *vicāra* as the sustained attention on the chosen object.[140] However, this interpretation overlooks the common meaning of *vitakka* and *vicāra* in the Nikāyas as conceptual thinking and reflecting.[141] I am not suggesting that there is no meditative process in which the mind places its attention onto a meditation objects and sustains it for a period of time. However, I do not think that *vitakka* and *vicāra* express this meditative procedure in the Nikāyas.

But before discussing *vitakka* and *vicāra* in the context of the first *jhāna*, let us first review few occurrences of *vitakka* and *vicāra* in the Nikāyas. No attempt will be made here to survey and discuss all the occurrences of *vitakka* and *vicāra* as I am concerned here with interpreting the existence of these two mental factors in the first *jhāna* and not in ordinary cognitive processes. To narrow the discussion, I shall confine it to a brief reflection on the common usage of *vitakka* and *vicāra* as 'discursive and conceptual thinking'.

In the Nikāyas, the terms *vitakka* and *vicāra* usually describe thinking and reflecting upon an issue (wholesome or unwholesome). Interestingly, the term *vitakka* appears many times by itself.[142] However, to the best of my knowledge, *vicāra* appears mostly, if not exclusively, with *vitakka*. It might be that the use of both terms together analyzes the process of thinking more accurately, while the use of *vitakka* alone designates 'thinking' in more general way.

Vitakka and *vicāra* are also connected to verbalization,[143] and they are defined as 'verbal formation' (*vacīsaṅkhāra*).[144] MN I.301 explains this by stating that 'first one thinks and reflects, and subsequently one breaks out into speech'.[145] Although the process of thinking is a prerequisite to the ability to talk, it is also important to note that thinking cannot occur without language as a precondition. That is, without words, concepts and syntax, the process of thinking is impossible; they are co-dependent processes. DN II.277 further explains that the origin of *vitakka* are 'words, conceptualization and mental proliferation' (*papañcasaññāsaṅkhā*).[146] It is stated that without *papañcasaññāsaṅkhā* there is no *vitakka*.[147] The compound *papañcasaññāsaṅkhā* is one of the most difficult compounds in the Nikāyas, and I will not discuss it here.[148] What is relevant to our discussion is the apparent question of whether all three mental phenomena (i.e., *papañca*, *saññā* and *saṅkhā*) must exist for *vitakka* to exist. Although DN II.277 explains that without *papañcasaññāsaṅkhā* there is no *vitakka*, this statement was made in a specific context – as an answer to a question concerning the origin of jealousy and avarice. In this context, it is clear that thinking is bound up with the tendency to proliferate mentally. However, *vitakka* and *vicāra* are not always connected to *papañca* (contrary to *saññā* and *saṅkhā*, which seem to be imperative to the process of thinking). According to Buddhist psychology, the tendency to proliferate (*papañca*) is a mental function which has no real purpose in the human mind except from creating suffering and perpetuating desire and aversion. *Vitakka*, on the other hand, can be a wholesome mental activity, conducive to liberation.[149]

Thus, it is interesting to reflect on the differences between *saññā*, *vitakka* and *papañca*. These terms seem to describe various stages in the process through which the world is created and made intelligible in the human mind.[150] They describe a gradation in the way we interpret experience; they are the three types of 'curtains' which mediate, according to Buddhist epistemology, as well as hinder, our direct perception of the nature of reality, thus creating suffering. I use the word 'mediate' in the same way the constructivists use it; that is, every experience of an unawakened person is touched by language and concepts in a deep way. Ordinary cognition interprets the flow of experience through discrete conceptual units (*saññā*), and then supplements further conceptual interpretation (*vitakka* and *papañca*). This process of interpretation is based upon our previous experiences, proclivities, preferences, view, misconceptions, desires and will.[151] Furthermore, according to Buddhist epistemology, one of the features of ordinary human cognition is to ascribe false reality to these concepts and thoughts, as though they describe the world. They are believed to relate to something real and to belong to a specific 'self'. This false identification creates suffering.[152] It also separates experience into perceiving subject and perceived objects, both of which are understood in Buddhist philosophy as mental fabrications.

It should be remembered, however, that words (*saṅkhā)*, concepts (*saññā*) and thoughts (*vitakka* and *vicāra*) are not problematic in themselves according to Buddhist psychology. When one understands their functional role, without considering them as referring to something real and without identifying with them, they are important cognitive faculties.[153] Sue Hamilton has explained clearly this cognitive process by explaining that

> [D]elineating and identifying things, verbally differentiating them – making them manifold – is the way we reify our experiences: by naming them as we do we as it were pin them down so they can become a real part of our total reality.[154]

However, I think Sue Hamilton has also expressed beautifully the necessity of the cessation of 'making manifold' through the thinking process by arguing that

> knowledge of the absence of activity gives one knowledge of what the nature of the activity usually is.[155]

In other words, the cessation of the thinking process, and the observation of this cessation, is an important realization for loosening attachment and clinging to subjective experience – experience that is based upon our thinking process. Seeing the cessation of thinking lends insight into the origin and nature of thinking, and therefore into the origin and manifestation of the sense of self. It allows one to see clearly how thinking creates subjective experience, and how this reality is insubstantial in nature.[156] I would argue that this insight occurs in the transition between the first and second *jhāna*, where *vitakka* and *vicāra* fade away.

To clarify this idea, and to reflect upon the advantages, disadvantages and limits of conceptual thinking, let us consider the first discourse of the *Sutta Nipāta*. This discourse describes a bhikkhu who becomes liberated. Although each verse of the sutta ends with affirming that this monk 'leaves this shore and the far shore as a snake leaves its old worn-out skin', it nonetheless seems to describe a gradual process of liberation from various disturbing emotions and cognitive misconceptions. I would suggest that the phrase repeated after each verse was added for mnemonic purposes, perhaps for helping the reciters to remember that these verses are part of the same discourse.

The sutta begins by describing the various disturbing emotions which a bhikkhu abandons on the path to liberation. These include anger (*kodha*), passion (*rāga*), craving (*taṇhā*) and conceit (*māna*). The sutta then continues by describing the overcoming of the various cognitive misconceptions. This portrayal presents a process in which conceptual thinking is utilized, but then has to be abandoned for clarity and insight to deepen. The first attitude that must be developed is that which 'does not find any essence in existences' (*nājjhagamā bhavesu sāraṃ*). We can assume that 'not finding essence in existences' can be achieved by contemplating the impermanent nature of all conditioned phenomena. For such contemplation one must use cognitive discursive faculties such as *vitakka* and *vicāra* (that seem to support the arising of *viveka*, 'discernment'). That is, one employs the power of conceptual thinking and reflecting for contemplating the transitory, dependent and unsatisfactory nature of phenomena.

The next verse makes it quite clear, however, that thinking should cease (*vitakkā vidhūpitā*) in order to attain liberation.[157] The subsequent verse goes even further and identifies that same 'thinking' with *papañca* by declaring that a monk 'overcomes all this *papañca*'[158] (presumably referring to *vitakka* from the previous verse). This is an intriguing statement, since as I pointed out earlier, thinking can be conducive to liberation, while *papañca* cannot. However, I believe that this verse suggests something more subtle. It implies that even though *vitakka* and *vicāra* have less 'suffering potential' than *papañca*, they still hinder our perception;[159] they tell a story about the experience and can create a sense of self. This is the reason why the Buddha declared that 'thoughts build the world'[160] and that one has to arrive at the 'end of the world' for attaining liberation.[161]

I would suggest that the difference between *vitakka* and *papañca* is a difference in intensity and the power of clinging and ignorance. Thoughts, either wholesome or obsessive, have always a point of reference – the self. In a very basic way, thinking is the way we create and sustain a sense of self. Descartes expressed this notion by declaring, 'Cogito, ergo sum' – I think, therefore I am. Thinking, even if it is wholesome, separates the flow of experience into a subjective 'I' who experiences an objective reality – a 'thinker' and a 'thought'. We can even go further and argue that most of our thoughts (if not all of them) are constructed in relation to a 'self'. They are the manifestation of wanting, planning and remembering, which has most frequently 'I', 'me' and 'mine' as their centre. According to Buddhist philosophy, concepts (*saññā*) and thoughts do not *describe* the world; they *create* the world. Put differently, thinking and conceptualizing do not refer to anything real 'out there'. This seems to be the reason for the statement in the next verse that 'having known with regard to the world that all this is unreal' (*sabbaṃ vitathamidanti ñatvā loke*) – that is, thoughts, concepts, ideas and so forth – one is liberated. In other words, for seeing reality as it is, thinking, which is a type of *papañca*, must cease.[162] Thus, the cessation of the thinking process is imperative for seeing the true nature of this mental phenomenon and for realizing how subjective experience and the sense of self originates and is sustained.[163]

Thus, this sutta delineates a gradual elimination of mental obstructions and cognitive misconceptions. First, one uses the power of thinking for abandoning certain misconceptions but subsequently even this wholesome type of thinking – which has both a relative value and serious limitations – must cease in order to see the nature of experience clearly. There are various modes of conceptuality, from the grossest ones, in which we conceive (*maññati*) reality from erroneous perspectives, to wholesome discursive thinking, to more subtle forms[164] where the defilements do not hinder our seeing, such as the perception of impermanence and not-self (*anicca-saññā, anattā-saññā*).[165] Anne C. Klein has made an observation about the Buddhist path that is applicable to the early teachings as well; she notes that the uniqueness of the Buddhist path is in harnessing conceptual thinking for experiencing non-conceptual state.[166]

We should bear in mind, however, that even if we argue that conceptual thinking must cease for liberation to occur, the thinking process will resume its activity after the liberation event. We can imagine that after one has seen the advantages, disadvantages and limits of the thinking process, by seeing directly its origination and cessation, thinking will no longer have the same delusive power. It is conceivable that since a liberated person will not ascribe trueness to this mental phenomenon, he or she will employ thinking and reflecting only wholesomely and beneficially, and only when the need arises. If we assume that thinking is a manifestation of wanting, we can speculate that a liberated person will have thoughts only when there is a need to respond to a situation or question. Otherwise, his mind will not produce any thoughts at all.

It appears from what I have discussed thus far that there are different types of *vitakka* and *vicāra*. What I seek to examine further is the nature of *vitakka* and *vicāra* in the first *jhāna*: what kind of thinking and reflecting can occur in this attainment and why? These questions are quite difficult to answer due to the absence of clear textual explanation. However, I do think it is possible to offer some reflections based on the texts, and in the following discussion, I shall offer three such reflections on the nature of *vitakka* and *vicāra* in the first *jhāna*.

As previously noted, *vitakka* and *vicāra* can be wholesome and beneficial (*kusala*) to the attainment of liberation. This is contrary to unwholesome mental proliferation (*papañca*), which is always an unbeneficial mental activity.

According to the *Dvedhāvitakka Sutta*, thoughts of renunciation (*nekkhamma vitakka*), of non-ill-will (*abyāpāda vitakka*) and of non-cruelty (*avihiṃsa vitakka*) are thoughts that can lead to *nibbāna*. These types of thoughts, contrary to other thoughts, can lead to the development of wholesome inclinations of mind:

> Bhikkhus, whatever a bhikkhu frequently thinks and reflects on, that will become the inclination of his mind. If he frequently thinks and reflects on thoughts of renunciation, he has abandoned the thought of sensual desire to cultivate the thought of renunciation . . . If he frequently thinks and reflects on thoughts of non-ill will . . . on thoughts of non-cruelty, he has abandoned the thought of sensual desire to cultivate the thought of cruelty to cultivate the thought of non-cruelty, and then his mind inclines to thoughts of non-cruelty.[167]

The *Dvedhāvitakka Sutta* also affirms that these types of thoughts do not lead to affliction; they aid wisdom, do not cause difficulties and lead to *nibbāna*.

Having said that, how are we to understand the existence of thoughts in the first *jhāna*? This is hard to answer. I believe that *vitakka* and *vicāra* of the first *jhāna* cannot be considered as tantamount to ordinary thinking and reflecting. I would suggest that developing thoughts of renunciation, of non-ill-will and of non-cruelty is preliminary to the attainment of the first *jhāna*. Their development is one of the means by which one can let go of *kāma* and other unwholesome states. This is the prerequisite for entering into this attainment.

While I think that *vitakka* and *vicāra* of the first *jhāna* designate some form of conceptual, intentional and dualistic perception, I would also suggest that this type thinking cannot be regarded as 'ordinary thinking process' that is mostly chaotic, excursive and excessive. Put differently, I would suggest that there is no 'train of thoughts' while one is in the first *jhāna*. This was made quite clear in the *Dvedhāvitakka Sutta*, where the Buddha explains that after he developed wholesome thoughts, he also understood that

> [t]his thought of renunciation has arisen in me. This does not lead to my own affliction . . . it aids wisdom, does not cause difficulties, and leads to *nibbāna*. If I excessively think and reflect upon this thought even for a night, even for a day, even for a night and day, I see nothing to fear from it.
>
> But with excessive thinking and reflecting, I might tire my body, and when the body is tired, the mind might become disturbed. When the mind is disturbed, it is far from being imperturbable. So I steadied my mind internally, quieted it and unified it and made it imperturbable.[168]

Here we find the notion that there is a difference between thinking and reflecting (*vitakka* and *vicāra*) and excessive thinking and reflecting (*anuvitakka* and *anuvicāra*). I propose to interpret 'excessive thinking and reflecting' as referring to what we call 'thinking' in ordinary language. That is, 'ordinary thinking' is mostly excessive since one fuels the arising thoughts with identification and clinging. However, I suggest that in the first *jhāna*, thoughts arise and pass away but without being continually fuelled by desire, aversion and other unwholesome mental states. In this *jhāna* attainment one begins to de-condition the tendency to sustain the thinking habits of commenting on and interpreting experience (that is, thinking about the present) and the tendency to think about the past and the future.

The Buddha further points at the drawback of excessive thinking and reflecting (even wholesome thinking): when one is occupied with excessive thinking and reflecting, the body is stressed and the mind is disturbed. A disturbed mind cannot see clearly the whole spectrum of phenomena since it is occupied solely by the content of his thinking (again, even if the content is wholesome). The aim of cultivating wholesome thoughts (such as thoughts of renunciation, of non-ill-will and of non-cruelty) is not the content, but for inclining the mind into an *attitude* of renunciation, an *attitude* of non-desire and an *attitude* of non-aversion to whatever is experienced. When these mental attitudes have been developed, there is no need for developing further these types of thoughts. Thus, my suggestion is that we should interpret the existence of *vitakka* and *vicāra* in the first *jhāna* as wholesome 'residues' of a previous development of wholesome thoughts. They denote the 'echo' of these wholesome thoughts, which reverberates in one who enters the first *jhāna* as wholesome attitudes towards what is experienced. This is the reason, I believe, that *vitakka* and *vicāra* are said to *accompany jhānic pīti* and *sukha*.

The *Sakkapañha Sutta* of the DN gives us another way to understand the nature of *vitakka* and *vicāra* in the first *jhāna*, which complements the earlier suggestion. This sutta draws a causal connection between *vitakka* and *chanda*, between thinking and intention. It reads, '[W]hen *vitakka* exists, *chanda* exists, when *vitakka* does not exist, *chanda* does not exist.'[169] *Chanda* has several meanings. It can be translated as 'intention', 'will' or 'desire', depending on the context. It can be wholesome[170] or unwholesome.[171] Thus, *kusala chanda* ('wholesome intention') is closely connected to *sammā saṅkappa* ('right intention'), one of the Eightfold Path factors. Since MN II.28 states that the second *jhāna* is where wholesome intentions (*kusala saṅkappa*) cease without any remnant, (*aparisesā nirujjhanti*) together with *vitakka* and *vicāra*, the implication is that in the first *jhāna*, wholesome intentions are still present.[172] In the context of the first *jhāna*, *vitakka* and *vicāra* seem to express the existence of right attitude and right intention. It should be noted that intention, just like thinking, is conceptual and dualistic. Both intention and thinking describe a relation between the mind and an object. In other words, they both have an intentional attitude towards something. We should bear this point in mind since the 'liberative reason' for which both wholesome intentions and conceptual thinking cease when one enters into the second *jhāna*, will become clearer here as well as in the chapter on the second *jhāna*.

My last reflection on *vitakka* and *vicāra* in the first *jhāna* will point at the shortcoming of *vitakka* and *vicāra* in the context of Buddhist meditation theory. The *Dantabhūmi Sutta* of the MN gives us interesting information which connects the *jhānas* with the practice of the *satipaṭṭhānas*:

> Having thus abandoned these five hindrances, imperfection of the mind that weakens wisdom, he abides observing the body as the body, ardent, fully

> aware, and mindful, having put away covetousness and grief for the world. He abide observing feelings as feelings . . . mind as mind . . . dhammas as dhammas, ardent, fully aware, and mindful, having put away covetousness and grief for the world.[173]

This description delineates the practice of observing body, feeling, mind and *dhammas* when the hindrances are abandoned, which clearly refers to the first *jhāna* (it becomes evident in the next paragraph of the same sutta). It expresses the notion that there is a transition from gross observation of the *satipaṭṭhānas* when the hindrances are still present in the mind, to a more subtle observation, when they are abandoned. That is, in the first *jhāna* one observes phenomena without desire, restlessness, aversion and so on. However, this sutta makes it very clear that this type of observation – observation that occurs while one is in the first *jhāna* – is only preliminary to a more refined observation of phenomena, namely, an observation without thinking and intending. This will be discussed in the next chapter.

Summary

Having said that and before we turn the attention to the nature and liberative value of the second *jhāna*, let me summarize my argument succinctly. Having explored the liberative value of the first *jhāna*, I have argued that only by entering the first *jhāna* one actualizes internally the 'middle path'. In other words, the first *jhāna* is the experiential actualization of a midpoint between asceticism[174] and indulgence, between sensual pleasure and bodily pain. This unique pleasurable experience allows the mind to let go of a rooted and basic tendency: the tendency to be attracted to sensual pleasures (*kāma*). This transformation becomes possible only by attaining a different type of pleasure and joy, a pleasure and joy which are wholesome and not connected to desire for sense pleasure and other unwholesome states. This is *jhānic pīti* and *sukha*.

I have also argued that the entrance into the first *jhāna* occurs through the practice of the four *satipaṭṭhānas*, the development of the qualities of the seven factors of awakening to some degree, the abandoning of the five hindrances and the development of discernment (*viveka*). *Viveka*, from which *pīti* and *sukha* of the first *jhāna* are born, arise through the observation of phenomena as prescribed in the *Satipaṭṭhāna Sutta*. I suggested that the cultivation of the quality of discernment enables the mind to change its inclinations and to let go of our basic unwholesome tendencies and desires. This letting go (*vossagga*) is the proximate cause for entering the first *jhāna*. Further, I have also observed that entering the first *jhāna* marks a transition from gross observation of the *satipaṭṭhānas* to a more subtle one: the practitioner can now observe phenomena without being hindered by unwholesome emotions and intentions. The next chapter will continue with exploring the nature and liberative significance of the second *jhāna*.

Notes

1 E.g., MN I.174: *bhikkhu vivicceva kāmehi vivicca akusalehi dhammehi savitakkaṃ savicāraṃ vivekajaṃ pītisukhaṃ paṭhamaṃ jhānaṃ upasampajja viharati.*

2 MN I.246–7: *Na kho panāhaṃ imāya kaṭukāya dukkarakārikāya adhigacchāmi uttarimanussadhammā alamariyañāṇadassanavisesaṃ. Siyā nu kho añño maggo*

bodhāyā"ti. Tassa mayhaṃ aggivessana etadahosi: abhijānāmi kho panāhaṃ pitusakkassa kammante sītāya jambucchāyāya nisinno vivicceva kāmehi vivicca akusalehi dhammehi savitakkaṃ savicāraṃ vivekajaṃ pītisukhaṃ paṭhamaṃ jhānaṃ upasampajja viharitā. Siyā nu kho eso maggo bodhāyāti. Tassa mayhaṃ aggivessana satānusāriviññāṇaṃ ahosi: esova maggo bodhāyāti.

3 E.g., MN I.181: *so iminā ca ariyena sīlakkhandhena samannāgato, iminā ca ariyena indriyasaṃvarena samannāgato, iminā ca ariyena satisampajaññena samannāgato.* See also MN I.356–7, where when one has gone through the gradual process of cultivation virtue, restraint of the senses, moderation in eating, wakefulness, possessing seven good qualities and then he attains the *jhānas* at will, which are the basis for the three types of knowledge. Note that the fourth *jhāna* is the basis for attaining liberation.

4 E.g., MN I.181: *nisīdati pallaṅkaṃ ābhujitvā, ujuṃ kāyaṃ paṇidhāya, parimukhaṃ satiṃ upaṭṭhapetvā.* See also MN III.3.

5 This gradual description occurs, for example, in MN I.179ff, I.268–70, I.271–7, I.346ff, III.1–5; III.33–6; III.134–6; DN I.63ff, III.270; AN II.208ff, V.206.

6 E.g., MN III.136: *so ime pañca nīvaraṇe pahāya cetaso upakkilese paññāya dubbalīkaraṇe.*

7 SN V.198: *katamañca bhikkhave, samādhindriyaṃ: idha bhikkhave, ariyasāvako vossaggārammaṇaṃ karitvā labhati samādhiṃ, labhati cittassekaggataṃ. So vivicceva kāmehi vivicca akusalehi dhammehi savitakkaṃ savicāraṃ vivekajaṃ pītisukhaṃ. Paṭhamajjhānaṃ upasampajja viharati.* See also SN V.197, and V.225.

8 *Vossagga* is from the Sanskrit verb *ava+sṛj*: to let go, abandon, relax, to give up etc.

9 SN IV.367.

10 E.g., MN I.11: *satisambojjhaṅgaṃ bhāveti vivekanissitaṃ virāganissitaṃ nirodhanissitaṃ vossaggapariṇāmiṃ.* See Also DN III.226; MN II.12; MN III.88; AN II.16. Gethin calls it the *viveka-nissita* formula and points out that it is employed on eighteen occasions: fourteen involve its application to the *bojjhaṅgas*, two to the factors of the path, one to the *indriyas* and one to the *balas* (2001, 163). He concludes that 'in the Nikāyas, the formula is in the first place to be associated with the *bojjhaṅgas* alone' (Gethin 2001, 165).

11 *Vossagga* has various meanings in the Nikāyas (e.g., S V 395; A IV 266; MN III 88). In this context, it seems that *vossaga* refers to some degree of 'relinquishment' or 'letting go', and not to complete and final 'relinquishment' (i.e., *nibbāna*). In other words, it refers to relinquishment of what is needed for attaining the *jhānas*. I also suggest that the four *jhānas* become the basis for further letting go that will incline the mind to the attainment of liberation.

12 MN III.92–4.

13 MN III.94.

14 At MN I.435, there is a slightly different description of the way one enters the first *jhāna*: 'with detachment from the foundation [of attachment] (*upadhivivekā*), with the abandoning of unwholesome states, with tranquilizing all coarse bodily [activities]' (*sabbaso kāyaduṭṭhullānaṃ paṭipassaddhiyā)*, one enters and abides in the first *jhāna*. Here the Buddha describes the first *jhāna* as the outcome of abandonment of all that causes suffering – *upadhi*, the foundation of *saṃsāra* and the cause of *dukkha*. See also MN I.454, MN II.260.

15 Note, that the term *nimitta* is the usual term that designates 'object', that is, an object of meditation (e.g., SN V.156 and MN I.273) or the object of the senses (e.g., SN III.10).

16 Liberation occurs when the various obstructions of mind are abandoned, and when the seven factors of awakening mature and are fulfilled: 'and what bhikkhus is the path crushing the army of Māra? It is the seven factors of awakening'. See, for example, SN V.99 (*katamo ca bhikkave, mārasenappamaddano maggo? Yadidaṃ sattabojjhaṅgā*) and SN V.329.

17 Gethin has observed concerning the term *vossagga* that 'its basic import of "release" or "letting go" as a term for the final goal of *nibbāna* or liberation seems clear' (Gethin 2001, 166).

18 E.g., DN I.73, DN I.157 and AN III.428–9.
19 MN III.136: *so ime pañca nīvaraṇe pahāya cetaso upakkilese paññāya dubbalīkaraṇe.* See also MN I.276; MN II.226–7; MN III.4; SN V.94, AN III.63–4; DN I.73–85; DN I.124–5; DN I.206–10.
20 Vism IV.104–5. Buddhaghosa considers the *nīvaraṇas* as specifically obstructing the unity of mind that tries to concentrate on the chosen meditation object.
21 See MN I.323 and SN V.127 where the Buddha states that the five *nīvaraṇas* are the cause and condition for lack of knowledge and vision *(ñāṇa-dassana)*.
22 SN V.92: *evameva kho bhikkhave, pañcime cittassa upakkilesā yehi upakkilesehi upakkiliṭṭhaṃ cittaṃ na ceva mudu hoti na ca kammaniyaṃ na ca pabhassaraṃ pabhaṅgu ca, na ca sammāsamādhiyati āsavānaṃ khayāya. Katame pañca: kāmacchando . . . vyāpādo . . . thīnamiddhaṃ . . . uddhaccakukkuccaṃ . . . Vicikicchā bhikkhave, cittassa upakkileso.* Although here these obstructions are called *upakkilesa*, it is the usual list of the five *nīvaraṇas*.
23 See, for example, MN III.3 and MN III.136.
24 See also SN V.225, which explains that after one has confidence (*saddha*) – whose energy (*viriya*) is aroused and mindfulness (*sati*) is established – he will gain *samādhi* and 'oneness of mind' (*cittassekaggataṃ*), though I do not see such 'oneness' as meaning absorption, only calm collectedness. See further discussion in chapter 4.
25 MN III.3: *so pacchābhattaṃ piṇḍapātapaṭikkanto nisīdati pallaṅkaṃ ābhujitvā ujuṃ kāyaṃ paṇidhāya parimukhaṃ satiṃ upaṭṭhapetvā, so abhijjhaṃ loke pahāya vigatābhijjhena cetasā viharati. Abhijjhāya cittaṃ parisodheti, byāpādapadosaṃ pahāya abyāpannacitto viharati sabbapāṇabhūtahitānukampī. Byāpādapadosā cittaṃ parisodheti thīnamiddhaṃ pahāya vigata thīnamiddho viharati ālokasaññī sato sampajāno, thīnamiddhā cittaṃ parisodheti uddhaccakukkuccaṃ pahāya anuddhato viharati ajjhattaṃ vūpasantacitto. Uddhaccakukkuccā cittaṃ parisodheti. Vicikicchaṃ pahāya tiṇṇavicikiccho viharati. Akathaṅkathi kusalesu dhammesu. Vicikicchāya cittaṃ parisodheti.*
26 E.g., MN III.3 and MN III.136.
27 SN V.95: *pañcassa nīvaraṇā tasmiṃ samaye na honti. Sattabhojjhaṅgā tasmiṃ samaye bhāvanāpāripūriṃ gacchanti.* Note that in the Chinese and Sanskrit versions of the *Satipaṭṭhāna Sutta*, the section about the contemplation of *dhammas* contains an observation of only the *nīvaraṇas* and the seven *bojjhaṅgas*. This might indicate that these two contemplations are the oldest.
28 See MN I.464, which states that only when *pīti* and *sukha* of the first *jhāna* are attained, the hindrances do not invade the mind and remain.
29 SN V.93: *ime kho bhikkhave, satta bojjhaṅgā anāvaraṇā anīvaraṇā cetaso anupakkilesā bhāvitā bahulīkatā vijjāvimuttikiriyāya saṃvattantīti.* See also V.126.
30 SN V.97: *pañcime, bhikkhave, nīvaraṇa andhkaraṇā acakkhukaraṇā aññāṇkaraṇā paññānirodhikā vighātapakkhiyā anibbānasaṃvattanikā.*
31 MN I.60. This type of contemplation, of seeing that the mind is free from hindrances, accords well with the instruction in the *Satipaṭṭhāna Sutta* of seeing the non-arising of the hindrances and the presence of the seven factors of awakening. See also SN V.127 where the Buddha explains that the *nīvaraṇas* are the cause and condition for the lack of knowledge and vision.
32 SN V.93.
33 See SN V.124ff, where only when the defilements are not present one can see realty as it actually is and the seven factors of awakening can manifest and realized.
34 PED, 638.
35 Vism IV.93. The *Niddesa* classified three types of *viveka*: *kāya-viveka*, *citta-viveka* and *upadhi-viveka* (Nd I 140) while the Paṭisambhidāmagga II 220 lists five types of *viveka*.
36 MMW.

37 SN V.301: *so vatāvuso bhikkhu cattāro satipaṭṭhāne bhāvento cattāro satipaṭṭhāne bahulīkaronto sikkhaṃ paccakkhāya hīnāyāvattissatīti, netaṃ ṭhānaṃ vijjati. Taṃ kissa hetu: "yaṃ hi āvuso cittaṃ dīgharattaṃ vivekaninnaṃ vivekapoṇaṃ vivekapabbhāraṃ.*

38 The Sutta Nipāta seems to connected *viveka* with (1) insight into the danger of sensual pleasures, (2) with seeing (*dassin*) and (3) with the attainment of liberation. E.g., Sn 772, 822, 851, 915 and 1065. See also *paviveka* at AN I.241.

39 See also AN III.423 which states that *sammā-diṭṭhi* needs to be fulfilled before *sammā-samādhi* (i.e., the four *jhānas*).

40 MN I.60.

41 See, for example, Sayalay 2005, 133 and also Snyder and Rasmussen 2009, 28.

42 Kv XVIII 8, p. 572. According Tse-Fu Kuan, this view was advocated also by the Sarvāstivādins but was negated by the Sautrāntikas (Kuan 2005, 299–300). Vism also points out that when entering the first *jhāna*, one is secluded from sense pleasures as object. Vism IV.83–4 points out that when entering the first *jhāna* one is secluded from sense pleasures as object. This statement might mean that one can have experience of sense objects without any desire.

43 E.g., MN I.295. Note that Kuan has maintained that since the *Kaṇṭaka Sutta* points out that sound (*sadda*) is a thorn (*kaṇṭaka*) for the first *jhāna*, it means that 'sound is not heard by one who attains the first *jhāna*' (Kuan 2012, 50). However, this conclusion is a bit strong for what is actually said in the sutta, meaning that certain things might agitate one who practices certain meditation (for example, if one practices restraining the senses, restless motion of sights is a thorn). This does not mean that one does not hear in the first *jhānas* or that moving sights are not present when one practices restraint.

44 E.g., MN III.114.

45 AN III.411.

46 AN III.411: *apica kho bhikkhave nete kāmā, kāmaguṇā nāmete ariyassa vinaye vuccanti.*

47 AN III.411: *Saṅkapparāgo purisassa kāmo, nete kāmā yāni citrāni loke. Saṅkapparāgo purisassa kāmo Tiṭṭhanti citrāni tatheva loke. Athettha dhīrā vinayanti chandanti.*

48 Tse-Fu Kuan has observed that the Sauntrātikas objected to the Sarvāstivādins and the Theravādins claims that the five classes of consciousness related to the body are absent in one who attained the *jhānas*, and consequently that bodily feelings are also absent (Kuan 2005, 299). Note that DN I 73f describes the bodily feelings one feels while abiding in the *jhānas*: *so vivicceva kāmehi vivicca akusalehi dhammehi savitakkaṃ savicāraṃ vivekajaṃ pītisukhaṃ paṭhamaṃ jhānaṃ upasampajja viharati. So imam-eva kāyaṃ vivekajena pītisukhena abhisanteti l parisanneti paripūreti parippharati. Nāssa kiñci sabbāvato kāyassa vivekajena pītisukhena apphuṭaṃ hoti.*

49 See, for example, MN I.504.

50 See also MN I.293, where it is stated that when one abandons the five *indiriyas* (which are the five sense bases), then one can know the four *arūpa samāpattis*. That is, it seems that these five faculties are still in operation when one attains the four *rūpa jhānas*. See AN III.428, which states that for entering the first *jhāna* one has to clearly see the danger in *kāma*.

51 See SN IV.236.

52 *Sukha* that lead to desire (*rajanīya*) is 'ordinary' *sukha*. See MN I.85.

53 MN II.261–2: *Aniccā bhikkhave, kāmā tucchā mosadhammā. Māyākatametaṃ bhik-khave, bālalāpanaṃ. Ye ca diṭṭhadhammikā kāmā, ye ca samparāyikā kāmā, yā ca diṭṭhadhammikā kāmasaññā, yā ca samparāyikā kāmasaññā, ubhayametaṃ māradheyyaṃ, mārassesavisayo, marassesanivāpo, mārassesagocaro. Etthete pāpakā akusalā mānasā abhijjhāpi byāpādāpi sārambhāpi saṃvattanti. Teva ariyasāvakassa idhamanusikkhato antarāyāya sambhavanti.* See also Sn 771–2, 948, 1098.

54 E.g., MN I.85–6, MN I.507–8.
55 A good example of this concern is the questions posed to the Buddha by various ascetics in the *Sutta Nipāta*. They are mainly concerned with abandoning sensual pleasures. E.g., Sn 1071, 1088, 1096.
56 See, for example, MN I.94, where the Nigaṇṭhas say to the Buddha that 'pleasure is not to be gained by pleasure; pleasure is to be gained by pain. For were pleasure to be gained through pleasure, then King Seniya Bimbisāra of Magadha would gain pleasure, since he abides in greater pleasure than the Venerable Gotama.' See also MN I.307–8.
57 Olivelle 1992, 144. See also Maitrī Upaniṣad I.3.
58 In MN I.92, the Buddha describes the Nigaṇṭhas' practice, as a practice of asceticism which causes pain (*opakkamikā dukkha tibbā kharā kaṭukā vedanā vedayanti*). See also MN I.246.
59 E.g., MN I.305–6: sensual pleasures are conceived by recluses and Brahmins to be the reason for a painful rebirth in the future.
60 MN I.171.
61 The root *tap* was used in the Nikāyas with reference to painful ascetic practices, practiced by some *samaṇas* and *brahmanas*. See, for example, DN I.161; MN II.199; SN I.29; SN IV.330.
62 Kaelber 1989, 49.
63 Note the metaphor the Buddha uses in MN II.225 to describe the right time for ascetic practices that cause pain, and the avoidance of such practices: 'Suppose, bhikkhus, an arrow smith were warming and heating an arrow shaft between two flames, making it straight and workable. When the arrow shaft had been warmed and heated between the two flames and had been made straight and workable, then at a later time he would not again warm and heat the arrow shaft and make it straight and workable.'
64 In the Nikāya, self-mortification is described by the Buddha in the phrase *attakilamathānuyoga* 'practicing self-exhaustion'. E.g., SN IV.330.
65 Kaelber 1989, 51.
66 Kaelber 1989, 45–61.
67 Kaelber 1989, 57, 58.
68 *Tattvārtha Sūtra* 8.2. Contrary to this view, the Buddha internalized and 'mentalized' *kamma*. *Kamma* was conceived as volition (*cetanā*) (AN III.414) – a mental attitude and not a physical matter. From that followed the view that the power to eliminate bad *kamma* and the *āsavas* is a mental power.
69 *Tattvārtha Sūtra* 9.3.
70 *Tattvārtha Sūtra* 9.8. Bronkhorst has also pointed out that in early Jainism, one must 'abstain from food and prepare for death in a position which is as motionless as possible' (Bronkhorst 1993, 36).
71 *Tattvārtha Sūtra* 9.9.
72 See *Tattvārtha Sūtra* 9.20–7.
73 *Tattvārtha Sūtra* (1994, 232).
74 E.g., MN I.454, where the Buddha refers to the sensual pleasures (*kāma*) as filthy, ordinary and ignoble pleasure (*mīḷhasukhaṃ puthujjanasukhaṃ anariyasukhaṃ*). See also other places where the Buddha states that *kāma* is a primary fetter: MN I.305–6; MN I.508; MN II.261–2; SN IV.330–1; Sn 50–1, 768, 771–3, 823, 945, 948, 1071.
75 MN I.454: *Yaṃ kho udāyi ime pañcakāmaguṇe paṭicca uppajjati sukhaṃ somanassaṃ, idaṃ vuccati kāmasukhaṃ mīḷhasukhaṃ puthujjanasukhaṃ anariyasukhaṃ na sevitabbaṃ na bhāvetabbaṃ na bahulīkātabbaṃ. Bhāyitabbaṃ etassa sukhassāti vadāmi*. See also MN III.233.
76 MN I.246–7.
77 Note, however, that in MN II.225, the Buddha permits the practice of asceticism for a certain purpose. But when this purpose is achieved, one should not continue to exert himself in what is painful.

78 MN I.454.
79 Sn 436: *kāma te paṭhamā senā.*
80 MN III.233–4: *idaṃ vuccati nekkhammasukhaṃ pavivekasukhaṃ upasamasukhaṃ sambodhisukhaṃ āsevitabbaṃ bhāvetabbaṃ bahulīkātabbaṃ. Na bhāyitabbaṃ etassa sukhassāti vadāmi.* See also MN I.454; DN III.131–2.
81 MN I.246.
82 See DN III.131–2.
83 I agree with Wynne's observation that there were different early Brahminic and Jain notions of the spiritual path, and that the meditation of the early Upaniṣads and *Mokṣadharma* were not part of the extreme asceticism of Jain (and the Ājīvika) practices. However, in the preceding examples (and in the Buddha's own spiritual journey), it is clear that in the Buddha's spiritual milieu, these ascetic notions and practices were not marginal but quite central. Thus, his own teaching was a rejection of asceticism and also of other ideas and practices, such as the ones taught by Āḷāra Kālāma and Uddaka Rāmaputta (Wynne 2007, 111–13).
84 MN I.341. These four kinds of persons appear also in MN I.411–2, while in MN I.342–4 the Buddha gives a detailed account of these types of persons.
85 MN I.341: *so anattantapo aparantapo diṭṭheva dhamma nicchāto nibbuto sītībhuto sukhappaṭisaṃvedī brahmabhūtena attanā.*
86 MN I.93: *atthi vo nigaṇṭhā, pubbe pāpaṃ kammaṃ kataṃ taṃ imāya kaṭukāya dukkarakārikāya nijjaretha. Yaṃ panettha etarahi kāyena saṃvutā vācāya saṃvutā manasā saṃvutā taṃ āyatiṃ pāpassa kammassa akaraṇaṃ. Iti purāṇānaṃ kammānaṃ tapasā vyantībhāvā, navānaṃ kammānaṃ akaraṇā āyatiṃ anavassavo. Āyatiṃ anavassavā kammakkhayo. Kammakkhayā dukkhakkhayo. Dukkhakkhayā vedanākkhayo. Vedanākkhayā sabbaṃ dukkhaṃ nijjiṇṇaṃ bhavissatī"ti.* Occur also in MN II.214 and AN I.220.
87 MN I.94: *sukhena sukhaṃ adhigantabbaṃ, dukkhena kho sukhaṃ adhigantabbaṃ. sukhena cāvuso gotama, sukhaṃ adhigantabbaṃ abhavissa, raja māgadho seniyo bimbisāro sukhaṃ adhigaccheyya, raja māgadho seniyo bimbisāro sukhavihāritaro āyasmatā gotamen* ti. See also MN II.36.
88 E.g., MN I.341: *so anattantapo aparantapo diṭṭheva dhamma nicchāto nibbuto sītībhuto sukhappaṭisaṃvedī brahmabhūtena attanā.* This description occurs in various places in the Nikāyas; see, for example, MN I.413; DN III.233; AN I.197; AN I.181; AN II.206. In AN IV.14 *sukhappaṭisaṃvedī* is also connected to *nibbāna*.
89 AN I.221: *catutthaṃ jhānam upasampajja viharati. So navañca kammaṃ na karoti purāṇañca kammṃ phussa phussa byantīkaroti.*
90 See SN IV.209: *tassa kāmasukhaṃ nābhinandato yo sukhāya vedanāya rāgānusayo so nānuseti.*
91 DN III.131–2.
92 DN III.132: *ime kho cunda cattāro sukhallikānuyogā ekattanibbidāya virāgāya nirodhāya upasamāya abhiññāya sambodhāya nibbānāya saṃvattanti.*
93 MN III.234: *sukhavinicchayaṃ jaññā, sukhavinicchayaṃ ñatvā ajjhattaṃ sukhamanuyuñjeyyā'ti.* The pleasure that needs to be cultivated is the pleasure of the *jhānas*, which are 'the pleasure of renunciation, the pleasure of peace, the pleasure of awakening'.
94 The *Kīṭāgiri Sutta* from the MN further elucidates of the role of certain kinds of feelings in the process of liberation and purification of mind. In this sutta the Buddha declares that 'when someone feels a certain kind of pleasant feeling, unwholesome states increase in him and wholesome states diminish; but when someone feels another kind of pleasant feeling, unwholesome states diminish in him and wholesome states increase'. After this statement, the Buddha encourages his disciples to 'enter upon and abide in such a kind of *sukha-vedanā*' (MN I.475 6).
95 See also MN I.464.

96 The *Visuddhimagga* enumerates five kinds of *pīti*. When the five types of *pīti* mature, there is bodily and mental tranquillity. When this is matured it perfects the threefold concentration – momentary (*khaṇika-samādhi*), access (*upacāra samādhi*) and absorption (*appaṇā samādhi/jhāna*) (Vism IV.99).
For a detailed discussion of *pīti* in the commentarial tradition see Cousins 1974, 120–1.

97 SN IV.236: *katamā ca bhikkhave nirāmisā nirāmisatarā pīti: yā kho bhikkhave khīṇāsavassa bhikkhuno rāgā cittaṃ vimuttaṃ paccavekkhato dosā cittaṃ vimuttaṃ paccavekkhato mohā cittaṃ vimuttaṃ paccavekkhato uppajjati pīti. Ayaṃ vuccati bhikkhave nirāmisā nirāmisatarā pīti.*
The same is said about *nirāmisā nirāmisataraṃ sukha* in SN IV.237.

98 In the Theravāda view this will be the experience of *lokuttara jhānas*.

99 Vism IV.100. See also the article by Tse-Fu Kuan that makes the observation that the Sarvāstivādins also distinguish the *sukha* faculty from *sukha* as a *jhāna* factor, but in a different manner from the Theravādins. The *Vibhāśa śāstra* refers to the *sukha* of the first two *dhyānas* as tranquillity (*prasrabdhi-sukha*), while the Dharmaskandha, a canonical Sarvāstivādin Abhidharma text, understands *sukha* of the third *jhāna* as feeling (*vedanā*), not as *prasrabdhi*. Note that the Theravādins and the Sarvāstivādins distinguish between the *sukhi*-indriya and the *sukha* of the *jhānas*. For a detailed discussion of *sukha* and *pīti* in Sarvāstivāda, Theravāda and Sautrātika, see Kuan 2005, 295–300.

100 MN II.203: *taṃ kiṃ maññasi māṇava, yaṃ vā tiṇakaṭṭhūpādānaṃ paṭicca aggiṃ jāleyya, yaṃ vā nissaṭṭhatiṇakaṭṭhūpādānaṃ aggiṃ jāleyya, katamo nu khvāssa aggi accimā ca vaṇṇimā ca pabhassaro cāti?*

101 MN II.203: *imehi kho māṇava, pañcahi kāmaguṇehi brāhmaṇo pokkharasāti opamañño subhagavaniko gathitol mucchito ajjhopanno anādīnavadassāvī anissaraṇapañño paribhuñjati.*

102 See also the *Pīti Sutta*, where the Buddha describes what it is like when one dwells in the '*pīti* of solitude' (*pavivekaṃ pītiṃ*) that presumably is *pīti* of the first *jhāna* (also according to AA III.303). On such an occasion, there is no physical or mental pain (*dukkhaṃ domanassaṃ*) or pleasure (*sukhaṃm somanassaṃ*) associated with desire for sense pleasures (*kāmūpasaṃhitaṃ*); physical or mental pain associated with the unwholesome (*akusala*); physical or mental pleasure associated with the unwholesome; and physical or mental pain associated with the wholesome (AN III 207).

103 SN III.232: *yo bhikkhave, cakkhusmiṃ chandarāgo, cittasse'so upakkileso. yo sotasmiṃ chandarāgo cittasse'so upakkileso yo ghānasmiṃ chandarāgo cittasse'so upakkileso yo jivhāya chandarāgo cittasse 'so upakkileso yo kāyasmiṃ chandarāgo, cittasse'so upakkileso, yo manasmiṃ chandarāgo cittasse'so upakkileso. yato kho bhikkhave, bhikkhuno imesu chasu ṭhānesu cetaso upakkileso pahīno hoti, nekkhammaninnaṃ cassa cittaṃ hoti. Nekkhammaparibhāvitaṃ cittaṃ kammaniyaṃ khāyati abhiññā sacchikaraṇiyesu dhammesūti.* See also DN III.239–40.

104 It is interesting to mention AN IV.415, where Udāyin asks Sāriputta about happiness that is not felt (*sukhaṃ yadettha natthi vedayitaṃ*). As an explanation, Sāriputta describes a situation in which one attains the first *jhānas* but is beset by attention and perception accompanied by sensual desire. This seems to contradict the various references that describe the attainment of the first *jhāna* as a state devoid of these very mental states. It seems that this is an 'unworthy *jhāna*', since in a 'worthy *jhāna*' there is no perception (*saññā*) of *kāma*, *byāpāda* and *vihiṃsa*. In a private correspondence, Peter Harvey has suggested to me that perhaps an 'unworthy *jhāna*' 'is an unstable state in which the mind is still flipping in and out of *jhāna*'. For the former possibility see DN I.182, which states that 'quite secluded from *kāma* and unwholesome states (probably perceptions of ill will and cruelty), he enters and abides in the first *jhāna* . . . and whatever perceptions of *kāma* that he previously had disappeared' (*so vivicceva kāmehi vivicca akusalehi dhammehi savitakkaṃ savicāraṃ vivekajaṃ pītisukhaṃ paṭhamaṃ jhānaṃ upasampajja viharati. Tassa yā purimā kāmasaññā sā nirujjhati*).

105 Note that *pīti* is a 'factor of awakening' (*bojjhaṅga*).
106 MN I.91.
107 It seems that something more peaceful than (mental) joy and (bodily) pleasure, and not sensual pleasures (i.e., *jhānic pīti* and *sukha*) is the attainment of liberation. It is not probable that the Buddha refers here to the *arūpa samāpatti* since they are mostly referred to as 'those peaceful liberations that transcends forms, the formless attainments' (*te santā vimokkhā atikkamma rūpe āruppā*). See, for example, SN II.123.
108 MN I.91: *yato ca kho mahānāma ariyasāvakassa appassādā kāmā bahudukkhā bahūpāyāsā, ādīnavo ettha bhiyyoti evametaṃ yathābhūtaṃ sammappaññāya sudiṭṭhaṃ hoti, so ca aññatreva kāmehi aññatra akusalehi dhammehi pītisukhaṃ adhigacchati aññaṃ vā tato santataraṃ, atha kho so anāvaṭṭī kāmesu hoti.*
109 E.g., SN IV.70–1.
110 E.g., MN I.141. Note that according to the commentary, Mahānāma was a 'once-returner' [MA II.61].
111 Only a 'non-returner' eradicated the desire of sense pleasures and aversion according to Buddhist theory of liberation.
112 See, for example, Hamilton's argument that 'knowing and seeing this process as it really is enable one to "uproot" the binding continuity tendencies of desires coupled with ignorance – both aspect of bondage' (Hamilton 2000, 122–3).
113 I wish to make clear that translating the term *yathābhūtaṃ* as 'things as they are', does not refer to knowledge about the ontology of reality, or reality in the scientific sense, but to knowledge about how *dukkha* arises and ceases; knowledge about the nature of experience which can liberate the mind from clinging.
114 SN II.117: *aññatreva āvuso nārada, saddhāya aññatra ruciyā aññatra anussavā aññatra ākāraparivitakkā aññatra diṭṭhinijjhānakkhantiyā atthāyasmato nāradassa paccattameva ñāṇaṃ.*
115 SN II.118. The same question was put to the venerable Musīla, and he gave the same answers as Nārada. However, contrary to Nārada who claimed he is not an Arahant, Musīla kept silent when Saviṭṭha said that he must be an arahants [SN II.117].
116 SN V.229–30: *idha bhikkhave, sekho bhikkhu idaṃ dukkhanti yathābhūtaṃ pajānāti. Ayaṃ dukkhasamudayoti yathābhūtaṃ pajānāti, ayaṃ dukkhanirodhoti yathābhūtaṃ pajānāti, ayaṃ dukkhanirodhagāminīpaṭipadāti yathabhūtaṃ pajānāti . . . sekho bhikkhu pañcindriyāni pajānāti: saddhindriyaṃ viriyindriyaṃ satindriyaṃ samādhindriyaṃ paññindriyaṃ, yaṃgatikāni yaṃparamāni yaṃbalāni yaṃpariyosānāni, naheva kho kāyena phusitvā viharati, paññāya ca ativijjha passati. Ayampi kho bhikkhave: pariyāyo: yaṃ pariyāyaṃ āgamma sekho bhikkhu sekhabhūmiyaṃ ṭhito sekhosmī'ti pajānāti.*
117 The *Kosambī Sutta* was interpreted in different ways. La Vallée Poussin, for example, has argued that Musīla represents those who know and thereby reach the goal (he identifies Musīla as a Sāṃkhya), while Nārada, strives to reach the goal through direct experience (and therefore he is a yogin, as defined in the Bhagavad Gīta). La Vallée Poussin has also contended that insight without meditation is possible and accessible to more than just a few. See Bronkhorst summary of La Vallée Poussin's argument in Bronkhorst 1993, 101–2. Gombrich has suggested, that Nārada interprets *paññā* in the narrow sense of intellection without a deeper realization (Gombrich 2002, 129). In a more recent article Bhikkhu Bodhi has demonstrated that the *Kosambī Sutta* does not present a tension between two competing visions – the cognitivists and pro-meditatie view of the path – but between a *sekha* and the *arahant*. Bodhi points out that 'by denying that he is an arahant [i.e., Nārada], he is insinuating that an *arahant* has not only directly cognized *nibbāna* but is capable of experiencing it in a meditative state so powerful that one seems to be making bodily contact with it' (Bhikkhu Bodhi 2003, 62).
118 Note that in MN II.15–6 and DN I.73–6, the Buddha describes the four *jhānas* elaborately and explains that the various *jhāna* factors should be experienced in such a way that they pervade the whole body. With reference to the first *jhāna*, the Buddha says

that 'there is no part of the whole body, un-pervaded by the joy and pleasure born of discernment' (*nāssa kiñci sabbāvato kāyassa vivekajena pītisukhena apphuṭaṃ hoti*).

119 MN I.504: *vigatapipāso ajjhattam vūpasantacitto vihareyya.*

120 MN I.504–5: *so aparena samayena kāmānaṃyeva samudayañca atthaṃgamañca assādañca ādīnavañca nissaraṇañca yathābhūtaṃ viditvā kāmataṇhaṃ pahāya kāmapariḷāhaṃ paṭivinodetvā vigatapipāso ajjhattaṃ vūpasantacitto viharāmi. So aññe satte passāmi kāmesu avītarāge kāmataṇhāhi khajjamāne kāmapariḷāhena pariḍayhamāne kāme paṭisevante. So tesaṃ na pihemi. Na tattha abhiramāmi. Taṃ kissa hetu: yā hayaṃ māgandiya ratī aññatreva kāmehi aññatra akusalehi dhammehi api dibbaṃ sukhaṃ samadhigayha tiṭṭhati, tāya ratiyā ramamāno hīnassa na pihemi, na tattha abhiramāmi.*

121 The *Tevijja Sutta* of the DN seems to contradict my argument, since the Buddha describes in this sutta how to achieve union with Brahmā by the attainment of the first *jhāna* as the basis (DN I.250). However, although the first *jhāna* seems to be a prerequisite for this union, the actual practice for being reborn in the presence of Brahmā is the practice of the four *Brahmā-vihāras* (DN I.251–2). Note also, that in the Nikāyas, to the best of my knowledge, there is only one occurrence where the *jhānas* are identified with the attainment of certain heavenly realms. I will discuss this issue later on.

122 MN I.506.

123 The Buddha further elucidates this abandoning process by a comparing it to the story a leper who habitually eases his wounds by cauterizing his sores on a charcoal pit as a medical intervention. After this leper has been cured of leprosy, he does not envy another leper who is easing his disease in the same way as he had previously. The cured leper has the capacity to abandon a lesser craving, easing bodily suffering on a charcoal pit, since he is now cured. MN I.506: *roge hi, bho Gotama, sati bhesajjena karaṇīyaṃ hoti, roge asati na bhesajjena karaṇīyaṃ hoti.*

124 There are three cosmological realms that are inhabited by different ranks of devas: the *kāma-dhātu* and *rūpa-dhātu* and the *arūpa*-dhātu. See the chart of the cosmological plains in Akira 1997, 58–9.

125 It is interesting to note that DN III.220 enumerates three abidings: deva-abiding, Brahmā abiding and Ariya-abidinig (*tayo-vihārā: dibbo-vihāro, buhmā-vihāro, ariyo-vihāro*). This classification of 'abidings' (*vihāra*) is interesting. According to this classification there is a deva abidings that refers to heavenly worlds of the *kāma-dhātu* ('the realm of divine sensual pleasures'). The Brahmā abiding seems to be a generic term for both *rūpa-dhātu* and the *arūpa-dhātu*. The Ariya-abiding (*ariyo-vihāro*), however, refers to the abidings of Noble Persons (*ariya*). I would propound that the *jhānas* are the *ariyo-vihāro*, mainly because what the Buddha states in the *Māgandiya Sutta* (that he surpasses 'divine pleasures' in the first *jhāna*), and because the third *jhāna* is described as an attainment in which one experiences pleasure (*sukha*) with the body, 'on account of which, the Noble Ones announce: He has a pleasant abiding'. E.g., MN I.159: *sukhañca kāyena paṭisaṃvedeti. Yantaṃ ariyā ācikkhanti' upekkhako satimā sukhavihārī'ti tatiyaṃ jhānaṃ upasampajja viharati.*

126 Taishō, 54, 55 (26?).

127 DDB "intelligent". <http://www.buddhism-dict.net/cgi-bin/xpr-ddb.pl?8c.xml+id('b8ce2')>

128 MN I.91.

129 Cousins 1994–6, 50. The Paṭisambhidāmagga was dated by A.K. Warder to be a composition from the third century and the early second century BCE (Ibid., 51).

130 Cousins 1994–6, 50.

131 Bhikṣu Thich Minh Chau 1991, 250.

132 In his article 'Thinking about Cessation', Daniel Stuart makes preliminary observations about the *jhānas* and the 'attainment of cessation' from studying the *Pṛṣṭhapālasūtra* of the (Mūla-) Sarvāstivādin Dīrghāgama. In this text, the attainment of cessation is attained immediately after the practice of the four *dhyānas*. Stuart

suggests that later on the *jhānas* and the attainment of cessation were separated. He states that 'the practice of the four *dhyānas* was one of the fundamental practices of the early tradition. Thus, the idea that liberation was attained directly from the fourth *dhyāna* is probably as old as the tradition itself.' He further posited that entering the attainment of cessation after the practice of the four *dhyānas*, was quite possibly one of the earliest Buddhist models of liberation (Stuart 2008, 24–5). In a more recent book he has stated that 'the idea that liberation was attained directly from the fouth dhyāna is probably as old as the tradition itself' (Stuart 2013, 44).

133 DN III.288: *Katame nava dhammā bahukārā? Nava yonisomanasikāramūlakā dhammā: yoniso manasikaroto pāmojjaṃ jāyati, pamuditassa pīti jāyati, pītimanassa kāyo passambhati, passaddhakāyo sukhaṃ vedeti, sukhino cittaṃ samādhiyati, samāhite citte yathābhūtaṃ jānāti. Yathābhūtaṃ jānaṃ passaṃ nibbindati, nibbindaṃ virajjati, virāgā vimuccati. Ime nava dhammā bahukārā.* See also SN II.30.

134 The reason I refer to these moments as 'similar' to *jhānic pīti* and *sukha* is because *jhānic pīti* and *sukha* are part of a particular body-mind experience that includes specific mental factors and the absence of others. Only this unique configuration of factors can be characterized as *jhāna*. However, this does not mean that one cannot otherwise experience pleasure and happiness that are not connected to sense gratification. Yet, in the absence of the other *jhāna* factors, these *pīti* and *sukha* are perhaps similar to the *jhānic* one, but not identical.

135 See also AN III.207.

136 See DN I.73.

137 SN IV.209: *tassa kāmasukhaṃ nābhinandato yo sukhāya vedanāya rāgānusayo so nānuseti.* This transformative process, in which the mind is independent from pleasant sense experiences, is depicted in the *Salla Sutta*: 'Being contacted by a painful feeling, a noble disciple does not seek delight in the pleasures of the senses. For what reason? It is because the instructed noble disciple knows of an escape from painful feeling other than sensual pleasures. Since he does not seek delight in the pleasures of the senses, the underlying tendency to lust for pleasant feeling does not lie behind this. He understands as it really is the origin and the passing away, the gratification, the danger, and the escape in the case of these feelings' (SN IV.209).

138 MN I.303–4.

139 See, for example, Griffiths 1983, 59.

140 For a detail study of these terms in the Abhidhamma and later Pāli texts, see Cousins 1992, 137–47. Cousins has summarized the Abhidhamma understanding of *vitakka* and maintained that *vitakka* is a faculty which in its weakest form is a tendency to speculate and fix upon ideas, and when it is strongly developed it is the ability to apply the mind and fix it on an object. *Vicāra* in its weakest form is the tendency of the mind to wander, but when it is developed, it is the ability to explore and examine the object (Cousins 1992, 153). See also Vism IV.88–91 and VI.67.

141 E.g., MN I.9; MN I.114–5; MN III.114; SN V.417–8.

142 E.g., *Dvedhāvitakka Sutta* and *Vitakkasaṇṭhāna Sutta* of MN.

143 E.g., SN IV.293.

144 MN I.301; SN IV.293.

145 MN I.301: *vitakketvā vicāretvā pacchā vācaṃ bhindati, tasmā vitakkvicārā vacīsaṅkhāro.*

146 DN II.277.

147 *papañcasaññāsaṅkhāya sati vitakka hoti, papañcasaññāsaṅkhāya asati vitakka na hoti.* See also MN I.112–3.

148 See Ñānananda 1971, 25.

149 E.g., SN V.417–8.

150 See, for example, MN I.111–12: 'Dependent on the eye and forms, eye consciousness arises. The meeting of the three is contact. With contact as a condition there is feeling. What one feels, that one perceives. What one perceives, that one thinks about. What

one thinks about, that one mentally proliferates. With what one mentally proliferates as the source, perceptions and notions tinged by mental proliferation beset a man with respect to past, future, and present forms cognizable through the eye.'

151 Note the well-known example of seeing a rope when it is dark and thinking it is a snake.

152 See SN IV.202, which points out that the notion 'I am'(*asmīti*), 'I am this' (*ayamahamasmīti*) and so forth are all forms of thinking (*maññita*) and that this type of thinking is fundamentally problematic. Wynne has pointed out that this sutta indicates that the various manifestations of the subjective aspect of self-consciousness – the 'I' as a quasi-independent observer of phenomena – arise in dependence on the conceptual activity of the mind. He further asserts that this implies that 'the subject of self-consciousness does not exist beyond particular cognitive events' (Wynne 2011, 131–2).

153 See, for example, DN I.202.

154 Hamilton 2000, 148.

155 Hamilton 2000, 133.

156 The *Sangīti Sutta* enumerates five results when one develops *samādhi*. The third result of developing and extending *samādhi* is mindfulness and clear awareness (*satisampajaññā*): when a monk knows the arising, remaining, and falling of feelings, perceptions and thoughts (*vitakka*) (DN III.223).

157 Sn 7: *yassa vitakkā vidhūpitā, ajjhattaṃ suvikappitā asesā.*

158 Sn 8: *sabbaṃ accagamā imaṃ papañcaṃ.*

159 Note that the tern *vikalpa* in Mahāyāna Buddhism seems to designate the same thing: erroneous thinking that originates from delusion, ignorance and desire. This 'thinking' is the cause of *saṃsāra*: 'the state of *saṃsāra* is merely the result of deluded thoughts (myi-bden-pais' 'du-ses)' (Gomez 1983, 89).

160 SN I.39–40*: nandi sambandhano loko vitakkassa vicāraṇaṃ.*

161 AN II.49: *gamanena na pattabbo lokassanto kudācanaṃ, na ca appatvā lokantaṃ dukkhā atthi pamocanaṃ.*

162 See the *Bāhiya Sutta* where the Buddha instructs Bāhiya that he must train himself in a way that in 'the seen there will be only the seen; in the heard, only the heard; in the sensed only the sensed; in the cognized, only the cognized' (Ud 1.10).

163 See Sue Hamilton's suggestion that 'by concentrating on gaining understanding of the nature of all things at the same time as working for stilling one's normal mental activity, one can see the way one's affective reaction to one's perceptions is something that arises because of *not* understanding that all things are similarly dependently originated and therefore impermanent and impersonal' (Hamilton 2000, 134).

164 E.g., DN I.186–7.

165 DN III.253.

166 Klein 1998, 207.

167 MN I.116: *yaññadeva bhikkhave bhikkhu bahulamanuvitakketi anuvicāreti tathā tathā nati hoti cetaso nekkhammavitakkañce bhikkhave bhikkhu bahulamanuvitakketi anuvicāreti, pahāsi kāmavitakkaṃ. Nekkhammavitakkaṃ bahulamakāsi. Tassa taṃ nekkhammavitakkāya cittaṃ namati. Abyāpāda vitakkañce bhikkhave bhikkhu bahulamanuvitakketi anuvicāreti, pahāsi byāpādavitakkaṃ. Abyāpādavitakkaṃ bahulamakāsi. Tassa taṃ abyāpādavitakkāya cittaṃ namati. Avihiṃsāvitakkañce bhikkhave bhikkhu bahulamanuvitakketi anuvicāreti pahāsi vihiṃsāvitakkaṃ. Avihiṃsāvitakkaṃ bahulamakāsi. Tassa taṃ avihiṃsāvitakkāya cittaṃ namati.*

168 MN I.116: *uppanno kho me ayaṃ nekkhammavitakko. So ca kho nevattavyābādhāya saṃvattati, na paravyābādhāya saṃvattati, na ubhayavyābādhāya saṃvattati, paññāvuddhiko avighātapakkhiko nibbānasaṃvattaniko. Rattiñcepi naṃ bhikkhave anuvitakkeyyaṃ anuvicāreyyaṃ neva tatonidānaṃ bhayaṃ samanupassāmi. Divasañcepi naṃ bhikkhave anuvitakkeyyaṃ anuvicāreyyaṃ neva tatonidānaṃ bhayaṃ samanupassāmi. Rattindivañcepi naṃ bhikkhave anuvitakkeyyaṃ anuvicāreyyaṃ neva*

tatonidānaṃ bhayaṃ samanupassāmi. api ca kho me aticiraṃ anuvitakkayato anuvicārayato kāyo kilameyya. Kāye kilante cittaṃ ūhaññeyya. Ūhate citte ārā cittaṃ samādhimhāti. So kho ahaṃ bhikkhave ajjhattameva cittaṃ saṇṭhapemi sannisādemi ekodiṃ karomi samādahāmi. Taṃ kissa hetu: mā me cittaṃ ūhaññī ti.

169 DN II.277: *vitakke sati chande hoti, vitakke asati chando na hotī.*

170 For example, *chanda* appears as a wholesome factor in the 'giving rise to the intention for the non-arising of un-arisen evil unwholesome states'. MN II.11: *anuppannānaṃ pāpakānaṃ akusalānaṃ dhammānaṃ anuppādāya chandaṃ janeti. Chanda* as a wholesome factor occurs also in SN I.202; AN IV.320.

171 *Chanda* as an unwholesome factor, occurs in DN I.25; SN IV.195; Sn 835. According to the *Sakkapañha Sutta*, *chanda*, as an unwholesome factor, is the cause for the arising of likes and dislikes (*piyāppiyaṃ*), which in turn is the cause for ill will (*issā*) and envy/stinginess/selfishness (*macchariyaṃ*).

172 'And where do these unwholesome intentions cease without a reminder? Their cessation is stated: quite secluded from the desire for sensual pleasures and unwholesome states, a bhikkhu enters upon and abides in the first *jhāna* . . . It is here that unwholesome intentions cease without a reminder' (MN II.27–8).

173 MN III.136: *So ime pañca nīvaraṇe pahāya cetaso upakkilese paññāya dubbalikaraṇe kāye kāyānupassī viharati ātāpī sampajāno satimā vineyya loke abhijjhādomanassaṃ. Vedanāsu vedanānupassī. . . citte cittānupassī. . . dhammesu dhammānupassī viharati ātāpī sampajāno satimā vineyya loke abhijjhādomanassaṃ.*

174 E.g., MN III.235–6.

3 The Second *Jhāna*

Non-discursive broad field of awareness

> Again, with the stilling of thought and reflection, a bhikkhu enters upon and abides in the second *jhāna*, which is [mental] joy and [bodily] pleasure born of *samādhi*, and has inner stillness and unification of mind, without thought and reflection.[1]

The Buddhist path to liberation is a progression from an ordinary mind filled with many moments of unwholesome states to a purified mind wholesome and free. It is a progression from a wrong perception of reality to a clear seeing of phenomena. The *jhānas*, I would suggest, exemplify this progression: when one progresses from one *jhāna* to the next, one purifies the mind from mental obstructions and actualizes the aim of Buddhist meditation. By progressing through the *jhānas*, insight (*vipassanā*) becomes deeper and reality is perceived more clearly. This chapter will offer an analysis of the second *jhāna* viewed as a progression from the previous *jhāna*. This analysis will also serve as a foundation for exploring the third and fourth *jhānas*.

Before we delve into exploring the nature and liberative value of the second *jhāna*, I would like to offer an observation. The second, third and fourth *jhānas* pose a problem if we consider Buddhist liberation as some kind of discursive wisdom. This notion of liberation has been presented, for example, by Paul Griffiths and Robert Gimello, who have argued that liberation is discursive knowledge brought about by *vipassanā* practice, which by itself is a conceptual reflection upon basic categories of Buddhist doctrine.[2] If the practice of meditation and the notion of liberation are conceived of in this manner, how are we to understand the second, third and fourth *jhānas*, in which discursive thinking are absent? What is the benefit in the cessation of discursive thinking for seeing the nature of reality and for attaining awakening? Moreover, how does the stilling of discursive thinking and reflecting come about according to the Pāli Nikāyas: is it a fruit of insight or the outcome of certain concentration exercises? And last, what happens in the mind when thinking fades away?

To offer a theory regarding these questions, let me begin by restating briefly the arguments concerning the disadvantages and limits of discursive thinking that were made in the previous chapter. These arguments are the basis and foundation for understanding the liberative value of the second *jhāna*. They also assist in interpreting the terms *samādhi* and *ekodibhāvaṃ* in the context of the *jhānas*.

I Introduction

In the previous chapter, I suggested that, ultimately, discursive thinking has serious limitations from a Buddhist perspective. Discursive thinking is a mental process that interprets experience based upon previous proclivities, misconceptions, desires and will. According to early Buddhist epistemology, the process of thinking can be said to be 'on top' of the process of perceiving and naming (*saññā*) that which we experience[3] (although perception itself can be distorted).[4] I have pointed out that although discursive thinking is useful in the preliminary stages of developing insight, it also has serious disadvantages according to the Nikāyas. Even when thinking is wholesome, it has a relative value in the context of Buddhist liberation theory.[5] I have argued that thinking is a manifestation of the sense of self; it is that which sustains, at least, the grossest sense of 'me' and 'I'. In other words, the notions 'I am', 'this is mine' and 'this is myself' are certain types of thoughts – thoughts with which we mistakenly identify and from which we interact with the world in a misconceived manner.[6] According to Buddhist psychology, this mistaken identification is that which causes suffering.[7] Therefore, I have suggested that experiencing the cessation of thinking when transitioning from the first *jhāna* to the second, lends insight into the origin and nature of the misconceived sense of self and the emptiness of thoughts. The cessation of the thinking process – accompanied by the observation of this cessation – is an important realization for loosening attachment and clinging to subjective experience and to a 'thinker'. I suggested that after one has seen the advantages, disadvantages and limits of the thinking process, by seeing directly its origination and cessation,[8] thinking will no longer have the same delusive power.

II The transition from the first *jhāna* to the second

From the perspective of the Nikāyas' meditation theory, the progression from the first *jhāna* to the second *jhāna* allows the practitioner to further establish mindfulness and develop insight into the true nature of experience. I propose viewing the transition from one *jhāna* to the next as a manifestation of insight into the nature of mind. I would argue that the fading away of thoughts and reflections is the actualization of loosening attachment to them; this is achieved by not following the trajectory of thoughts. Thoughts are sustained by a continual identification with their content. Once one sees thoughts as they are – that is, penetrates their impermanent nature and lack of inherent existence, thereby seeing directly that they are not 'me', 'mine' or 'myself' (AN II.45) – thoughts are abandoned. In other words, only when one does not goad thoughts through identification, and does not nourish the thinking mind to sustain a sense of existence (*bhava*) and worthiness, can thoughts be naturally stilled. When they are stilled in this way (contrary to their stilling by vigorous one-pointed concentration), their cessation has a liberative value.[9] This is implied in the description of the second *jhāna* from the *Dantabhūmi Sutta*.

Also, a beautiful verse from the Udāna emphasizes this process; when one does not follow out thoughts, thoughts cease:

> Trivial thoughts, subtle thoughts,
> when followed, they stir up the mind.
> Not understanding these thoughts,
> one runs here and there,
> the mind out of control.
> But understanding thoughts,
> one who is ardent, mindful,
> restrains them.
> When, followed, they stir up the mind,
> one who is awakened
> abandons them without a trace.[10]

The second *jhāna* is also essential for properly establishing mindfulness. As pointed out by Rupert Gethin, the texts distinguish between the initial stages of the establishing of mindfulness, which are preparatory in nature, and the proper establishing of mindfulness. He has observed that

> [i]n order to practice the *satipaṭṭhānas* the bhikkhu requires concentration; in order to acquire concentration he practices the *satipaṭṭhānas*. Stated without paradox, this means that the texts distinguish between the initial stages of the establishing of mindfulness, which are preparatory in nature, and the establishing of mindfulness proper.[11]

Observation of the four *satipaṭṭhānas* can and should be practiced in various stages of the path. It should be practiced from the outset, when the mind has not yet abandoned the hindrances or developed fully the seven factors of awakening. This level of observation is preparatory in nature, but it also that which allows the practitioner to develop discernment (*viveka*);[12] this quality aids the process of purifying the mind from the various unwholesome states, thereby slanting into the attainment of the first *jhāna*.[13] In the previous chapter, I showed that abiding in the first *jhāna* enables one to observe the four *satipaṭṭhānas* without being hindered by mental proliferation and unwholesome states. Nevertheless, the Buddha clearly states that observing the four *satipaṭṭhānas* in the first *jhāna* is still preliminary. Mindfulness is established and fulfilled properly only when one enters and abides in the second *jhāna* (and presumably when one abides in the third and fourth *jhānas*). This kind of observation is depicted clearly in the *Dantabhūmi Sutta*:

> [C]ome bhikkhu, abide observing the body as the body but do not think thoughts connected with the body; abide observing feelings as feelings but do not think thoughts connected with feelings; abide observing mind as mind but do not think thoughts connected with the mind; abide observing *dhammas* as *dhammas* but do not think thoughts connected with *dhammas*. With the stilling of thoughts and reflections he enters upon and abides in the second *jhāna*.[14]

This passage explains the initial difference between observing the four *satipaṭṭhānas* when one abides in the first *jhāna* and the observing the four *satipaṭṭhānas* while one abides in the second *jhāna*. It also elucidates how the transition between the two occurs: when the practitioner does not react or cling to experience by thinking and commenting about it, thoughts fade away, and one enters naturally into the second *jhāna*.

Whereas the Theravāda tradition explains the entrance into each *jhāna* as a process of concentrating on the *paṭibhāga nimitta* ('counterpart sign'),[15] this sutta connects the attainment of the *jhānas* with perfecting the practice of observing experience (what is traditionally called *vipassanā* meditation). It is interesting to note that the account from the *Dantabhūmi Sutta* also indicates clearly that one does not emerge from each of the *jhānas* for the sake of contemplating the *jhāna* factors; rather, one actually observes phenomena while in the *jhānas*.[16]

Thus, it is plausible to argue that the second *jhāna*, along with the following two, are the optimal states for seeing experience clearly. They are the actualization of developing insight (*vipassanā*) and wisdom (*paññā*). In the first *jhāna*, the practitioner observes phenomena without being hindered by the *nīvaraṇas* (or any other unwholesome states that obstruct wisdom);[17] in the second *jhāna*, the practitioner observes phenomena without being hindered by conceptual thinking, mental interpretation and intentionality. As observed before, thinking might be beneficial in certain stages of the path, but it also filters our perception of reality by interpreting what is being experienced according to conditioned tendencies, views and memories. In just the same way, while intention can be wholesome and directed to wholesome action, it also implies that there is a preference towards something; this is a movement of becoming (*bhava*). In the first *jhāna*, this intentionality is wholesome, that is, one's intentions are directed to the correct path to awakening. However, the second *jhāna* is where *kusala saṅkappa* (wholesome intentions) cease without a remainder (*aparisesā nirujjhanti*).[18] Importantly, according to Buddhist philosophy, wholesome intentions create *kamma*[19] and yield the fruit of *upadhi* (the substrate for existence and *dukkha*), just as unwholesome intentions do.[20] This seems to be the reason why wholesome intentions must cease for attaining liberation. A mind with no intention, an unmovable mind, resembles the mind of a liberated person[21] – one who does not create *kamma*. I would also suggest that the cessation of intention, accomplished while one is abiding in the three higher *jhānas*, de-conditions the tendencies to prefer, to like and to dislike.

To sum up this point, the *Dantabhūmi Sutta* delineates the way one transitions and progresses from the first *jhāna* to the next and correlates this transition with the development of insight and the establishing and grounding of mindfulness (*sati*).

III *Samādhi* and *vipassanā*

The fading away of *vitakka* and *vicāra* seems to be the proximate cause for entering into the second *jhāna*. The cessation of discursive thinking is also the condition for the arising of three mental qualities that were not present in the mind prior to entering into the second *jhāna*. These are *samādhi*, *ajjhattaṃ sampasādanaṃ* ('inner stillness') and *cetaso ekodibhāvaṃ* ('unification of mind'). These three factors are obviously related and indicate a certain quality of mind that cannot manifest when discursive thinking (not perception) is still active. From this supposition, two interesting questions arise: do *samādhi* and *ekodibhāvaṃ* designate a one-pointed concentration, that is, a one-pointed absorption in which the mind is disconnected from sense experience? Or perhaps these terms indicate a spacious and open mind, a quality of mind that allows one to perceive experience without being obscured by likes and dislikes, interpretation, aversion and wanting?

The assumption that *samādhi* designates a one-pointed concentration of mind is founded upon the common dichotomy, which I would argue is misconceived, between *samatha* meditation and *vipassanā* meditation. According to this dichotomy, *samatha* meditation is described as means for attaining *samādhi* through one-pointed concentration, and *vipassanā* meditation is described as means for attaining insight by observing the changing phenomenal field.

Here, I would merely like to emphasize again that the concept of 'access concentration' (*upacāra samādhi*) and the correlation of the *jhānas* with 'absorption concentration' (*appaṇā samādhi*) are both products of the commentarial tradition. In the Nikāyas, there is no mention whatsoever of this classification of two types of *samādhi* together with the view that the *jhānas* are not necessary for liberation (since *upacāra samādhi* is enough for insight practice and for the attainment of liberation). Furthermore, Buddhaghosa's classification and systematization of the path into *sīla*, *samādhi* and *paññā* led to the view that the development of *samādhi* is not the outcome of insight (although it might be a basis for insight practice) or the manifestation of insight. Those who embrace Buddhaghosa's structure of the Buddhist path fully[22] will also ascertain that one can achieve *samādhi* (i.e., attain the *jhānas*) by concentrating on various synthetic objects of meditation; such objects do not reveal anything about the nature of experience. Thus, the common interpretation of *samādhi* is that it is a mental quality which has nothing to do with the development of insight into the true nature of phenomena,[23] although it can be used, if wished, as a basis for insight practice.[24]

This sort of interpretation of *samādhi* (and the *jhānas*) seems to derive from two preconceptions. The first assumption is the notion that genuine Buddhist practice is a conceptual reflection upon basic categories of Buddhist doctrine.[25] The second assumption is the view that *vipassanā* mediation, as Buddhist practice par excellence, does not lead to the 'cessation of normal intellectual operations'[26] since this is not the aim of Buddhist meditation. We can see that these assumptions are interconnected and place great emphasis on the power and significance of discursive thinking for attaining the Buddhist *summum bonum*. Therefore, for one who holds the preceding views about the nature of Buddhist practice and goal, the first *jhāna* is still in accordance with this notion, while the second, third and fourth *jhānas* are at odds with it.

Contrary to the aforementioned assumptions, we have seen in our analysis that according to the Nikāyas the attainment of the first two *jhānas* enables mindfulness (*sati*) to be further developed and established. I have also postulated, based on textual analysis, that the *jhānas* themselves exemplify the optimal state for observing phenomena clearly and directly. Moreover, although the practice of *vipassanā*[27] as the practice of observing the four *satipaṭṭhānas* does partially employ concepts and propositions of Buddhist doctrine in its preliminary stages, it is quite problematic to assert that the practice of observing these four categories of experience always involves conceptual thinking.

We are left, then, with the need to offer an alternative interpretation of the term *samādhi*, as it appears in relation to the *jhānas* and the earlier argument. Re-thinking and re-interpreting the meaning of such an important term might assist in understanding the correlation between path elements, which can appear irreconcil-able when one holds the preceding conceptions about the Buddhist path. For this study, two applications of the term *samādhi* are relevant. The first refers specifi-cally to a quality of mind that arises when *vitakka* and *vicāra* fade away, specifi-cally when one enters into the second *jhāna*. The second is *sammā-samādhi*, which is one of the factors of the Eightfold Path. I would suggest that the former signifies the development of the *samādhi bojjhaṅga* ('awakening factor') and the initial development of *sammā-samādhi*; in contrast, *sammā-samādhi* refers to the situa-tion where one attains the fourth and final *jhāna* and fulfils the seven factors of awakening as 'awakening factors' (*bojjhaṅgas*). In other words, the concept of *sammā-samādhi* contains within it the previous development of the *samādhi bojjhaṅga* together with the purification (*parisuddhi*) and fulfilment of the other awakening factors, most importantly, *sati* and *upekkhā*.

Although *sammā-samādhi* refers to the attainment of the four *jhānas* as a whole, I have decided to discuss it in this chapter, since this chapter is dedicated to the concept of *samādhi* in the *jhāna* attainments. Here, I have two primary objectives. First, I show that the presence of *samādhi* (and *ekodibhāvaṃ*) in the second *jhāna* is the actualization of insight. I contend that these two qualities express the ability of the mind to know experience directly. Second, I will argue that *sammā-samādhi* symbolizes the fulfilment of the Eightfold Path and the ability to perceive the nature of phenomena, meaning that no phenomena is viewed or grasped at, as 'me' or 'mine'.

I want to preface this discussion by highlighting two interesting observations made by Stuart Sarbacker and Anne Klein; these observations will be echoed in my analysis and interpretation of the next three *jhānas*. Sarbacker has observed that the mind, according to both Buddhist and Hindu texts, can be knowing and discriminative despite being non-discursive.[28] Following his observation, I hope to show that in the Nikāyas, both the quality of *samādhi*, which manifests in the second *jhāna*, and the concept of *sammā-samādhi* denote this type of non-discur-sive awareness. This is contrary to the common interpretation of *samādhi* as one-pointed concentration that has nothing to do with insight. Second, I believe that Klein's observation that there are 'degrees' of conditioning is pertinent to our discussion and very sensitive and insightful with regard to the process of Buddhist meditation. Klein suggests that the grey area between the conditioned and the unconditioned is mental quiescence which is 'an ameliorating connection between these two oppositionally framed categories'.[29] I would suggest that the *jhānas*, as *sammā-samādhi*,[30] function as such a connection. *Samādhi* describes a quality of mind that although conditioned, aids the process of de-conditioning, thereby allowing the mind to perceive phenomena without being tinged by tendencies, preferences and 'self-view'. This will demonstrate further that the dichotomy between *samatha* (as the *jhānas*) and *vipassanā* (as the four *satipaṭṭhānas*) has no firm basis in close textual analysis; all the more so, the view that the *jhānas* are a separate meditation technique, not required for attaining liberation, is unfounded. Hopefully, this will offer insight into the vision of liberation and the potentiality of mind according to the Pāli Nikāyas.

IV *Samādhi, ekodibhāvaṃ, sati* and *paññā*

In the Nikāyas, the compound *sammā-samādhi* refers specifically to the attainment of the four *jhānas* as a whole:

> And what, friend, is right *samādhi*? Here, separated from the desire for sensual pleasures, separated from [other] unwholesome states, a bhikkhu enters upon and abides in the first *jhāna*, which is [mental] joy and [bodily] pleasure born of *viveka*, accompanied by thought and reflection. With the stilling of thought and reflection, a bhikkhu enters upon and abides in the second *jhāna*, which is [mental] joy and [bodily] pleasure born of *samādhi*, inner stillness and unification of mind, without thought and reflection. With the fading away of [mental] joy, a bhikkhu abides in equanimity, mindful and fully aware. [Still] experiencing pleasure with the body, he enters upon and abides in the third *jhāna*, on account of which noble ones announce: 'abiding in pleasure, one is equanimous and mindful'. With the abandoning of pleasure and pain, and with the previous disappearance of joy and grief, a bhikkhu enters upon and abides in the fourth *jhāna*, which is neither-painful-nor-pleasurable, and has purity of mindfulness and equanimity. This is called right *samādhi*.[31]

The *Mahācattārīsaka Sutta* clarifies that *sammā-samādhi* is a quality achieved by the support and development of the other seven factors of the Eightfold Path:

> Bhikkhus I shall teach you noble right *samādhi* with its support and requisites . . . What bhikkhus is noble right *samādhi* with its support and requisites, that is, right view, right intention, right speech, right action, right livelihood, right effort, and right mindfulness? Unification of mind equipped with these seven factors is called noble right *samādhi* with its support and requisites.[32]

From the first passage, it is quite clear that the four *jhānas* are one of the factors of the Eightfold Path, and therefore an essential component of the Buddhist path to liberation. The second passage indicates that the four *jhānas* can only be attained by the development of the other seven path-factors. The later statement is further strengthened by the *Micchatta Sutta* from the AN, which points out that the ten qualities of the Tenfold Path are gradually developed from one another. Each quality gives rise (*pahoti*) to the next quality[33]

> From right view, right intention originates; from right intention, right speech originates; from right speech, right action originates; from right action, right livelihood originates; from right livelihood, right effort originates; from right effort, right mindfulness originates; from right mindfulness, right *samādhi* originates; from right *samādhi*, right knowledge originates; from right knowledge, right release originates.[34]

Even if we are cautious in taking this statement at face value, that is, as describing a strict causal relationship between the qualities, it does point at the importance of developing certain qualities first as a foundation and condition for other qualities (as with the '*bojjhaṅga* process formula'). It is also significant that both the *Mahācattārīsaka Sutta* and the *Micchatta Sutta* (and other suttas as well),[35] clearly state that *sammā-samādhi* can be achieved only by the previous development of the other seven path-factors, which then serve as its support, requisite and foundation. In our context, what is of importance is that *sammā-sati* is one of the qualities that supports *samādhi*, and not *vice versa*. This is further supported by the *Cūḷavedalla Sutta* of the MN, which states that the 'signs' (*nimitta*) of *samādhi* are the four *satipaṭṭhānas*,[36] not the *kaṣinas* or the *brahma-vihāras*, for example. This was also pointed out by Vetter, who argued that *sammā-sati* is perfected just before one enters into the *jhānas*.[37] In light of this, it can be inferred that only when the practitioner develops the four *satipaṭṭhānas*, that is, observes experience and its characteristics and establishes right *sati* to a certain degree, *sammā-samādhi* can be fulfilled and perfected.[38]

From this, it is hard to understand how the idea that the four *jhānas* can be bypassed on the path to liberation was conceived by the Theravāda tradition. It seems to me that the commentarial distinction between 'ordinary' *jhāna* and *lokuttara-jjhāna* was created for dealing exactly with this problem: how to reconcile their view that one can achieve liberation without the *jhānas* with the explicit description in the Nikāyas that *sammā-samādhi* is another name for the attainment of the four *jhānas*. However, as I have shown in the Introduction, this distinction cannot be found anywhere in the Nikāyas. The only type of *jhānas* the Nikāyas (and the Āgamas) record are the four gradual attainments that should be attained on the path to liberation. There are no references to the Abhidhammic idea that the *jhānas* are also a label for the moment one attains one of the four stages of awakening, in which a particular set of *jhāna* factors corresponds to each of the four stages of awakening.[39]

As to how the Pāli Nikāyas understand the liberative value of *samādhi* specifically, SN IV.144 has an interesting perspective. This sutta explains that the attainment of *samādhi* (and while we can assume that the sutta refers here to *sammā-samādhi*, it also may refer to *samādhi* of the second *jhāna* as a factor of awakening) leads to seeing experience manifest: 'Monks, develop *samādhi*. When a monk has *samādhi*, [things] appear as they are."[40]

The *Samādhibhāvanā Sutta* further explains that the quality of *samādhi* allows the practitioner to understand things as they are, and more specifically, it allows one to understand the origination and cessation of the five aggregates. The point is to understand the nature of self:

> Monks, develop *samādhi*. A bhikkhu who has *samādhi* understand things as they really are. And what does he understand as it really is? The origin and the passing away of form . . . feeling . . . perception . . . volitional formations . . . and consciousness.[41]

Both suttas expound that one who has *samādhi* can understand the dependent and transitory nature of experience.[42] The striking point for our purpose is that the development of *samādhi* enables one to see the dynamics of experience. These suttas do not portray the quality of *samādhi* as an absorption disengaged from experience or as a state of mind which narrows the field of awareness. On the contrary, *samādhi* is depicted as a broad field of awareness, knowing but non-discursive.

However, even if *samādhi* refers to a mind focused a small range of related objects, I will argue, that contrary to the traditional view that characterizes the quality of *samādhi* in the *jhānas* as states of absorption – absorption that does not allow for insight to arise – the Nikāyas consider the quality of *samādhi* in the *jhānas* as what allows the meditator to see the dynamics of experience, even if this dynamic is 'on a small sample of "reality" '.[43] In other words, *sammā-samādhi* (i.e., the four *jhānas*) are not states of one-pointed absorption; rather, they states of a stable, discerning and focused mind, either on a broad phenomenal field or on a sample of it.[44]

That said, how can the qualities of *samādhi* and *ekodibhāvaṃ* be understood as the actualization of insight as I have already suggested? How do the seemingly disparate qualities such as *samādhi*, *ekodibhāvaṃ*, *sati* and *paññā* actually interrelate?

The term *samādhi* is a complex concept in Indian contemplative traditions. It has various descriptions and characteristics depending on which text one studies. In Buddhist (and Hindu) texts, the term *samādhi* refers to a spectrum of higher or altered states of consciousness. It is also associated in later Buddhist texts and in non-Buddhist meditative traditions with the development of special powers,[45] the possibility of being reborn in higher cosmological realms[46] and even with liberation itself.[47] In the Buddhist context, it is usually translated as 'concentration' and interpreted, together with terms such as *ekodibhāvaṃ* and *ekaggata*, as signifying 'one-pointed concentration' of mind. More specifically, this means a one-pointed absorption into a certain object of meditation, probably the sensation of the breath or one of the *kaṣinas*. In the Nikāyas, the term *samādhi* is used in reference to both states of consciousness that are desirable, such as the *samādhi bojjhaṅga*, *animitta samādhi*, *suññata samādhi* and *appaṇihita samādhi*,[48] and to attainments that are not specifically conducive to liberation, such as the 'one-sided *samādhi*' (*ekaṃsabhāvito samādhi*)[49] and the 'two-sided *samādhi* (*ubhayaṃsabhāvito samādhi*).[50] However, since the focus of this study is the nature of the *jhāna* attainments, I shall confine my analysis of *samādhi* to its appearance in connection with the second *jhāna* and to its related terms *ekodibhāvaṃ and ekaggata/ekaggacittā.*

Let us first begin with discussing the correlation of *samādhi, ekodibhāvaṃ* and *ekaggacittā* to the practice of the four *satipaṭṭhāna*. The Satipaṭṭhāna Saṃyutta has an interesting and illuminating account that sheds light on the significance of these qualities for observing and understanding experience:

> Come friends, dwell observing the body as body, ardently, fully aware with unified and clear mind, calm and with oneness of mind, in order to know the body as it really is. Dwell observing feeling as feeling . . . dwell observing mind as mind . . . dwell observing phenomena as phenomena ardently, fully aware with unified and clear mind, calm and with oneness of mind, in order to know phenomena as it really is.[51]

This passage points at an interesting perspective: to really know experience, full awareness (*sampajānā*) and effort (*ātāpino*) are not enough. For understanding the nature of phenomena, the mind has to be unified (*ekaggacittā*) and clear. It has to be 'one-natured' (*ekodibhūtā*). This statement conflicts with the view that 'oneness of mind' (*ekaggacittā/ekodibhāvaṃ*) actually characterizes a type of mystical experience that has nothing to do with knowing and understanding experience in the Buddhist sense.[52] This is because it refers to a state of mind that is disconnected from sense experience. For example, in his article 'Mysticism and Meditation', Gimello has suggested that 'oneness' is a characteristic of all mystical experiences. He claims that it would be fruitless to distinguish between varieties of 'oneness', due to the fact that these differences seem to be the outcome of doctrinal interpretation. His argument is that 'there must be some common factor in all of these experiences'.[53] Gimello provides this analysis – of a shared characteristic of mystical experience – in order to demonstrate that Buddhist meditation is not 'a form of mysticism or a means by which to attain mystical experience'[54] (i.e., the experience of oneness/the *jhānas*). Thus, he divides the Buddhist meditative path into *samatha*[55] and *vipassanā*; having done so, he contends that only *vipassanā* meditation is genuinely Buddhist. He further argues that *vipassanā* meditation has nothing to do with 'mystical experience'[56] or with the quality of 'oneness' (contrary to *samatha* meditation). That is, Gimello argues that discernment or *vipassanā* meditation does not lead to the 'feeling of oneness', since it is a different category of religious experience.[57]

His argument cannot be substantiated when we consider what has been established thus far. The Nikāyas clearly correlate the practice of '*vipassanā*' (as the observation of the four *satipaṭṭhānas*) with the attainment of the *jhānas* and hence with developing *samādhi*[58] and *ekodibhāvaṃ*. We should also bear in mind that the Buddha used known terms and concepts while changing their meaning to suit his own understanding. Therefore, his use of *samādhi*, *ekaggata* and *ekodibhāvaṃ* might very well have a distinct meaning in the Nikāyas; this use is not necessarily the same as their use in other Śramaṇic traditions, nor can we assume that it is similar to the way they were used in later texts or in other contemplative traditions. I would suggest that in the Nikāyas, the term *samādhi* together with *ekodibhāvaṃ* imply an intimate relationship and closeness with experience. It is 'being-at-one-with' that which one is experiencing. This is implied in the earlier description from the

Satipaṭṭhāna Saṃyutta: for knowing phenomena as it really is, we need to be 'one with' it. However, we should bear in mind that in this context, being-at-one-with experience does not mean absorption, but close contact with what presents itself to awareness devoid of discursive interpretation and mental reactions

Contrary to Gimello's argument that genuine Buddhist meditation does not lead to the 'quality of oneness'. SN V. 144 (as SN V.150 and MN III.136) makes the opposite claim by connecting the practice of the *satipaṭṭhānas* with the presence of the qualities of *samādhi* and *ekodibhāvaṃ*. Even though the description from SN V. 144 does not identify this attainment as the second *jhāna*, we are justified in assuming that it does portray the attainment of the second *jhāna* with a different emphasis in mind. In other words, it is likely that this passage describes the second *jhāna* in a slightly different way than the formulaic description. If we accept this premise, it means that when one attains the second *jhāna*, a different type of knowing occurs: knowing that is associated with *samādhi* and *ekodibhāvaṃ*.

To sum up, SN V.144 points out clearly that having such qualities of mind means that one is in a better position to observe and know experience.[59] It also indicates that this knowing of phenomena occurs despite the fact that discursive thinking is absent – even better, one knows clearly the nature of phenomena because of it. SN V.144 also integrates qualities such as *samāhita*, *ekaggacittā* and *ekodibhāvaṃ* with the practice of *satipaṭṭhāna*. I would also emphasize that from the preceding discussion, *samādhi* cannot be viewed as a quality that 'immunizes' the meditator against disturbances or functions merely as an extraordinary 'data' for the meditator to scrutinize, as Gimello has put it.[60] On the contrary, *samādhi* and *ekodibhāvaṃ* are the actualization of insight – of knowing experience clearly. Here we see how mindfulness, insight and *samādhi* are interrelated and complementary in the Nikāyas' conception of the nature of the meditative practice.

At this point, based on the preceding analysis, I would like to offer a more precise definition of *samādhi* and *ekodibhāvaṃ* in the context of the *jhānas*. How are we to understand the quality of mind they actually describe? What will be a meaningful and precise translation of these two significant terms?

Samādhi literally means 'together' or 'joining'. It can also mean 'being-at-one-with', especially when it is combined with terms such as *ekodibhāvaṃ*. As I have already pointed out, in the Theravāda Buddhist tradition, the idea of 'oneness' (*ekodibhāvaṃ* and *samādhi*) was usually understood to denote one-pointed concentration that has nothing to do with insight. However, as I have just shown, being-at-one-with is exactly that which allows the mind to know the nature of phenomena. That is, the quality of 'oneness' and 'being one with' one experiences does not refer to mental absorption;[61] it does not mean that when 'oneness of mind' is experienced in the second *jhāna* the practitioner abides in a state of mind in which the senses are withdrawn. It also does not refer to 'feeling' in the ordinary sense of the word. The feeling (*vedanā*) one experiences in the second *jhāna* is spiritual pleasure (*nirāmisa sukha*) – the same type of feeling one has experienced in the previous *jhāna*. In other words, *samādhi* and *ekodibhāvaṃ* do not refer to the 'feeling tone' (*vedanā*) of the experience; rather, they refer to a different mode of being *with* experience.

I would suggest that *samādhi* and *ekodibhāvaṃ* signify a close and intimate contact with experience. This kind of contact occurs when mental interpretation and the fluctuation of ordinary cognition have ceased. We can say that when thinking, interpretation and intention are still present in the mind, one cannot be with experience fully and intimately. This is because every moment of ordinary sense experience is tinged by conditioned habits of commenting on and interpreting experience based on previous memories. I might even suggest that the type of knowing that occurs in the second, third and fourth *jhānas* is empty of the notion of subject and object. When thoughts subside, the mind does not tell a story about the experience and does not re-create the sense of 'I-ness'. Experience is known just as it is: impermanent (*aniccā*) and not-self (*anattā*).

Samādhi also seems to denote an undisturbed and unshakable state of mind (*samāhita*); that is, a stable and unshakable awareness of phenomena. Given the preceding, it seems that the common interpretation of *samādhi* as 'concentration' or as 'one-pointed concentration' is not only narrow but also misleading. However, I also think that it will be impossible to find an appropriate translation of *samādhi* without losing its multi-layered meaning. Therefore, I suggest leaving it un-translated, just as we do with other complicated terms such as *jhāna* and *nibbāna*.

V ***Ekodi, ekagatta*** **and** ***samādahāti***

I would like to conclude our discussion on the second *jhāna* by considering three occurrences in which *ekodi*, *ekagatta* and the verb *samādahāti* are associated, quite oddly I think, with the first *jhāna*. If these records are authentic or correct, the suggestions I have already made might be weakened. This is because I have associated these qualities with the cessation of discursive thinking and intention; such cessation occurs only in the transition into the second *jhāna*. However, it still needs to be noted that there are only three suttas in the four primary Nikāyas that connect the terms *ekodi*, *ekagatta* and *samādahāti* with the first *jhāna*. Furthermore, both Martin Stuart-Fox and Govid Chandra Pande have already pointed out the anomalies of these three records.[62]

In one of these records, from the *Savitakka Sutta*, *ekodi* and *samādahāti* are related to the attainment of the first *jhāna*. Two things should be pointed out here: the first is that this record is not attributed to the Buddha himself, and the second is that the description is logically problematic.[63] In this sutta, Moggallāna describes how the Buddha came to him by means of spiritual power and said,

> Moggallāna, Moggallāna . . . steady your mind in the first *jhāna*, unify your mind in the first *jhāna*, stable your mind in the first *jhāna*.[64]

Here we have a peculiar reference to *cittaṃ ekodi karohi* and *samādhahāti* with reference to the first *jhāna*. This contrasts how these are referred to in numerous other suttas; in other suttas, the qualities of oneness and *samādhi* are said to arise only when one enters the second *jhāna*. It is also interesting that this passage records an instruction 'to make the mind one' (*cittaṃ ekodi karohi*) and does not describe the mind as already having the quality of oneness or *samādhi*. In this passage, the Buddha supposedly instructs Moggallāna to develop these qualities while he is in the first *jhāna* as an antidote to Moggallāna's dilemma, expressed in his statement, that while he was abiding in the first *jhāna* he was assailed by perception and attention accompanied by sense desire.[65] Logically, this statement is inconsistent: how can Moggallāna state that he is detached from *kāma* and other unwholesome states[66] and, at the same time, declare that he is beset by the same hindrances he just abandoned? In view of this inconsistency, it might be reasonable to suggest that this record is corrupted. It should also be noted that the instruction to unify the mind (*cittaṃ ekodiṃ karohi*) is repeated without distinction for each *jhāna* in this sutta. Martin Stuart-Fox has suggested that this repeated sentence is the consequence of a faulty memorization; he further postulates that the reference to Moggallāna seems to indicate the lateness of this sutta.[67]

I tend to accept Martin Stuart-Fox's conclusion. However, if we do not accept the argument that this sutta was corrupted due to faulty memorization or any other reason, it might be that the Buddha's instructions imply that one should make an effort to unify the mind while abiding in the first *jhāna*. Put differently, this sutta points out that the mind is *not* unified in the first *jhāna*. Therefore, one has to make an effort to develop these qualities in order to progress to the second *jhāna*. I would suggest that this is another way to instruct the practitioner to observe the four *satipaṭṭhānas* without thinking thoughts connected with body, feeling, mind and *dhammas*. It might be a different formulation of the instructions given in the *Dantabhūmi Sutta*.[68]

The other two references in which the term *ekagatta* is mentioned as a quality of the first *jhāna* are from the *Mahāvedalla Sutta* (MN I.294) and the *Anupada Sutta* (MN III.25). As I have already pointed out, both Martin Stuart-Fox and Govid Chandra Pande have discerned correctly the anomalies of these two records. In the *Mahāvedalla Sutta*, there is a discrepancy in Sāriputta's answer concerning the first *jhāna*. His description of the first *jhāna* is identical to the formulaic one, but when he lists the factors of the first *jhāna*, immediately after he depicts his own attainment, he mysteriously adds *ekagatta* as one of the qualities although he did not mention it before.[69]

The account from the *Anupada Sutta* is also problematic. It states that there are sixteen *dhammas* present in the first *jhāna*: *vitakka, vicāra, pīti, sukha, citteka-gatta, phassa, vedanā, saññā, cetanā cittaṃ, chanda, adhimokkha, vīriyaṃ, sati, upekkhā, manasikāra*. To the best of my knowledge, these *dhammas* do not occur in any other sutta as factors of the first *jhāna*. The reason for this is the obvious fact that some of the factors, according to Buddhist thought, cannot coexist with other factors in this list. For example, *upekkhā* and *chanda* cannot arise at the same moment of consciousness.[70] Also, to claim that *citta-ekagatta* (together with *samādhi*) can characterize a state of mind in which *vitakka* and *vicāra* are still present is problematic in my view. In light of all this, Pande's suggestion that both suttas seem to be of late composition, probably an early Abhidhammic text, seems to be very plausible.[71]

Notes

1 MN I.174: *puna ca paraṃ bhikkhave bhikkhu vitakkavicārānaṃ vūpasamā ajjhattaṃ sampasādanaṃ cetaso ekodibhāvaṃ avitakkaṃ avicāraṃ samādhijaṃ pītisukhaṃ dutiyaṃ jhānaṃ upasampajja viharati.*
2 Gimello 1978, 188; Griffiths 1981, 618.
3 E.g., MN I.112.
4 AN II.52.
5 E.g., SN II.66.
6 In Sn 1119 the Buddha instructs Mogharāja to destroy the view of one's self (*attānudiṭṭhaṃ ūhacca*) so he could cross beyond death (*evaṃ maccutaro siyā*). It is plausible to argue that a 'view' (*diṭṭhi*) is a type of thought.
7 E.g., MN I.111–12.
8 See, for example, AN II.45: 'And what is the development of *samādhi* that, when developed and pursued, leads to mindfulness and clear knowing? . . . Thoughts are known to him as they arise, known as they persist, known as they fade away. This is the development of *samādhi* that, when developed and pursued, leads to mindfulness and clear knowing.' *Katamā ca bhikkhave samādhibhāvanā bhāvitā bahulīkatā satisampajaññāya saṃvattati . . . Viditā vitakkā uppajjanti viditā upaṭṭhahanti. Viditā abbhatthaṃ gacchanti. Ayaṃ bhikkhave samādhibhāvanā bhāvitā bahulīkatā satisampajaññāya saṃvattati.*
9 E.g., AN II.14. This view of how to still thoughts is also presented by the Korean Master Chinul. In his work 'Secret on Cultivating the Mind' (Susim Kyŏl) Chinul explains, 'Do not fear the arising of thoughts: only be concerned lest your awareness of them be tardy.' It is also said, 'If we are aware of thought at the moment it arises, then through that awareness it will vanish' (Buswell 199, 107).
10 Ud.34: *khuddā vitakka sukhumā vitakka, anugatā manaso uppilāvā. Ete avidvā manaso vitakke, hurā huraṃ dhāvati bhatacitto. Ete ca vidvā manaso vitakke, ātāpiyo saṃvaratī satīmā; anugate manaso uppilāve, asesamete pajahāsi buddho'ti.*
11 Gethin 2001, 53.
12 SN V.301.
13 See SN V.143 where the Buddha declares that based upon *sīla*, one should develop the four *satipaṭṭhānas*. By this development, one should expect only growth in wholesome states, not decline. These wholesome states seem to be the four *jhānas*, as the foundation on which *nibbāna* might be realized.
14 MN III.136: *Tamenaṃ tathāgato uttariṃ vineti: ehi tvaṃ bhikkhu, kāye kāyānupassī viharāhi. Mā ca kāyūpasaṃhitaṃ vitakkaṃ vitakkesi. Vedanāsu vedanānupassī viharāhi. Mā ca vedanūpasaṃhitaṃ vitakkaṃ vitakkesi. Citte cittānupassī viharāhi. Mā ca cittūpasaṃhitaṃ vitakkaṃ vitakkesi. Dhammesu dhammānupassi viharāhi. Mā ca dhammūpasaṃhitaṃ vitakkaṃ vitakkesī'ti. So vitakkavicāranaṃ vupasamā ajjhattaṃ sampasādanaṃ cetaso ekodibhāvaṃ avitakkaṃ avicāraṃ samādhijaṃ pītisukhaṃ dutiyaṃ jhānaṃ upasampajja viharati.*
15 E.g., Pa-Auk Sayadaw 2003, 56.
16 In her article on *dhyāna* in the *Abhidharmakośabhāṣya*, Karin Meyers points out that 'the AKBh is clearly of the view that one can and should practice *vipaśyanā* while in *dhyāna*'. Meyers 'The Pleasant Way'. Retrieved April 15 2012, 12.
17 E.g., MN III.136.

18 MN II.28.
19 Wholesome *saṇkhāras* also lead to meritorious destination (SN II.82).
20 See MN III.73.
21 E.g., MN III.244.
22 A more dominant path structure in the Nikāyas is the one that depicts a gradual training path: the training in morality (*sīla-khandha*); the practice of guarding and restraining the impressions brought about by sense experience (*indriya-saṃvara*); and the practice of full awareness *sampajāna*. See, for example, MN I.179ff, I.268–70, I.271–7, I.346ff, III.1–5; III.33–6; III.134–6; DN I.63ff, III.270; AN II.208ff, V.206.
23 E.g., Gimello 1978, 184.
24 See, for example, Gimello's argument that the practice of *vipassanā* is an intellectual operation that might be performed upon mystical experiences (i.e., the *jhānas* and the *arūpa samāpattis*) (Gimello 1978, 189).
25 E.g., Gimello 1978, 188.
26 Gimello 1978, 188.
27 Note that the term *vipassanā-bhāvanā* does not appear in the Nikāyas material, only in the commentarial tradition.
28 Sarbacker 2005, 37.
29 Klein 1992, 295.
30 E.g., MN III.252.
31 E.g., MN III.252: *Katamo cāvuso, sammāsamādhi: idhāvuso, bhikkhu vivicceva kāmehi vivicca akusalehi dhammehi savitakkaṃ savicāraṃ vivekajaṃ pitisukhaṃ paṭhamaṃ jhānaṃ upasampajja viharati. Vitakkavicāranaṃ vūpasamā ajjhattaṃ sampasādanaṃ cetaso ekodibhāvaṃ avitakkaṃ avicāraṃ samādhijaṃ pitisukhaṃ dutiyaṃ jhānaṃ upasampajja viharati. Pītiyā ca virāgā upekkhāko ca viharati. Sato ca sampajāno sukhaṃ ca kāyena paṭisaṃvesedeti. Yantaṃ ariyā ācikkhanti upekkhāko satimā sukhavihārīti tatiyaṃ jhānaṃ upasampajja viharati. Sukhassa ca pahānā dukkhassa ca pahānā pubbeva somanassa domanassānaṃ atthaṃgamā adukkhaṃ asukhaṃ upekkhā sati pārisuddhiṃ catutthaṃ jhānaṃ upasampajja viharati. Ayaṃ vuccatāvuso sammāsamādhi.* See also SN V.9 and SN V.196.
32 MN III.71: *ariyaṃ vo bhikkhave, sammāsamādhi desessāmi sa-upanisaṃ saparikkhāraṃ*... *katamo ca, bhikkhave, ariyo sammāsamādhi sa-upaniso saparikkhāro? Seyyathidaṃ sammāsdiṭṭhi, sammāsaṅkappo, sammāvācā. Sammākammanto, sammā-āvījo, sammāvāyāmo, sammāsati. Yā kho, bhikkhave, imehi sattāṅgehi citassa ekagatta parikkhatā. Ayaṃ vuccati, bhikkhave, ariyo sammāsamādhi sa-upaniso saparikkhāro itipi.* This statement appears also in SN V.21, AN IV.40, DN II.216–7, DN III.252–3. See also AN V.214.
33 This 'hierarchy' also appears in reference to the development of the seven factors of awakening, an issue I have mentioned before.
34 AN V.212: *sammādiṭṭhikassa bhikkhave sammāsaṅkappo pahoti, sammāsaṅkappassa sammāvācā pahoti, sammāvācassa sammākammanto pahoti, sammākammantassa sammā ājīvo pahoti, sammā ājīvassa sammāvāyāmo pahoti, sammā vāyāmassa sammāsati pahoti, sammāsatissa sammā samādhi pahoti, sammāsamādhissa sammāñāṇaṃ pahoti, sammāñāṇissa2 sammāvimutti pahoti.* See also AN V.214 and DN II.217.
35 See also AN IV.337.
36 MN I.301.
37 Vetter 1988, 3–32.
38 E.g., DN III.242.
39 See my discussion in the Introduction. Note, however, that in Vibaṅga 265, it is said that one gains the first stage of awakening by any of the four *lokuttara jhānas*.
40 SN IV.144: *samādhiṃ bhikkhave bhāvetha, samāhitassa bhikkhave bhikkhuno yathābhūtaṃ okkhāyati.* See also AN IV.337, AN II.45, SN III.14, SN IV.78, SN IV.80, SN IV.144 and SN V.414 (*samādhi* leads to understanding the Four Noble Truths). It is

interesting to note Robert Buswell's observation that according to Tsung-mi, the fifth patriarch of the Hua-yen School in China, *samādhi* is actually an abbreviation for both *samādhi* and *prajñā* (Ch'an-yuan chi tu-hsu 1, *T* 48.399a18) (Buswell 1987, 329).

41 SN III.13–14: *samādhiṃ bhikkhave, bhāvetha. Samāhito bhikkhave, bhikkhu yathābhūtaṃ pajānāti. Kiñca yathābhūtaṃ pajānāti? Rūpassa samudayañca atthagamañca, vedanāya samudayañca atthagamañca, saññāya samudayañca atthagamañca, saṃkhārānaṃ samudayañca atthagamañca, viññāṇassa samudayañca atthagamañca.* See also SN IV.80, AN II.202 and AN II.45, which call for the observation of the rise and fall of the five aggregates: *samādhibhāvanā bhāvitā bahulīkatā āsavānaṃ khayāya saṃvattati.* DN II.216 also explains that when the practitioner observes the four *satipaṭṭhānas* internally, he develops right *samādhi* and right clarity. From that right *samādhi* and right clarity, one gains knowledge and vision about the external bodies of others. These insights arise when one develops *samādhi* through the practice of the four *satipaṭṭhānas*, which were taught by the Buddha.
Here we find an explanation about the problematic instruction in the *Satipaṭṭhāna Sutta* to observe internally and externally the four *satipaṭṭhānas*.

42 SN IV.78 also states that only when the mind has gladness, mental happiness and tranquillity, the mind is free from *dukkha*. This freedom from *dukkha* enables the mind to be truly concentrated (*samādhiyati*) and to see phenomena as it is.

43 I am grateful to Peter Harvey for pointing out this observation.

44 See, for example, Vism XI, which clearly sees the *jhānas* as states that do not allow for the meditator to see change or different objects. For Buddhaghosa (as for contemporary meditation teacher such as Pa-Auk Sayadaw), meditation practice such as element meditation cannot lead to *jhāna* since one observes different objects.

45 Gimello 1978, 183. Gustaaf Houtman has also indicated that in Burma, the practice of concentration (i.e., the *jhānas*) was perceived as a way to obtain special powers such as healing, supernatural abilities, alchemical and mundane success. He points out that the government 'was not pleased with the unorthodox concentration meditator whose aspirations to power introduce an element of political instability. Many concentration meditation practitioners, both laymen and monks, have been arrested over the last few years, and the powers derived from concentration meditation, such as those of flight and transformation are censored from Burmese films'(Houtman 1990, 184).

46 Sarbacker 2005, 91, 128.

47 E.g., Yoga Sūtra 1.51; 3.3.

48 E.g., DN III.219. The *animitta samādhi* and *suññata samādhi* are also declared in the Nikāyas as 'deliverances of mind' (*cetovimutti*) (MN I 296–8).

49 DN I.153.

50 DN I.155.

51 SN V. 144: *etha tumhe āvuso, kāye kāyānupassino viharatha, ātāpino sampajānā ekodibhūtā vippasannacittā samāhitā ekaggacittā kāyassa yathābhūtaṃ ñāṇāya. Vedanāsu vedanānupassino viharatha, ātāpino sampajānā ekodibhūtā vippasannacittā samāhitā ekaggacittā vedanānaṃ yathābhūtaṃ ñāṇāya. Citte cittānupassino viharatha, ātāpino sampajānā ekodibhūtā vippasannacittā samāhitā ekaggacittā cittassa yathābhūtaṃ ñāṇāya. Dhammesu dhammānupassino viharatha, ātāpino sampajānā ekodibhūtā vippasannacittā samāhitā ekaggacittā dhammānaṃ yathābhūtaṃ ñāṇāya.*

52 Gimello 1978, 184.

53 Gimello 1978, 177. See his basic features of mystical experiences in Gimello 1978, 178.

54 Gimello 1978, 179.

55 For Gimello, the four *jhānas* and the four *arūpa samāpatti* are part of the same meditative procedure that he calls 'absorption'; moreover, as he puts it, 'these eight levels of absorption fall also under another, perhaps better known, meditative rubric – that of "concentration" or "collectedness" (*samādhi*) – a term which is in many circumstances synonymous with *samatha*' (Gimello 1978, 182–3).

56 Gimello 1978, 188

57 Gimello 1978, 188. Note also, that the classification of certain experiences as 'mystical' or not-mystical, as with the religious category 'mysticism', is extraneous to Buddhist analysis and its framework.

58 See also SN V.151–2.

59 See also AN V.3: '[F]or one who attains the imperturbable [mind], there is no need for the intentional thought: "may I know and see things as they really are". Monks, this is the natural way, when one has attained the imperturbable [mind], one knows and sees things as they really are.' (*Samāhitassa bhikkhave na cetanāya karaṇīyaṃ 'yathābhūtaṃ taṃ jānāmi passāmī'ti. Dhammatā esā bhikkhave yaṃ samāhito yathābhūtaṃ jānāti passati*).

60 Gimello 1978, 184.

61 E.g., as a yogic absorption into the true Self (*puruṣa*) that is separated from experience (*prakṛti*).

62 Pande [1957]1999, 134, 138; Stuart-Fox 1989, 89–90.

63 SN IV.263.

64 SN IV.263: *moggallāna, moggallāna . . . paṭhame jhāne cittaṃ saṇṭhapehi, paṭhame jhāne cittaṃ ekodiṃ karohi, paṭhame jhāne cittaṃ samādahāti.*

65 SN IV.263: *tassa mayhaṃ āvuso iminā vihārena viharato kāmasahagatā saññāmanasikārā samudācaranti.*

66 SN IV.263: *so khvāhaṃ āvuso vivicceva kāmehi vivicca akusalehi dhammehi savitakkaṃ savicāraṃ vivekajaṃ pītisukhaṃ paṭhamaṃ jhānaṃ upasampajja viharāmi.*

67 Stuart-Fox 1989, 89–90.

68 See MN III.136.

69 MN I.294.

70 Note also that *upekkhā* is always described as a quality which arises only when one enters into the third *jhāna.*

71 Pande [1957]1999, 134, 138.

4 Awakening-*Jhāna* Factors

Before passing on to the analysis of the third and fourth *jhānas*, this chapter will call attention to the noticeable parallelism between the development of the seven factors of awakening (*bojjhaṅgas*) and the attainment of the first three *jhānas*. This will be done by a close textual analysis of what Rupert Gethin has termed 'the *bojjhaṅga* process formula'.[1] My aim is to demonstrate the essential connection and interdependency of these two unique Buddhist models. I hope to show that the seven factors of awakening (*bojjhaṅgas*) and the four *jhānas* should be construed as parallel models of spiritual ascension. In other words, they should be viewed as different formulations or expressions of the same spiritual process. I shall illustrate that by showing how by progressing from one *jhāna* to the next, the mind develops and gradually fulfils the seven factors of awakening. I will suggest that one cannot develop and fulfil the qualities of the seven *bojjhaṅgas,* as 'factors of awakening', without attaining the *jhānas*. Correspondingly, one cannot attain the *jhānas* without the fulfilment of the seven *bojjhaṅgas*. Looking at both models in parallel will enable us to understand more clearly the process of liberation as it is envisioned in the Pāli Nikāyas.

As pointed out by Rupert Gethin, the parallelism between the seven *bojjhaṅgas* and the attainment of the *jhānas* is not accidental.[2] Looking at the four *jhānas* in parallel with the *bojjhaṅga* process formula can shed light on several issues. Among these issues is the similitude between certain *jhānic* and *bojjhaṅga* factors, which at first glance seem to designate different mental qualities. Parallel comparison will also show that the *bojjhaṅga* process formula presents a process-oriented perspective in which the 'factors of awakening' can be developed in various levels of stability and strength. This will support my contention that the *bojjhaṅgas* can be developed to a certain extent before one attains the *jhānas* but they can be fulfilled as 'factors of awakening' only when the *jhānas* are attained. Lastly, paralleling the two models will clarify the obscure relation between the second and third *jhānas*. This last point will be addressed here only succinctly since it will be discussed thoroughly in the next chapter.

I The *bojjhaṅga* process formula and *sati*

Looking at the seven factors of awakening[3] in parallel with the four *jhānas* follows Gethin's observation that the successive development of the seven *bojjhaṅgas* corresponds with the model of the four *jhānas*.[4] SN V.331–3 will be our source text for this analysis. It lays out the *bojjhaṅga* process formula by describing the seven factors of awakening as qualities that are cultivated and fulfilled successively.[5] In my view, this presentation of the *bojjhaṅgas* (contrary to the 'bare' list)[6] is meaningful, since it describes more precisely the subtle spiritual process taking place in the mind-body complex when one observes phenomena, abandons unwholesome states, cultivates wholesome qualities and progresses on the path of awakening. It also lends insight, I believe, into the mechanism of the *jhānas* as a process in which the factors of awakening are developed successively until full completion as 'factors of awakening'. When this occurs, which I would argue does so in the fourth *jhāna*, the mind might slant and slope into the attainment of *nibbāna*.[7]

The *bojjhaṅga* process formula explains that each *bojjhaṅga* serves as a condition for the arising of the next *bojjhaṅga*. This, however (as with the successive descriptions of the eightfold and tenfold paths),[8] should not be mistaken as describing a strict causal relationship between the *bojjhaṅgas*. It is obvious that this process is more complex. However, it does show that certain qualities are seen as the foundation and condition for the arising and development of other qualities, most likely as their proximate causes.

The *bojjhaṅga* process formula starts with a straightforward statement that the practice of observing the four *satipaṭṭhānas* (what we traditionally call *vipassanā* meditation) is aimed at the establishment (*upaṭṭhitā*), arousal (*āraddha*) and fulfilment (*pāripūri*) of mindfulness (*sati*)[9] as a foundation for the arousal (*āraddha*), development (*bhāveti*) and 'fulfilment by development' (*bhāvanāpāripūri*) of the other factors of awakening:

> And how Ānanda, are the four establishing of mindfulness developed and cultivated so they fulfil the seven factors of awakening? Whenever, Ānanda, a bhikkhu dwells observing the body as a body,[10] on that occasion, un-muddled mindfulness is established in that bhikkhu. Whenever, Ānanda, un-muddled mindfulness has been established in a bhikkhu, on that occasion, the awakening factor of mindfulness is aroused by the bhikkhu; on that occasion the bhikkhu develops the awakening factor of mindfulness; on that occasion, the awakening factor of mindfulness goes to fulfilment by development in the bhikkhu.[11]

The use of three different nouns in this context points at the process-oriented perspective of this description. Although the description of how each *bojjhaṅga* is developed is different (since it is a successive process in which each *bojjhaṅga* is founded upon the previous one), it is identical with regard to the processive nature of their fulfilment: each quality goes through the process of arousal and development until it is fulfilled and perfected. This is noteworthy for several reasons. It emphasizes the multilevel nature of the awakening factors, and in my view, it also emphasizes the multilevel nature of any other wholesome quality or unwholesome factors. By explicating the process, it shows that each quality can be developed on various levels of stability, strength, steadiness, breadth and depth.

The repeated description of each of the *bojjhaṅgas* as a quality that goes through arousal and development shows that each quality is developed gradually until it is fulfilled as a factor of awakening. What is particularly important is that the *bojjhaṅga* process formula accentuates that a quality becomes an 'awakening factor' (i.e., a *bojjhaṅga*) only when the practitioner develops it to a certain degree of stability and steadiness. It seems that the first level of development, when a quality is said to be established (*upaṭṭhitā*) is when a quality has been aroused and sustained in the mind to a certain extent. However, it is not yet steady, strong or continual enough to be called a 'factor of awakening' (*bojjhaṅga*). One can have moments of mindfulness, tranquillity or equanimity, but more effort and cultivation (*bhāvanā*) are needed for making a quality an 'awakening factor' – that is, stable, strong and continuous in the mind.[12] By the continuous practice of 'remembering' (*sati*) to cultivate and sustain these wholesome qualities (and this is why 'mindfulness' is the foundation for the entire practice)[13] one fulfils and perfects these wholesome qualities as 'factors of awakening'. It should also be noted, however, that the preceding account indicates clearly that even when a quality becomes a *bojjhaṅga*, the practitioner still needs to develop it further until it is completely fulfilled or purified.

In light of this, I would suggest that the formulaic description of the *jhānas* delineates specifically the moment when a factor of awakening is established as one of the 'awakening factors'. I believe that this observation can explain why mindfulness (*sati*) does not appear as one of the qualities of the first and second *jhānas*. This is an important point, since when we parallel the *bojjhaṅga* process formula with the attainment of the *jhānas*, the first question that comes to mind is why *sati* is not listed as one of the qualities of the first and second *jhānas* when it is obvious that one cannot attain the first *jhāna* without developing mindfulness first. We have seen in Chapter 2 that numerous suttas in the Nikāyas describes a gradual path to liberation; in this description, it is clear that one needs to develop mindfulness to a certain extent for attaining the first *jhāna* (and consequently the other three *jhānas* and liberation):[14]

> Possessing this aggregates of noble virtue, and this noble restraint of the faculties, and possessing this noble mindfulness and full awareness, he resorts to a secluded resting place . . . Having thus abandoned these five hindrances, imperfections of the mind that weaken wisdom, quite secluded from *kāma* and unwholesome states, he enters upon and abides in the first *jhāna*.[15]

From this description of the gradual path to liberation, we can safely argue that before one abandons the hindrances and enters into the first *jhāna*, mindfulness[16] and full awareness (*sampajāna*) have already been established to a high degree.[17]

Suppose we accept the suggestion that the formulaic description of the *jhānas* refers to the moment when a wholesome (*kusala*) quality is established as a 'factor of awakening' (and accompanied by other qualities that support its sustainment). Having accepted this supposition, it is plausible to argue that until the attainment of the third *jhāna*, *sati* (and *upekkhā*), are not yet *bojjhaṅgas*. This is why they are not mentioned as factors of the first two *jhānas*.[18] This does not mean, however, that the practitioner did not develop mindfulness (and equanimity) or that mindfulness is not technically present in these attainments. It does mean, however, that it is yet to be called an awakening factor. I would further argue that only in the fourth and final *jhāna* are they fulfilled and perfected (*pāripūri*) as ones.

II ***Dhamma-vicaya***

After mindfulness has been established, the *bojjhaṅga* process formula continues by explaining that

> [d]welling thus mindfully, he discriminates that *dhamma*[19] with wisdom, examines it, makes an investigation of it . . . on that occasion, the bhikkhu develops the awakening factor of discrimination of states (*dhamma-vicaya*).[20]

The awakening factor 'discrimination of *dhammas*'[21] (*dhamma-vicaya*) does not appear as such in the description of the *jhānas*. Furthermore, holding the view that the *jhānas* are in conflict with discrimination and wisdom, one might argue that this quality cannot be developed and sustained when one attains the *jhānas*. However, I would contend the opposite. I suggest that the quality of *dhamma-vicaya* is analogous in nature to the quality of *viveka* of the first *jhāna*. We have seen in Chapter 2 that the first meaning of *viveka* in Sanskrit is 'discrimination'[22] and that this interpretation of *viveka* is supported by SN V.301, which clearly states that the quality of *viveka* is developed by the practice of observing the four *satipaṭṭhānas*.[23] It seems that the cultivation of the four *satipaṭṭhānas* develops the ability to discern the mechanism of mind and body, thereby arousing *viveka*. Thus *viveka*, just as *dhamma-vicaya*, seems to designate the ability to discern the true nature of phenomena. I therefore suggest that SN V.301 portrays the same process as the earlier account from the *bojjhaṅga* process formula. Both passages explain that when one develops mindfulness, the mind is able to discern and discriminate phenomena clearly, and both passages associate these two qualities with discursive discernment (*vitakka*, *vicāra*, *pavicarati*).[24] Therefore, I will argue that the quality of *viveka* of the first *jhāna* (from which *pīti* and *sukha* are born) is similar to the quality of *dhamma-vicaya*. That is, both *dhamma-vicaya* and *viveka* are qualities conditioned by the previous development of mindfulness, and both qualities refer to some kind of wholesome discursive discernment of that which one experiences (*dhamma*).[25]

Furthermore, the preceding description of discriminating *dhamma* with wisdom (*dhammaṃ paññāya pavicināti*) might very well refer to a mind in which the hindrances (*nīvaraṇas*) are no longer present. The hindrances are identified time and again in the *suttas* as that which obstructs wisdom;[26] they are described as 'the makers of blindness, causing lack of vision, lack of knowledge, destroyers of wisdom, tending one to vexation, not conducive to [the attainment] of *nibbāna*'.[27] Thus, it seems that the ability 'to discern phenomenon with wisdom' (*dhammaṃ paññāya pavicināti*)[28] can veritably occur only when the five hindrances cease to arise and clear seeing is not obstructed.[29] This seems to be possible only when one attains the *jhānas* – more accurately, when one dwells in the first *jhāna*, where the *nīvaraṇas* are no longer present, but wholesome discursive discernment is still operative.

III *Viriya*

According to the *bojjhaṅga* process formula, the *dhamma-vicaya* factor of awakening serves as a foundation and condition for the arising of the next awakening factor: the 'awakening factor of energy' (*viriya-sambojjhaṅga*). Similar to *dhamma-vicaya*, energy does not appear as one of the *jhāna* factors explicitly. Nevertheless, it is reasonable to maintain that, similar to *dhamma-vicaya,* energy is aroused as a *bojjhaṅga* when one abandons the five hindrances (and more specifically 'sloth and torpor') while entering into the first *jhāna*. According to SN V.105–6, what prevents the hindrance 'sloth and torpor' (*thina-middha*) from arising is the cultivation of the element of arousal (*ārambhadhātu*), the element of endeavour (*nikkhamadhātu*) and the element of exertion (*parakkamadhātu*).[30] Interestingly, SN V.104 explains that these same three 'elements' are the nutriment for the arising of the awakening factor of energy:

> There are, bhikkhus, the element of arousal, the element of endeavour, the element of exertion: frequently giving attention to them is the nutriment for the arising of the un-arisen awakening factor of energy and for the fulfilment by development of the arisen awakening factor of energy.[31]

It ensues from these two suttas that the abandonment of 'sloth and torpor' means that one has developed the element of arousal, the element of endeavour and the element of exertion. When these elements are aroused, they act as a nutriment for the arising of *viriya* as an awakening factor (*viriya-sambojjhaṅga*). In other words, it is only when one enters and abides in the first *jhāna*, in which sloth and torpor have ceased, that one has aroused and perhaps even has fulfilled, the awakening factor of energy.

IV *Pīti*

The '*bojjhaṅga* process formula' further explains that after the awakening factor of energy has been aroused, 'spiritual joy' (*nirāmisa pīti*) arises:

> Whenever Ānanda, spiritual joy (*pīti-nirāmisā*) arises in a bhikkhu whose energy is aroused, on that occasion, the awakening factor of joy (*pīti-sambojjhaṅga*) is aroused by the bhikkhu.[32]

The important implication of this depiction is that the *bojjhaṅga* process formula makes it unequivocally clear that *pīti-sambojjhaṅga* is actually *nirāmisa pīti*. I would like to point out that *nirāmisa pīti* is a different designation for *jhānic pīti*.[33] This identification, between the awakening factor *pīti* and the *pīti* of the first two *jhānas*, means that the awakening factor *pīti* can only arise and become fulfilled when one enters and abides in the first and second *jhānas*.

V *Passadhi*

When one has established the awakening factor of (spiritual) joy, the *bojjhaṅga* process formula explains that it serves as a foundation for the arousal of the awakening factor of tranquillity (*passadhi-sambojjhaṅga*):

> For one whose mind is uplifted by [spiritual] joy, the body becomes tranquil and the mind becomes tranquil. Whenever, Ānanda, the body becomes tranquil and the mind becomes tranquil, in a bhikkhu whose mind is uplifted by [spiritual] joy, on that occasion, the awakening factor of tranquility is aroused.[34]

Since we have already established the identity between *pīti-sambojjhaṅga* and *jhānic pīti*, we can safely maintain that the awakening factor of tranquillity must arise in the first or second *jhānas*. It is therefore reasonable to suggest that the awakening factor of tranquillity might be a different appellation for the experience of 'inner stillness' (*ajjhattaṃ sampasādanaṃ*) in the attainment of the second *jhāna*. This parallelism, between *passadhi-sambojjhaṅga* and *ajjhattaṃ sampasādanaṃ*, can assist in clarifying the latter. This is significant, since we have no clear explanation in the Nikāyas as to the nature of 'inner stillness'. If we identify the awakening factor *passaddhi* with *ajjhattaṃ sampasādanaṃ*, we can understand the latter as relating to stillness of *both* body and mind (*kāyopi passambhati, cittampi passambhati*). I would suggest that *passadhi-sambojjhaṅga* and *ajjhattaṃ sampasādanaṃ* refer to a general sense of well-being when the in-and-out breathing tranquillizes (*kāyopi passambhati*) conjointly with the tranquilization of the thinking and intending processes (*cittampi passambhati*)[35] in the second *jhāna*.[36] It also elucidates the relation between spiritual joy (*jhānic pīti*) and the resultant arising of mental and physical tranquillity or 'inner stillness' in the attainment of the second *jhāna*. It seems that the *bojjhaṅga* process formula, just as the *jhāna* model, describes a process in which the mind (and the body) is first energetic, uplifted and joyful but gradually becomes more contented, calm and balanced.

VI *Samādhi*

The *bojjhaṅga* process formula further explains how these qualities function as a condition for the arising of *samādhi*.[37] At this point, I think it is safe to postulate that *samādhi* is aroused and fulfilled as an awakening factor when one attains the second *jhāna*. The *bojjhaṅga* process formula explains that

> [F]or one whose body is tranquil and who [experiences] pleasure (*sukhino*) the mind has *samādhi*. Whenever, Ānanda, the mind has *samādhi* in a bhikkhu

> whose body is tranquil and who [experiences] pleasure, on that occasion, the awakening factor of *samādhi* is aroused by the bhikkhu.[38]

Again, this description appears tantamount to the experience of the second *jhāna*.[39] Furthermore, since we have already established the identity between *pīti-sambojjhaṅga* and *jhānic pīti*, it is reasonable to argue that the experience of pleasure (*sukhino*) in this context, refers to 'spiritual [bodily] pleasure' (*nirāmisa sukha*), that is, *jhānic sukha*. What is interesting, however, is that although the *bojjhaṅga* process formula mentions the experience of *sukha* here, this factor is not listed as one of the *bojjhaṅgas*. This absence is especially odd since *nirāmisa pīti* is recognized as a *bojjhaṅga*. Nevertheless, I think there is a simple explanation for this. I would suggest that the *bojjhaṅga* list has to do with mental qualities rather than physical ones.[40] Since *jhānic sukha*[41] seems to refer to the experience of physical pleasure exclusively,[42] it is not listed as one of the *bojjhaṅgas*. Yet, the *bojjhaṅga* process formula does not exclude this important and valuable factor from its account, and indicates that this type of pleasurable spiritual physical experience accompanies the development of the other factors of awakening. As to the reason why *sukha* is mentioned only in the account of *samādhi*, there is no apparent explanation for this. I think that even though the *bojjhaṅga* process formula mentions *sukha* only at this point of its analysis, it is possible to surmise that *sukha* is experienced before; in other words, it is experienced in conjunction with the experience of *pīti-sambojjhaṅga*.

Having said that, it is also unclear how body-mind tranquillity (*passadhi-sambojjhaṅga*) can be experienced together with (spiritual) bodily pleasure. Are they not contradictory? How can body-tranquillity be experienced with (spiritual) bodily pleasure? To the best of my knowledge, there is no plain answer to this question in the Nikāyas. My own interpretation to this ostensible problem is that the awakening factor of tranquillity (*passadhi-sambojjhaṅga*) pertains to the aggregate (*khandha*) of *rūpa* and to the aggregate of *saṅkhāra*,[43] while the experience of pleasure (*sukhino*), refers to the 'feeling tone' (*vedanā*) of the experience. If one follows this line of reasoning, it explains how body-mind tranquillity (*passadhi-sambojjhaṅga*) can be experienced together with (spiritual) bodily pleasure, as the formula states: when the process of breathing has been quieted down in the second *jhāna*, jointly with the fading away of discursive thinking, one experiences body-mind tranquillity; at the same time, the practitioner experiences pleasure with the body (*sukha-vedanā*). In other words, *passadhi-sambojjhaṅga* and *sukha* quite possibly refer to distinct processes according to Buddhist psychology.

VII *Upekkhā*

We have now arrived at the final account from the *bojjhaṅga* process formula, the description on the arousal of the last awakening factor: the *upekkhā-sambojjhaṅga*. The *bojjhaṅga* process formula concludes its depiction on the fulfilment of the seven factors of awakening by explaining that when the awakening factor of *samādhi* goes to fulfilment by development (most probably when one dwells in the second *jhāna*). On that occasion,

> [H]e becomes one who observe closely and thoroughly[44] the imperturbable mind. Whenever, Ānanda, a bhikkhu becomes one who observes closely and thoroughly the imperturbable mind, on that occasion, the *upekkhā* awakening factor is aroused by the bhikkhu; on that occasion the *upekkhā* awakening factor goes to fulfilment by development in the bhikkhu.[45]

Up to this point, we have seen a noticeable parallelism between the development of the first six *bojjhaṅgas* and the attainment of the first and second *jhānas*. In light of this, I would argue that the final account from the *bojjhaṅga* process formula implies that the arousal of *upekkhā*, as a factor of awakening, occurs when one enters into the third *jhāna*, an attainment characterized by the full expression of *sati*, *sampajāna* and *upekkhā*.[46] More particularly, I would suggest that this description/prescription expresses the way that one progresses from the second *jhāna* to the third, thereby illuminating the relation between these two *jhāna*-states. I will offer some preliminary reflections here, while a full discussion will be offered in the chapter on the third *jhāna*.

A close reading of the final account from the *bojjhaṅga* process formula reveals and elucidates a few things. First, it points out that the arousal of *upekkhā* as factor of awakening is conditioned by the previous fulfilment of *samādhi* as an awakening factor. The description/prescription points out that *upekkhā* is aroused as a *bojjhaṅga* when *samādhi* serves as a foundation for 'becoming one who observes closely and thoroughly the imperturbable mind' (*samāhitaṃ cittaṃ sādhukaṃ ajjhupekkhitā hoti*). This statement is interesting since it emphasizes that that which arouses *upekkhā* as a *bojjhaṅga* is the attention and close observation of a specific phenomenon: the 'imperturbable mind' (*samāhitaṃ cittaṃ*). For arousing *upekkhā* as a factor of awakening, one must turn one's attention to the mind itself, characterized here as *samāhitaṃ*. This specification raises an obvious question: what is an 'imperturbable mind' and when does the mind become identified as *samāhitaṃ* according to Buddhist analysis?

I think that this statement should be understood as referring to the observation of the *jhānic* mind, and more specifically, to the observation of the quality of mind in the second *jhāna*.[47] This conclusion is supported in two ways: (1) the designation *samāhitaṃ* is associated in the Nikāyas with the attainment of the *jhānas*[48] and (2) the evident parallelism between the fulfilment of *samādhi* as a *bojjhaṅga* and the attainment of the second *jhāna*. Following this, I propose a fourfold argument: first, the description 'imperturbable mind', in this context, refers specifically to the quality of mind in the second *jhāna*. Second, the '*bojjhaṅga* process formula' connects the arousal of *upekkhā* with the attainment of the third *jhāna*. Third, the entrance into the third *jhāna* is brought about by the practice of observing one of the *satipaṭṭhānas*, namely, the mind (*citta*). Fourth, although *upekkhā* is aroused as a *bojjhaṅga* in the third *jhāna*, it is only fulfilled as one in the fourth and final *jhāna*.

To conclude, in this chapter I attempted to show an essential connection and interdependency between two unique Buddhist models: the fourfold *jhāna* model and the '*bojjhaṅga* process formula'. Given this analysis, I hope I have shown that it is possible to argue convincingly that the attainment of the *jhānas* is interlinked and interconnected with the development of the seven factors of awakening. That is, the development and fulfilment of the qualities of the seven *bojjhaṅgas*, as 'factors of awakening', are mutually connected with the attainment of the *jhānas*. It may be deduced, based on this premise, that the development of the *bojjhaṅgas* and the attainment of the *jhānas* are parallel models of spiritual ascension, different formulations of the same spiritual process.

Notes

1 Gethin 2001, 168.

2 Gethin 2001, 170. On page 181, he also states that the *bojjhaṅga* list 'links directly into arrange of ideas associated with the *jhānas* and is intended to characterize a particular variety of *jhāna*'.

3 For a comprehensive treatment of the seven factors of awakening in the Nikāyas, see Gethin 2001, 146–83. I will parallel the formulaic description of the *jhānas* to the *bojjhaṅga* process formula, and not only the 'introduction to the *jhāna* formula' (e.g., DN I.73).

4 Gethin 2001, 170–1, 181.

5 This process is depicted in other suttas as well. Gethin has pointed out that 'the process formula should be regarded as a significant and characteristic treatment of the *bojjhaṅga* is surely confirmed by the way the Vibhaṅga singles it out at the opening of the *suttanta-bhājaniya* for the *bojjhaṅgas*' (Vibh 227) (Gethin 2001, 169).

6 By a 'bare' list, I mean a list of the *bojjhaṅgas* without any explanation to their development or an elaboration as to their relation with each other. See, for example, MN II.12.

7 SN V.72: "While one is developing these seven factors of *awakening*, one's mind is liberated from the *āsava* of attachment for sensual pleasures, from the *āsava* of becoming, from the *āsava* of ignorance . . . They lead to awakening, bhikkhu, therefore they are called factors of awakening (*tassime sattabojjhaṅge bhāvayato kāmāsavāpi cittaṃ vimuccati.*" *Bhavāsavāpi cittaṃ vimuccati. Avijjāsavāpi cittaṃ vimuccati . . . bodhāya saṃvattantīti kho bhikkhu, tasmā bojjhaṅgāti vuccantīti*). See also SN V.81–2; 87–8; 97–8.

8 E.g., AN V.212.

9 We should bear in mind that according to the *Ānāpānasati Sutta*, 'when mindfulness of breathing is developed and cultivated . . . it fulfils the four *satipaṭṭhānas*' (MN III.82).

10 The same is repeated with regard to observing the other three *satipaṭṭhānas*. Therefore, it seems that one can choose any of the four *satipaṭṭhānas* as a vehicle for the establishment of mindfulness. However, it should be noted that the '*bojjhaṅga* process formula' also indicates that for arousing *upekkhā* as an awakening factor, one has to observe the mind. This will be discussed later on in this chapter.

11 SN V.331: *kathaṃ bhāvitā ca ānanda, cattāro satipaṭṭhānā kathaṃ bahulīkatā sattasambojjhaṅge paripūrenti. Yasmiṃ samaye ānanda, bhikkhu kāye kāyānupassī viharati upaṭṭhitā tassa tasmiṃ samaye sati hoti asammuṭṭhā. Yasmiṃ samaye ānanda, bhikkhuno upaṭṭhitā sati hoti asammuṭṭhā, satisambojjhaṅgo tasmiṃ samaye bhikkhuno āraddho hoti. Satisambojjhaṅgaṃ tasmiṃ samaye bhikkhu bhāveti. Satisambojjhaṅgo tasmiṃ samaye bhikkhuno bhāvanāpāripūriṃ gacchati.*

12 This recognition is part of the practice given in the *Satipaṭṭhāna Sutta* (MN I.61–2).

13 Note, however, that this is only a preliminary meaning of the term *sati*. When it is further developed, it can be described as 'mindfulness' and even 'present awareness'.
14 See the discussion on this path structure in the chapter on the first *jhāna*.
15 E.g., MN I.181. See also MN III.3. In other descriptions of the *jhānas*, the Buddha makes a declaration about mindfulness before he enters the first *jhāna* that 'mindfulness was established and not lost' (*upaṭṭhitā sati asamuṭṭhā*); e.g., MN I.21, 117.
16 The proximate cause for entering into the first *jhāna* is the abandonment the five hindrances; for abandoning the hindrances, one has to develop mindfulness through observing phenomena and their characteristics.
17 Note our previous discussion on *sammā-sati* as the foundation of *sammā-samādhi*, which means that *sati* is a preliminary quality to the attainment of the *jhānas*.
18 See, for example, SN V.150–1, which states that if the bhikkhu's mind does not become *samādhiyati*, his corruptions (*upakkilesa*) are not abandoned and he does not realize the characteristic of that (i.e., the characteristic of body, feeling, mind and *dhammas*). Through the observation of the four *satipaṭṭhānas*, 'that foolish, unaccomplished, unskillful bhikkhu does not gain pleasant abiding in this very life, nor does he gain the awakening factor of mindfulness' (*sa kho so bhikkhave, bālo avyatto akusalo bhikkhu naceva lābhī hoti diṭṭhadhammasukhavihārānaṃ, na lābhī satisambojjhaṅgassa*). Note that the VRI edition reads *satisampajañña* instead of *satisambojjhaṅga*. However, both seem to suggest that through the development of the four *satipaṭṭhānas* one attains *samādhi* and then, it would seem, attains the third *jhāna*.
19 Note Gethin's observation that it is not clear to what 'that *dhamma*' is referring. In his notes he mentions that Vibh-a 312 refers *taṃ dhammaṃ* back to the initial *sati-sambojjhaṅga* (Gethin 2001, 147).
20 SN V.331: *yasmiṃ samaye ānanda, bhikkhu tathā sato viharanto taṃ dhammaṃ paññāya pavicināti. Pavicarati parivīmaṃsamāpajjati . . . dhammavicayasambojjhaṅgaṃ tasmiṃ samaye bhikkhu bhāveti.*
21 See Gethin's observation about the translation of *vicaya* as 'discrimination' rather than 'investigation' (Gethin 2001, 152).
22 MMW.
23 'Indeed friends, when that bhikkhu is developing and cultivating the four establishments of mindfulness, it is impossible that he will give up the training and return to the lower life. For what reason? Because for a long time his mind has slanted, sloped, and inclined towards *viveka*' (SN V.301).
24 See also SN V.104, which states that the nutriment for the arising of *dhamma-vicaya* is the discrimination between the wholesome and unwholesome and so forth.
25 I think that the quality of *dhamma-vicaya* and *viveka* connote the process of discerning what is present and absent from the mind. In the context of the first *jhāna*, one discerns that the unwholesome (*akusala*) has been abandoned (i.e., the five hindrances), while certain wholesome (*kusala*) qualities are present. This type of discernment is discursive in nature.
26 E.g., MN III.136 and SN V.96.
27 SN V.97: *pañcime bhikkhave, nīvaraṇā andhakaraṇā acakkhukaraṇā aññāṇakaraṇā paññānirodhiyā vighātapakkhiyā anibbānasaṃvattanikā.* See also MN I.323.
28 I believe that the reference here to *dhamma* in the singular is to the investigation of each of the four *satipaṭṭhāna* separately.
29 See also SN V.121–4, which describes the hindrances as those qualities that obstruct one from knowing and seeing as it really is one's own good, or the good of others, or the good of both.
30 SN V.105–6.
31 SN V.104: *atthi bhikkhave, ārambhadhātu nikkhamadhātu parakkamadhātu. Tattha yonisomanasikārabahulīkāro, ayamāhāro anuppannassa vā viriyasambojjhaṅgassa uppādāya uppannassa vā viriyasambojjhaṅgassa bhāvanāpāripūriyā.*

32 SN V.332: *Yasmiṃ samaye ānanda, bhikkhuno āraddhaviriyassa uppajjati pīti nirāmisā, pītisambojjhaṅgo tasmiṃ samaye bhikkhuno āraddho hoti. Pītisambojjhaṅgaṃ tasmiṃ samaye bhikkhu bhāveti.*

33 SN IV.236.

34 SN V.332: *yasmiṃ samaye ānanda, bhikkhuno pītimanassa kāyopi passambhati, cittampi passambhati, passaddhisambojjhaṅgo tasmiṃ samaye bhikkhuno āraddho hoti.*

35 It is interesting to note in this regard SN IV.59 (and the identical sutta from Ud 81) where the Buddha describes the attainment of *nibbāna* as a process: 'When there is no wavering, there is tranquillity (*passaddhi*); when there is tranquillity, there is no inclination (*nati*); where there is no inclination, there is no coming and going; where there is no coming and going, there is no passing away and being reborn; there is neither here nor beyond nor in between the two. This itself is the end of suffering.' Tranquillity is a mental state that arises when one sees reality clearly. That is, when the mind does not waver and nothing obstructs clear seeing (e.g., SN V.123). Furthermore, this tranquillity is the cause and condition for the cessation of the inclinations (*nati*). According to SN II.67, the inclinations are the cause for the 'whole mass of suffering'.

36 Note that in AN I.43 the Buddha states that mindfulness of body results in tranquillity of both body and mind (*kāyopi passambhati, cittampi passambhati*), and to the quieting of *vitakka* and *vicāra*. Although MN I.301 states that *vedanā* and *saññā* are *citta-saṅkhāra*, this statement, to the best of my knowledge, appears only in this sutta. I would argue that it is a bit odd and should be taken cautiously; instead, I would suggest that it is more reasonable that 'tranquillity of mind' (*cittampi passambhati*) refers to the quieting of *vitakka* and *vicāra* rather than to tranquillity of *vedanā* and *saññā*. What is more, it seems reasonable to suggest that the description from the *bojjhaṅga* process formula parallels the instructions on developing mindfulness of breathing (*ānāpāna-sati*). In this practice, it seems that tranquilization (*passambhayaṃ*) of body and mind corresponds to the practice (*sikkhati*) of breathing in and out while tranquilizing body and mental formation (*kāya saṅkhāra* and *citta-saṅkhāra*). For mindfulness of breathing, See, for example, MN III.82–3; MN I.425; SN V.311–2.

37 A similar description of a successive development of wholesome qualities is depicted in a slightly different way in other suttas. It occurs in relation to the entrance into the first *jhāna* (e.g., DN I.73) and in connection with the 'spheres of liberation'. These spheres of liberation refers to the understanding of the spirit and letter of the Dhamma: 'Bhikkhus, there are these five spheres of liberation where the un-liberated mind of a monk dwelling attentive, ardent and resolute finds liberation, or where the *āsavas* that are not yet wholly destroyed become wholly destroyed, where the unsurpassed and unattained security from bondage is attained . . . gladness (*pāmojjaṃ*) arises; on account of this gladness, [mental] happiness (*pīti*) arises; on account of *pīti*, the body becomes tranquil (*passaddha-kāya*); on account of a tranquil body, the practitioner experiences [spiritual bodily] pleasure (*sukha*); on account of *sukha*, the mind attains *samādhi*' (AN III.21, DN III.241–4 and DN III.288).

38 SN V.332: *yasmiṃ samaye ānanda, bhikkhuno passaddhakāyassa sukhino cittaṃ samādhiyati, samādhisambojjhaṅgo tasmiṃ samaye bhikkhuno āraddho hoti. Samādhisambojjhaṅgaṃ tasmiṃ samayo bhikkhu bhāveti.*

39 Note that Buddhaghosa considers that when bodily and mental tranquillity matures, it perfects 'threefold concentration, that is, momentary concentration, access concentration and absorption concentration' (Vism IV.99). This means that for perfecting the *samādhi bojjhaṅga* one does not need to attain the *jhānas*, as momentary concentration or access concentration are enough.

40 Note that the 'awakening factor of tranquillity' refers to both mental and physical tranquillity.

41 In other contexts, *sukha* might refer to *nibbāna* (MN I.508). However, in the context of the *jhānas* (and the '*bojjhaṅga* process formula'), it is clear that *sukha* is a type of *vedanā*.

42 The description of the third *jhāna* explicitly states that one experiences 'pleasure with the body' (*sukhañca kāyena paṭisaṃvedeti*) (e.g., MN I.174).

43 My suggestion here is different from the Dhammasaṅgaṇi's classification, which considers *kāya-passaddhi* as tranquillity of *vedanā, saññā* and *saṅkhāra*. See Gethin 2001, 155.

44 I avoided translating the terms *ajjhupekkhitā* as 'one who closely looks on with equanimity', because it is more of a figurative translation. The root meaning of *ikkhati* means to 'look' or 'observe'. The compound *ajjhupekkhitar* is composed from *adhi+upa+ikkh. Adhi* is a prefix of direction and it can mean 'here', while the prefix *upa* denotes nearness or close touch. Thus, I have translated *ajjhupekkhitar* as 'one who observes closely'.

45 SN V.332: *samādhisambojjhaṅgo tasmiṃ samaye bhikkhuno bhāvanāpāripūriṃ gacchati. So tathā samāhitaṃ cittaṃ sādhukaṃ ajjhupekkhitā hoti. yasmiṃ samaye ānanda, bhikkhu tathā samāhitaṃ cittaṃ sādhukaṃ ajjhupekkhitā hoti, upekhāsambojjhaṅgo tasmiṃ samaye bhikkhuno āraddho hoti. Upekhāsambojjhaṅgaṃ tasmiṃ samaye bhikkhu bhāveti. Upekhāsambojjhaṅgo tasmiṃ samaye bhikkhuno bhāvanāpāripūriṃ gacchati.*

46 Note, however, that both *upekkhā* and *sati* seem to be aroused as awakening factors in the third *jhāna*; it is only in the fourth *jhāna* that they are fulfilled and perfected (*pāripūri*) as ones.

47 See the discussion on SN V.144 in the previous chapter.

48 E.g., MN I.21; AN II.14–15; AN IV.176;

5 The Third *Jhāna*

Establishing a specialized form of awareness

> With the fading away of joy, a bhikkhu abides in equanimity, mindful and fully knowing. [Still] experiencing pleasure with the body, he enters upon and abides in the third *jhāna*, on account of which the noble ones announce: 'abiding in pleasure, one is equanimous and mindful'.[1]

The previous chapters that analyzed the first and second *jhānas* have also argued for their liberative value in the path to awakening. This was made possible by analyzing diverse passages on the nature of these two *jhāna* attainments (and their specific factors). Unfortunately, the Nikāyas contain only a few explicit references to the liberative value of the third *jhāna*. However, we do have some interesting references that can shed light on the nature of this attainment and through which we can extract some illuminating conclusions on its liberative value. In this chapter I will explore further the preliminary inquiry and tentative arguments I put forth in the previous chapter concerning the final account from the '*bojjhaṅga* process formula'. This will assist in understanding the nature of this attainment as the intensification of insight engendered by observing the *jhānic* mind. A close analysis of the final account from the *bojjhaṅga* process formula will also clarify the way one progresses from the second to the third *jhāna*; analysis of this progression reinforces my argument that the *jhānas* are the fruit of insight.

The first part of this chapter will attempt to show that the third *jhāna* marks the moment in the Buddhist path when the last factor of awakening is aroused (although not yet fully fulfilled), namely, the awakening factor of equanimity (*upekkhā-sambojjhaṅga*). I will suggest that it is aroused as a *bojjhaṅga* together with the establishment of mindfulness as a 'factor of awakening'. I will argue that the final account from the *bojjhaṅga* process formula indicates that progression from the second *jhāna* to the third is brought about by the actualization of insight. As I have already argued and continue to do so in this chapter, the progression from one *jhāna* to the next is the way by which one develops and fulfils gradually the seven *bojjhaṅgas* as 'awakening factors'. I propose to look at this spiritual ascension as a process of 'resetting' the mind to wholesomeness; a process in which the mind is purified from mental states that obstruct clear seeing until the mind is free from reinforcing the latent tendencies (*anusaya*), from affective reactions rooted in desire and aversion, and from wrong perception of experience. This process actualizes the full manifestation of the awakening factors, enabling them to be fully obvious. In the second part of this chapter, I will offer a theory regarding the nature and liberative value of the third *jhāna*, by considering various textual materials that seem to delineate this *jhānic* attainment.

Before proceeding to demonstrate the essential connection between the arousal of *upekkhā* as a factor of awakening and the attainment of the third *jhāna*, I would like to reflect for a moment on the relation between the second and third *jhānas* and what it can expose about the misconceived idea, in my view, that the Nikāyas present two meditative procedures, that is, *samatha* meditation (as the *jhānas*) and *vipassanā* meditation (as the observation of the four *satipaṭṭhānas*). It is important to notice that the *jhānas* themselves contain qualities that are traditionally associated with both types of meditation. The second *jhāna* is characterized by qualities associated traditionally with *samatha* meditation (*samādhi* and *ekodibhāvaṃ*), while the third and fourth *jhānas* are characterized by qualities associated with *vipassanā* meditation (*sati*, *sampajāna* and *upekkhā*). The Nikāyas' path-structure becomes more intricate and interesting, when these observations about the second and third *jhānas* are coupled with the analysis from the previous chapter. Analysis in previous chapters clearly showed, first, that the development of *sammā-sati* (as the fruit of observing the four *satipaṭṭhānas*) functions as a foundation and condition for the establishment of *sammā-samādhi* (i.e., the attainment of the four *jhānas*); second, that the establishment of mindfulness proper is linked with the attainment of the *jhānas*.[2] I believe it becomes gradually evident that the *jhānas* are integral to the Nikāyas' vision of liberation, and that the structure of the path is more complex than the common hierarchal-polarized model of the path in which the development of the *jhānas* is preliminary, at best, to the practice of *vipassanā*. The following discussion will attempt to show further that these path elements – *satipaṭṭhāna* and the *jhānas* – are woven together in a complex structure of successive interdependent development, development through which the mind is in inclined towards the attainment of *nibbāna*.

The third *jhāna* is characterized by four qualities: three mental and one physical. These are *upekkhā*, *sati*, *sampajāna* and *sukha*, respectively. As I have already mentioned, the Nikāyas do not contain many additional references on the nature of the third *jhāna* per se. However, analyzing the final account from the *bojjhaṅga* process formula[3] will shed light on several issues, among them the way one progresses from the second *jhāna* to the third. Understanding this progression ensues from clarifying the linkage between the fulfilment of *samādhi* as a factor of awakening (which I have suggested is fulfilled in the second *jhāna*) and the arousal of *upekkhā* as a *bojjhaṅga*. This is significant, since the causal relation between the second and third *jhānas* is not easily discerned. Understanding the connection between these two attainments is especially problematic when one interprets *samādhi* (and *ekodibhāvaṃ*) as signifying a narrow field of awareness that has nothing to do with insight into the nature of phenomena.[4] One who holds this view encounters an obvious problem in explaining how the second *jhāna* can condition and result in the attainment of the third *jhāna*, an attainment characterized by the full expression of *upekkhā*, *sati* and *sampajāna* – qualities associated mainly with 'insight practice'. How is it possible for these qualities to be fully expressed in the attainment of the third *jhāna* without developing insight into the nature of phenomena? What is one mindful of, knows fully and equanimous about, if not experience as it presents itself?

I think the key to understand the relation between the two attainments has to do with the nature of *samādhi* (and the second *jhāna* in general) and with the means by which one progresses from one *jhāna* to the next. Only if we recognize that *samādhi* of the second *jhāna* denotes a broad field of awareness, knowing but non-discursive, can we easily see the essential connection between the fulfilment of *samādhi-sambojjhaṅga* (presumably in the second *jhāna*), and the arousal of *upekkhā-sambojjhaṅga* (presumably in the third *jhāna*). In Chapter 3, I show that the second *jhāna* is where the mind is not hindered by discursive thinking.[5] I argue that in the second *jhāna* one is in a better 'position' (than the previous *jhāna* and ordinary cognition) to perceive experience clearly, as the mind is not obstructed by mental interpretation and preferential attitudes. As I explain in my analysis of the second *jhāna*, it is precisely because discursive thinking is absent that one knows the nature of experience more clearly. Given that, I have suggested that the qualities of *samādhi* and *ekodibhāvaṃ* of the second *jhāna* signify a close and intimate contact with experience.[6] This seems to explain why SN V.144 and SN V.150–1 associate the qualities of *samāhitaṃ* and *ekodibhāvaṃ* with the practice of observing the four *satipaṭṭhānas*: these two qualities allow experience to be known directly and intimately, thereby assisting in intensifying insight into the dynamic of experience.

What is more, one cannot find in the Nikāyas the notion that for progressing from one *jhāna* to the next, one needs to emerge from each of the *jhāna* attainments and then concentrate time and again on the *paṭibhāga nimitta* (which can be the breath, one of the *kaṣinas* etc.).[7]

I The progression from the second *jhāna* to the third as the outcome of insight

The final description/prescription from the *bojjhaṅga* process formula portrays how the last awakening factor, the *upekkhā-sambojjhaṅga*, is aroused and fulfilled. It explains that when the awakening factor of *samādhi* reaches fulfilment by development (most probably when one dwells in the second *jhāna*), on that occasion

> [H]e becomes one who observe closely and thoroughly the imperturbable mind. Whenever, Ānanda, a bhikkhu becomes one who observes closely and thoroughly the imperturbable mind, on that occasion, the *upekkhā* awakening factor is aroused by the bhikkhu; on that occasion the *upekkhā* awakening factor goes to fulfilment by development in the bhikkhu.[8]

In the previous chapter, I argue that there is a noticeable parallel between the development of the first six *bojjhaṅgas* and the attainment of the first and second *jhānas*. My reasoning identifies the close observation of the 'imperturbable mind' (*samāhitaṃ cittaṃ*) as what arouses *upekkhā* as a *bojjhaṅga*. I argue that close observation of the imperturbable mind refers specifically to the quality of mind in the second *jhāna*. Therefore, I maintain that the entrance into the third *jhāna* is brought about by the practice of observing one of the *satipaṭṭhānas*, namely, the mind (*citta*).

A close analysis of the final account from the *bojjhaṅga* process formula supports my hypothesis on the mechanism by which one progresses from *jhāna* to *jhāna*. Such analysis presents a similar view to that portrayed in the *Dantabhūmi Sutta*. I not only suggest that both the *Dantabhūmi Sutta* and the *bojjhaṅga* process formula associate the progression from one *jhāna* to the next with the actualization of 'the practice of insight', I also suggest that both understand the attainment of the *jhānas* as the outcome of insight into the nature of phenomena. In my view, the *bojjhaṅga* process formula shows us once again that the *jhānas* and the practice prescribed in the *Satipaṭṭhāna Sutta* should not be viewed as two distinct meditative paths.

If we accept that *samādhi* is fulfilled as a *bojjhaṅga* in the second *jhāna*, it is easy to demonstrate that the *bojjhaṅga* process formula delineates the same process as the *Dantabhūmi Sutta* does. It suffices to read the final description closely to see this clearly:

> On that occasion (i.e., the attainment of the second *jhāna*), the awakening factor *samādhi* goes to fulfilment by development in the bhikkhu. He becomes one who observes closely and thoroughly the imperturbable mind (i.e., he observes the nature of mind in the second *jhāna*). Whenever, Ānanda, a bhikkhu becomes one who observes closely and thoroughly the imperturbable mind (i.e., implements the instruction given in the Satipaṭṭhāna Sutta), on that occasion, the *upekkhā* awakening factor is aroused by the bhikkhu (thereby one enters naturally into the third *jhāna*).[9]

To me, the meditative process depicted in this passage seems perspicuous: that is, arousing *upekkhā* as a factor of awakening (thereby entering into the third *jhāna*) one needs to actualize the instructions specified in the section on 'observing mind as mind' (*citte cittānupassī*) in the *Satipaṭṭhāna Sutta*. In this section, the sutta explicitly instructs the practitioner 'to know the imperturbable mind as an imperturbable mind' (*samāhitaṃ vā cittaṃ samāhitaṃ cittanti pajānāti*).[10] It is therefore plausible to assert that this contemplative instruction should be put into practice when one attains and dwells in the second *jhāna*. This seems a logical conclusion since where else could this instruction be carried out, other than in the attainment of the second *jhāna* itself?

I will therefore contend that the preceding prescription indicates that the practitioner needs to know the nature of mind in the second *jhāna*, otherwise, one will not ground mindfulness (*sati*) and full knowing (*sampajāna*); will not stabilize equanimity, and therefore, will not proceed to the next *jhāna* where these three qualities are fully expressed. Realizing that such a surpassed state of mind (i.e., the second *jhāna*) is conditioned and impermanent[11] leads to the further stabilization and grounding of equanimous and impartial observation (*upekkhā*) of phenomena (in this case the observation of mind as it is in the second *jhāna*). This is accomplished while abiding[12] in this attainment (as prescribed in the *Dantabhūmi Sutta*). When *upekkhā* is thus obvious and strong, one has aroused it as a factor of awakening, thereby attaining the third *jhāna*. In this *jhāna* attainment, *upekkhā*, *sati* and *sampajāna* are further brought out and established.

II The attainment of the third *jhāna* as the actualization of insight

Sati and *upekkhā* are important qualities in the Nikāyas that are found in various contexts. Here. I will restrict my reflection to their nature in the third *jhāna* alone. I will first suggest that *upekkhā*, as a '*jhāna*-awakening factor', denotes a balanced and impartial attitude towards experience. It refers to the ability to observe experience without preference and identification. When *upekkhā* as a '*jhāna*-awakening factor' is combined with *jhānic-sati* and *sampajāna*, I believe it relates to experience without making it 'I' or 'mine'. According to the formulaic description of the third *jhāna*, the full manifestation of *upekkhā* occurs when *pīti* fades away. Gethin has observed that *pīti* is seen as enlivening the mind to such an extent that *upekkhā*, 'although technically present in the first and second *jhānas*, is not fully obvious'.[13] He has observed that in reference to the attainment of the third *jhāna*,

> *[U]pekkhā* plays a significant part in the process of the mind's becoming stiller, less agitated and more settled, and so less prone to becoming unbalanced or obsessed. Once again this is not seen as implying indifference or insensitivity; on the contrary this is what allows the mind to become fully sensitive and effective. The process is seen as being completed in the fourth *jhāna* by the coupling of *upekkhā* and *sati*.[14]

What this means is that the third *jhāna* is where *upekkhā*, *sati* and *sampajāna* are fully obvious, strong and continuous. It means, as observed by Gethin, that one has established sensitivity to experience and, at the same time, an attitude of non-identification with that experience, namely, without the superimposition of 'me' and 'mine'. This is made possible by fully knowing (*sampajāna*) the impermanent nature of experience.[15] Yet, we should also bear in mind that the process of fulfilling these qualities is gradual, and that Gethin was correct in his observation that 'the process is seen as being completed in the fourth *jhāna* by the coupling of *upekkhā* and *sati*'.[16] Furthermore, I think Gethin's observation related to *upekkhā* is relevant also to *sati* and *sampajāna*: these qualities are technically present in the first and second *jhānas* (and to some degree also before), fully obvious in the third *jhāna* but perfected and fulfilled only in the attainment of the fourth and final *jhāna*.

Taking all of this into consideration lends insight into the reason why the second *jhāna* serves as a foundation for *sati*, *upekkhā* and *sampajāna*. When thoughts subside and mental preferences have ceased, the mind is not conditioned by habitual reaction-and-appropriation patterns. Now, one can observe closely and know thoroughly the nature of mind as it is in the second *jhāna*, without evoking habitual identification and clinging (especially to such a pleasant state). Note AN V.3, which explicates that

> [F]or one who attains the imperturbable [mind], there is no need for the intentional thought: 'may I know and see things as they really are'. Monks, this is the natural way, when one has attained the imperturbable [mind], one knows and sees things as they really are. For one who knows and sees things as they really are there is no need for the intentional thought: 'may I become disenchanted, may I be free from desire'. Monks, this is the natural way, when one knows and sees things as they really are, one becomes disenchanted and free from desire.[17]

When the second *jhāna* is attained, experience is seen clearly, that is, seeing the nature of mind in the second *jhāna* itself. When it is known as it is (*yathābhūtaṃ pajānāti*) – conditioned (*saṅkhata*) and not-self (*anattā*) – *upekkhā*, *sati* and *sampajāna* can manifest fully as the fruit of non-clinging and of not ascribing false substantiality to a conditioned phenomenon. This moment of deep insight into the nature of a surpassed state of mind, marks the attainment of the third *jhāna* as the actualization of insight, the actualization of wisdom-awareness.

It is also interesting to reflect here on the statement made in the *Cūḷavedalla Sutta*, that even the latent tendencies (*anusaya*) to aversion and desire do not underlie the first three *jhānas*.[18] This means that the third *jhāna* is a significant moment in the spiritual path. If we attempt to understand the liberative value of the third *jhāna* and abstract its nature, we can conceptualize that the third *jhāna* proceeds with the process of de-conditioning the tendency to prefer, to compare, to interpret and to react; a spiritual process that commences when one starts to walk the Buddhist path, enhances when one attains the *jhānas* and ends when one attains awakening. In the third (and fourth) *jhāna* one can further deepen insight into the nature of experience by embodying an awakened perspective. By being fully present, knowing and equanimous with manifested experience, one embodies an awakened awareness. By attaining the third (and fourth) *jhānas*, the mind becomes intimately familiar with a different mode of being.

What I am suggesting is that the third *jhāna* signifies another step in the deconstruction of the fabricated sense of self. In this *jhāna* attainment, one can have sense experience without the affective reactions rooted in desire and aversion, reactions that sustain the sense of a specific self that prefers this and is averse to that. This, I believe, is an important step in the deconstruction of the origination of *dukkha*: when the mind is devoid of habitual reactivity, one can deconstruct the re-created sense of self that defines itself by habitual reactivity and also is fixated on certain desired conditions. I suggest construing the third *jhāna* as a clarified perception of reality. This specialized form of awareness is beginning to become established in the third *jhāna*, and according to the *Paṭhamāhuneyya Sutta*, it is that which entitles one to the designation 'worthy of offerings, worthy of gifts, worthy of donation, worthy of being honoured, unsurpassed, the world's field of merit'. This sutta gives us an interesting perspective on the third *jhāna*, elucidates the odd statement from the formulaic description of the third *jhāna* that 'the noble ones announce: 'abiding in pleasure, one is equanimous and mindful'.[19] The *Paṭhamāhuneyya Sutta* explains that abiding in equanimity, mindfulness and full knowing are ennobling:

> Monks, herein a monk on seeing a form with the eye he is neither elated or sad; rather he abides in equanimity, mindful and fully knowing. On hearing a sound with the ear . . . ; on smelling a smell with the nose . . . ; on tasting a taste with the tongue . . . ; on touching a touchable with the body . . . ; on cognizing a mental phenomenon with the mind he is neither elated or sad; rather he abides in equanimity, mindful and fully knowing. Monks, a monk who possesses these six things is worthy of offerings, worthy of gifts, worthy of donation, worthy of being honoured, unsurpassed, the world's field of merit.[20]

This passage does not explicitly state that this is a description of the third *jhāna*. However, in my opinion, it clearly does refer to it. The fact that the passage states that one 'abides' (*viharati*) in equanimity, mindfulness and full knowing (the same phrasing as the formulaic description of the third *jhāna*) is a strong indication that this passage refers specifically to the experience of the third *jhāna*.[21] The *Paṭhamāhuneyya Sutta* also elucidates the odd reference in the formulaic description of the third *jhāna* about the ariyas; it points out that the actual abiding in a state of mind in which *upekkhā*, *sati* and *sampajāna* are fully expressed is ennobling.[22] If we recall the discussion on the first *jhāna*, I have demonstrated that the assumption that one is cut off from sense experience while in the *jhānas* is misconceived. This is further supported in the above passage from the *Paṭhamāhuneyya Sutta*, which seems to be another example of the *jhānic* experience: it is an experience where one has full contact with sense experience but lacks any mental reactions of liking and disliking. In the third *jhāna*, one is present with whatever contacts the senses, knows their nature fully and therefore remains completely equanimous in the midst of it.

I suggest that the third (and fourth) *jhānas* can be entitled 'the dwelling of the nobles' (*ariyo-vihāro*)[23] precisely because the *jhānic* mind lacks any unwholesome cognitive states and affective reactions rooted in desire, aversion and ignorance. In other words, the third *jhāna* and certainly the fourth *jhāna* (where *avijjā* and the latent tendency to *avijjā* are absent as well as desire and aversion)[24] are ennobling since they simulate the noble mind. Although the *jhānas* are conditioned states (as all experiences are), they are 'less' conditioned than other experiences. I have mentioned in chapter 3 Klein's interesting reflection that the grey area between the conditioned and the unconditioned is mental quiescence which is 'an ameliorating connection between these two oppositionally framed categories'.[25] I suggested that the *jhānas* function as such a connection. They aid significantly to the process of de-conditioning. They enable the mind to perceive reality without imposing on the experience the notion of 'I', 'me' or 'mine', thereby familiarizing itself with an awakened perspective.

To conclude, the power of the *jhānas* – all four of them – is the fact that one abides (*viharati*) in them for a period of time. This allows the practitioner to experience fully and intimately a different mode of being, very different from ordinary cognition in which the mind constantly reacts, interprets, rejects and desires. Knowing intimately that there is a different mode of being in the world, a mode of being that is simply aware, knowing and equanimous, is the liberatory value of the third (and fourth) *jhānas*. Attaining these states is the way to uproot our deep tendencies of mental reactivity and identification with experience. By allowing experience to be simply seen, the mind becomes closely in touch with the taste of freedom.

With these thoughts in mind, let us proceed to the analysis of the fourth and final *jhāna*.

Notes

1 MN I.174: *bhikkhu pītiyā ca virāgā upekkhāko ca viharati, sato ca sampajāno, sukhañca kāyena paṭisaṃvedeti yaṃ taṃ ariyā ācikkhanti 'upekkhāko satimā sukhavihārī'ti tatiyaṃ jhānam upasampajja viharati.*
2 MN III.136.
3 Gethin 2001, 168.
4 See, for example,, Gunaratana 1999, 79.
5 E.g., MN II.28.
6 See, for example, AN V.3, which will discuss later on in this chapter.
7 E.g., Vism XVIII.3. Note that the Nikāyas do not ever express the view that for integrating insight practice with the *jhānas*, one has to emerge from a *jhāna* attainment for contemplating (discursively) the *jhāna* factors.
8 SN V.332: *samādhisambojjhaṅgo tasmiṃ samaye bhikkhuno bhāvanāpāripūriṃ gacchati. So tathā samāhitaṃ cittaṃ sādhukaṃ ajjhupekkhitā hoti. yasmiṃ samaye ānanda, bhikkhu tathā samāhitaṃ cittaṃ sādhukaṃ ajjhupekkhitā hoti, upekhāsambojjhaṅgo tasmiṃ samaye bhikkhuno āraddho hoti. Upekhāsambojjhaṅgaṃ tasmiṃ samaye bhikkhu bhāveti. Upekhāsambojjhaṅgo tasmiṃ samaye bhikkhuno bhāvanāpāripūriṃ gacchati.*
9 SN V.332.
10 MN I.59.
11 See SN V.181, which explains that *sampajāna* is the ability to know the arising, presence and passing away of feeling (*vedanā*), thoughts (*vitakka*) and apperception (*saññā*). Since this quality manifests fully in the third *jhāna*, it demonstrates that the third *jhāna* is the actualization of understanding conditionality and impermanence. See also AN II.45, which calls this type of observation *samādhi-bhāvanā bhāvitā bahulīkatā satisampajaññāya saṃvattati.*
12 Note the statement in the *Satipaṭṭhāna Sutta* that one 'abides observing mind as mind' (*citte cittānupassī viharati*) (MN I.59).
13 Gethin 2001, 159.

14 Gethin 2001, 159.
15 Note that according to SN III.131, when one has seen the rise and fall of the five aggregates, which are the Buddhist analysis of subjective conditioned experience, it is only then that one can eradicate the conceit, intention and underlying tendency 'I' am with regard to the five aggregates. Note that SN V.180–1 points out the establishment of *sati* means that one sees form, feeling, *citta* and *dhamma* as they are, without clinging or aversion; at the same time, the establishment of *sampajāna* means that one knows the impermanent and insubstantial nature of feeling, perception and thoughts. This is a slightly different formulation than the five aggregates, but it refers to the same experiential aspect of human beings.
16 Ibid.
17 AN V.3: *Samāhitassa bhikkhave na cetanāya karaṇīyaṃ 'yathābhūtaṃ taṃ jānāmi passāmī'ti. Dhammatā esā bhikkhave yaṃ samāhito yathābhūtaṃ jānāti passati. Yathābhūtaṃ bhikkhave jānato passato na cetanāya karaṇīyaṃ, nibbindāmi, virajjāmī'ti. Dhammatā esā bhikkhave yaṃ yathābhūtaṃ jānaṃ passaṃ nibbindati virajjati.*
18 MN I.303–4.
19 E.g., MN I.174: *yaṃ taṃ ariyā ācikkhanti 'upekkhāko satimā sukhavihārī'ti tatiyaṃ jhānam upasampajja viharati.*
20 AN III.279: *idha bhikkhave bhikkhu cakkhunā rūpaṃ disvā neva sumano hoti na dummano. Upekkhako viharati sato sampajāno. Sotena saddaṃ sutvā neva sumano hoti na dummano. Upekkhako viharati sato sampajāno. Ghānena gandhaṃ ghāyitvā neva sumano hoti na dummano. Upekkhako viharati sato sampajāno. Jivhāya rasaṃ sāyitvā neva sumano hoti na dummano. Upekkhako viharati sato sampajāno. Kāyena phoṭṭhabbaṃ phusitvā neva sumano hoti na dummano. Upekkhako viharati sato sampajāno. Manasā dhammaṃ viññāya neva sumano hoti na dummano. Upekkhako viharati sato sampajāno. Imehi kho bhikkhave chahi dhammehi samannāgato bhikkhu āhuneyyo hoti pāhuneyyo dakkhiṇeyyo añjalikaraṇīyo anuttaraṃ puññakkhettaṃ lokassāti.* See also DN III.250.
21 E.g., *bhikkhu pītiyā ca virāgā upekkhāko ca viharati, sato ca sampajāna . . .*
22 See also DN III.113, which states that *ariya* supernormal power (*iddhi*) is the abiding in equanimity, mindfulness and full knowing. This is the noble supernormal power that is free from the *āsavas* and free from clinging.
23 See the threefold classification into *dibbo vihāra, Brahmā-vihāra and Ariyo-vihāro* in DN III.220. I suggest that the last one refers specifically to the *jhānas*, while the first kind refers to 'divine pleasures' (*dibba-sukha*) attained in heavenly worlds of the *kāma-dhātu* and the *the rūpa-dhātu* and the *arūpa-dhātu*. The *Brahmā-vihāra* refers to the attainment of specifically the Brahmā world.
24 MN I.303–4.
25 Klein 1992, 295.

6 The Fourth *Jhāna*

Non-reactive and lucid awareness of the phenomenal field

> With the abandoning of pleasure and pain and with the previous disappearance of gladness and discontent, a bhikkhu enters upon and abides in the fourth *jhāna*, which is neither-painful-nor-pleasurable and has complete purity of mindfulness and equanimity.[1]

Throughout the previous chapters, I state that what I seek to demonstrate in my analysis of the *jhānas* is that this model of four successive states exemplifies a gradual development of an awakened awareness of experience. I suggest that the *jhānas* designate a gradual spiritual ascent in which each step signifies a more clarified perception of experience. This position contrasts with the traditional Buddhist conception that views the *jhānas* as altered states of consciousness disconnected from sense experience and therefore not relevant for seeing reality clearly. Relatedly, following Rupert Gethin, I suggest that by progressing from one *jhāna* to the next, the mind gradually develops the seven factors of awakening until they are fulfilled as 'awakening factors' (*bojjhaṅgas*). Put simply, I argue that the *jhānas* actualize the aim of Buddhist meditation: they purify the mind from that which obstructs clear seeing and fulfil those qualities that can awaken the mind. My suggestion was that through the attainment of the *jhānas,* one can experience intimately a different mode of being; this mode is very different from ordinary cognition, in which the mind constantly reacts, interprets, rejects and desires. By progressing through the *jhānas* one gradually de-conditions the tendency to prefer, compare, interpret and react. Although the process of de-conditioning culminates in the attainment of *nibbāna*, it deepens when one attains the four *jhānas*.

In this chapter, I wish to continue this argument by further demonstrating that the process of purifying the mind's perception of experience arrives at an important moment when one enters into the fourth and final *jhāna*. In the previous chapter, I suggest that in the third *jhāna*, a specialized form of awareness is beginning to be established. In this chapter, I attempt to show that this specialized form of awareness becomes fully grounded in the fourth and final *jhāna*. I will argue that the fourth *jhāna*, although conditioned and impermanent (as all experiences and insights are), is nonetheless further rectifying the connection between the conditioned and unconditioned by familiarizing the practitioner with an awakened awareness of phenomena. In other words, the fourth *jhāna* is an attainment, dare we say, that resembles or anticipates an awakened mind.

I The entrance into the fourth *jhāna*

Let us begin our exploration of the fourth *jhāna* by analyzing the opening statement of the formulaic description of the fourth *jhāna*:

> With the abandoning of pleasure (*sukha*) and pain (*dukkha*) and with the previous disappearance of gladness (*somanassa*) and discontent (*domanassa*), a bhikkhu enters upon and abides in the fourth *jhāna*.[2]

Before looking at the oddity of this statement and trying to shed some light on it, I would like to make two preliminary remarks. First, it is important to note that when *dukkha* and *sukha* are coupled with *somanassa* and *domanassa*, they refer specifically to bodily pleasure and bodily pain; at the same time, *somanassa* and *domanassa* designate gladness and discontent, respectively.[3] Second, this description is interesting since it seems to indicate that the fourth *jhāna* is the moment where the movement between two extremes ceases: the movement between mental and physical pleasure on the one end and mental and physical pain at the other end – that is, as I shall demonstrate, between desire and aversion. It seems that the entrance into the fourth *jhāna* marks a point in the spiritual path were one embodies equilibrium in both body and mind.

The opening statement of the formulaic description of the fourth *jhāna* is odd first and foremost because we already know that bodily pain ceases to arise when one attains the first *jhāna*.[4] We know that the first, second and third *jhānas* are characterized specifically as physically pleasurable. What is more peculiar is the statement that for entering into the fourth *jhāna*, one 'abandons' (*pahānā*) [bodily] pleasure (*sukha*) and [bodily] pain (*dukkha*): how can one 'abandon' bodily pleasure and bodily pain when these bodily-sensations (*kāyika-vedanā*) can only cease (*nirodha*) or disappear (*atthagama*) due to various causes and conditions?[5] Finally, why the sudden reference to gladness (*somanassa*) and discontent (*domanassa*), when these two mental factors are not mentioned in any of the descriptions of the previous three *jhānas*? When, then, did they disappear? How did their disappearance come to be? Why does their disappearance condition the attainment of the fourth *jhāna*? In other words, what is the spiritual and emotional process this statement is trying to convey?

Since they are related, let us begin with the first and second issues. According to Buddhist theory, it would be incorrect to say that one 'abandons' (*pahāna*) bodily pleasure or bodily pain. As noted earlier, these sensations arise and cease due to certain causes and conditions (we can say that they are 'old *kamma*', *vipāka*). Therefore, to state that one 'abandons' them seems inconsistent with the Buddhist view. What is more, the verb *pajahati*, in its various forms and inflections in the Nikāyas, usually appears in contexts where the abandonment of unwholesome states is described;[6] it refers to the letting go of *akusala dhammas* (which *sukha-vedanā* and *dukkha-vedanā* are not), an abandonment brought about by insight into the nature of phenomena. Thus, all this seems to suggest is that the use of the term *pahāna* here implies that what one actually abandons, before entering into the fourth *jhāna*, is unwholesome reactions to pleasant and painful feelings.

That is, one does not abandon the sensations themselves but the *desire* for pleasant feelings (*vedanā*) and *aversion* to painful ones. Following this, I will contend that abandoning these unwholesome habitual reaction-patterns to pleasant and painful sense experiences is the proximate cause for entering into the fourth and final *jhāna*.

This interpretation finds support in the *Cūḷavedalla Sutta*, which indicates that, when one attains the first three *jhānas*, not only aversion and desire but also the latent tendencies (*anusaya*) to aversion and desire are abandoned.[7] The sutta then associates the abandonment of ignorance (*avijjā*) with the attainment of the fourth *jhāna*. It heralds that by abiding in the fourth *jhāna* 'one abandons ignorance, and the underlying tendency to ignorance does not underlie that'.[8] This makes it very clear that ignorance, the wrong perception of experience – wrong perception that gives rise to desire for impermanent and unreliable things, and aversion to unpleasant and painful ones – is not present in any level in the attainment of the fourth *jhāna*. Since desire and aversion, as the active aspects of ignorance, are abandoned when one enters the fourth *jhāna* – by developing insight into the nature of experience – one finally breaks free of ignorance by experiencing a different mode of being in the world of phenomena. This mode of being is untainted by emotional reactions and cognitive overlays based on a wrong perception of the nature of experience.

This last point is also demonstrated implicitly in verses 1106–7 from the *Sutta Nipāta*. Even though these verses do not mention the fourth *jhāna* explicitly, it seems obvious that they do refer to the *jhānas*, and more specifically, to the fourth *jhāna*. I suggest that the reason the fourth *jhāna* is not specifically mentioned in this context is due to the simple fact that the *Sutta Nipāta* is less systematic in its teachings than are the four primary Nikāyas. In other words, what received a systematic presentation in the four primary Nikāyas is still in a seed-form in the *Sutta Nipāta*. However, it is clear from *Sutta Nipāta* 1105, which opens this sutta, that the verses that follow describe the *jhānic* process.

In this discourse, Udaya questions the Buddha about the nature of liberation. He specifically asks the Buddha to explain 'the breaking of ignorance' for 'one who attained *jhāna*, seated, free from defilements' (*jhāyiṃ virajaṃ āsinaṃ*). As a response to Udaya's question, the Buddha states that

> [T]he abandonment of both the desire for sensual pleasures, said the Blessed One to Udaya, and discontent, and the dispelling of sloth and the hindrance of worry,
>
> I tell [you], that liberation by perfect knowledge, the breaking of ignorance, is pure mindfulness and equanimity, preceded by examination of phenomena.[9]

Though this description is not identical to the formulaic description of the fourfold *jhāna* model (or to the fourth *jhāna* specifically) it seems clear that these verses make reference to the attainment of the *jhānas* – especially in light of Udaya's question. These verses seem to illustrate, albeit in a different formulation, the beginning and ending of the *jhānic* process (from the abandoning of the *nīvaraṇas*, the examination of *dhammas* up to the fulfilment of *upekkhā* and *sati* in the fourth *jhāna*). What is particularly interesting in this account is the Buddha's statement that 'pure mindfulness and equanimity' (*upekkhāsatisaṃsuddhaṃ*), which quite evidently refers to the attainment of the fourth *jhāna*,[10] is 'where' the breaking of ignorance (*avijjāya pabhedanaṃ*), 'liberation by perfect knowledge' (*aññāvimokkhaṃ*), happens. In other words, the sutta propounds that this *jhānic* attainment is the point where the breaking of ignorance can happen; when the active aspects of ignorance are abandoned, one actualizes and embodies wisdom (*paññā*). Furthermore, when one embodies wisdom, the underlying tendency to ignorance does not underlie this mode of being.

Considering all the preceding, I propose to read the formulaic description of the fourth *jhāna* in this way:

> With the abandonment of [the desire] for pleasure and [aversion] to pain, and with the previous disappearance of [the inner movement between] gladness and discontent, a bhikkhu enters upon and abides in the fourth *jhāna*.

II Wholesome gladness (*somanassa*) and discontent (*domanassa*)

As already observed, there is no apparent explanation why gladness (*somanassa*) and discontent (*domanassa*) are suddenly mentioned in the formulaic description of the fourth *jhāna*, especially since the descriptions of the other three *jhānas* do not. SN V.213–14 makes things even more complicated when it states that the pain faculty (*dukkha-indriya*), the discontent faculty (*domanassa-indriya*), the pleasure faculty (*sukha-indriya*) and the gladness faculty (*somanassa-indriya*)[11] cease without a remainder (*aparisesaṃ nirujjhati*) when one enters into the first, second, third and fourth *jhānas*, respectively.[12] The difficulty with this account is the statement that *sukha-indriya* ceases (not abandoned) when one enters into the third *jhāna*, while gladness (*somanassa*) ceases when one enters into the fourth *jhāna*. This is problematic for two reasons: first, it contradicts the opening statement of the fourth *jhāna*, which states plainly that *somanassa* (together with *domanassa*) disappears prior to the attainment of the fourth *jhāna* and not when one enters into the fourth *jhāna*. Second, as we already know, *sukha* is very much present in the third *jhāna*. *Sukha* does not cease when one enters into the third *jhāna*, as stated in SN V.213–14, but only when one enters into the fourth and final *jhāna*.

Looking at this discrepancy, there is no plausible way to reconcile SN V.213–14 and the formulaic description, except from concluding that one of them is faulty. Based on Tse-Fu Kuan's observation, in his article 'Clarification on Feelings in Buddhist Dhyāna/Jhāna Meditation', I believe we can safely conclude that SN V.213–14 is not a reliable account. Tse-Fu Kuan has pointed out that according to the *Aviparītaka Sūtra* (and other later texts translated into Chinese), *sukhi-indriya* is that which ceases at the fourth *jhāna* and not *somanassa*.[13] This means that the Chinese accounts complement the formulaic description of the third and fourth *jhānas* (in both the Pāli and Chinese versions), while SN V.213–14 does not. Given that, it seems reasonable to contend that the Chinese sources preserved the correct version of this process. Accepting the Chinese version also clarifies the statement that both *domanassa* and *somanassa* disappear prior to entering into the fourth *jhāna*; that is, they disappear when one enters into the second and third *jhānas*, respectively, while *sukha* is that which ceases (*nirujjhati*) (though not abandoned) when one enters into the fourth and final *jhāna*.

Having said that, how are we to understand the disappearance of *domanassa* and *somanassa* in a way that will clarify our understanding of the *jhānic* process, the nature of the fourth *jhāna* and the way by which one progresses into this attainment? Although this statement seems out of place at first sight, in point of fact, it gives us additional information on the process of insight, the very insight that arises prior to the attainment of the fourth *jhāna* and by which one attains this state. The *Saḷāyatanavibhanga Sutta*[14] is a helpful discourse in understanding this spiritual-psychological process. It clarifies the nature of *jhānic domanassa, somanassa* and *upekkhā* as wholesome mental factors that arise from insight into the nature of experience. It also explains the connection between the disappearance of *domanassa* and *somanassa* and the fulfilment of *upekkhā*.

The *Saḷāyatanavibhanga Sutta* classifies gladness (*somanassa*), discontent (*domanassa*) and equanimity (*upekkhā*) into two types. The aim of this classification is to discern between the wholesome and the unwholesome as a guide for the practitioner. The sutta directs the practitioner to explore gladness, discontent and equanimity by seeing clearly when these mental factors arise from ignorance or when they arise from insight. The sutta then depicts a gradual process of cultivation in which wholesome gladness, discontent and equanimity are developed by the abandoning and surmounting unwholesome gladness, discontent and equanimity. That is, by the abandonment of the unwholesome, the wholesome can unfold and be revealed.

The *Saḷāyatanavibhanga Sutta* defines two types of gladness, discontent and equanimity: (1) those based on 'worldly life' (*gehasitāni*), and (2) those based on renunciation (*nekkhammasitā*). In this context, the classification between 'worldly life' and 'renunciation' should not be understood to refer to the external conditions of life, meaning whether a person has a family and lives at home or if one wears robes and lives as a monk or a nun. It refers to a mental attitude: whether the Dhamma was actually internalized or not.[15] Wearing robes does not transform a person into a liberated person (although it is a beneficial and helpful condition to do so), only the abandonment of unwholesome states transforms one into a real renunciant. This point is exemplified by the way the *Saḷāyatanavibhanga Sutta* characterizes gladness, discontent and equanimity based on worldly life and gladness, discontent and equanimity based on renunciation. The former are mental states that are rooted in ignorance, arising from not seeing experience as it is; in contrast, the latter are mental states that arise from insight into the nature of sense experience.[16]

Given this basic definition, it can be suggested that 'gladness based on renunciation' is gladness that arises from knowing experience as it is (and not from pleasant experiences). I would suggest that this type of wholesome mental gladness is similar in nature to *jhānic pīti*. If we recall our discussion on *pīti* of the first two *jhānas*, the Buddha explains that it is like the fire that burns independent on fuel.[17] That is, *pīti* of the first two *jhānas* arises due to clear seeing of reality and is not dependent on the obtainment of desired experiences or objects. This is similar to the way '*somanassa* based on renunciation' is described: when one sees the true nature of sense experience, one experiences mental gladness that is not connected to specific pleasurable experiences and is not associated with any unwholesome states such as desire and clinging. Thus, both *jhānic pīti* and '*somanassa* based on renunciation' describe a joyful wholesome mental state that originates from insight into the nature of experience.[18] Interestingly, both *jhānic pīti* and '*somanassa* based on renunciation' cease when one enters into the third *jhāna*. The reason seems to be that these two mental factors enliven the mind to such an extent that *upekkhā* cannot be fully obvious and strong. This again suggests that '*somanassa* based on renunciation' might be another designation for *jhānic pīti* or perhaps very similar mental state.

According to the *Saḷāyatanavibhanga Sutta*, 'discontent based on worldly life' arises when one desires unobtainable delightful and gratifying sense experiences. In other words, this type of discontent arises when one desires what is unreliable, impermanent and subject to change.[19] On the contrary, 'discontent based on renunciation' is discontent that arises from seeing with wisdom that sense experiences are impermanent, not worth holding on to. The sutta explains that when this insight arises, it arouses longing for 'supreme liberations' (*anuttaresu vimokkhesu*). This longing conditions the arising of 'discontent based on renunciation'; it is discontent that arises due to clear seeing of the disadvantage of sense experiences and as it originates from wisdom, it is devoid of aversion.

The question relevant for our discussion is what kind of discontent is present in the attainment of the first *jhāna* and ceases in the attainment of the second *jhāna*? From reading the description of the *jhānic* process depicted in the *Cūḷavedalla Sutta*, it is evident that the type of discontent that arises when one attains the first *jhāna* is what the *Saḷāyatanavibhanga Sutta* calls 'discontent based on renunciation'. This is clear from the almost verbatim depiction of *jhānic domanassa* from the *Cūḷavedalla Sutta* to the description of '*domanassa* based on renunciation' from the *Saḷāyatanavibhanga Sutta*. In the *Cūḷavedalla Sutta* the wise nun Dhammdinnā explains to Visākha:

> Here friend Visākha, separated from the desire for sensual pleasures, separated from [other] unwholesome states, a bhikkhu enters upon and abides in the first *jhāna*, which is joy and [bodily] pleasure born of *viveka*, accompanied by thought and reflection . . . Here a bhikkhu considers thus: 'when shall I enter upon and abide in that base that the noble ones now enter upon and abide in'? In one who thus generates a longing for supreme liberations, discontent arises with that longing as condition. With that he abandons aversion, and the underlying tendency to aversion does not underlie that.[20]

It is obvious that both the *Cūḷavedalla Sutta* and the *Saḷāyatanavibhanga Sutta* describe the same type of discontent: (1) it is discontent that arises when one abandons the unwholesome; (2) it is conditioned by the arising of wholesome longing for liberation, longing that arises when one understands the unreliable nature of sense experience. The two accounts actually complement one another. The *Saḷāyatanavibhanga Sutta* points out clearly that this type of discontent or better put, sadness. Arises from seeing the nature of sense experiences,[21] while the *Cūḷavedalla Sutta* connects the arising of this wholesome discontent or sadness with the attainment of the *jhānas*. The latter also associates this type of discontent with the abandonment of aversion. This is an interesting and important point, especially for understanding the liberative value of the *jhānas*. It points out that discontent that arises from ignorance (i.e., from holding on to impermanent delightful sense experiences) leads to the arising of aversion when these experiences fade away or cannot be obtained. Grieving about the passing away of desired experiences or from not obtaining what one desires arouses and perpetuates the arising of aversion. However, when one realizes with proper wisdom that everything is transient, suffering and subject to change, one arouses longing for liberation, longing that conditions the arising of wholesome discontent or sadness; this, in turn, conditions the abandonment of aversion (*paṭigha*) as a result of this insight.

What all this means is that *jhānic* discontent is beneficial for two reasons: first, it is discontent that motivates a person to carry on the effort to become liberated by acknowledging that true happiness cannot arise dependent on sense experience. Second and relatedly, this wholesome discontent aids in the abandonment of aversion since it originates from clear seeing of the unreliability of phenomena. When this type of discontent arises in the mind, obvious and latent aversion is not present.[22] For our investigation it is of interest to note the following: according to the *Cūḷavedalla Sutta*, this type of discontent or sadness – discontent which the *Saḷāyatanavibhanga Sutta* calls 'discontent based on renunciation' – arises when one enters into the first *jhāna* and as the *Aviparītaka Sūtra* states, this type of discontent, ceases when one attains the second *jhāna*.[23]

III *Upekkhā*

We already established that *somanassa* and *domanassa* 'based on renunciation' can be seen as parallel designations for *jhānic somanassa* and *domanassa*, namely, wholesome gladness and discontent that arise from insight into the nature of sense experience. Following this, it is plausible to further argue that '*upekkhā* based on renunciation' must be another title for *jhānic upekkhā* (and *upekkhā-sambojjhaṅga*). Yet, this identification might be problematic when we compare the analysis from the *Saḷāyatanavibhanga Sutta* with a description from the *Potaliya Sutta*.

But before setting about discussing this problem, let us first examine the analysis from the *Saḷāyatanavibhanga Sutta*, which further differentiates '*upekkhā* based on renunciation' into two types: The first is '*upekkhā* that is diversified, based on diversity' (*upekkhā nānattā nānattasitā*), and the second is '*upekkhā* that is unified, based on unity' (*upekkhā ekattā ekattasitā*).[24] According to the *Saḷāyatanavibhanga Sutta*, '*upekkhā* based on diversity' is *upekkhā* regarding forms, sounds, odours, flavours and tangibles,[25] while '*upekkhā* based on unity' is *upekkhā* regarding the four *arūpa samāpattis*.[26] This distinction is important since it seems to imply that while '*upekkhā* based on renunciation and unity' concerns the four *arūpa samāpattis*, '*upekkha* based on renunciation and diversity' is *upekkhā* that is present in the *jhānas*.

This identification between *upekkha* based on renunciation and diversity and *upekkhā* of the *jhānas* is not trivial; it touches upon the nature of the fourth *jhāna* and its liberative value. It raises the question of whether the fourth *jhāna* is one-pointed meditative absorption, disconnected from sense experience and therefore not necessary for the attainment of awakening, or whether the fourth *jhāna* is a broad field of awareness, non-discursive but in direct contact with the changing phenomenal field.

From what has been described and analyzed until now about the nature of the *jhānas*, it follows that *upekkha* based on renunciation and diversity should be seen as a different designation for *jhānic upekkhā*. This means that *upekkhā* of the (third) and fourth *jhāna* is based on diversity of sense experience and not on one-pointed absorption. What I am arguing again is that the fourth *jhāna* (and the other three *jhānas* as well) are not disconnected from sense experience. On the contrary, these attainments arise from seeing the nature of experience clearly (*vipassanā*).

Yet, the identification of *upekkha* based on renunciation and diversity with the *upekkhā* of the fourth *jhāna* encounters a problem when we read the *Potaliya Sutta*. Contrary to the *Saḷāyatanavibhanga Sutta*, the *Potaliya Sutta* proclaims that *upekkhā* based on diversity is associated with ignorance regarding the nature of sensual pleasures. For the *Potaliya Sutta*, a noble disciple should develop '*upekkhā* that is unified'; this is because it is only then that clinging (*upādānā*) to material things of the world (*loka-āmisa*) utterly ceases without a remainder.[27] In other words, for the *Potaliya Sutta*, any *upekkhā* that is based on diversity of sense experience cannot be considered wholesome.

The discrepancy between the two suttas did not escape the eyes of the commentator on the *Potaliya Sutta*. The commentary states that since the *Potaliya Sutta* claims that *upekkhā* based on diversity is connected to unwholesome states of mind, *upekkhā* of the fourth *jhāna* must be *upekkhā* based on unity (MA III.43). Note that this statement reflects the traditional view that the *jhānas* are wholesome states of mind but also trance-like attainments, absorptions that are disconnected from sense experience. For the commentator on the *Potaliya Sutta*, *upekkhā* that arises in the *jhānas* must be a wholesome mental factor, but it also must be based on unity of perception and not on the diversity of sense experience.

Having said that, the account from the *Potaliya Sutta* and the commentator's solution are problematic for two reasons: first, it contradicts the clear statement in the *Saḷāyatanavibhanga Sutta* that *upekkhā* based on unity is *upekkhā* regarding the four *arūpa samāpattis*.[28] Moreover, this statement in the *Saḷāyatanavibhanga Sutta* seems more valid and reasonable than suggesting that *upekkhā* of the *jhānas* is based on unity. Contrary to the *jhānas*, the four *arūpa samāpattis* are states which transcend form (*rūpa*). That is to say, they transcend diversity (*nānatta*) of sense contact; therefore, they are said to be based on unity of perception. The association of *upekkhā* based on unity with the attainment of the *arūpa samāpattis* is also reinforced by a description from the *Mahānidāna Sutta* of the DN, which delineates the 'seven stations of consciousness'. For our discussion, the portrayal of the 'station of consciousness' that corresponds to the first *arūpa samāpatti* is particularly relevant. The *Mahānidāna Sutta* states that those beings who reach 'space that is infinite' are those

> [W]ho pass beyond all perception of form, by the vanishing of the perception of resistence and by non-attention to the perception of diversity (*nānattasaññānaṃ*).[29]

It is clear from this description that 'the non-attention to the perception of diversity' (*nānattasaññānaṃ amanasikārā*), which characterizes the first *arūpa samāpatti* (and all the other *arūpa samāpattis* as well), means that these attainments are based on unity (*ekattasitā*) of perception. In all the formless attainments, one passes beyond all perception of form (*sabbaso rūpasaññānaṃ samatikkamā*) by the disappearance of sense stimuli.[30] This, of course, supports the *Saḷāyatanavibhanga Sutta* statement that *upekkhā* based on unity (*upekkhā ekattā ekattasitā*) refers to the attainment of the *arūpa samāpattis* (the formless attainments).

Given that, I will argue that what the *Potaliya Sutta* calls '*upekkha* based on diversity' actually parallels what the *Saḷāyatanavibhanga Sutta* designates as '*upekkha* based on worldly life',[31] which is also based on diversity of sense experience but is rooted in ignorance. Thus, it should be justified in arguing that the type of *upekkhā* that is present in the *jhānas*, while fully perfected in the fourth *jhāna*, is '*upekkha* based on diversity [of experience] and renunciation (i.e., on insight into the nature of experience)'.

At this point, I want to draw out the implications and meanings of what we have discussed until now with regard to the nature of *upekkhā* in the fourth *jhāna*. In light of the preceding discussion, we can deduce three things about the nature of *jhānic upekkhā*: the first is that it arises from insight into the nature of sense experience. The second is that it becomes fully fulfilled only when *somanassa* and *domanassa* based on renunciation fade away. And the third is that this type of *upekkhā* goes beyond the six sense objects.[32] Before offering an interpretation for the latter, which seems to me important and in need of clarification, I wish to first look at the description from the *Saḷāyatanavibhanga Sutta* of how this type of *upekkhā* becomes fully grounded and fulfilled (contrary to its mere arising). This will further aid in understanding the nature of *jhānic upekkhā* and the meaning of it being perfected in the fourth and final *jhāna*.

The *Saḷāyatanavibhanga Sutta* delineates a clear process of how wholesome qualities arise in dependence on the abandonment of unwholesome factors. However, it also points out how certain wholesome qualities are fulfilled only when certain *other wholesome* qualities are abandoned (this is contrary to wholesome qualities that can accompany each other to perfection, like *sati* and *upekkhā*). This process of abandonment is demonstrated by a concise utterance in the *Saḷāyatanavibhanga Sutta*: 'by depending on this, abandon that' (*tatridaṃ nissāya idaṃ pajahathāti*).[33] The sutta explains this utterance by stating that depending on 'gladness based on renunciation' one abandons and surmounts 'gladness based on worldly life'.[34] The same holds for discontent and equanimity based on worldly life: they are abandoned by the arising of discontent and equanimity based on renunciation. The significance of this description is that it points out that through the actual arising of wholesome states of mind, one can abandon unwholesome states. This line of reasoning is similar to my argument about the spiritual significance of the first *jhāna*: experiencing *jhānic pīti* and *sukha* is that which enables one to abandon the desire for sense gratification (*kāma*). In other words, for entering into the first *jhāna* one has to cultivate insight regarding the nature of sense pleasure; however, only the actual experience of a different kind of pleasure and joy – one that is not connected to unwholesome states – enables the mind to let go of ingrained mental tendency to desire pleasurable sense experiences.

In the same way, the process of abandoning unbeneficial gladness, discontent and equanimity is initiated by the development of insight into the nature of sense experience but ends when their wholesome counterparts fully arise. That is, the complete abandonment of unwholesome gladness, discontent and equanimity seems to be brought about by the full expression and manifestation of wholesome gladness, discontent and equanimity. When these wholesome qualities are fully realized and grounded in the mind, unwholesome states cannot find footing anymore.

Nevertheless, for certain wholesome qualities to be fulfilled, certain other wholesome states must be surmounted. The *Saḷāyatanavibhanga Sutta* observes that for wholesome gladness to be fully experienced, wholesome discontent must be surmounted. Furthermore, for wholesome *upekkhā* to be fully fulfilled and grounded, wholesome gladness must be surmounted. This is a gradual and dependent process:

> By depending and relying on the six kinds of gladness based on renunciation, abandon and surmount the six kinds of discontent based on renunciation. It is thus they are abandoned; it is thus they are surmounted. By depending and relying on the six kinds of equanimity based on renunciation, abandon and surmount the six kinds of gladness based on renunciation. It is thus they are abandoned; it is thus they are surmounted.[35]

This prescription/description construes a certain aspect of the *jhānic* process. It elucidates the statement that one of the conditions for entering into the fourth *jhāna* (where *upekkhā* is fulfilled and perfected) is that *somanassa* and *domanassa* must fade away. In other words, for *upekkhā* to become purified (i.e., fully grounded) one must surmount and abandon wholesome discontent and gladness. This sutta also corroborates the description from the *Aviparītaka Sūtra* that points out that the cessation of *jhānic domanassa* and *somanassa* is a gradual and conditioned process where *domanassa* ceases before *somanassa*, and both cease before one can attain the last two *jhānas* (where *upekkhā* is now obvious and strong). Furthermore, I suggest that this account implies that wholesome *upekkhā* can be present in conjunction with *jhānic domanassa* and *somanassa*, but it cannot be said to be fully perfected until they fade away.

Now we can turn to the final aspect of '*upekkhā* based on renunciation and diversity' (i.e., *jhānic upekkhā*) as *upekkhā* that 'goes beyond the six sense objects'.[36] This is an intriguing statement. What does it mean that one goes beyond (*ativattati*) forms, sounds, odours, flavours, tangibles and mental phenomena (*dhamma*) while not being disconnected from them? How can we understand this statement so it will take us one step further in deciphering the phenomenology of the fourth *jhāna* and its significance for the attainment of liberation?

I will begin this investigation by looking at the way the *Saḷāyatanavibhanga Sutta* describes '*upekkhā* based on worldly life'. Understanding the difference between the two types of *upekkhā* – that which is based on worldly life and that which is based on renunciation – will illuminate the statement that '*upekkhā* based on diversity and renunciation' is grounded upon the diversity of sense experience but at the same time goes beyond them.

The *Saḷāyatanavibhanga Sutta* explains that *upekkhā* based on worldly life arises in

> [A] foolish infatuated ordinary person who has not conquered [his] limits (*anodhijinassa*) and the fruit [of action] (*avipākajinassa*) and who is blind to the disadvantage [of sense experience]. Such equanimity as this, does not go beyond (*nātivattati*) form' etc.[37]

According to this description *upekkhā* based on worldly life is *upekkhā* rooted in ignorance with regard to the nature of sensory experience. This description points out that this type of *upekkhā* does not go beyond (*nātivattati*) the objects of the senses; this is because one does not understand their disadvantage and unreliable nature. A person who lacks this wisdom is an ordinary person (*puthujjanassa*). This implies that *upekkhā* based on worldly life is not really the type of *upekkhā* that one aims at developing on the path to awakening (namely, *upekkhā-sambojjhaṅga*). I would suggest the preceding paragraph connotes the following: although one might think one is experiencing unfeigned equanimity, one's mind is still entangled in the experience in some level. This is why one is bound to the laws of cause and effect: one's mind is not free from subtle reactivity that creates imprints in the mind, imprints that will yield results (*kamma*). Thus, the obvious question is why this type of mental factor that is rooted in confusion (*moha*) and ignorance (*avijjā*) is called *upekkhā* at all, when *upekkhā* usually refers to a wholesome mental quality that arises from insight.

There seems to be two possible explanations. The first is that the term '*upekkhā* based on worldly life' actually refers to indifference masked as equanimity. It might be that since there is no term for indifference as such in the Nikāyas, the sutta describes this mental state as *upekkhā* rooted in ignorance. The preceding description implies that indifference can be identified mistakenly by an ordinary person as *upekkhā*. The second option, which I think is more likely, is that this type of mental state is a gross type of equanimity. That is to say, this type of equanimity manifests as non-reactivity on the surface of the mind, while subtle forms of reactivity operate in a deeper level.[38] I suggest that this type of equanimity is still tainted by wrong perception of reality. In other words, on a subtle level, the mind still reacts according to underlying habitual patterns of aversion and desire and a distorted perception that considers phenomena to have some inherent existence.

To put the matter a little differently, we can say that we all experience moments in which we are somewhat equanimous in the face of certain experiences, meaning we are not overwhelmed or completely captivated by the objects of the senses, be they pleasant or painful. However, if there is no penetrative insight into the unreliability of sense experience, if there is no real insight into the nature of phenomena and its selflessness, these moments are only superficially equanimous. This gross level of equanimity needs to be further deepened by the development of deep and penetrative wisdom. It cannot be considered perfect or complete (*parisuddhi*), since it does not originate from clear and transformative insight but only from partial and incomplete understanding. According to the earlier description, when this type of *upekkhā* arises, the mind still creates *kammic* results (*vipāka*). Thus, this *upekkhā* is associated with intention; moreover, even if the intention (*cetanā*) is wholesome and operates as an underlying tendency that is not completely conscious or obvious, it still creates impressions in the mind and sustains habitual patterns of desire and aversion that have the potential to cause *dukkha*.

Having said that, we now have a better understanding of what it means that '*upekkhā* based on diversity and renunciation' goes beyond the six sense objects.[39] I believe that the key to understanding this statement is the meaning of the verb *ativattati* in light of the preceding analysis. An ordinary person has not yet conquered the limits of ordinary attitudes towards sense experience; such a person continues to desire, reject and identify with seeing, hearing, smelling, tasting, touching and cognizing. By contrast, a person who attains this type of *upekkhā* has gone beyond ordinary limitations; that is, he or she experiences the sensory world without clinging or attaching to the flow of experience, without being ignorant as to their fleeting and empty nature and without identifying these experiences as 'me', 'mine' or 'I' (including to the quality of *upekkhā* itself). This *upekkhā* transcends the seductiveness of sense experiences by seeing them as they actually are.[40] This seems to suggest that when this type of *upekkhā* is fully perfected in the attainment of the fourth *jhāna*, one does not re-create mental impressions, which means that one does not create *kamma* (while one is dwelling in the fourth *jhāna*).

The last point I wish to mention is how *upekkhā* is described in the *Dhātuvibaṅga Sutta*. This discourse can assist in comprehending how *upekkhā* is purified (*parisuddhi*) and what this purification means. The *Dhātuvibaṅga Sutta*, albeit in a different formulation, describes the practice of observing phenomena as the *Satipaṭṭhāna Sutta* does. It also (1) delineates the process of liberation by describing the insights that arise from such observation; (2) depicts the actual state of mind that originates from such a practice and consequent insights; (3) lays out the possibility of attaining liberation from such a state; and (4) portrays the nature of a liberated mind. I do not wish to enter into a deep analysis of this complex and interesting discourse, for my concern here is only the nature of *jhānic upekkhā*. To narrow the discussion, I would like to examine only what the *Dhātuvibaṅga Sutta* says about the purified (*parisuddhi*) *upekkhā*, which quite clearly evinces the nature of *upekkhā* of the fourth *jhāna*.

According to the *Dhātuvibaṅga Sutta*, a purified *upekkhā* remains after one has progressively developed insight into the nature of phenomena, that is, after one has understood the impersonal and conditioned nature of experience. According to the sutta, the first step in the process of insight is 'seeing as it is with proper wisdom' (*yathābhūtaṃ sammappaññāya daṭṭhabbaṃ*) that each of the elements cannot be regarded as 'me', 'mine' or 'myself'.[41] This allows the mind to become dispassionate (*cittaṃ virājeti*) towards the elements, meaning towards the physical aspect of experience. When the mind is thus dispassionate, a purified and bright (*parisuddhaṃ pariyodātaṃ*) consciousness (*viññāṇaṃ*) is established.

This purified consciousness has a particular function according to the *Dhātuvibaṅga Sutta*: it can cognize the 'feeling tone' of experience free from any type of clinging and identification since one has understood the conditioned nature of experience. In other words *viññāṇa*, in this context, designates the faculty of clear and purified discernment; it clearly refers to the ability to know the way feelings (*vedanā*) arise from contact between a sense door and a corresponding object. A purified consciousness is the faculty of discernment free from craving (*taṇhā*) and clinging (*upādānā*).[42] In this context, a purified consciousness refers specifically to the faculty of knowing (*pajānāti*) the conditioned nature of every type of experience.[43]

The sutta then explains that when this insight is gained, what remains is *upekkhā* that is 'purified and bright, malleable, wieldy and radiant'.[44] As already pointed out, it is safe to infer that this sutta refers to *upekkhā* of the fourth *jhāna*, which is also characterized as *parisuddhi* in the formulaic descriptions. This identification is further strengthened when we recognize that a similar depiction is made in various suttas in respect to the nature of mind as one finally attains the fourth *jhāna*.[45] For our purpose what is interesting and illuminating is that this type of *upekkhā* is likened to refined gold that can be moulded into any kind of ornament. It can be directed wisely for the purpose of understanding the conditioned nature of very subtle states of mind (the *arūpa samāpattis*); that is, one does not confuse these exalted states of mind (if attained) with *nibbāna*. But more importantly, when *upekkhā* is thus purified,

> [O]ne does not form any condition or generate any volition tending towards being or non-being. Since he does not form any condition or generate any volition tending towards either being or non-being, he does not cling to anything in the world. When he does not cling, he is not agitated. When he is not agitated, he attains *nibbāna*.[46]

The point is clear. A purified *upekkhā* – *upekkhā* of the fourth *jhāna* – is vital for the attainment of *nibbāna*. I would say that this type of *upekkhā* denotes a profoundly wise relation to experience, not tainted by any kind of wrong perception and mental reactivity rooted in craving (*taṇhā*). This is not some superficial or momentary equanimity towards experience; rather, it is a profound and deep impartial attitude that is grounded in clear seeing of the conditioned and empty nature of every type of experience.

What I am arguing is that attaining the fourth *jhāna* means that one has perfected this transformative quality (and hence, it can be recognized now as *upekkhā-sambojjhaṅga*). In other words, *jhānic upekkhā* is an essential quality for attaining *nibbāna*. Perfecting this quality seems to mean that one is in the best possible position for attaining liberation. When this quality is perfected, the mind does not cling to anything in the world; there is no tending towards being or non-being. It is the actualization of the middle way (a middle point between likes and dislikes, being and non-being). Thus, *upekkhā* (and *sati*) are characterized as purified or perfect (*parisuddhi*) because they are the actualization and embodiment of wisdom-awareness. This is why *Sutta Nipāta* 1107 declares that the attainment of pure *upekkhā* and *sati* (*upekkhāsatisaṃsuddhaṃ*) is the 'breaking of ignorance' (*avijjāya pabhedanaṃ*): it is a state of mind in which no reactivity rooted in nescience (*avijjā*), conscious and latent, is present. Therefore, it resembles and anticipates an awakened cognition. Dwelling in such a state, where *sati* and *upekkhā* are finally purified, stable and strong – that is, fulfilled as 'awakening factors' – might finally break ignorance completely.

IV *Sati*

With these reflections and suggestions in mind, let us now consider the second quality that is said to be perfected in the fourth *jhāna*, namely, *sati*. *Sati* is a central concept in Buddhist theory and practice. Therefore, much has already been written on it, regarding the variety of contexts it occurs in Buddhist texts (i.e., the suttas, the Abhidharma and later commentarial and exegetical literature), the various definitions it has received in these Buddhist literary genres and its application in meditative practice. This interest became even more widespread in the last decade when the practice of 'mindfulness' (*sati*) became common in contemporary psychology. Clearly, no attempt will be made here to survey and discuss the various uses and contexts of this concept in Buddhist textual traditions, nor would I offer a comprehensive review of *sati* in the Pāli Nikāyas. Various scholars have already offered extensive analyses of these occurrences;[47] moreover, it is beyond the scope of this study. Here, I offer an interpretation of *sati* in one particular context – the fourth and final *jhāna* – based on definitions of *sati* offered by Bhikkhu Bodhi, Rupert Gethin and Anālayo. This interpretation, however, is by no means a definitive account of *sati* in all Buddhist texts and contexts. Yet, I will argue that this particular understanding of *sati* should be recognized as describing the nature of *sati* as a *bojjhaṅga*. The following interpretation is established on what has already been discussed in this study on the phenomenology of the *jhānic* process, the mental qualities it involves, the multidimensional nature of these mental qualities and their gradual development and maturation.

The ongoing discussion and debate in modern scholarship as to the nature of *sati* in Buddhist theory of mind and the meditative procedure, produced different definitions of this term, some incongruous with others. Nevertheless, offering a satisfying description of the nature of *sati* in the (third) and fourth *jhānas* is less problematic than we would expect in light of this debate. This is because the fourth *jhāna* is the climax of specific mental cultivation. The fourth *jhāna* (as the previous ones) is a wholesome state, involving only specific mental and physical factors. That said, one must acknowledge that *sati* can be described slightly differently in other stages of the path and in different cognitive contexts. In other words, *sati* is a multidimensional and versatile concept in Buddhist theory of mental development (in the Nikāyas and in other Buddhist textual traditions). It can be cultivated in various levels and it can be associated with, or free from, certain mental factors. I would suggest that the reason *sati* incurred various descriptions and interpretations in Buddhist texts resulted from the following situation: the fact that *sati* can be cultivated in diverse ways[48] and in various levels of stability, strength, steadiness, breadth and depth, and it can arise in conjunction with wholesome and unwholesome factors.[49] That is, the description of *sati* seems to be dependent upon the technique one is utilizing for its development, the stage of the path a particular text is discussing, the level of stability *sati* has developed and its associated mental factors in a particular cognitive occurrence.

Given that, it is interesting to ask: how does *sati* function when it arises in conjunction with unwholesome mental factors (e.g., the five *nīvaraṇas*)? How does it function when it arises in a completely wholesome stream of consciousness, associated with specific mental qualities such as *upekkhā*? How does it function when it arises in association with ethically indeterminate factors such as *vitakka* and *vicāra* (in a wholesome and unwholesome stream of consciousness)? And lastly, what happens to the function of *sati* when these mental capacities (i.e., *vitakka* and *vicāra*) fade away? Before offering a definition of the nature of *sati*, as what I will call a '*jhāna*-awakening factor', and before discussing its mode of function in the fourth *jhāna*, a few general words on *sati* are in order.

In the Buddhist context, *sati* was translated in various ways such as 'memory', 'remembrance', 'recollection', 'mindfulness', 'bare attention', 'presence' or 'present awareness'. *Sati* is the Pāli term for the Sanskrit word *smṛti*, which originates from the root *smṛ*. This root involves two basic notions: 'to remember' and 'to have in mind'. In Indian culture the term *smṛti* has a specific use: it refers to a class of historical narratives such as the epics, the myths, traditional law, public and domestic rituals and grammar.[50] In other words, texts not 'revealed' (*śruti*) by the sages (*ṛṣi*) but 'remembered' and kept in mind. Dreyfus has pointed out that 'within the Buddhist context, this word has usually a related but more restrained meaning and refers to the quality of mind when it is recollecting or keeping in mind an object'.[51]

The relation between *sati* and the process of memory has prompted various suggestions;[52] however, I believe that Bodhi was correct in observing that although the meaning of *sati* as 'memory' is preserved in the Buddha's discourses in certain contexts, 'we should not give this excessive importance'.[53] He further argued that

> [T]o designate the practice that became the main pillar of his meditative system, he chose the word *sati*. But here *sati* no longer means memory. Rather, the Buddha assigned the word a new meaning consonant with his own system of psychology and meditation. Thus it would be a fundamental mistake to insist on reading the old meaning of memory into the new context.[54]

It is plausible that the Buddha used the term *sati* specifically because the term *smṛti* was associated with the idea that everything that is not the Veda cannot be a source of real knowledge.[55] That is, his choice of using the term *sati*, which is a key term in his theory and practice of meditation, might have been his way of separating himself completely from Vedic ideas while granting *sati* a central role in the way of gaining immediate knowledge of the nature of phenomena.

In his book on the *Satipaṭṭhāna Sutta*, Anālayo makes this observation about the connotation of *sati* as memory in the Nikāyas:

> *[S]ati* is not really defined as memory, but as that which facilitates and enables memory. What this definition of *sati* points to is that, if *sati* is present, memory will be able to function well.[56]

If *sati* no longer has the simple meaning of memory or remembrance, what is it exactly? First, we should bear in mind that the Pāli Nikāyas do not offer a comprehensive definition for the term *sati*. As previously noted, in certain places, it is defined as that which facilitates basic mental activities as remembering;[57] as such, it is connected to the practice of recollection (*anussati*).[58] Other descriptions of *sati* describe it as that which guards the mind against unwholesome states.[59] The latter definition is important since *sati* is a necessary component of Buddhist meditation practice; it supports the contemplative process of recognizing what is wholesome (*kusala*) and what is unwholesome (*akusala*) and underpins the abandonment of the latter. As pointed out by Bodhi, in this process of discrimination, *sati* works in unison with right view and right effort.[60] This evaluative quality of *sati* in the Buddhist meditative practice is sometimes pretermitted by contemporary *vipassanā* teachers who defined it solely as 'bare attention', accentuating the pre-conceptual element of Buddhist meditation, while identifying *sati* with a brief moment of pre-conceptual attention (an issue I will address later).[61] The last recurrent context in which *sati* is a prominent factor is, of course, the (third) and fourth *jhānas,* where it is characterized as purified or fulfilled (*parisuddhi*).

It is obvious from looking at these various contexts that they reflect different cognitive events and different levels of mental development. What makes this situation even more complicated is the fact that we cannot find a clear and precise description of *sati* in any of these contexts. Despite this, we can construe its function and nature from looking at the *Satipaṭṭhāna Sutta*. As Gethin has pointed out, it seems the Nikāyas prefer to describe *sati* by the actual practice of *satipaṭṭhāna*, which is seen as the method by which *sati* is established.[62] This sutta (together with the *Mahāsatipaṭṭhāna Sutta*) became in modern times the main sutta for the practice of meditation, viewed as the discourse that lays out the practice of mindfulness (or in its traditional appellation: *vipassanā-bhāvanā*).[63] It is interesting, however, that although the name of the sutta contains the word *sati*, the sutta itself does not use this term very frequently.

The actual practice in this sutta is usually designated by the verb *anupassati* ('to observe') and not as 'mindfulness or insight practice' (e.g., *vipassanā-bhāvanā*), which is a modern usage. In other words, the practice in this sutta is not formulated by the instruction to 'be mindful' of body, feelings, states of mind and mental phenomena (the four *satipaṭṭhānas*); rather, it is by the instructions to observe (*anupassati*) and know (*pajānati*) these various phenomena factorized in these teachings into four categories of experience. The four *satipaṭṭhānas* are a process of setting up *sati* through direct and specific observation of the phenomenal field. This type of observation (guided by various techniques) is the means by which the practitioner develops *sati* (and ways of looking that free the mind from clinging). It seems plausible to suggest, then, that *sati*, in its refined and fulfilled mode, must contain an element of insight infused within it from the simple fact that it is developed and established by a specific type of observation or a way of looking: observation that allows one to see (*anupassati*) and know (*pajānati*) the true nature of the phenomenal field. We can therefore conclude that the act of observing (*anupassanā*) is the practice while *sati* is the quality developed (in various levels of stability, strength, breadth, depth and continuity) as a result of such observation. Gethin has put it quite clearly when he states that

> [T]he four *satipaṭṭhānas* are, then, four *anupassanās,* four activities the purpose of which is to bring *sati* into 'service'. That is, in the process of watching the body, feelings, mind and *dhammas*, *sati* stand near, manifests and is established.[64]

At this point I would like to emphasize again two points that have been discussed in previous chapters and should be recalled here again. First, the practice of *satipaṭṭhāna* is a gradual practice. Second, the Nikāyas clearly correlate the gradual maturity of this practice with the attainment of the *jhānas* and the development of *samādhi*.[65] We have seen that the *jhānas* appear as the outcome of a recurrent and gradual path-structure that consists essentially of the abandoning of the five hindrances by the practice of *sīla*, the training in restraining sense impressions and the preparatory development of *sati*.[66] We have also seen that the *Dantabhūmi Sutta* clearly points out that prior to the attainment of the *jhānas*, the practice of *satipaṭṭhāna* is preliminary.[67] In light of the analysis of the *Dantabhūmi Sutta*, I have suggested that it is only by abiding in the *jhānas* that one can observe phenomena clearly and lucidly. This, I have argued, occurs in a gradual manner since each *jhāna* signifies a more clarified perception of experience; when the mind is not conditioned by habitual reaction-patterns of likes and dislike (conscious and latent), not conditioned by unwholesome mental states, and when the awakening factors arrive at full maturation, only then can one finally see clearly the nature of experience. The implication of all this is that the practice of *satipaṭṭhāna* and the attainment of the *jhānas* are woven together in a complex structure of successive interdependent development, development through which the mind is in inclined into the attainment of *nibbāna*. In other words, the progression from one *jhāna* to the next should be seen as the actualization of insight meditation and not as a separate meditation technique.

For now, we can conclude that *sati* is a multidimensional and versatile concept. *Sati* – as all other *kusala dhammas* – has a wide spectrum: one is not with or without *sati*[68] but rather one can have various degrees of *sati*. Secondly, *sati* (just as the practice of *satipaṭṭhāna*) is cultivated gradually and in various levels of stability, depth and continuity.[69] Lastly, different cognitive contexts modify *sati*'s mode of function. The latter was observed by Anālayo, who wrote that

> [T]his mental quality of *sati* has a broad variety of possible applications. Within the context of the *satipaṭṭhāna*, *sati* can range from the coarsest activities, such as defecation and urination, all the way up to the most sublime and exalted state, when *sati* is present as a mental factor during the breakthrough to *nibbāna*.[70]

All this entails that the interpretation of *sati* is a sensitive endeavour. One is obligated to take into consideration the specific cognitive-affective contexts of *sati* and the level of stability, strength, depth and continuity this quality has developed.

Despite these words of precaution, I do believe that previous scholars have been successful in offering a good working definition of *sati* as a fundamental mental quality in the path of transforming the cognitive process from ordinary to awakened by means of practicing *satipaṭṭhāna* and by fulfilling the seven factors of awakening. I believe that these definitions are applicable (with minor refinements) to the nature and function of *sati* in the fourth *jhāna*, which I believe is a key mental (and physical) context for attaining awakening. I will refer here specifically to suggestions made by Bodhi which I find discerning and helpful.

In a recent article on *sati*, Bodhi maintains that

> [T]o establish mindfulness is not to set about remembering something that occurred in the past, but to adopt a particular stance towards one's present experience. I characterize this as a stance of *observation* or *watchfulness* towards one's own experience. One might even call this as a stance of *sati* a 'bending back' of the light of consciousness upon the experiencing subject in its physical, sensory and psychological dimensions.[71]

He further explains that *sati* makes the objective field 'present' to awareness as an expanse of phenomena exhibiting their own distinctive phenomenal characteristics, as well as patterns and structures common to all conditioned phenomena. This, he suggests, means that *sati* might be characterized simply as 'lucid awareness'. He explains:

> *Sati* makes the apprehended object stand forth vividly and distinctly before the mind. When the object being cognized pertains to the past – when it is apprehended as something that was formerly done, perceived, or spoken – its vivid representation takes the form of memory. When the object is a bodily process like in-and-out breathing or the act of walking back and forth, or when it is a mental event like a feeling or thought, its vivid presentation takes the form of lucid awareness of the present.[72]

Bodhi's main arguments are helpful for the present enquiry and can be summed up as follows: *sati* is a mental quality that enables the mind to bring into focus the experiential field. It can be characterized as a particular stance towards experience,[73] constituting lucid awareness of the present whether it is a sensation, emotion or memory. Furthermore, *sati* has varying layers of conceptual content ranging from 'heavy' to 'light' to 'zero', depending on the particular type of *satipaṭṭhāna* being practiced.[74]

With these definitions in mind, let us proceed to analyzing the nature and function of *sati* in the fourth and final *jhāna*, taking into consideration that it is a unique mental and physical position – the culmination of a spiritual ascent – where the process of purifying the mind's perception of experience arrives at a potentially transformative moment.

IV The nature and function of *sati* in the fourth *jhāna*

I mentioned earlier the observation made by Bodhi that many contemporary *vipassanā* teachers define *sati* as 'bare attention', identifying it with a brief moment of pre-conceptual awareness. For Bodhi, this definition is acceptable only if we take it as a pragmatic definition rather than definitive or theoretical.[75] According to Bodhi, the reason why it cannot be regarded as definitive is because this definition conflates two mental factors: the first one is the immediate pre-conceptual apprehension of an object that comes into the range of cognition (*manasikāra*),[76] and the second is *sati*. Bodhi correctly observes that the first is an automatic and ethically indeterminate cognitive process while the second is a quality of mind that the practitioner has to cultivate (*bhāvetabba*).[77] In other words, *manasikāra* is a spontaneous and automatic function exercised whenever an object contacts one of the sense-doors while *sati* supervenes, according to Bodhi, at a later stage, 'sustaining attention on the object and making it appear vividly to lucid cognition'.[78]

Bodhi's observation is perceptive and important but it seems to overlook a situation where the two might not be as distinct as they are in ordinary consciousness. For example, I would hypothesize that these two mental functions might not be so distinguishable in a state of mind where the conceptual content is very light (meaning perception (*saññā*) is at work but discursive and conceptual thinking is not)[79] and where the mind is free temporarily (or permanently) from emotional reactive patterns. What I am suggesting (and will elaborate later) is that in this cognitive-emotive context, *manasikāra* and *sati* might not be so distinct in contrast to how they are during ordinary cognitive process. It is interesting that Bodhi himself points out that the initial task of *sati* is to observe experience as free as possible from distorted conceptual overlays.[80] Several questions arise from this statement: what happens when this initial task of *sati* arrives at full completion? What are the theoretical and practical differences between *manasikāra* and *sati* when distorted conceptual and affective overlays fade away? How should we understand the function of *sati* when it is fully matured in a wholesome, non-discursive and non-reactive field of awareness? Can we define it then as 'bare awareness', namely, as non-discursive lucid awareness of the phenomenal field?

It seems obvious that the mode of function of *sati* in a wholesome, non-discursive and non-reactive stream of consciousness is quite different from its mode of function in an ordinary mind where unwholesome states arise alternately with wholesome ones, and where the mind discursively interprets experience based on deep physical, mental and emotional habits. When the mind is not yet wholesome and calm (i.e., not free from the various hindrances and other unwholesome states that obstruct clear seeing), *sati* must operate as a guard against unskilful tendencies, thereby assisting the meditative practice of recognizing the wholesome (*kusala*) and the unwholesome (*akusala*) with the intention of abandoning the latter. As mentioned earlier, in an ordinary cognitive process *sati* works in unison with right view (that which aids the process of evaluating between the wholesome and unwholesome), right effort (that which cultivates the wholesome and abandons the unwholesome) and right intention.

Another important point that should be remembered is the versatility and multidimensionality of *sati*. This versatility is illustrated by Bodhi's observations that *sati* has varying layers of conceptual content ranging from 'heavy' to 'light' to 'zero', depending on the particular type of *satipaṭṭhāna* being practiced.[81] This observation is self-evident when one reads the *Satipaṭṭhāna Sutta*. Certain practices in this discourse use conceptualization extensively. In these types of techniques, *sati* is associated and works closely with discursive and conceptual thinking.[82] In these practices the practitioner uses thoughts and concepts frequently as an aid for bringing and keeping the mind on the body, feelings, mind and mental phenomena. This indicates that *sati*, as pointed out by Bodhi, cannot be regarded as non-discursive and non-conceptual by its nature.[83] To put it differently, I would say that in an ordinary cognitive process, *sati* requires continuous cultivation by various techniques; many of these techniques concern concepts and discursive thoughts, and some even use verbal formulations. In such contexts, right effort, right view and right intention must accompany *sati*.

Yet, we should bear in mind that in other stages of the path, when the conceptual content is very light and the mind contains only wholesome factors, *sati* does not need the 'assistance' of any type of thinking and intention in order to maintain awareness on the phenomenal field. In these unique occasions, *sati* is finally fully developed in a stream of consciousness that is free from mental obstructions and cognitive overlays. It seems plausible to characterize *sati* during such a higher level occasion as 'bare awareness' of the phenomenal field. It is bare in the sense that it is free from affective or cognitive overlays; it is free from the medium of discursive thoughts and conceptual constructions; it is free from mental and physical reactivity rooted in desire, aversion and ignorance. Therefore, it is free from clinging and identification. On such an occasion, I would argue, the aim of Buddhist meditation has been achieved to a very high extent (this is because the final aim is, of course, *nibbāna* – the permanent cessation of unwholesomeness).

It is clear, I think, by now that *sati*'s mode of function in a wholesome, non-discursive and non-reactive field of awareness is different from its mode of function during an ordinary cognitive process. What I am suggesting is that the attainment of the fourth *jhāna* marks an important moment in the Buddhist path to awakening. At this point in the spiritual path a specialized form of awareness has been fully established – a form of awareness that resembles an awakened awareness. I would further suggest that the purification of *sati* in the fourth *jhāna* actually means there is no deliberate or intentional effort to bring *sati* into service. This is because it has already been fully developed as a sustained and lucid awareness; that is, it is fulfilled as an awakening factor. In other words, in the fourth *jhāna*, *sati* as a sustained and lucid awareness of the phenomenal field becomes an 'automatic' function; it is automatic in the sense that it does not require deliberate and intentional effort.

In addition, following the latter proposition, I contend that in the fourth *jhāna* the automatic apprehension of an object and the sustained awareness (*sati*) of that activity are almost indistinguishable. My point is that these two mental processes are not 'spaced', as in an ordinary mind, by discursive and conceptual thinking and emotional reactions. Thus, it is the case that *manasikāra* and *sati* are differentiated by the fact that the former is always an automatic process (i.e., the initial adverting of attention to an object) and, by contrast, *sati* (i.e., the lucid awareness of this process of attention) is originally a cultivated quality.[84] Nevertheless, I would argue, that in the fourth *jhāna*, both mental factors arise automatically and in such proximity and continuity that they can almost be looked at as one single event. In short, the lucid and vivid awareness (*sati*) of what contacts the senses arises immediately after an object comes into the range of cognition, unintentionally and free from any hindrances. In other words, there is no pause between the moment an object contacts the sense-doors and when *sati* comes into play. This seems to mean that there is no mental gap in which the experiential act (i.e., seeing, hearing etc.) can be ascribed to a subjective 'I' by conceptual and affective overlays. At this attainment there is no fabrication of a sense of self. The experiential act is seen as conditioned and empty of self. This, however, does not mean that this state itself is a completely unfabricated state, as all moments of experience are fabricated.

However, I would suggest that it fabricates much less. Hence, it can be the spring board to awakening: it sees its own fabrication and therefore can see clearly the origin of *dukkha*.

To sum up, this unique mental setting allows the practitioner to be deeply familiarized with a clear, lucid and non-reactive awareness of experience for a prolonged period of time,[85] free from emotional and cognitive overlays that create a sense of a subjective 'I' separated from the objective field, and hence, free from the duality of subject and object. In the fourth *jhāna*, the initial task of *sati* has arrived at full completion. Bodhi has beautifully described this mode of function even though he does not ascribe it to the nature of *sati* in the fourth *jhāna*. He explains that

> [B]y bringing into focus the experiential field, *sati* illuminates objects without the usual overlay of distorted conceptual elaborations that obscure their real nature.[86]

I would suggest that this description relates unintentionally to the function of *sati* in the fourth *jhāna* (and it would seem to me, to awakened awareness as well). I am suggesting that *sati* of the fourth *jhāna* not only helps keep cognitive distortions in check as specified by Bodhi;[87] rather, it should also be accredited as that which facilitates insight or wisdom by functioning as lucid and bare awareness of the phenomenal field. In the fourth *jhāna*, *sati* serves (*upaṭṭhāna*) the mind not as a guard against the unwholesome but as that which allows insight to manifest through a sustained attention of what presents itself to awareness. At this moment, this attention is free from ignorance and reactive tendencies of desire and aversion; this is because *upekkhā* has also been fulfilled as an awakening factor.[88]

I will provisionally reflect, following these observations, that the preceding analysis seems to imply that consciousness (*viññāṇa*) in the fourth *jhāna* might not be shaped by conditioned psychological settings or conceptual structures (an issue I will offer some further reflections later on). This, I would hypothesize, can be described as the best possible 'position' for attaining awakening.

V *Vedanā* of the fourth *jhāna*

The last factor I wish to discuss is the 'feeling tone' (*vedanā*) of the fourth-*jhāna* experience. While the first three *jhānas* are characterized as pleasurable (*sukha*), the fourth *jhāna* is characterized as *adukkhaṃ-asukhaṃ* – 'neither-painful-nor-pleasant'. According to Buddhist analysis of experience, *vedanā* is the term for the 'feeling tone' of every moment of experience; it is born out of contact between an object and a sense door.[89] Buddhist analysis discerns three types of *vedanā*: painful, pleasant and neither-painful-nor-pleasant[90] while assuming that it has both mental and physical facets.[91] *Vedanā*, according to Buddhist psychology, is central in determining the reactions to our experiences. Our reactions to the different types of feelings can sustain and recondition three kinds of underlying tendencies: the underlying tendency to desire (*rāgānusayo*), the underlying tendency to aversion (*paṭighānusayo*) and the underlying tendency to ignorance (*avijjānusayo*).[92] When these reactive tendencies are not abandoned, they condition the arising of craving (*taṇhā*) and clinging (*upādānā*). Yet, a wise relation to the different types of feelings and sensations (*vedanā*) can uproot these same underlying tendencies; therefore, it can stop the origination of *dukkha*.[93]

According to the *Cūḷavedalla Sutta*, the underlying tendency to desire underlies most pleasant feelings, while the underlying tendency to aversion underlies most painful feelings.[94] This process is described in detail in the *Salla Sutta*, which explains that, when an ordinary person (*puthujjana*) experiences painful feelings, the mind harbours aversion towards that feeling. When one harbours aversion towards painful feelings, the underlying tendency to aversion (*paṭighānusayo*) lies behind this. When an ordinary person feels a pleasant feeling (or when one seeks delight in sensual pleasures as an escape from painful feelings), the mind seeks delight in that pleasant feeling; here the underlying tendency to desire (*rāgānusayo*) lies behind these feelings.[95] The *Salla Sutta* further explains that the underlying tendency to ignorance underlies most 'neither-painful-nor-pleasant' feelings when one does not understand:

> [A]s it really is the origin and the passing away, the gratification, the danger, and the escape in the case of these feelings (painful and pleasant), the underlying tendency to not-know (*avijjānusayo*) in regard to neither-painful-nor-pleasant feeling lies behind this.[96]

We might say that when one does not understand the impermanent and conditioned nature of *vedanā*, the underlying tendency to ignorance lies behind all three types of feelings. However, it seems that the preceding passage wishes to emphasize something particular about neither-painful-nor-pleasant feelings: this type of feeling does not create strong reactions in the mind such as strong aversion and desire; hence, the skilful way to relate to this type of feeling is to observe and know its impermanent and conditioned nature.[97] We can also say that this type of feeling is very subtle; thus, it can arise and pass away unnoticed. When one does not recognize the arising and passing away of this subtle feeling, it perpetuates a lack of clarity and ignorance with regard to experience; therefore, ignorance (*avijjā*) will lie behind this type of feeling.

It is interesting to note a further point made by the *Pahāna Sutta*: if one finds delight even in that 'peaceful feeling of neither-painful-nor-pleasant' (*adukkhamasukhaṃ santaṃ*), one is not free from *dukkha*.[98] In other words, when subtle delight arises as conditioned by this type of feeling (it seems that delight arises when the experience is not painful or unpleasant and not only when the experience is obviously pleasant), the underlying tendency to desire can lie behind it as well. We might articulate this process by saying that when a person is not observant enough, this subtle feeling of neither-painful-nor-pleasant can arise and pass away unnoticed and unrecognized. When this occurs, one cannot see the subtle reactivity that might arise as a result of that feeling tone. Not knowing that a certain type of feeling is present in a certain moment of experience means that ignorance as to the nature of experience is functioning and further implanted in the mind. This, it would seem to me, is the reason why the Nikāyas associate ignorance or 'no-recognition' (*avijjā*) specifically with the arising of neither-painful-nor-pleasant feeling.

What is particularly significant in the exploration of the nature of *jhānic* 'feeling-tones' is the assertion made in the *Cūḷavedalla Sutta* that these underlying tendencies – the underlying tendency to desire, to aversion and to ignorance – do not underlie *all* pleasant, painful and neither-painful-nor-pleasant feelings.[99] There are certain kinds of pleasant, painful and neither-painful-nor-pleasant feelings that do not sustain or create desire, aversion and ignorance, and these feelings do not embody these tendencies. We can imagine that feelings felt by an awakened person do not condition any unwholesome reactions; this is because these feeling are not rooted in desire, aversion and ignorance but in seeing clearly. When feelings arise in an awakened person due to various causes and conditions,[100] they do not condition any (new) underlying tendencies; they do not produce any unwholesome mental patterns;[101] they do not produce new *kamma*. This seems a plausible depiction of an awakened mind-set, since one becomes an arahant only when the underlying tendencies are completely eradicated.[102]

The second experiential context in which these three underlying tendencies do not underlie pleasant, painful and neither-painful-nor-pleasant feelings is, according to the *Cūḷavedalla Sutta*, the attainment of the *jhānas*. I would suggest that the account from the *Cūḷavedalla Sutta* aims at clarifying the abstruse process of how the mind becomes purified and free. It points out that by attaining the *jhānas* one can abandon desire, aversion and ignorance by actualizing profound wholesomeness.[103] This description further deepens our understanding of the liberative value of *jhānic* states. We now know that the *jhānas* are completely wholesome; moreover, when one abides in them, the mind does not produce desire, aversion and clinging both on the surface of the mind and in its deeper levels. Given that, I would argue that the notion that the *jhānas* have delusive power is quite problematic. On the contrary, they seem to have the uttermost potential to eradicate delusion completely.

We have seen in previous chapters that *jhānic* feelings are very different from ordinary feelings. I have shown that *jhānic sukha* originates from insight into the nature of experience and not from pleasant sense experience. More so, *jhānic sukha* (and *pīti*) aids the process of de-conditioning the tendency to desire by familiarizing the practitioner with a different mode of being in the world. I discuss this issue at length in Chapter 2 on the first *jhāna*, so I shall not repeat the argument here. As to the liberative function of painful (*dukkha*) feelings in the attainment of the *jhānas*, this is more problematic. It is clear that the first three *jhānas* are physically pleasurable, while the last *jhāna* is neither-painful-nor-pleasant. That is to say, one does not experience any physically (*kāyika*) painful sensations while in the *jhānas*. However, we might suggest that *jhānic domanassa* (discontent or sadness) can be classified as an unpleasant mental (*cetasika*) *vedanā*,[104] an unpleasant feeling that in an ordinary cognitive-emotive context can arouse aversion (and originate from ignorance). However, we have seen that *jhānic domanassa*, contrary to *domanassa* based on 'worldly life' (*gehasitāni*), is a wholesome discontent that arises from wholesome longing for liberation when one understands the unreliable nature of sense experience. This wholesome discontent is connected, according to the *Cūḷavedalla Sutta*, with the abandonment of aversion; this is because, when this type of discontent arises in the *jhānic* mind, aversion – obvious and latent – is not present.[105] In other words, in the *jhānas* one does not recondition the tendency to reject the unpleasant.

This characteristic is reflected in both the *Pahāna Sutta* and the *Salla Sutta* that associate both the abandonment of aversion and its underlying tendency with non-reactiveness to unpleasant feelings. What I am trying to suggest is that, when '*domanassa* based on renunciation' arises in the attainment of the first *jhāna*, the mind which is now wholesome and non-reactive does not harbour aversion towards this type of feeling. Since one does not harbour aversion towards this type of discontent, the underlying tendency to aversion (*paṭighānusayo*) does not lie behind this feeling. This, I would argue, aids significantly to the de-conditioning of the tendency to push away the unpleasant.

Having said that, let me offer some concluding reflections, specifically on the nature and liberative value of neither-painful-nor-pleasant feeling that accompanies the fourth-*jhāna* experience. As previously pointed out, the *Cūḷavedalla Sutta* indicates that the underlying tendency (*anusaya*) to ignorance (*avijjā*) does not underlie this type of feeling.[106] This statement is not surprising in light of the analysis of the *jhānas* thus far and from the analysis of the opening statement from the formulaic description of the fourth *jhāna*. I have already demonstrated that the use of the term *pahāna* in the opening statement suggests that before entering into the fourth *jhāna*, what one abandons are the unwholesome reaction-patterns to pleasant and painful feelings. One does not abandon the sensations themselves but the *desire* for pleasant feelings and *aversion* to painful ones. This process is delineated in greater detail in the *Salla Sutta*, which explains that

> [When] one knows as it really is the origin and the passing away, the gratification, the danger, and the escape in the case of these feelings (painful and pleasant), the underlying tendency to ignorance (*avijjānusayo*) in regard to neither-painful-nor-pleasant feeling does not lie behind this.[107]

It would seem to me that this description specifies the *jhānic* process implicitly and corresponds with the *Cūḷavedalla Sutta* account of the *jhānas*. It points out that abandoning the unwholesome habitual reaction-patterns to pleasant and painful experiences is the proximate cause for entering into the fourth and final *jhāna*, which is characterized as neither-painful-nor-pleasant. I have suggested that the description concerning the process through which one attains the fourth *jhāna* implies that this attainment can be recognized as the moment when one actually breaks ignorance: the latent tendency to ignorance does not underlie the type of feeling that is present in the fourth[108] *jhāna* while the active aspects of ignorance are also abandoned (i.e., desire and aversion). Hence, one actualizes and embodies wisdom (*paññā*).[109] Although this wisdom (as any other wisdom) is conditioned and impermanent, it has the potent ability to finally purify and awaken the mind.

VI Conclusion

From a Buddhist perspective, each moment of experience, as experienced by an unskilled ordinary person, can potentially sustain and recondition the underlying tendencies (*anusaya*) and other unwholesome mental and physical patterns. However, when one does not react to sense experience according to these tendencies and patterns of behaviour, a moment of experience holds the potential to liberate the mind. I wish to emphasize two points: first, the feeling of neither-painful-nor-pleasant, as experienced in the fourth *jhāna*, is the embodiment of seeing experience as it is (as expressed in the earlier passage from the *Salla Sutta*). Second, since *sati* and *upekkhā* are purified in the fourth *jhāna*, one does not perpetuate or recondition ignorance as one has grounded a specialized form of awareness: non-reactive and lucid awareness of the phenomenal field. Thus, in the fourth *jhāna* one does not find delight in its accompanied feeling since one has seen the impermanent and conditioned nature of all phenomena, including neither-painful-nor-pleasant *vedanā*.[110] What I am suggesting is that the fourth *jhāna* is characterized as neither-painful-nor-pleasant feeling because this instance reflects the embodiment of non-reactivity. It can be conceptualized as the embodiment of non-wanting, the embodiment of wisdom; it does not condition ignorance, confusion or lack of clarity; it is the bodily manifestation of an un-preferential attitude towards experience. Furthermore, the attainment itself seems to be the best possible situation for abandoning ignorance completely; this is because one has actualized a clear, lucid and non-reactive field of awareness, free from emotional and cognitive overlays.

It can be concluded at this point that since the *jhānic* mind is free from any unwholesome reactivity, the underlying tendencies do not lie behind these feelings. This, I would suggest, is what ameliorates the link between an ordinary mind that is dominated by deeply rooted mental and physical patterns of reactivity and an awakened mind that is permanently free from all unwholesome tendencies and predispositions. In other words, the fourth *jhāna* anticipates an awakened awareness for an unawakened practitioner.

To sum up, I am propounding that the fourth *jhāna* is the optimal experiential event for the utter de-conditioning of unwholesome tendencies of mind and for the transformation of deep epistemological structures. This is because one embodies and actualizes an awakened awareness of experience. Given that the fourth *jhāna* is not momentary but an attainment in which one enters into (*upasampajja*) and abides (*viharati*) in it for a sustained period of time, this means that the mind can become intimately familiar with an awakened and free mode of being. It is, therefore, the threshold of awakening.

Notes

1 MN I.174: *puna ca paraṃ bhikkhave bhikkhu sukhassa ca pahānā dukkhassa ca pahānā pubbeva somanassadomanassānaṃ atthagamā adukkhaṃ asukhaṃ upekkhāsatipārisuddhiṃ catutthaṃ jhānaṃ upasampajja viharati.*

2 MN I.174: *puna ca paraṃ bhikkhave bhikkhu sukhassa ca pahānā dukkhassa ca pahānā pubbeva somanassadomanassānaṃ atthagamā . . . catutthaṃ jhānaṃ upasampajja viharati.*

3 See SN V.210. In SN IV.208–10 the Buddha proclaims that there are two types of *vedanā*: physical and mental (*dve vedanā vediyati kāyikañca cetasikañca*).

4 Note also that according to AN III.207, when '*pīti* of solitude' (*pavivekaṃ pītiṃ*) arises, which quite obviously refers to *pīti* of the first *jhāna* (also according to AA III.303), there is no physical or mental pain associated with the wholesome and unwholesome.
5 E.g., SN V.213–6.
6 E.g., MN I.60; MN III.4; SN IV.7.
7 MN I.303–4.
8 MN I.304: *idhāvuso visākha bhikkhu sukhassa ca pahānā dukkhassa ca pahānā pubbeva somanassadomanassānaṃ atthagamā adukkhaṃ asukhaṃ upekkhāsatipārisuddhiṃ catutthaṃ jhānaṃ upasampajja viharati. Avijjaṃ tena pajahati. Na tattha avijjānusayo anusetīti.*
9 Sn 1106–7: *pahānaṃ kāmacchadānaṃ, (udayāti bhagavā) domanassāna cūbhayaṃ; thinassa ca panūdanaṃ, kukkuccānaṃ nivāraṇaṃ, upekkhāsatisaṃsuddhaṃ, dhammatakkapurejavaṃ; aññāvimokkhaṃ pabrūmi, avijjāya pabhedanaṃ.* Note that this seems to describe the attainment of the first *jhāna*, where one abandons the hindrances and *kāma* and still has *vitakka* and *vicāra* as the faculties that investigate phenomena, and the fourth *jhāna*, where *sati* and *upekkhā* are purified. Although it does not correspond verbatim to the formulaic description of these two attainments, it nonetheless seems to describe them all the same.
10 MN I.174: *upekkhāsatipārisuddhiṃ catutthaṃ jhānaṃ upasampajja viharati.*
11 See SN V.209 for an explanation on each of these faculties.
12 According to SN V.215 the *upekkhā indriya* ceases without a remainder in *saññāvedayitanirodha*. Gethin has pointed out that the Abhidhamma (and other Buddhist Sanskrit sources) classify *upekkhā* in two ways: as *upekkhindriya* and *tatramajjhattatā* ('balance of mind'). The first is defined as *adukkhamasukhā* and treated as a *vedanā*, while the second is defined as a skilful mental equilibrium and treated as a *saṅkhāra*. The later was associated with the *jhānas*, the four *brahma-vihāras* and the awakening factors. This clear-cut distinction between two types of *upekkhā* is not evident in the Nikāyas. However, I believe, Gethin has observed correctly that, in the Nikāyas, *upekkhindriya* is a type of *vedanā* (*adukkhamasukhā*), while in other contexts, to understand *upekkhā* as simply not-painful-and-not-pleasant feeling would seem to be inadequate. It is obvious, then, that *upekkhā* as a '*jhāna*-awakening' factor is a skilful mental equilibrium classified under the aggregate of *saṅkhāra* (Gethin 2001, 157). Note that according to Buddhaghosa, there are several other kinds of *upekkhā*. There is *upekkhā* in *samatha* and *upekkhā* in *vipassanā*. When calm is developed or when there is right understanding of the present moment, *upekkhā* performs its function. See Vism IV.157–71; XXI.18. However, this classification is also absent from the Nikāyas.
13 Kuan 2005, 290–1.
14 MN III.215–22.
15 See, for example, verse 267 from the Dhammapada, which proclaims that a real monk is one who abandons unwholesome states: 'But he who is above good and evil and lives the spiritual life; who wanders in the world with knowledge, he indeed, is called a bhikkhu' (*yo'dha puññaṃ ca pāpaṃ ca bāhetvā brahmacariyavā. Saṃkhāya loke carati, sa ve bhikkūti vuccati*). See also MN I.282ff.
16 See MN III.217–8.
17 MN II.204.
18 MN III.217–8.
19 MN III.218.
20 MN I.303–4: *idhāvuso visākha bhikkhu vivicceva kāmehi vivicca akusalehi dhammehi savitakkaṃ savicāraṃ vivekajaṃ pītisukhaṃ paṭhamaṃ jhānaṃ upasampajja virahati . . . idhāvuso visākha bhikkhu iti paṭisañcikkhati: 'kudassu nāmāhaṃ tadāyatanaṃ upasampajja viharissāmi, yadariyā etarahi āyatanaṃ upasampajja viharantī'ti. Iti anuttaresu vimokkhesu pihaṃ upaṭṭhāpayato uppajjati, pihappaccayā domanassaṃ. Paṭighaṃ tena pajahati. Na tattha paṭighānusayo anuseti.*

21 MN III.218. This discontent arises from understanding all sense experiences). See also MA V.22.
22 MN I.304.
23 Note that SN V.213–14 also indicates that the grief faculty (*domanassa-indriya*) ceases when one enters the second *jhāna*.
24 MN III.220: *atthi bhikkhave, upekkhā nānattā nānattasitā. Atthi upekkhā ekattā ekattasitā.*
25 MN III.220.
26 MN III.220.
27 MN I.364.
28 MN III.220.
29 DN II.69: *sattā sabbaso rūpasaññānaṃ samatikkamā paṭighasaññānaṃ atthaṅgamā nānattasaññānaṃ amanasikārā 'ananto ākāso'ti ākāsānañcāyatanūpagā.*
30 See also MN I.293, where it is states that a purified mind-consciousness (*mano-viññāṇa*) knows the four *arūpa samāpattis* when it has given up the five faculties (*pañca indriya*). This supports, again, the *Saḷāyatanavibhanga Sutta* analysis that the four *arūpa samāpattis* are attainments that one attains when sense stimuli are overcome. This is not said anywhere in the Nikāyas with regards to the four *jhānas*.
31 MN III.219.
32 MN III.219.
33 MN III.220.
34 MN III.220.
35 MN III.220: *tatra bhikkhave, yāni cha nekkhammasitāni somanassāni, tāni nissāya tāni āgamma, yāni cha nekkhammasitāni domanassāni. Tāni pajahatha, tāni samatikkamatha. Evametesaṃ pahānaṃ hoti, evametesaṃ samatikkamo hoti. Tatra bhikkhave, yā cha nekkhammasitā upekkhā, tā nissāya tā āgamma yāni cha nekkhammasitāni somanassāni tāni pajahatha, tāni samatikkamatha. Evametesaṃ pahānaṃ hoti, evametesaṃ samatikkamo hoti.*
36 MN III.219: *evametaṃ yathābhūtaṃ sammappaññāya passato upapajjati upekkhā yā evarūpā upekkhā dhammaṃ sā ativattati.*
37 MN III.219: *upapajjati upekkhā bālassa mūḷhassa puthujjanassa anodhijinassa avipākajinassa anādīnavadassāvino assutavato puthujjanassa. Yā evarūpā upekkhā, rūpaṃ sā nātivattati.*
38 See, for example, SN II.67 where the Buddha describes two layers of intending. When the obviously intended process ceases, the underlying tendency to prefer and intend can still operate and function as a basis for the proliferation of consciousness, and, therefore, sustain the existence of *dukkha*. For complete cessation of *dukkha*, all levels of intending must stop.
39 MN III.219.
40 MN III.219: *evametaṃ yathābhūtaṃ sammappaññāya passato upapajjati upekkhā yā evarūpā upekkhā dhammaṃ sā ativattati.*
41 MN III.240–2.
42 MN III.242–3.
43 Note that this is similar to the *Mahāvedala Sutta*: *vijānāti vijānātīti kho āvuso, tasmā viññāṇanti vuccati. Kiñca vijānāti: sukhantipi vijānāti, dukkhantipi vijānāti, adukkhamasukhantipi vijānāti. Vijānāti vijānātīti kho āvuso, tasmā viññāṇanti vuccatīti* (MN I.292).
44 MN III. 243: *athāparaṃ upekkhāyeva avasissati parisuddhā pariyodātā mudu ca kammaññā ca pabhassarā ca.*
45 E.g., MN I.182: *so evaṃ samāhite citte parisuddhe pariyodāte anaṅgaṇe vigatūpakkilese mudubhūte kammaniye ṭhite āneñjappatte pubbenivāsānussatiñāṇāya cittaṃ abhininnāmeti.* See also MN II.38, II.226, III.136; DN I.76.
46 MN III.244: *so neva taṃ abhisaṅkharoti, nābhisañcetayati bhavāya vā vibhavāya vā. So anabhisaṅkharonto anabhisañcetayanto bhavāya vā vibhavāya vā na kiñci loke upādiyati. Anupādiyaṃ na paritassati, aparitassaṃ paccattaṃyeva parinibbāyati.*

47 The concept of *sati* is discussed at length in the last issue of *Contemporary Buddhism* 12 (2011) and especially by Bodhi 2011, 12–39; see also Anālayo 2003, 46–66; Gethin 2001, 36–44; Bhikkhu Sujato 2005, 111–23; Shulman 2010, 393–420; Olendzki 2011, 61, 64–70; Kuan 2005.

48 According to the *Satipaṭṭhāna Sutta*, one can cultivate *sati* in different ways, for example, by observing the breath, repulsiveness of the body, by contemplating death or by knowing states of mind (*citta*) as states of mind.

49 It should be noted that in the Abhidhamma, *sati* is a 'wholesome universal', meaning it is only present in a wholesome state of mind. However, in the Abhidharmakośa, *sati* is considered among the universal mental factors, and it arises in an unwholesome stream of consciousness. See Olendzki 2011, 67.

50 Larson 1993, 374.

51 Dreyfus 2011, 45.

52 For example, Shulman suggests an interesting relation between *sati* and memory in the practice of Buddhist meditation (Shulman 2010, 408).

53 Bodhi 2011, 22. Gethin has also observed that 'it is clear from the notion of *satipaṭṭhāna* that what the Nikāyas mean by "remembering" is rather more than simply the ability to recall information from the distant past' (Gethin 2001, 36).

54 Bodhi 2011, 22; Dreyfus 2011, 47. Anālayo suggests something different. He argues that '*sati* is not really defined as memory, but as that which facilitates and enables memory'(Anālayo 2003, 47).

55 In the Hindu traditions, the concept of *smṛti* as 'memory' was not considered as a means or a source of knowledge by most Indian philosophical schools, although it was viewed as an important dimension of cognition. The Mīmāṃsakas also contended that *smṛti* does not give any new information, and hence, is not a valid source of knowledge (Larson 1993, 37–56). Later Buddhist thought followed this line of reasoning and did not consider *smṛti* as a *pramāṇa* since it involves thoughts and construction (*vikalpa*).

56 Anālayo 2003, 47. He also argues that, in the context of *satipaṭṭhāna*, *sati* 'is not concerned with recalling past events, but functions as awareness of the present moment'.

57 E.g., MN I.356.

58 E.g., AN III.284.

59 E.g., MN III.136and SN IV.194.

60 See Bodhi 2011, 26.

61 For a fuller discussion on this issue, see Bhikkhu Bodhi 2011, 27–32.

62 Gethin 2001, 36.

63 It should be noted, however, that the *Satipaṭṭhāna* and *Mahāsatipaṭṭhāna Suttas* were probably important throughout the history of the Theravāda tradition and not only in modern times. It is not clear how these discourses were used exactly, but it seems likely that they were significant. This historical observation is founded on the fact that the *Mahāsatipaṭṭhāna Sutta* has many palm leaf copies in the 'Guardian of the Flame Collection', a collection containing five hundred manuscripts from Sri Lanka. This collection is the largest known collection of Sri Lankan manuscripts. According to Berkwitz, 'the multiple manuscripts of these titles (in which the *Mahāsatipaṭṭhāna Sutta* is one) speaks of their importance in Sri Lankan monastic culture' (Berkwitz 2009, 42).

64 Gethin 2001, 32. Bhikkhu Bodhi explains that '*upaṭṭhāna* means, firstly, "setting up, establishing", which is what one does with mindfulness'. Already in the Nikāyas the word is closely connected with *sati*. The compound *satipaṭṭhāna* is itself composed of *sati* and *upaṭṭhāna*. The four *satipaṭṭhānas* are the four establishments of mindfulness, a process of setting up mindfulness (Bhikkhu Bodhi 2011, 25).

65 See also SN V.151–2. All this has been pointed out by Gethin, who has concluded that the establishing of mindfulness is seen as presupposing a certain degree of concentration (*samādhi*), but this concentration itself is the outcome of the preparatory practice

of the establishing of mindfulness. He has pointed out that 'in opposing the four *satipaṭṭhānas* to the five *nīvaraṇas*, it once more associates the practice of the *satipaṭṭhānas* with the practice of the *jhānas*' (Gethin 2001, 58).

66 E.g., MN I.181. See also SN V.143, where the Buddha declares that, based upon *sīla*, one should develop the four *satipaṭṭhānas*. By this development, one should expect only growth in wholesome states, not decline. These wholesome states seem to be the four *jhānas*, as the foundation on which *nibbāna* might be realized. See the discussion on this path structure in the chapter on the first *jhāna*.

67 MN III.136ff.

68 Here I mean that 'one is not with or without *sati*' in the context of practice, as there are for sure instances where one does not have *sati* at all. After all, *sati* is a cultivated factor, not necessarily present in all moments of consciousness.

69 I have showed in my analysis of the '*bojjhaṅga* process formula' that *sati* (just as the other factors of awakening) is fulfilled in a gradual manner: it is first established (*upaṭṭhitā*), then aroused (*āraddha*) and then fully fulfilled (*pāripūri*). I have argued that *sati* is technically present in the first and second *jhānas* (and to some degree even before), fully obvious in the third *jhāna* but perfected and fulfilled only in the attainment of the fourth and final *jhāna*.

70 Anālayo 2003, 267.

71 Bodhi 2011, 25. Gethin has concluded that *sati* watches over the mind, it is a form of presence of mind (Gethin 2001, 32).

72 Bodhi 2011, 25–6.

73 For Bodhi, this aspect of *sati* provides the connection between its two primary canonical meanings: as memory and as lucid awareness of present happenings. Bodhi 2011, 25.

74 Bodhi 2011, 31.

75 Bodhi 2011, 27.

76 Bodhi 2011, 30.

77 Bodhi 2011, 28.

78 Bodhi 2011, 30. See Olendzki, who observed that *sati*, according to the Pāli Abhidhamma, 'is a mental state that arises over and above basic levels of attention' (Olendzki 2011, 61).

79 Note that according to the *Poṭṭhapāda Sutta* perception (*saññā*) functions in the *jhānas*. However, it is not ordinary but 'true' (*sacca*) and 'subtle' (*sukhuma*). DN I.182–3.

80 Bodhi 2011, 32.

81 Bodhi 2011, 31.

82 E.g., the practice of visualizing the decaying process of a corpse (MN I.58).

83 Bodhi 2011, 28.

84 Bodhi 2011, 30.

85 I have already suggested that the *jhānas* are not momentary attainments. This is clear by the way these experiences are described: the practitioner enters and abides (*viharati*) in these attainments for a period of time. I have argued that this is one of their liberative strengths and benefits.

86 Bodhi 2011, 32.

87 Bodhi 2011, 32.

88 I would further suggest that the fulfilment of *sati* in the fourth *jhāna* means that the quality of *sampajāna* (which is present in the third *jhāna* but not mentioned in the fourth *jhāna*) is now intrinsic to *sati* as the aspect of knowing experience as it is. That is, the fulfilment of *sati* as a factor of awakening in the fourth *jhāna* might mean that *sati* does not refer only to the quality of presence of mind but also has a wisdom aspect in it: knowing the nature of each phenomenon.

89 E.g., SN IV.214–5. Note that some feelings (*vedanā*) originate from *kamma* but some feelings originate from different physical disorders, from change of climate, from careless behaviour and by assault. SN IV.230–1.

90 SN IV.204ff.
91 SN IV.208–9 and IV. 231.
92 E.g., SN IV.205, 208 and 209; MN I.303.
93 E.g., SN IV. 205 and 209
94 MN I.303–4. The *Pahāna Sutta* further states that the underlying tendency to ignorance should be abandoned in regard to neither painful nor pleasant feeling together with the underlying tendencies to lust and aversion. The reason given for this is that this is how a practitioner is called: 'one who sees rightly. He has cut off craving, severed the fetters, and by completely breaking through conceit, he has made an end to suffering.' SN IV.205: *acchecchi taṇhaṃ, vāvattayī. Saññojanaṃ sammāmānābhisamayā antamakāsi dukkhassāti.*
95 According to the instruction given in the *Salla Sutta*, a noble disciple feels painful feelings as like a dart but since he does not harbours aversion towards it: 'he feels (only) one feeling-a bodily one, not a mental one' (SN IV.209: *so ekaṃ vedanaṃ vediyati kāyikaṃ, na cetasikaṃ* and SN IV.206–7). Since he knows an escape other than sensual pleasures, a noble person does not harbour aversion towards painful feelings. I would suggest this means that one knows *jhānic* pleasure, which is not connected to sense pleasures; therefore the underlying tendency to desire does not underlie that.
96 SN IV.208: *so tāsaṃ vedanānaṃ samudayañca atthagamañca assādañca ādīnavañca nissaraṇañca yathābhūtaṃ nappajānāti. Tassa tāsaṃ vedanānaṃ samudayañca atthagamañca assādañca ādīnavañca nissaraṇañca yathābhūtaṃ appajānato yo adukkhamasukhāya vedanāya avijjānusayo so anuseti.* This is also stated in MN I.303, MN III.286 and SN IV.205.
97 The *Daṭṭhabba Sutta* instructs that one should see the painful ones as like a dart, the pleasant ones as painful and neither-painful-nor-pleasant feeling as impermanent (SN IV.207).
98 SN IV.205.
99 MN I.303.
100 See, for example, SN IV.214–5.
101 E.g., MN III.286–7.
102 E.g., Sn 14 and 369; MN I.47; MN I.109–110.
103 MN I.303–4.
104 See SN IV.232, where *domanassa* is classified as an *indriya* under the category of *vedanā.*
105 MN I.304.
106 This is clearly stated in MN I.303, and I would argue that this is implied in SN IV.208–9.
107 SN IV.209.
108 It should be clear that I am not suggesting that the latent tendencies are rooted completely in the *jhānas* but that during the experience of the *jhānas*, these latent tendencies do not underly these particulat moments of experience.
109 We should bear in mind that *paññā* is also a conditioned and impermanent *dhamma.*
110 SN IV.207: *adukkhamasukhā vedanā aniccato diṭṭhā hoti.*

7 Morality (*sīla*), Wisdom (*paññā*) and the Attainment of the *Jhānas*

> In this way Ānanda, it may be understood how this is a designation for this Noble Eightfold Path: 'the divine vehicle' . . . :
>
> Its qualities of trust and wisdom
> are always yoked evenly together.
> Conscience is its pole, mind its yoke-tie,
> Mindfulness the watchful charioteer.
> The chariot's ornament is virtue,
> Its axle is *jhāna*, energy its wheels;
> Equanimity keeps the burden balanced,
> Desirelessnsess serves as upholstery.[1]

In the course of this study I made the point that, if one reads the Nikāyas closely, some key terms such as *jhāna*, *ekodibhāvaṃ*, *viveka* and *samādhi* might have different meanings than the way they are conceptualized traditionally. We have seen evidence for this in each chapter and in reference to other terms as well. This observation has led me not only to rethink the interrelation between these qualities (and the whole *jhānic* process) and other key terms (and mental processes) in the Nikāyas' path-model, such as *satipaṭṭhāna, vipassanā* and *paññā*, but also to offer a new perspective on their nature and mutual dependency.

I have already discussed the reciprocity and essential connection between the attainment of the *jhānas* and the development of the seven factors of awakening, and the clear correlation between the *jhānas* and the gradual maturity of the practice of *satipaṭṭhāna* in the Nikāyas' teaching of meditation. In this chapter I wish to further emphasize the interrelation between the attainment of the *jhānas* and the development of *sīla*; I also wish to offer some reflections on the nature of 'wisdom' (*paññā*) in the Nikāyas' vision of spiritual liberation and its dependency on the attainment of the fourth *jhāna*. This will be anchored in the discussion on the problematic identification of *paññā* – as liberating insight – with the understanding of the Four Noble Truths.

In his conclusion to his monumental work *The Buddhist Path to Awakening*, Rupert Gethin points out that a path to awakening is a process of change and development. He observes that this process of transformation involves coming to know the relationship between unawakened mind and the awakened mind. This process postulates that some kinds of ordinary mind actively perpetuate the defilements; at the same time, it postulates that other kinds of ordinary mind 'actually approximate rather closely to the waking mind itself'.[2] Following that, Gethin postulates that the task of the Buddhist spiritual path is to maximize these *kusala* or 'skilful' tendencies. He further observes that the Buddhist solution for maximizing these skilful tendencies is to practice calm (*samatha*) and concentration (*samādhi*). Stilling the mind, Gethin explains, allows the natural skilful tendencies to grow and strengthen; at the same time, the mind becomes clearer. In other words, Gethin concludes, one must cultivate the *jhānas*; it is in these states that the skilful tendencies – the *bodhi-pakkhiyā dhammā* – are fully activated.[3]

Gethin's conclusion has echoes in my analysis of the *jhānas* and in my suggestions regarding their transformative power. But there are differences. Gethin and other interpreters of the Nikāyas emphasize the calming and one-pointed concentration aspects of the *jhānas* and *samādhi* and argue as to what degree of concentration one needs for practicing *vipassanā* for the attainment of liberation.[4] In contrast, I have offered a different perspective on the *jhānas*, their phenomenology and their relation to the practice of *satipaṭṭhāna*. I have argued that the common interpretation of the *jhānas* as one-pointed absorption, a narrow field of awareness, absorbed in a single object of meditation (possibly a synthetic one) seems to be misleading and even erroneous. I have demonstrated in the preceding chapters that the various descriptions of the *jhānas* and the combination of *jhānic* factors in each *jhāna*-state imply that *jhānic* mind is a broad field of awareness, observant of the changing phenomenal field. This observation was further established when we saw that the Nikāyas clearly correlate the gradual maturity of the practice of *satipaṭṭhāna* with the attainment of the *jhānas* and the establishment of *samādhi*.[5]

The premise that the *jhānas* can be practiced and attained separately from the development of *sīla* and the practice of *satipaṭṭhāna* has led to conclusions about the *jhānas*. Based on this premise, the *jhānas* are viewed as unnecessary for the attainment of liberation, as they have no real liberative value; as such, one can develop insight and attain *nibbāna* on the basis of lower levels of concentration (i.e., 'access concentration'). However, unlike the view that the Nikāyas present two distinct and even contradictory meditative procedures (i.e., *samatha* meditation and *vipassanā* meditation), I have attempted to demonstrate in the course of this study that the four *jhānas* should not be conceived as meditative techniques at all. They are not concentration exercises that one can choose to practice as a basis for insight meditation (and only if one wishes or is able to); rather, the four *jhānas* are the actualization and embodiment of insight practice.[6] In other words, the *jhānas* are not separated and distinguished from the practice of *satipaṭṭhāna*; they are the fruit of this type of *bhāvanā*, which includes not only calming the mind but also insight into the nature of experience. I have argued that the fourfold *jhāna* model exemplifies a gradual development of an awakened awareness of reality, showing how the *jhānic* process designates a gradual spiritual ascent in which each *jhāna* signifies a more clarified perception of experience. What I wish to argue further here is that the *jhānas* – particularly the fourth and final *jhāna* – exemplify the ideal mind, in the Nikāyas' theory of spiritual development. It expresses, I believe, what I will call 'wisdom-awareness'.[7]

I *Sīla* and the attainment of the *jhānas*

Before moving on to offer some reflections on the nature of wisdom (*paññā*) in the Nikāyas' vision of spiritual liberation and its relation to the attainment of the fourth *jhāna*, let me first discuss the interrelation between *sīla* and the attainment of the *jhānas*. The Nikāyas' theory of mental development associates the attainment of the *jhānas* not only with the practice of *satipaṭṭhāna* and the deepening of insight (*vipassanā*) but also with the cultivation and embodiment of *sīla*. That is, the *jhānas* in the Nikāyas' path theory are not some meditative states that can be attained independently from other path-factors. More importantly, the *jhānas* have an important and imperative liberative role in the path itself: by progressing through the *jhānas*, one gradually de-conditions the unwholesome tendencies, purifies the mind from unethical demeanour and fulfils those qualities that can awaken the mind. In other words, the *jhānas* actualize the aim of Buddhist practice, which includes both the development of morality and insight.

It can be argued that some 'altered states of consciousness' (or what some would call mystical experiences) are not necessarily dependent upon the development of morality. However, I believe that the *jhānas* cannot be reckoned as such states in the Nikāyas' vision of inner cultivation. It seems that for the Nikāyas, the attainment of the *jhānas* is not separated from the ethical dimension of the path. I have already showed that the Nikāyas do not make any references to attaining the *jhānas* as a result of merely practicing concentration techniques on some 'neutral' object of meditation such as the *kaṣinas*. If we recall our discussion on one of the most recurrent path structures in the Nikāyas, it is obvious that the attainment of the *jhānas* occurs only after one has developed ethical behaviour, abandoned unwholesome states and possessed certain wholesome qualities. The *jhānas*, so it seems, cannot be attained without possessing those qualities that constitute the Buddhist spiritual path: noble virtue (*sīla*), noble restraint of the faculties, noble mindfulness and full knowing.[8] Only then, the hindrances (which obstruct wisdom and might cause one to act unethically in body, speech and mind) are abandoned,[9] and one can enter into the first *jhāna*. Hence, the first *jhāna*, I have already argued, is attained by releasing and letting go of the foothold of an unwholesome mind. What I wish to emphasize further here is that the *jhānas* (all four of them) exemplify an ethical mind.

The *Pāsādika Sutta* gives a clear indication of the close relationship and dependency between the attainment of the *jhānas* and ethical development. The sutta classifies two different kinds of life devoted to pleasure, positioning them in opposition.

The first is 'low, vulgar, worldly, ignoble and not conducive to welfare . . . not leading to *nibbāna*',[10] while the second kind is entirely conducive to *nibbāna*.[11] The former is pleasure and delight arising from killing living beings, in taking that which is not given, in telling lies and in the pleasures of the five senses.[12] These four types of behaviour are associated with unethical ways of life and are not what the followers of the Buddha are devoted to. However, the four kinds of life devoted to pleasure that the followers of the Buddha are devoted to are the four *jhānas* 'which are entirely conducive to disenchantment, to dispassion, to cessation, to tranquilly, to realization, to awakening, to *nibbāna*'.[13] Positioning the two kinds of life devoted to pleasure as opposing directions expresses, I believe, something important about the *jhānas*: they are closely linked with and dependent upon moral prerequisites. If killing, taking that which is not given, telling lies and delighting in the pleasures of the five senses are morally problematic (the latter in the sense of not being conducive to the cessation of *dukkha*), the four *jhānas*, on the other hand, are ethical states of mind that are entirely conducive to the elimination of suffering (in oneself and others) and the attainment of awakening.[14]

This close connection between the attainment of the *jhānas* and the cultivation of ethical intentions is evident when we read the *Samaṇamaṇḍikā Sutta*. In this sutta, the Buddha explains 'where' and 'when' unwholesome and unskilful intentions (*akusala-saṅkappā*) such as the intention to delight in sensual pleasures, the intention of ill will and the intention of cruelty cease without a trace. He explains that

> [S]eparated from the desire for sensual pleasures, separated from [other] unwholesome states, a bhikkhu enters upon and abides in the first *jhāna* . . . It is here that unwholesome intentions cease without a remainder.[15]

Here we find the notion that the attainment of the first *jhāna* is closely associated with perfecting ethical intentions. The sutta associates an ethical mind – the progression in the development of thoroughgoing and profound ethical attitudes – with the attainment of the first *jhāna*. According to the *Samaṇamaṇḍikā Sutta*, the first *jhāna* is 'where' one abandons unethical intentions and perceptions; this abandonment, therefore, allows wholesome intentions (*kusalasaṅkappā*) to be fully realized.[16] In other words, in the first *jhāna* one has actually fulfilled 'right intention' (*sammā saṅkappa*) – the second factor in the Eightfold Path.

However, what is even more interesting is the Buddha's statement that these wholesome intentions cease when one progresses further and enters into the second *jhāna*.[17] This is an odd and engrossing statement: why must these wholesome intentions cease after they have arisen? Is it not the aim of the Buddhist path to cultivate exactly this wholesome mind-set?[18] An answer to this question is actually given a few passages before in the same sutta when the Buddha explains why wholesome habits (*sīlā*) also cease without a remainder when one progresses in the spiritual path. He explains that the cessation of wholesome *sīla* means that 'a bhikkhu is virtuous, but he does not identify with his virtue'.[19] This is an enlightening explanation. It lends insight into the nature of an awakened mind that has fulfilled wholesomeness. As I understand this statement, it does not imply that one lacks moral habits and wholesome intentions when one has finally developed these qualities by practicing the path; rather, it wishes to emphasize that, in more advanced stages of the spiritual path, one transcends the dualistic structure of grasping intentionality in which one identifies with wholesome habits and qualities of mind. What this answer is pointing at is that the perfection of *sīla* means that one actually embodies these qualities without considering them as 'I' or 'mine'. One's mode of being is completely wholesome, free from any grasping relations even to wholesome habits and intentions: one is a *sīlavā*; that is, one is not one who consists of *sīla* (*no ca sīlamayo*). I would suggest that this non-dual ethical mode of being is experienced in the attainment of the second, third and fourth *jhānas*, while finding completion and immovability in the attainment of awakening.

II The nature of the fourth *jhāna* and its liberative importance

Let me take a sidetrack for a moment to offer some further reflections and remarks that might illuminate to a greater degree the nature of the fourth *jhāna* and its liberative importance. This will serve as a foundation for discussing the nature of wisdom (*paññā*) and its relation to this attainment.

In her interesting PhD dissertation on 'Vipassanā Meditation and the Microsociology of Experience', Michal Pagis observes that although all self-cultivating practices are based on theories, general knowledge and rules, their main aim is to enter a mode of experience that is non-verbal and non-discursive. Pagis makes this further observation: she acknowledges that this process of cultivation starts in cultural and social setting and in rigorous process of training anchored in abstract rule and guidance of a specific discourse (as, for example, the teaching on the Four Noble Truths and dependent origination).[20] She then observes that real change – the remodelling of the way we experience life – occurs not in processes that are anchored in abstract thought[21] but in embodied feeling.[22] Pagis has further suggested that self-cultivation is 'a process based on new forms of interaction with the world, forms that de-stabilize the consistency given to the self and allow for self-transformation'.[23] She uses the idea of 'firstness' – of the American philosopher Charles Sanders Peirce – to explain this notion and to emphasize the important role of this phenomenological category for inner transformation.

For Peirce, 'firstness' 'is the felt quality in *toto*: present, immediate, uncategorized, pre-reflective, the manifold of sensuous impressions before thought'.[24] Following this portrayal, Pagis has observed that

> [T]aken to the extreme, self-cultivation requires a temporal return to 'firstness', to a mode of freshness, life, freedom. The free is that which has not another behind it, determining its actions.[25]

It seems to me that this depiction highlights a meaningful aspect of the fourth-*jhāna* phenomenology and liberative value. I would suggest that the fourth *jhāna* can be reckoned as a temporal return to firstness: a post-conceptual state,[26] free from conceptual overlays and mental and physical unwholesome habitual propensities. As we have seen in the previous chapter, the fourth *jhāna* can be characterized as complete openness to the influx of experience, free from grasping and any type of reactivity (mental or physical, latent or obvious). I have showed that in the fourth *jhāna*, the manifold of sensuous impressions is perceived by non-reactive (*upekkhā*) lucid and vivid awareness (*sati*), free from any hindrances and mental faculties that obstruct a clear perception of phenomena. This, it would seem to me, can be identified with Peirce's idea of temporal return to firstness: a return to a different mode of being in the world, not contingent upon erroneous perception and grasping intentionality, but as the *Poṭṭhapāda Sutta* states, on 'true and subtle' perception (*sukhumasaccasaññī*).[27]

More explicitly, the type of perception (*saññā*) that is present in the fourth *jhāna* recognizes the manifold sense experience but in a very different way than ordinary conceptual thought does. In Buddhist psychology conceptual thought is linked with 'conceiving' (*maññati*) – a mental process that interprets experience from erroneous perspectives, particularly from the perspective of an enduring self. I would suggest that the fourth *jhāna* marks the realization and actualization of a mind that knows directly *aniccā* and *anattā* with regard to all phenomena (forms, sounds, odours, flavours etc.).[28] In the fourth *jhāna* one enters a mode of experience that is free from the standpoint of an 'I'; it is free from 'conceiving' (*maññati*).

III The fourth-*jhāna* as a non-dual experience

I have so far tried to show that the fourth *jhāna* is a mode of awareness where there is no mental gap in which the experiential act (i.e., seeing, hearing etc.) is ascribed to a subjective 'I' by conceptual and affective overlays. What I wish to argue here is that the fourth-*jhāna*-mode-of-awareness is a specific instance of non-dual experience. Yet, it is important to recognize that this type of non-duality as observed by Olendzki has nothing to do with the relationship between consciousness (as a subject) and the object cognized by it, but it is 'only about the object and the illusory sense of being a person who stands in relation to it'. Although Olendzki does not discuss the *jhānic* experience, I believe that his analysis will give us an interesting perspective with which we can understand the phenomenology of the fourth *jhāna*. According to Olendzki the 'subject' in this duality is

> [T]he point where desire is generated towards the object of experience. By liking or not liking the object, a subject who likes or does not like the object is created. It is craving, manifesting as clinging, that leads to the becoming of a self (*attā-bhāva*), and it is only when one has becomes a self, a subject, there can then also be suffering.[29]

I would suggest that the type of non-dual experience portrayed by Olendzki is actually experienced in the fourth *jhāna* (and permanently, I might hypothesize, by an awakened person). This seems a plausible interpretation following the analysis I have offered of the *jhānic* process and the phenomenology of fourth *jhāna*. We have seen that in the fourth *jhāna* there is no construction of a self; there is no movement of likes and dislikes which concoct a sense of self. The analysis of the fourth *jhāna* showed, that in this attainment, one is free from grasping intentionality, as it is the apogee of a spiritual process in which the mind has been clarified and purified from desire, aversion and ignorance and from conceptual and affective overlays that distorted our perception. Furthermore, I have demonstrated that attaining this state means that one does not recondition the unwholesome latent tendencies (*anusaya*). Although technically it is a conditioned state, it is not subject to conditioning in the normal way. This implies that consciousness (*viññāṇa*) of the fourth *jhāna* is not shaped by conditioned psychological setting or conceptual structures. It can be described as liberated (*vimuttaṃ*) even if this event is conditioned and not permanent.[30] We might also speculate, following the later suggestion that the fourth *jhāna* anticipates, for an unawakened practitioner, the awakened cognition described in AN II.25:

> Thus, monks, the Tathāgata is a seer, but when he sees, he does not conceive regarding the seen. He does not conceive about the 'unseen'. He does not conceive about what 'to-be-seen'. He does not conceive about a seer. When hearing, he does not conceive regarding the heard. He does not conceive about the 'unheard'. He does not conceive about what 'to-be-heard'. He does not conceive about a hearer. When sensing, he does not conceive regarding the sensed. He does not conceive about the 'unsensed'. He does not conceive about what 'to-be-sensed'. He does not conceive about one who senses. When cognizing, he does not conceive regarding what is cognized. He does not conceive about the 'un-cognized'. He does not conceive about what 'to-be-cognized'. He does not conceive of one who cognizes. Thus, monks, the Tathāgata, being such like with regard to all phenomena that can be seen, heard, sensed and cognized is 'Such'. And I tell you: There's no other 'Such' greater or more sublime.[31]

IV 'Liberating insight' (*paññā*) and the fourth *jhāna*

Following the preceding, I wish to offer two related arguments about the nature of wisdom or 'liberating insight' (*paññā*) in the Nikāyas' vision of liberation, and its interrelation with and mutual dependency on the attainment of the fourth *jhāna*. First, I wish to argue that for the Nikāyas the mind becomes purified and free not through specific cognitive content but through a gradual replacement of unwholesome (*akusala*) mind-moments by wholesome (*kusala*) ones. This purification of awareness arrives at an important moment in the attainment of the fourth *jhāna*. Second and related, I wish to further accentuate that the fourth *jhāna* – as a purified and ideal mind – should be recognized as 'wisdom-awareness': a specialized form of awareness that resembles and anticipates an awakened awareness.[32]

Having said that, let me start from the first issue. The mind is a stream of moments of consciousness that exists in dependency on the momentary existence of an object of consciousness. However, what I wish to argue is that the purification of mind, meaning the grounding of a clarified perception of experience, does not rely on certain objects or content of mind. Purification of mind in the Nikāyas' model of a spiritual cultivation concerns the gradual replacement of unwholesome (*akusala*) mind-moments by wholesome (*kusala*) ones. This is how an ordinary mind is transformed into an awakened awareness:[33] one will become awakened when one will cultivate and develop dependently arising wholesome (*kusala*) qualities that replace the unwholesome ones. An example of such a wholesome dependently arising process leading to liberation is expressed in the *Upanisā Sutta*:

> Thus, bhikkhus, with trust as proximate cause, gladness; with gladness as proximate cause, happiness; with happiness as proximate cause, tranquility; with tranquility as proximate cause, pleasure; with pleasure as proximate cause, *samādhi*, with *samādhi* as proximate cause, seeing and knowing [things] as they are; with seeing and knowing [things] as they are as proximate cause, disenchantment; with disenchantment as proximate cause, dispassion; with dispassion as proximate cause, liberation; with liberation as proximate cause, the knowledge of destruction.[34]

Though slightly different from the process delineated in the fourfold *jhāna* model, this passage seems to reflect the same process of resetting the mind to wholesomeness. I suggest that the term *samādhi* in the preceding description from the *Upanisā Sutta* refers to *sammā-samādhi* – namely, the attainment of the fourth and final *jhāna*. In other words, when the fourth *jhāna* is established and one fulfils *sammā-samādhi* as a path-factor, one arouses a 'proximate cause' (*upanisā*) for 'seeing and knowing [experience] as it is' (*yathābhūtañāṇadassanaṃ*).

Furthermore, consider *sati* and *upekkhā*, which are the first and last awakening factors and are the two qualities that are present in full capacity in the fourth *jhāna*. The purification of these two factors seems to be the key qualities for awakening the mind. The centrality of these two mental factors is evidenced also in *Sutta Nipāta* 855, which describes the 'greatest man' (*uttamaṃ naraṃ*) as one who is always mindful and equanimous (*upekkhako sadā sato*). More importantly, according to this sutta, the fulfilment of these qualities means that one 'does not conceive (*maññate*) [of himself] as equal, superior or inferior and therefore there is no pride [in him]'.[35] That is to say, when one fulfils (or purifies) *sati* and *upekkhā*, one is free from self-reference and comparison attitudes; one is free from *māna*. In other words, one realizes *anattā* by actualizing a mode of being that is free from self-centredness.

What I am trying to illustrate is the following: if one cannot relate differently to experience, then it is not relevant to the path of liberation whether or not one understands impermanence (*aniccā*) and not-self (*anattā*) as the truth of how things are. If this understanding is not actualized and grounded as a mode of being, real transformation cannot occur. Not-clinging and not-identifying with impermanent and empty phenomena (the five aggregates)[36] is the final aim of the Buddhist path. And here, I believe, is the liberative role and value of the *jhānas*: the experience of the fourth *jhāna* is a way of being in the world of phenomena without clinging, rejecting or identifying with any experience, physical or mental. The fourth-*jhāna* experience is the actualization of *anattā*; therefore, it is the understanding of *aniccā* and *dukkha*.

V *Paññā* in the Theravāda tradition

At this point, I would like to turn the attention to the interpretation of *paññā* in the Theravāda tradition and to say a few words about the problems it evokes. According to the traditional Theravāda understanding, the term *paññā* refers to what the Buddha realized on the night of his awakening. This 'liberating insight' is seen as the understanding of the Four Noble Truths in one moment of mind.[37] However, some Buddhologists tend to agreed that the Four Truths were not among the earliest components of the Buddha's awakening. Although the first discourse the Buddha gave, the *Dhammacakkappavattana Sutta*, presents them, it seems probable that they were not part of the earliest form of this sutta.[38]

For example, Schmithausen argues that even though the fourfold insight into the *āsavas* and the realization of the Four Truths are both probably old and were incorporated into the text at the time of composition,[39] there are problems with this theory if 'we try to understand it as referring to a psychologically plausible process'.[40] According to Schmithausen, it is hardly conceivable that knowledge of the Four Truths would have a direct psychological effect in eradicating craving or the *āsavas*.[41] Instead, he suggests that insight into the Four Truths was considered as having an effect on the destruction of craving, possibly because of influences from Vedic beliefs in the magical powers of truth and knowledge.[42] In Schmithausen's view, passages in which the Four Truths lead to liberating insight are not 'the original account of enlightenment'.[43]

Bronkhorst offers an argument with the same line of thought. He argues that the description of liberation that depicts a realization of the Four Truths does not fit the description of the Four Truths with reference to the *āsavas* (the recognition of the *āsavas*, their origin, their cessation and the path leading to their cessation).[44] This is because 'the connection between their knowledge and the destruction of the intoxicants is not clear'.[45] He further suggests that the Four Truths were added later in order to explain Buddhist liberating insight (*paññā*/*prajñā*) to other traditions. Bronkhorst points out that while other *śramaṇas* acknowledged liberation in life when one realizes the nature of the self (*ātman*), the Buddhists did not;[46] therefore, the tradition inserted the Four Truths in place of the term *paññā* wherever possible in order to explain what is meant by liberating insight.[47] Following Schmithausen's line of reasoning, Bronkhorst has also argued that the destruction of the *āsavas* by *paññā* and the identification of *paññā* with the Four Truths cannot be reconciled;[48] he maintains that the Four Truths are actually useful knowledge for the Buddhist aspirant at the beginning of the path before he becomes liberated.[49] He suggests that *paññā* was not intended to refer to the Four Truths;[50] he also suggests that insight in the early Buddhist texts was not described in any explicit form[51] but was quite possibly 'unspecified and un-specifiable kind of insight'.[52] For Bronkhorst, *paññā* is insight into the attainment of the *jhānas* and its possibilities.[53]

Adding to both Bronkhorst and Schmithausen's hypothesis, in her study on the Four Truths in the Nikāyas and the Theravāda sources, Carol Anderson suggests that

> [T]he four noble truths were introduced into what became the canonical writing first in relation to attaining the *jhānic* states and to the eradication of the *āsavā,* and later in the context of the Buddha's biographies, such as the *Dhammacakkappavattana-sutta.*[54]

These studies all argue convincingly, I believe, that the identification of liberating insight (*paññā*) with the Four Truths is problematic.[55] It seems that the centrality of the Four Noble Truths in the Buddhist tradition and its identification with the content of mind at the moment of awakening was a later development;[56] yet, by 'later', I do not mean necessarily after the Buddha's death, but it might be so. As for why the Four Truths became synonymous with the content of mind at the moment of liberation and a sufficient knowledge for the attainment of *nibbāna* (meaning, one does not need to attain the *jhānas* at all), this might have been the outcome of two historical processes. First, as Bronkhorst has suggested, the Buddhist tradition has been influenced by mainstream meditation traditions in which liberation in life was always accompanied by an explicit 'liberating insight'.[57] Second, insight became specified as a specific content when Buddhist monasticisms became more scholastic and less meditative. This last argument is also raised by Alexander Wynne. Wynne argues that in the early period, before the first schism, there was a tendency towards intellectualism; this tendency led to theories such as the one in which the Four Noble Truths and the teaching of dependent origination are the content of liberating insight.[58]

Given the preceding, I think it is very plausible to argue that the Four Truths were added to various suttas after the description of the attainment of the four *jhānas* for various reasons. First, they were an attempt to explain what type of liberating insight (*paññā*) Buddhism advocates for delineating Buddhist philosophical identity. This might have been a way for certain elements in the monastic institution to respond to arguments against the efficacy of meditation alone for attaining liberation. Second, it might be the result of a gradual decline in the practice of meditation in Buddhist circles and the growth of intellectual tendencies. It seems plausible to postulate that the emphasis in the Theravāda tradition on theoretical learning led to the idea that knowledge of the Four Truths is liberating. Wisdom (*paññā*) was recognized as a certain discursive and conceptual knowledge rather than 'yogic insight' (a specific type of awareness, possibly the fourth-*jhāna*-awareness). This might have originated the idea that *paññā-vimutti* arahants 'includes those who attain Arahantship either as a dry insight meditator (*sukha-vipassaka*) or after emerging from one or another of the four *jhānas*'.[59]

In light of this, I wish to make the suggestion that for the Nikāyas *paññā*, in its deepest sense, relates to a different phenomenological category than a conceptual or discursive insight. In other words, the content of mind is irrelevant for the attainment of complete liberation; this is because what is truly significant is the mode of awareness, the mode of knowing.

VI Wisdom or insight in the Nikāyas

The previous discussion raises a few important questions: is there any cognitive content that can transform the mind? In other words, what kind of mental content can transform our misconception of reality and our superimposition of independent separateness onto the various aspects of our experience? How is it possible to transform ignorance-based cognitive and affective processes into a liberated mind, free from misconceptions, delusions, anxieties, fear, attachments, aversion, hatred and other states that cause disease and suffering? How can one deconstruct the sense of self without going beyond mental structures such as thinking and conceptualizing, which lie at the basis of this mental construction?

It is not possible to discuss these issues at length in the present study. However, I will tentatively argue that it is possible to grasp every type of cognitive content – even those that can be classed under the category of *paññā* in certain stages of the path (as for example the development of 'right view' (*sammā-diṭṭhi*) or the perception (*saññā*) of impermanence). That is, the content itself, which might be conducive at a certain point in the spiritual path as a catalyst for right action in body, speech and mind and to abandon the unwholesome, can also become the object of attachment. Therefore, what is actually liberating is not the content but the quality of awareness that perceives this content. That is, the content or object of mind has no particular significance for the cessation of *dukkha*. What is crucial is the quality of awareness, the mode of knowing any content or object.

This might be the reason why wisdom (*paññā*) and insight (*vipassanā*) are not usually specified in terms of a specific content. This might imply that what we call wisdom or insight in the Nikāyas' spiritual path is the actual ripening and fulfilment of certain wholesome qualities in the mind, qualities that enable one to see experience clearly, free from distorted perception and self-centred mental fabrications. It would seem that when the mind is fully impregnated by fully matured *sati* and *upekkhā*, as occurs in the fourth *jhāna*, one actualizes wisdom as 'wisdom-awareness'; this is a specialized form of awareness in which 'even though the object of awareness is something as ordinary as the sensation of breathing, the moment is profoundly transformative'.[60]

Interestingly, in the Abhidhamma system of thought, wisdom (*paññā*), as pointed out observantly by Andrew Olendzki, is impermanent and tenuous, arising from certain causes and conditions.[61] What is more, we all tend to experience such momentary moments of (conditioned) wisdom (just like we experience moments of equanimity, mindfulness and happiness). Yet the arising of these qualities in an ordinary mind can be described as brief glimpses.[62] These brief glimpses of a different way to relate to experience cannot transform the habitual reactivity of mind, uproot the sense of an enduring self or eradicate ingrained tendencies and perceptions that maintain ignorance, namely, the sense of permanency, of an 'I', of an observer. In other words, we all experience moments of deep equanimity and lucid awareness free from emotional overlays, namely, moments of clarity and non-clinging (moments unconditioned by desire, aversion and delusion); nevertheless, these are usually short mind-moments that arise and pass away quickly. These moments are not steady enough to transform the mind. In this regard, Olendzki's observation seems significant for understanding the phenomenology and liberative value of the fourth *jhāna*. He points out that

> [I]f the wholesome attention can be sustained moment after moment, the entire stream of consciousness becomes purified of its naturally-arising toxins and wholesome dispositions are reinforced while their unwholesome counterparts atrophy.[63]

In the discussion of the nature of the fourth *jhāna* in the previous chapter, it is clear that the fourth-*jhāna*-mode-of-awareness expresses a mind that does not grasp at anything, while rejecting nothing. That is, in the fourth *jhāna* one is free from clinging or identifying with impermanent and empty phenomena.[64] I have also argued that the power of the *jhānas* is found in their description as attainments in which one 'enters into and abides in' (*upasampajja viharati*). Abiding in such modes of awareness for a prolonged period of time explains, I believe, their efficacy: they are not momentary, but attainments through which one becomes deeply familiar and closely in touch with a different mode of knowing. In the fourth *jhāna*, one experiences, moment after moment, a lucid (*sati*) and non-reactive (*upekkhā*) awareness, not conditioned by desire, aversion and ignorance. Experiencing this specialized form of awareness means that one does not become entrenched in sense objects, in their attractiveness or unattractiveness. Instead, the mind sees phenomena as they are: changing and empty of inherent existence. The fourth *jhāna* should be recognized as the actualization of wisdom. Phenomenologically, in this attainment one abides in a mode of awareness that is free from the effort to have, to hold or reject.[65] In this mode of being, desire, aversion and delusion have no footing; this is because one has grounded *sati* and *upekkhā* as an 'awakening-*jhāna*-factor'. In the fourth *jhāna* one does not cling to anything in the world; there is no tending towards being or non-being.[66] When

> [O]ne does not think, and one does not plan, and one does not have an underlying tendencies [towards anything], no basis exist for the maintenance of consciousness . . . such is the cessation of this whole mass of suffering.[67]

What I am arguing is that by experiencing this mode of being, one actualizes and embodies wisdom (*paññā*) as a wise-awareness. Thus, I wish to suggest that for the Nikāyas, liberating insight (*paññā*) is not some 'knowledge of' or specific cognitive content; rather, it is a specific type of wholesome awareness that is radiant, lucid and non-reactive.

In the fourth *jhāna* one actualizes wisdom also in the sense of abandoning.[68] After all, the purpose of *paññā* – in Buddhist theory of liberation – is abandoning what causes *dukkha*. A passage from MN seems to express this idea and its purifying power:

> [I]f nothing is found there to delight in, welcome, and hold to, this is the end of the underlying tendency to lust, of the underlying tendency to aversion, of the underlying tendency to views, of the underlying tendency to doubt, of the underlying tendency to conceit, of the underlying tendency to desire for being, of the underlying tendency to ignorance; this is the end of resorting to rods and weapons, of quarrels, brawls, disputes, recrimination, malice, and false speech; here these evil unwholesome states cease without a remainder.[69]

To sum up, when one abides in the fourth *jhāna* for multiple mind-moments, wisdom (*paññā*), as a specific stance and attitude towards experience, becomes intimate and transformative and might finally purify the entire stream of consciousness of 'its naturally-arising toxins'. It might finally break ignorance completely and awaken the mind.

Notes

1 SN V.5–6: *Iminā kho etaṃ ānanda pariyāyena veditabbaṃ yathā imassetaṃ ariyassa aṭṭhaṅgikassa maggassa adhivacanaṃ brahmayānaṃ . . . yassa saddhā ca paññā ca – dhammā yuttā sadā dhuraṃ, hiri īsā mano yottaṃ – sati ārakkhasārathī. Ratho sīlaparikkhāro – jhānakkho cakkavīriyo, Upekhā dhurasamādhi – anicchā parivāraṇaṃ.*

2 Gethin 2001, 344.

3 Gethin 2001, 345. Gethin also observes that the *bojjhaṅga* list focuses on *bodhi* as a kind of *jhāna* (Ibid., 181).

4 Gethin 2001, 345.

5 See, for example, SN V.151–2.

6 At this point I wish to mention AN II.45, which talks of different results that develop out of *samādhi*. I wish to claim that all four possible outcomes seem to me as actually describing, in different ways, the deepening of insight and the attainment of liberation. I would say that the first one (*diṭṭhadhammasukhavihārāya*) describes the emotive and physical aspects of the four *jhānas*. This is connected to the development of insight (e.g., SN III.168–9) and is a description of a pleasant abiding in which the Buddha dwells (e.g., MN I.23, III.153). The second one (*ñāṇadassanapaṭilābhāya*) usually refers to the moment one attains one of the four paths (including Arahantship). Although it is not clear what exactly is attained in this second option. However, it is clear that because the sutta is using the terms *ñāṇa-dassana*, it refers to some kind of insight into the nature of experience. This is because the purification of *ñāṇa-dassana* is the aim of the path (e.g., MN I.150). The third one (*satisampajaññāya*) seems to refer, at least, to the third *jhāna*-awareness in which *upekkhā*, *sati* and *sampajāna* are fully expressed and, therefore, are ennobling (AN III.279). It states that in this *samādhi*, one understands the impermanent nature of feeling, perception and thoughts. Clearly, this *samādhi* is part of

insight practice. The fourth one (*āsavānaṃ khayāya*) clearly refers to complete liberation by understanding the nature of the five aggregates.

7 If by the practice of mindfulness, the practitioner re-educates the mind not to react instinctively out of greed, hatred and delusion, then the attainments of the *jhānas* take the practitioner to another level. The *akusala* states do not arise anymore; therefore, we can say that *dukkha* is absent (temporarily) (e.g., MN I 89–90).

8 E.g., MN I.181. See the full discussion of this path structure in chapter 2 on the first *jhāna*. See a similar view also in AN V.2–4.

9 For example, when the desire for sense pleasures or ill will is present in the mind (the first two hindrances), one can act in a way that can harm oneself and others.

10 DN III.130: *cattāro'me cunda sukhallikānuyogā hīnā gammā pothujjanikā anariyā anatthasaṃhitā na nibbidāya na virāgāya na nirodhāya na upasamāya na abhiññāya na sambodhāya na nibbānāya saṃvattanti.*

11 DN III.131.

12 Ibid.

13 DN III.131–2: *cattāro'me cunda sukhallikānuyogā ekantanibbidāya virāgāya nirodhāya upasamāya abhiññāya sambodhāya nibbānāya saṃvattanti. Katame cattāro? Idha cunda bhikkhu vivicceva . . . catutthaṃ jhānaṃ upasampajja viharati. ayaṃ catuttho sukhallikānuyogo.* The sutta further indicates that those who are given to these four forms of pleasure seeking can expect four benefits: the attainment of stream entry, once-returnership, non-returnership and arahantship by the destruction of the different fetters (DN III.132).

14 See also AN I.53.

15 MN II.27–8: *ime ca thapati, akusalasaṅkappā kuhiṃ aparisosā nirujjhanti: nirodhopi nesaṃ vutto. Idha thapati bhikkhū vivicceva kāmehī vivicca akusalehī dhammehī savitakkaṃ savicāraṃ vivekajaṃ pitisukhaṃ paṭhamaṃjhānaṃ upasampajja viharati. Etthete akusalasaṅkappā aparisesā nirujjhanti.*

16 These are the intention of renunciation (*nekkhamma-saṅkappo*), the intention of non-ill will (*abyāpāda-saṅkappo*) and the intention of non-cruelty (*avihiṃsā-saṅkappo*). E.g., MN II.28.

17 MN II.28.

18 Note that the Buddha points out that the practice of the path *is* for the cessation of wholesome intentions; this means that this is not some 'side effect' but part of the practice. MN II.28: *kathaṃ paṭipanno ca thapati, kusalānaṃ saṅkappānaṃ nirodhāya paṭipanno hoti.*

19 MN II.27: *ime ca thapati, kusalasīlā kuhiṃ aparisesā nirujjhanti: nirodhopi nesaṃ vutto, idha thapati, bhikkhu sīlavā hoti no ca sīlamayo.*

20 Pagis 2008, 60.

21 In contrast to Pagis, I believe abstract thought has an important place in Buddhist contemplative path. E.g., SN V.418.

22 Pagis 2008, 59–60. Her study aims at illustrating that *vipassanā* meditation focuses on the pre-verbal and non-conceptual forms of self-awareness, ones that resist articulation, contexts or causation (Ibid.).

23 Pagis 2008, 60.

24 Daniel 1984, 239.

25 Pagis 2008, 60–1. Pagis cites from Peirce 1965, 302.

26 I have taken the term 'post-conceptual' from Janet Gyatso, who has referred to this type of experience in her article 'Healing Burns with Fire: The Facilitation of Experience in Tibetan Buddhism'. In this article she has analyzed Tibetan treatment of meditative experiences. She has pointed out that although in many instances Tibetan commentators grant that 'meditative experience is framed and interpreted through conceptual categories, we cannot deny that these same commentators will still maintain that the final fruit is, nonetheless, a direct realization of a primordial reality'. What is interesting is her clarification that Tibetan commentators would grant 'various kinds of immediacy that

are projected at the end of these paths represent what we might call a "post-conceptual" immediacy rather than a pre-conceptual one. This is an immediacy or naturalness that is won, like the acquisition of bodily skills, through a process of habituation. It is the fruit of a course of training' (Gyatso 1999, 138–9).

27 See DN I.182–3 where the Buddha describes the nature of perception in the *jhānas* as 'true and subtle' (*sukhumasaccasaññī*). In other words, perception operates in the *jhānas* but conceptuality does not.

28 We can say that, in the fourth *jhāna*, subtle forms of perception operate since the defilements do not hinder seeing, hearing so on, and one has the perception of impermanence and not-self (*anicca-saññā, anattā-saññā*).

29 Olendzki 2011, 68.

30 An example of such mode of consciousness and its relation to the attainment of *nibbāna* appears in SN III.53–4 and in SN II.67. Note also that the term *vimutti* appears in different contexts in the Nikāyas and apparently signifies different spiritual achievements; some are permanent and 'unshakable' (*akuppā*) and some are temporary (*sāmayika*). See De Silva 1978, 120.

31 AN II.25: *Iti kho bhikkhave tathāgato daṭṭhā daṭṭhabbaṃ diṭṭhaṃ na maññati. Adiṭṭhaṃ na maññati. Daṭṭhabbaṃ na maññati. Daṭṭhāraṃ na maññati. Sutā sotabbaṃ sutaṃ na maññati. Asutaṃ na maññati. Sotabba na maññati. Sotāraṃ na maññati. Mutā motabbaṃ mutaṃ na maññati. Amutaṃ na maññati. Motabbaṃ na maññati. Motāraṃ na maññati. Viññātā viññātabbaṃ viññātaṃ na maññati. Aviññātaṃ na maññati. Viññātabbaṃ na maññati. Viññātāraṃ na maññati. Iti kho bhikkhave tathāgato diṭṭhasutamutaviññātabbesu dhammesu tādīyeva tādī. Tamhā ca pana tāditamhā añño tādī uttaritaro vā paṇītataro vā natthīti vadāmīti.*

32 Note that according to MN I.293, the purpose of *paññā* is not only special knowledge (*abhiññā*) and full knowledge (*pariññā*); most importantly, it is abandoning (*pahāna*) (the unwholesome).

33 E.g., SN IV.78.

34 SN II.31–2: *saddhūpanisaṃ pāmujjaṃ. Pāmujjūpanisā pīti. Pītūpanisā passaddhi. Passaddhūpanisaṃ sukhaṃ. Sukhūpaniso samādhi. Samādhūpanisaṃ yathābhūtañāṇa dassanaṃ. Yathābhūtañāṇadassanūpanisā nibbidā. Nibbidūpaniso virāgo. Virāgūpanisā vimutti. Vimuttupanisaṃ khaye ñāṇanti.* See also DN III.288.

35 Sn 855: *upekkhako sadā sato na loke maññate samaṃ, na visesī na nīceyyo, tassa no santi ussadā. Upekkhā*, as an important quality of a 'true brahmin', appears also in Sn 911–2.

36 If we look at the fourth *jhāna* from the perspective of the five aggregates, which are a way to describe the 'how' of experience, we can say that in the fourth *jhāna* the aggregate of consciousness (*viññāṇa*) is not shaped by a psychological setting or conceptual construction; this is because the latent and active aspects of ignorance are not present. We know that the aggregate of *viññāṇa* is operative from the simple fact that without contact with some objects of experience, one will not experience feelings (*vedanā*). Yet, in the fourth *jhāna* one feels neither-painful-not-pleasant feeling (*vedanā*); this means that there is a conscious experience. According to DN I.182–3, the perception (*saññā*) of the *jhāna* is 'subtle and true' (i.e., not coloured by unwholesome latent tendencies and not added by affective and cognitive overlays). As to the *saṅkhāra* aggregate, the associated mental factors present in the fourth *jhāna* are purified *upekkhā* and *sati*. While *saṅkhāra*s are that which shape the experience; we might say that the presence of purified *upekkhā* and *sati* in the fourth *jhāna* means that the experience has the least possibility of being fabricated.

37 Gethin 1998, 192. Gethin explains that the path-moment (*magga*) according to the Theravada sources, 'is understood as being immediately followed by a transcendent *jhāna* of similar qualities, this time termed 'fruit' (*phala*)' (Ibid.). Note that this model of the path is not evident in the Nikāyas. Vin I.11.1 suggests that the Four Noble Truths

are the content of the Buddha's liberating insight. Vin I.1.4 states that the doctrine of dependent origination was discovered soon after his awakening.

38 A full discussion of this issue appears in Anderson (2001, 15–21). See also Williams and Tribe, who point out the anomaly of the *Dhammacakkappavattana Sutta*; that is, this sutta does not mention the idea of *anattā*, which is considered to be the unique discovery of the Buddha at awakening (Williams and Tribe 2000, 57).

39 Schmithausen 1981, 206.

40 Schmithausen 1981, 207.

41 Schmithausen further maintains that in the first truth, the relation between the realization and the ending of craving is evident: the understanding that all existence is suffering can be understood as stopping all craving to such existence. However, the cessation of craving as a result of the understanding of the set of the four truths appears to be unnecessary for that purpose (Schmithausen 1981, 208). Schmithausen points out that insight into the *āsavas*, their origination, their cessation and the path leading to their cessation is incoherent. He explains that since *avijjā* seems to be the origin of the *āsavas* but, at the same time, it is also one of them (Schmithausen 1981, 205).

42 Schmithausen 1981, 211.

43 Schmithausen 1981, 205. See also Bronkhorst 1993, 103.

44 E.g., MN I.23; DN I. 83–4 AN I.165 etc.

45 Bronkhorst 1993, 104). See also Schmithausen's conclusion that this description is not the original account of awakening (Schmithausen 1981, 205).

46 Bronkhorst 1993, 99.

47 Bronkhorst 1993, 108. Schmithausen also points out that the association of *paññā* and the Four Truths indicates the motivation of the early Buddhists to find a psychologically plausible relation between the content of liberating insight and its effect (Schmithausen 1981, 214).

48 Bronkhorst 1993, 104.

49 Bronkhorst 1993, 104–5.

50 Bronkhorst 1993, 108. Bronkhorst also suggests that the Buddhist texts leave the possibility that originally, the liberating insight was not described in any explicit form (Bronkhorst 1993, 100). Alexander Wynne also concludes that 'we can discount the notion that the earliest conception of liberating insight was the insight into the Four Noble Truths.' He further states that 'the content of liberating insight in the earliest teaching is unclear' (Wynne 2007, 107).

51 Bronkhorst 1993, 100.

52 Bronkhorst 1993, 108.

53 Bronkhorst 1993, 108–9.

54 Anderson 2001, 148–9.

55 While I cannot argue the case fully here, I will also contend that the identification of *paññā* with understanding dependent origination is also problematic. There are at least three places in the Nikāyas that identify the understanding or dependent-origination – the understanding that 'whatever is subject to origination is all subject to cessation' (*yaṃ kiñci samudayadhammaṃ, sabbaṃ taṃ nirodhadhammaṃ*) – with the *dhamma-cakkhu* and the attainment of stream-enterer and *not* with the attainment of Arahantship. See, for example, SN IV.423, MN I.501 and AN IV.209–10. Note that Carol Anderson also points out that it is only once that the commentaries define the *dhamma-cakkhu*, as the elimination of the *āsavas*, meaning the attainment of Arahantship (Ps III 92 [on MN I.380]) (Anderson 2001, 149).

56 Both Schmithausen and Bronkhorst conclude that the four truths were not central in the earliest period of Buddhist teaching (Bronkhorst 1993, 107; Schmithausen 1981, 203). Carol Anderson, who studied the Four Truths in the Pāli Canon, suggests that 'the four noble truths are a vehicle for the establishment of the Buddha's teaching (*sāsana*) in the

cosmos – and they come to symbolize the moment of enlightenment that is possible for anyone who follows the Buddha's teachings'(Anderson 2001, 21).

57 Bronkhorst 1993, 111.

58 Wynne 2007, 125.

59 See, for example, DA II.511 and MA to MN I 477. Also, the notion that the first *jhāna* is a sufficient basis for the attainment of *nibbāna* appears, to the best of my knowledge, only in two places in the Nikāyas: in MN I.435 and in AN IV.423. In both suttas, the first *jhāna* (as the other three *jhānas*) is a basis for seeing (*samanupassati*) impermanence, suffering and not self with regard to the five aggregates. From this, it might be inferred that there is a possibility of achieving *nibbāna* on the basis of the first *jhāna* alone (or the second or third *jhānas*). However, although this option seems theoretically possible, since the first *jhāna* is a state in which one is detached from what obstructs clear seeing (i.e., the *nīvaraṇas*), I could not find a description in the Nikāyas where someone actually attained *nibbāna* by only gaining the first *jhāna*. Even more to the point, although the young Gotama attained the first *jhāna* while sitting under the cool shade of the rose-apple tree, this attainment was not sufficient for him to attain *nibbāna*, although it showed him the correct path – the path to complete awakening. A plausible interpretation of the description of the first *jhāna* as a point where one understands the impermanence of the five aggregates, might well be a description of eliminating *sakkāyadiṭṭhi* but not the elimination of *māna*, which seems to need the purification of *upekkhā* and *sati* (Sn 855); this occurs only in the attainment of the fourth and final *jhāna*. In this regard it is interesting to mention Khemaka's observation that he himself does not regard any of the five aggregates as 'I am', but there is still a residue of *māna* in him: the desire 'I am' and the underlying tendency 'I am' in connection to the five aggregates (*pañcasupādānakkhandhesu aṇusahagato 'asmi'ti māno 'asmi'ti chando 'asmi'ti anusayo asamūhato*). In other words, it is possible to eliminate this last defilement and become an arahant only when ignorance and the underlying tendency to ignorance are absent; this seems to occur in the fourth *jhāna*.

60 Olendzki 2011, 64.

61 Olendzki 2011, 65.

62 Olendzki 2011, 65.

63 Olendzki 2011, 65.

64 Note that my interpretation of the fourth *jhāna* experience is not 'mystical' in the sense of direct contact with ultimate reality or with reality beyond the perceived world. It is direct contact with reality as it is: the reality of the world of the sensed but free from craving, aversion, identification and ignorance.

65 This interpretation of the nature of awareness of the fourth *jhāna* finds resonance in the way the Dzogchen tradition describes natural awareness. In a paper presented in the 11th Annual Conference of Asian Studies in Israel, Eran Laish describes this mode of awareness in the writings of the Dzogchen teacher Longchen Rabjampa as 'essentially open and primordially pure from all conceptual designations and perceptual limitations it transcends the dualistic structure of grasping intentionality, in which a subject is directed toward an object which absorbs open awareness into a grasping relation' (Laish 2012, 3). According to Laish, in Dzogchen practice, one returns to this natural mode of being as an open space in which the expressions of the livelihood of awareness are spontaneously present. Such a return, Laish argues, 'is possible only through a radical shift of being, moving from the desiring and reactive fragmented subject to a receptive and spacious subjectivity which is given to itself immediately in its wholeness, both self and other, inner and outer alike' (Laish 2012, 10). Although Dzogchen language is quite different than that that of the Nikāyas, it seems to bear some resemblance to an awakened awareness and the way one can realize it.

66 MN III.244.

67 SN II.66: *no ceva ceteti, no ca pakappeti, no ca anuseti, ārammaṇametaṃ na hoti viññāṇassa ṭhitiyā . . . evametassa kevalassa dukkhakkhandhassa nirodho hotī'ti.*

68 Note that according to MN I.293, the purpose of *paññā* is not only special knowledge (*abhiññā*) and full knowledge (*pariññā*) but most importantly, abandoning (*pahāna*).

69 MN I 113: *ettha ce natthi abhinanditabbaṃ abhivaditabbaṃ ajjhosetabbaṃ, esevanto rāgānusayānaṃ esevanto paṭighānusayānaṃ. Esevanto diṭṭhānusayānaṃ. Esevanto vicikicchānusayānaṃ. Esevanto mānānusayānaṃ. Esevanto bhavarāgānusayānaṃ. Esevanto avijjānusayānaṃ. Esevanto daṇḍādānasatthādāna kalahaviggahavivāda tuvantuvampesuññamusāvādānaṃ. Etthete pāpakā akusalā dhammā aparisesā nirujjhantī 'ti.*

8 Reconsidering *Samatha-bhāvanā*, *Vipassanā-bhāvanā* and *Paññā-vimutti*

> In that case, Vaccha, develop further two qualities: serenity (*samatha*) and insight (*vipassanā*). When these two things are developed further, they will lead to the penetration of many elements.[1]

> And what, bhikkhus, is the path leading to the unconditioned? Serenity and insight: this is called the path leading to the unconditioned.[2]

In earlier chapters I mentioned the prevalent view of the *jhānas* as not liberative or distinctively Buddhist. This view is based on the premise that the *jhānas* are a borrowed element from Indian contemplative traditions, a meditative technique (*samatha-bhāvanā*) that yields various mystical experiences and spiritual powers, but which is not conducive (or necessary) to liberation. A common supposition, shared by Theravāda thinkers and most Buddhologists, is that the *jhānas* are diametrically opposed to the practice of *vipassanā* (*vipassanā-bhāvanā*). This supposition considers *vipassanā* as the only Buddhist innovation and therefore the only practice that brings about the attainment of awakening. Stuart Sarbacker defines this division in his book *Samādhi: The Numinous and the Cessative in Indo-Tibetan Yoga*:

> In samatha one is approximating the qualities of a divinity, the very basis of the idea of the numinous. In theory, through meditative powers, the yogin ascends the very divine hierarchy, gaining along the way numerous experiences and ultimately a range of powers of perception and action . . . In vipaśyanā, we have the understanding or wisdom . . . yielding the cessation of suffering and the state of nirvāṇa in all its ineffability.[3]

This idea is rooted in classical Buddhist phenomenology of meditation. However, an in-depth analysis of the *jhānas* in the Pāli Nikāyas shows there is a solid basis for arguing that the *jhānas* are essential for attaining liberation in the Nikāyas' theory of spiritual cultivation. The fourfold *jhāna* model cannot be found in any early non-Buddhist texts.[4] A phenomenological analysis of the fourfold *jhāna* model demonstrates that it embodies a distinct Buddhist view of mental cultivation; that is, by progressing through the *jhānas*, insight (*vipassanā*) becomes deeper and experience is perceived more and more clearly until an awakened awareness is anticipated by an unawakened practitioner.

In this chapter, I wish to discuss several issues that emerge from the arguments I have made in the course of this study. These issues can be formulated in several questions: can we consider the *arūpa samāpattis* to be a type of *jhāna*, as the later Buddhist tradition has maintained? That is, are both sets of attainments, namely, the *arūpa samāpattis* and the four *jhānas*, similar in nature? Second, can we find in the Pāli Nikāyas concrete references to the view that one can attain *nibbāna* without the attainment of the four *jhānas* (a common view in the various Buddhist traditions)? In other words, what is the relation between the attainment of the *jhānas* and the attainment of Arahantship as a *pannā-vimutti* ('liberated by wisdom')?

In discussing these questions, I shall argue three points. First, I argue that the four *jhānas* and the *arūpa samāpattis* should not be considered as part of the same meditational process. They are not similar in nature: while the *jhānas* exemplify a distinctly Buddhist view of mental cultivation (as the fruit of what we call 'insight practice'), the *arūpa samāpattis* do not – they are attained through some form of concentration exercise. Second and related, I will reason that the classical Buddhist division into the 'path of serenity' (*samatha bhāvana*) and the 'path of insight' (*vipassanā-bhāvanā*) is a later development that is not evident in the Pāli Nikāyas. This classical division seems to be the outcome of the misconceived idea that the *jhānas* and the *arūpa samāpattis* are part of the same meditation procedure. Third, we will see that the Nikāyas do not envision liberation without the attainment of the four *jhānas*. That is, while one can surely be liberated without attaining the four *arūpa samāpattis*, the Nikāyas do make it evident that one cannot become awakened without attaining the four *jhānas*. Put differently, we cannot find evidence in the Nikāyas to support the view that some *pannā-vimutti* arahants are liberated without attaining the complete set of the four *jhānas* as 'dry insight' (*sukkha-vipassaka*) arahants.[5]

I The *jhānas* and the *arūpa samāpattis*

The interpretation of the *jhānas* as uniquely Buddhist and essential to the attainment of awakening – the interpretation offered in this book – stands in opposition to the traditional Buddhist view that associates the four *jhānas* with the four *arūpa samāpattis*. In classical Buddhist meditation theory, the four *arūpa samāpattis* are usually seen as following the process of meditation that starts with the four *jhānas*; as a result, the *jhānas* are regarded as attainments one must pass through on the way to the 'formless attainments' (*arūpa samāpattis*).[6] This view is based on the assumption that the *jhānas* are similar in nature to the *arūpa samāpattis*, where the only difference between the two is the intensity of concentration and abstraction attained. Linking the two sets of attainments into one process of meditation seems to be the main reason why the *arūpa samāpatti* are called *arūpa jhānas* in Buddhist commentarial literature. Indeed, this designation is maintained today by Buddhist meditation teachers and scholars.[7] Nevertheless, to the best of my knowledge, this designation does not appear even once in the Nikāyas.

Since the *jhānas* and the *arūpa samāpattis* are set up in classical Buddhist meditation theory as one process, they are considered as belonging to the same 'meditation vehicle' called *samatha-yāna*. This is a meditative technique that aims at increased mental absorption and quietude of all mental events by means of maximal one-pointed concentrated absorption.[8] For the Theravāda tradition, both sets of attainments are designated as 'absorption *samādhi*' (*appaṇā samādhi*),[9] given that one is completely absorbed in one object of meditation (usually the *kaṣina* but not exclusively)[10] and disconnected from sense experience.[11] Winston King has provided a clear statement about the two sets that recapitulates the traditional Theravāda view:

> The *jhānas* and the formless (immaterial) states . . . refer specifically to those meditative states most radically separated from ordinary consciousness by their deep inward abstraction from outer stimuli . . . the viewpoint adopted here is that the jhānic series of meditative attainments represent the Indian yogic heritage taken over and adapted by Buddhism . . . Indeed, 'jhānic' as a characterization adjective applies equally well to the four jhānas *and* to the four immaterial states.[12]

However, just from reading the formulaic description of the *jhānas* and the *arūpa samāpattis*, one can see a clear difference between the two. As I see this, the formulaic description of the four *jhānas* points at the quality of awareness and the feeling tone (*vedanā*) of each *jhāna* experience; moreover, this is done without referring to a specific content or object of mind. In contrast, the formulaic descriptions of the four *arūpa samāpattis* describe a specific mental content and object of perception. This is evident by the fact that each one of the 'formless attainments' is called by the name of its objective sphere: the 'sphere of Infinite Space' (*ākāsānañcāyatana*), the 'sphere of Infinite Consciousness' (*viññāṇañcāyatana*), the 'sphere of nothingness' (*ākiñcaññāyatana*) and the sphere of 'neither-perception-nor-non-perception' (*nevasaññānāsaññāyatana*). What is more, there is no indication in the Nikāyas either that one is cut off from sense stimuli while abiding in the four *jhānas*, or that one attains the *jhānas* by fixing the mind on an unchanging object of awareness; nevertheless, there is clear evidence in the Nikāyas that for attaining the *arūpa samāpattis* the meditator must transcend all perception of form and diversity of sense contact. The *arūpa samāpattis* are said to be based on unity of perception, meaning the mind is fixed on single unchanging object of consciousness while being disconnected from sense experience.[13] Hence, in contrast to the process of the four *jhānas*, the process expressed by the four *arūpa samāpattis* is one in which the meditator is detached from external stimuli, and constructs an experience that has a specific abstract content. Sarbacker offers a keen observation of these attainments; he notes that in this meditative practice the meditator suppresses the content of consciousness in order to concentrate on a particular object.[14] He further adds that in this practice, the meditator 'brings stability due to its condensing and habitual formation of energy'.[15]

Given the obvious dissimilarities between the formulaic descriptions of the four *jhānas* and the four formless attainments, and the fact that the Nikāyas never name the latter as *jhānas*, the question that needs addressing is why the tradition has associated – and continues to associate – the two sets of attainments by considering them both as part of the same meditation system? This question is especially intriguing when we acknowledge that the fourfold *jhāna* model is described in the Nikāyas as the unique discovery (and teaching) of the Buddha, while the last two *arūpa samāpattis* are clearly depicted as attainments Gotama learned from other teachers before his awakening.

I think that the main reason for the problematic association of the *jhānas* with the *arūpa samāpattis* is due to the fact that some suttas describe the attainment of the four *arūpa samāpattis* immediately after the four *jhānas*.[16] Importantly, this does not necessarily mean that the two sets of attainments have a similar nature. However, I would suggest that for Buddhaghosa, and subsequent generations of Buddhist thinkers and meditation teachers, this implied that the *arūpa samāpattis* and the *jhānas* do in fact have similar natures and are part of the same meditation process. Consequently, since the last two *arūpa samāpattis* were taught to Gotama before his awakening by other teachers, the association of the *arūpa samāpattis* with the *jhānas* led to the view that both sets of attainments originated from non-Buddhist meditative sources; hence, both are not really necessary for the attainment of *nibbāna*, the *summum bonum* of the Buddhist path. I would also postulate that the fact that, quite early in the history of the Theravāda tradition, the rigorous practice of meditation became primarily an ideal for most monastics contributed to this association. Since most Buddhist scholars did not practice meditation intensely (i.e., did not practice *satipaṭṭhānas* intensely), meditative attainments became mainly a matter of theoretical conceptualization. I will discuss this issue more at length later.

It is also important to bear in mind that although the *arūpa samāpattis* appear in various suttas after the four *jhānas*, the formless attainments also appear as part of a meditation model in which the four *jhānas* are absent completely. This meditative process is called 'the eight liberations' (*aṭṭha vimokkha*) and is described in many suttas:

> Ānanda, there are these eight liberations. What are they? Possessing form, one sees form. That is the first. Not perceiving material forms in oneself, one sees them outside. That is the second. Thinking: 'It is beautiful', one becomes intent on it. That is the third. By completely transcending all perception of matter . . . thinking: 'Space is infinite', one enters and abides in the sphere of Infinite Space. That is the fourth. By transcending the sphere of Infinite Space, thinking: 'consciousness is infinite', one enters and abides in the sphere of Infinite Consciousness. That is the fifth. By transcending the sphere of Infinite Consciousness, thinking: 'There is no thing', one enters and abides in the sphere of Nothingness. That is the sixth. By transcending the sphere of Nothingness, one reaches and abides in the sphere of Neither-Perception-Nor-Non-Perception. That is the seventh. By transcending the sphere of Neither

Perception-Nor-Non-Perception, one enters and abides in the Cessation of Perception and Feeling.[17] That is the eighth liberation.[18]

As we can see from this description, the four *arūpa samāpattis* are attained through a meditational process that does not involve the attainment of the four *jhānas*. That is, the account of the 'the eight liberations', affirms that one can attain the four formless attainments without going through the four *jhānas* at all.

A key difference in the representation of the four *jhānas* and the four formless attainments in the Nikāyas is self-evident, when we read the Buddha's own spiritual journey as depicted in the *Ariyapariyesanā Sutta*. This sutta tells us that Gotama attained the last two formless attainments before his awakening while practicing with two teachers, Āḷāra Kālāma and Uddaka Rāmaputta.[19] Āḷāra Kālāma taught Gotama the 'sphere of nothingness' (the third *arūpa samāpatti*);[20] Uddaka Rāmaputta taught him the sphere of 'neither-perception-nor-non-perception' (the fourth *arūpa samāpatti*).[21] What is of interest to our discussion is the obvious fact that there is no reference in the *Ariyapariyesanā Sutta* (or in any other sutta for that matter) that Gotama (or his teachers) attained the two higher 'formless states' by going through the four *jhānas*. It is not possible to determine what the specific practices were that Āḷāra Kālāma or Uddaka Rāmaputta taught the Bodhisatta. Nevertheless, it is plausible to presume that they did not achieve these attainments based on the four *jhānas*. This is evident from the simple fact that it is not mentioned in this sutta (or in other sutta);[22] moreover, the fourfold *jhāna* model appears in the Nikāyas as the unique discovery and teaching of the Buddha. Persuasive also is Wynne's argument that these two teachers taught early Brahminic goals[23] based on the practice of 'element meditation' and the *kaṣinas* practice.[24]

The different representation of the *jhānas* and the formless attainments is also seen in the Buddha's affirmation in the *Ariyapariyesanā Sutta* that the seventh and eighth formless attainments do not lead to *nibbāna*;[25] rather, they merely lead to reappearance in a corresponding cosmological realm, which implies that the other two formless attainments do not lead to *nibbāna* either.[26] This statement is in complete opposition to various declarations in the Nikāyas that the four *jhānas* are conducive to awakening.[27] The experience of the seventh and eighth formless attainments did not lead the Bodhisatta to *nibbāna*, although they did enable him to understand that these lofty states are not *nibbāna*, contrary to his two teachers, who presumably thought that these attainments constituted complete liberation. Nevertheless, his memory of spontaneously attaining the first *jhāna*, years before, had a crucial and transformative impact on his spiritual path and his understanding of what would lead him (and others) to complete freedom. After years of unfruitful practice, this particular memory steered him to the correct path to awakening; that is, it allowed him to attain the first *jhāna* again, and then, for the first time, the other three *jhānas* and finally *nibbāna*. This is depicted in a well-known story from the *Mahāsaccaka Sutta*.[28]

The last statement in the preceding description, combined with other statements in the Nikāyas about the conducive nature of the four *jhānas*,[29] indicates clearly the difference between the role and significance of the four *jhānas* in the Nikāyas' teaching compared to that of the four *arūpa samāpatti*. The latter 'do not lead to disenchantment, to dispassion, to cessation, to peace, to direct knowledge, to awakening, to *nibbāna*';[30] in contrast, the former do indeed 'slant, slope, and incline [the practitioner's mind] towards the [the attainment] of *nibbāna*'.[31] Most importantly, the four *jhānas* are delineated in the Nikāyas as the unique discovery of the Awakened One and as something taught only by him.[32] SN I.48 declares this very clearly:

> The one with great wisdom,
> have found an opening in the obstruction;
> The Buddha, the withdrawn, the bull among men, the sage,
> awakened to the *jhānas*' (*jhānambujjhā buddho*).[33]

Another interesting example of the different status of the four *jhānas* and the four *arūpa samāpattis* in the Nikāyas' teaching is seen in the *Anāthapiṇḍikovāda Sutta*. In this example, the *jhānas* are clearly distinguished from the *arūpa samāpattis* (and other experiences, ordinary or lofty). In this sutta, Sāriputta instructs Anāthapiṇḍika in the most profound teaching, the practice of non-clinging to any type of experience or attainment. In his instructions, Sāriputta lays out all the possible experiences and objects that one can cling to: sense organs, corresponding objects, six types of consciousness, six types of sense contact, six types of feelings, the five elements, the four *arūpa samāpattis* and so forth. Although Sāriputta mentions that one should train (*sikkhitabba*) not to cling (*na upādiyissāmi*) to any of the these, there are three things that are missing from his comprehensive list of objects of clinging: the four *jhānas*, the 'attainment of cessation' and *nibbāna*. This is interesting and illuminating. It seems to suggest that these three attainments can be the object of clinging when they arise as an idea in the mind; in spite of this, when one abides (*viharati*) in these states, they do not contain any type of clinging. In other words, one does not need to 'practice non-clinging' when one abides in these states, since clinging is completely absent. To put the matter a little differently, from this sutta we can surmise that the four *jhānas*, the attainment of cessation and certainly *nibbāna* are special attainments. That is, they are devoid of clinging by their nature; hence, they are very different from any other possible attainments and experiences that can be accompanied by clinging (*upādāna*).[34] The difference between the three, however, is that the first two are conditioned and impermanent while the latter is not. Yet, even though the four *jhānas* are conditioned and impermanent states, it does seem that both the *jhānas* and the attainment of cessation aid the process of de-conditioning the habitual tendency to cling to experience; they contribute to the cessation of *dukkha* – something that cannot be said about the attainment of the *arūpa samāpattis*.[35] What I am trying to suggest, then, is that one can cling to the memory of the *jhānas* (if the *jhānas* can be attained more than once before awakening) or to the idea of the *jhānas*, but one is free from clinging (and any other unwholesome states) while abiding in the these attainments.

These observations should be added to important historical studies that explore the origin of the *arūpa samāpattis* in the setting of early Indian contemplative traditions. Although these studies offer different suggestions, all agree that the *arūpa samāpattis*, in contrast to the four *jhānas*, are not originally or distinctively Buddhist.[36] Bronkhorst has suggested that the four formless attainments have similar features to Jain meditation. He observes that this list of meditational states agrees well with what he calls 'mainstream meditation', namely, a process which aims to stop mental activity. He distinguishes the *jhānas* from the *arūpa samāpattis* and argues that the formless attainments entered Buddhism from the Jain tradition or related circles.[37] Because they entered Buddhism from an outside tradition, they had to be integrated into the Buddhist canon; hence, they were placed on top of the four *jhānas* in the 'nine successive states' (*anupubbavihāra*).[38]

Alexander Wynne, however, offers a compelling and interesting argument that connects the formless attainments with *kaṣinas* practice and 'element meditation'.[39] He suggests that formless attainments were borrowed from early Brahminism[40] (not Jainism) as a form of meditation that aims to reverse the process of cosmic creation through inner concentration.[41] Wynne has also maintained that the four *jhānas* appear to be in accordance with the teaching of the Buddha; in particular, Wynne states that 'this scheme (i.e., the four *jhānas*) must go back in substance, and perhaps in word, to the Buddha.'[42] Tilmann Vetter, who also studied early Buddhist meditation, claims that the path of the four *jhānas* contains elements belonging to an early period;[43] Vetter maintains that the four *arūpa samāpattis* are more artificial forms of meditation that originated in non-Buddhist circles.[44] Vetter bases his argument upon Bronkhorst's article 'Dharma and Abhidharma', which shows that the four *arūpa samāpattis* do not appear in the oldest Abhidharma lists; these lists are older than the Abhidharma Piṭaka of the various schools and appear in the *suttas*.[45] In a more recent article, Daniel Stuart makes preliminary observations about the *jhānas* and the attainment of cessation from studying the *Pṛṣṭhapālasūtra* of the (Mūla-) Sarvāstivādin Dīrghāgama. He points out that in the *Pṛṣṭhapālasūtra*, the attainment of cessation is attained immediately after the four *dhyānas*; he concludes that, later on, the set of the four *arūpa samāpattis* separated the *jhānas* from the attainment of cessation. He makes this conclusion:

> The practice of the four *dhyānas* was one of the fundamental practices of the early tradition. Thus, the idea that liberation was attained directly from the fourth *dhyāna* is probably as old as the tradition itself.[46]

All this seems to imply that the association of the four *jhānas* with the formless attainments is questionable and even dubious; it might even be an artificial product. It is quite obvious that there was a way to attain the *arūpa samāpattis* without going through the four *jhānas*, and unlike the *jhānas*, the *arūpa samāpattis* have a non-Buddhist origin; moreover, they seem to reflect a different meditative direction.

At this point we can conclude that the association of the fourfold *jhāna* model with the *arūpa samāpattis* contributed to two related misconceptions: first is the interpretation of the *jhānas* as an inherently non-Buddhist meditative technique; second is the characterization of the *jhānas* as 'absorption concentration' (*appaṇā samādhi*) – meditative states disengaged from sense experience. What becomes clear, then, is that this problematic association is the source of the prevailing idea of the *jhānas* as not relevant to 'seeing [things] as they are' (*yathābhūta*). This conduced to their marginal role in later theories of meditation in the various Buddhist traditions, theories that viewed the *jhānas* (along with the *arūpa samāpattis*), as attainments not relevant to the process of releasing conditioned modes of perception.[47]

II *Samatha-bhāvanā* and *vipassanā-bhāvanā*

Losing sight of the inherent phenomenological difference between the *jhānas* and the *arūpa samāpattis* and their distinct representation in the Nikāyas, resulted, as we have seen above, in their being set up into one process of meditation called *samatha-yāna* or *samatha-bhāvanā*. This meditation process is seen in the Theravāda and other Buddhist traditions as a meditative path which is separated, and distinguished from, the practice of *satipaṭṭhāna*, which is called *vipassanā-bhāvanā* or *vipassanā-yāna*. This polarized model of the meditative path aroused tension over the manner in which the *jhānas* can be combined and integrated into the practice of *satipaṭṭhāna*. While there is unanimous agreement in Buddhist scholarship, and within the Buddhist tradition, that the *arūpa samāpattis* are not necessary for liberation, the issue of the four *jhānas* is much more challenging due to the simple fact that *sammā-samādhi*, one of the factors of the Eightfold Path, is another designation for the attainment of the four *jhānas*.[48] Hence, rendering the *jhānas* as similar in nature to the *arūpa samāpattis* engendered an obvious problem: how a meditative absorption in one object of awareness, absorption disconnected from experience, can be integrated with a meditative technique that aims at seeing (*vipassanā*) the true nature of phenomena? In other words, how can we integrate *sammā-samādhi* with *sammā-sati* if these two path-factors are seen as two different types of meditation techniques, directed to two different perceptual aims?

This problem has produced different responses from early times until today. It created various theories and a large amount of research, and it is evident that quite a few modern scholars have come up with the theory that there appear to be at least two paths to liberation in the Nikāyas. Some have argued that one path is more 'Buddhist' than the other,[49] while others have advocated that there are an old *jhāna* path, which was taught by the Buddha, and a new *jhāna* path, which is not the original teaching of the Buddha. Paul Griffiths for example has claimed that *samatha* meditation has a different aim from that of *vipassanā* meditation. According to Griffiths, the attempt to reconcile the two methods of meditation and to integrate them into a single process of liberation is especially difficult, since one is a meditative method of intense concentration, which leads to a total cessation of all physical and mental processes, while the other meditative method is an intellectual analysis, which leads to knowledge and to power over the world.[50]

Gimello has examined these two types of meditations through the types of 'obstacles' each of them removes. He has suggested that *samatha* meditation almost entirely removes obstacles such as anger, hate and desire, whereas *vipassanā* meditation removes the aforementioned obstacles as well as the intellectual obstacles – the misperceptions of self and reality. Nirvana, Gimello stated, is attained only when both kinds of obstacles are removed.[51] However he has also argued that

> [T]he transports of *samatha, dhyāna*, and *samādhi* serve primarily the purposes of immunizing the meditator against such disturbance (i.e. *agitation from within and distraction from without*) and of honing his faculties of attention . . . It is especially to be emphasized that *samādhi* and its associated experiences are not themselves revelatory of the truth of things, nor are they sufficient unto liberation from suffering.[52]

Another theory was presented by Schmithausen who has argued that there are two traditions in the Pāli Nikāyas: one which he calls the 'negative intellectualist'[53] and one which he describes as the 'positive mystical'[54] tradition. Schmithausen has separated the path into two 'currents' of liberation,[55] which correspond to La Vallée Poussin's division into the 'rationalist' conception of liberation and the 'mystic' one.[56] Tilmann Vetter has concluded that although the path to liberation in the Buddha's teaching was considered manifold, not all paths are from the same time or were preached by the Buddha. He has argued that the path of the four *jhānas* and the path of discriminating insight (without the attainment of the *jhānas*) both contain elements belonging to an early period,[57] while the path in which one progresses through the four *jhānas*, the four *arūpa samāpattis* and finally achieves the state of *saññāvedayitanirodha* was not taught by the Buddha, at least not in the early phase of his teaching career. He suggested that the *jhāna* path was probably too difficult for the Buddha's disciples, and hence afterwards, the Buddha introduced a simpler method, 'judging the constituents of the person as non-self'.[58] Stuart Sarbacker, in a more recent book, has suggested that although the two different types of meditation (i.e., *samatha* and *vipassanā*) are important and complementary, *samatha* is characterized by the development of what he calls 'numinous', while *vipassanā* is characterized by liberating drive.[59]

This debate is not confined to the academic study of Buddhist meditation. We have seen in the introduction that the Theravāda tradition has also tried to settle this dilemma by integrating the *jhānas* and the practice of insight into one process:[60] a gradual path of meditative practice, the aim of which is *nibbāna*. Yet, given that the *jhānas* were perceived as states of absorptions, which can be attained independently of the development of wisdom (*paññā*), the practice of *samatha* was regarded as optional and only preliminary to the practice of *vipassanā*. We have seen that according to Buddhaghosa some practitioners develop deep states of concentration, such as the *jhānas* and the *arūpa samāpattis*, and then embark into insight practice, while others develop only 'access concentration' (a level of concentration before the attainment of the first *jhāna*) which Buddhaghosa considered as sufficient for the practice of *vipassanā* and the attainment of *nibbāna*.[61]

For most contemporary Theravāda thinkers and meditation teachers (which mainly base their teaching on Buddhaghosa's *Visuddhimagga*),[62] the attainment of the various *jhānic* states (and for most Buddhist teachers, the *arūpa samāpattis* are a kind of *jhāna*)[63] are not necessary for liberation; they can be used as a basis for insight practice, but only if one wishes or is able to.[64] A clear statement that reflects the notion that the *jhānas* are preliminary to the practice of *vipassanā* was made by Pa-Auk Sayadaw one of the leading *jhāna* masters in present day Theravāda, in his book *Knowing and Seeing*:

> When a yogi has reached the fourth *jhāna* using *ānāpāna-sati*, and has developed the five masteries, the light of concentration is bright, brilliant and radiant, and he can, if he wishes, moves on to develop Vipassanā meditation. The yogi can, on the other hand, continue to develop Samatha meditation.[65]

Pa-Auk Sayadaw's explanation reflects the idea that the attainment of the four *jhānas* is separate from the development of insight (although the object of meditation might be the same) and preliminary to the practice of *vipassanā*. It illustrates the common hierarchal model of the path in which the *jhānas* can be attained separately from the practice of *satipaṭṭhānas* and prior to the establishing of wisdom.[66] Furthermore, Pa-Auk Sayadaw uses *ānāpāna-sati* in the practice of the *jhānas*, not for developing insight, but rather for developing concentration and absorption. That is, *ānāpāna-sati* can be used, as in Pa-Auk Sayadaw's system, as a basis for *samatha* meditation. In this regard it is interesting to bring Erik Braun's statement, in connection to Ledi Sayadaw's presentation of meditation (which is relevant to understanding Pa-Auk Sayadaw's system as well), that 'it is noteworthy that mindfulness, contrary to presentations by many later meditation teachers, is not a quality emphasized as more properly in the domain of insight practice. In fact, it also lays the basis for calming meditation.'[67]

As for Mahāsi Sayadaw, one of the most influential meditation teachers in the twentieth century, he has advocated that one does not need to attain the *jhānas* or 'access concentration' for attaining *nibbāna*, since 'momentary concentration' (*khaṇika-samādhi*) is sufficient.[68] This latter view was also presented by Buddhadāsa who stated that 'deep concentration (and he clearly refers here to the *jhānas*) is a major obstacle to insight practice. To practice introspection one must first return to the shallower level of concentration'[69] (i.e., momentary or access concentration). Ven. Sri Ñāṇārāma Matara, a respected meditation teacher from Sri Lanka, has also explained that momentary concentration has the same strength as access concentration and is enough for insight practice and for the attainment of Arahantship.[70]

All the different theories about the relationship between the practice of *samatha* and the practice of *vipassanā* assume the phenomenological sameness of the *jhānas* and the *arūpa samāpattis*. What is more significant is that the preceding views are all based on the assumption that, in the Pāli Nikāyas, the Buddha actually taught two distinct meditative procedures, namely, *samatha-bhāvanā* and *vipassanā-bhāvanā*. However, it should be clearly pointed out that the commonly used idioms *samatha-bhāvanā* and *vipassanā-bhāvanā* (which express this idea) cannot be found in the Nikāyas. Moreover, there is no clear correlation in the Nikāyas, to the best of my knowledge, between the term *samatha* and the attainment of the *jhānas* (or to the expression *sammā-samādhi*); at the same time, the term *vipassanā* is never defined as the practice of *satipaṭṭhāna* or associated with the term *sammā-sati*.[71] The word *vipassanā* does not even occur in the *Satipaṭṭhāna Sutta* or the *Mahāsatipaṭṭhāna Sutta*, the foundational texts for the 'practice of insight'. What we do find in the Nikāyas is the terms *samatha* and *vipassanā* but without the adjunct *bhāvanā*. Interestingly, the term *vipassanā*, which became synonymous in contemporary Theravāda with 'Buddhist practice', occurs in the Nikāyas less than the term *samatha*; moreover, when it does occur in the suttas, in most cases, it is part of the pair *samatha-vipassanā* and has no apparent spiritual or meditative precedence[72] over *samatha*.[73]

In light of all this, I wish to suggest that the meditation model that distinguishes between *samatha-bhāvanā* and *vipassanā-bhāvanā* has its roots in the Theravāda commentarial tradition, the Aṭṭhakathā, and not in the Nikāyas.[74] I would further propound, following Thanissaro Bhikkhu, that the terms *samatha* and *vipassanā* do not designate specific practices in the Nikāyas; rather, these are viewed as qualities of mind[75] fulfilled through the cultivation (*bhāvanā*) of the various path-factors, including *sammā-sati* and *sammā-samādhi*. In other words, the terms *samatha* and *vipassanā* should not be identified with *sammā-samādhi* and *sammā-sati*, respectively, but should be seen as terms designating a mind that fulfilled the whole Eightfold Path. Consequently, and following the analysis of the *jhānas* offered in this study, we might construe the attainment of the fourth *jhāna*, the apex of a gradual development of an awakened awareness of phenomena, as constituting the fulfilment of both *samatha* and *vipassanā*. These two qualities can be associated with the attainment of the fourth *jhāna*; this is because attaining this state means that one's mind is free from what obstructs clear seeing (*vipassanā*) and is completely peaceful and un-agitated (*samatha*) due to the absence of mental reactivity and any unwholesome mental states.

III *Paññā-vimutti*

I have already mentioned the traditional Theravāda idea that one can 'bypass' the attainment of the *jhānas* on the path to liberation.[76] In the Pāli commentaries, those who attain Arahantship without attaining the *jhānas* are called 'dry insight' arahants (*sukkha-vipassaka*). This type of arahant is classified under the category of 'liberated by wisdom' (*paññā-vimutti*).[77] The commentaries explain that *paññā-vimutti* arahants includes 'those who attain Arahantship either as a dry insight meditator or after emerging from one or another of the four *jhānas*'.[78]

It is obvious that the idea of dry insight arahants reflects the traditional conjecture that the *jhānas* can be attained without the practice of *satipaṭṭhāna* and the development of *paññā*; in contrast, *paññā*, a specific liberating knowledge, can be developed without the attainment of the *jhānas*. However, we have seen in the course of this study that this conjecture is problematic in light of a close analysis of the Nikāyas. Moreover, as we shall see, while the Nikāyas clearly present the option that one can be liberated without attaining the *arūpa samāpattis* (and the attainment of cessation), there is no support for the idea that some *paññā-vimutti* arahants attain *nibbāna* without entering and abiding in the four *jhānas*. Even the term *sukkha-vipassaka*, which describes this idea, cannot be found in the suttas; rather, it seems to emerge for the first time in the early Pāli commentaries.

Before discussing particular suttas that served as a foundation for the idea of *sukha-vipassaka*-arahants, a few words on the classification of liberated (*vimutti*) persons in the Nikāyas are in order. This is a complex issue. The term *vimutti*, which means 'liberation' or 'freedom', appears in different contexts and apparently signifies different spiritual achievements; some of these are temporary (*sāmāyikaṃ*), while others are permanent (*akuppā*).[79] This is also seen in the Nikāyas' system of categorization of spiritual achievements in which the term *vimutti* refers to those who are fully liberated as well as to persons who have 'still work to do'.[80] The *Kīṭāgiri Sutta* enumerates seven types of people in relation to spiritual progress: 'one liberated in both ways' (*ubhatobhāgavimutto*),[81] 'one liberated by wisdom' (*paññāvimutto*),[82] a 'body witness' (*kāyasakkhī*), 'one attained to view' (*diṭṭhappatto*), 'one liberated by faith' (*saddhāvimutto*), a Dhamma follower (*dhammānusārī*) and a 'faith follower' (*saddhānusārī*).[83] These definitions introduce important technical terminology[84] that should be subject to a deeper investigation elsewhere.[85] For our present inquiry, suffice it to say that *kāyasakkhi diṭṭhappatta* and *saddhāvimutti* may comprise the Noble Persons belonging to *sotāpatti*, *sakadāgāmin* and *anāgāmin*; in contrast, *saddhānusārī* (and according to De Silva also *dhammānusārī*) have not made any special spiritual progress.[86] Furthermore, it is obvious that the last five types of persons are not fully liberated and, therefore, still have work to do to attain complete liberation; in contrast, the first two types, the *ubhatobhāgavimutti arahants* and the *paññā-vimutti arahants*, are fully liberated, since their 'taints are completely destroyed by seeing with wisdom'.[87] For this study, only *paññā-vimutti* arahants are of interest; this is because the Theravāda tradition considers *ubhatobhāgavimutti arahants* as having attained the four *jhānas*, the *arūpa samāpattis* and the attainment of cessation.[88]

The origin of the idea that some *paññā-vimutti* arahants attain Arahantship as 'dry insight meditators' (*sukkha-vipassaka*), namely, without entering and abiding in the four *jhānas* is interesting; this is because there is no evidence for this in the Nikāya's delineation of *paññā-vimutti* arahants. The *Kīṭāgiri Sutta* explicates:

> What kind of person is a *paññā-vimutti*? Here, some person does not contact with the body and abide in those liberations that are peaceful and formless, transcending forms, but his taints are utterly destroyed by his seeing with wisdom.[89]

It is clear from this description that a *paññā-vimutti* arahant does not attain 'those liberations (*vimokkhā*) that are peaceful (*santā*) and formless (*āruppā*), transcending forms (*atikkamma rūpe*)' (i.e., the *arūpa samāpattis* and presumably the attainment of cessation),[90] yet there is no indication that this type of arahants does not attain the four *jhānas*. Similarly, this possibility does not appear in any way in the

Susīma Sutta,[91] which is also considered as presenting the idea that one can become an arahant without the attainments of the four *jhānas*.

The *Susīma Sutta* tells us the story of Susīma. Susīma is a wanderer who joined the Buddhist order after realizing that wanderers from other sects did not enjoy the honour and support the laity gave to followers of the Buddha. After ordination into the Buddha's *saṅgha*, he enquires about the spiritual attainments reached by a group of bhikkhus who have declared Arahantship. He asks them if they achieved five special powers (traditionally called 'higher knowledges' [*abhiññā*]): (1) the iddhis (*iddhi-vidha*), spiritual powers such as to walk through wall and so on; (2) the divine ear (*dibba-sota*); (3) the power to know other beings states of mind (*ceto-pariya-ñāṇa*); (4) the ability to recollect past lives (*pubbe-nivāsānussati*); and (5) the divine eye (*dibba-cakkhu*). The bhikkhus all reply that they do not possess any of the five *abhiññā*. Then Susīma inquires further:

> '[D]o you venerable ones abide in those liberation that are peaceful and formless, transcending forms, having touched them with the body?'
> *'No Friend.'*
> 'Here now, venerable ones: this answer and the non-attainment of those states, how could this be, friend?'
> *'We are liberated by wisdom (paññāvimuttā), friend Susīma.'*[92]

From the bhikkhus' answers, we learn that since they do not possess the five spiritual powers, or the 'formless (*āruppā*) liberations', they identify themselves as 'liberated by wisdom' (*paññāvimuttā*). In other words, they are arahants but not *ubhatobhāgavimutti* arahants. Interestingly, nothing is said about their attainment (or non-attainment) of the four *jhānas*. From this exchange, we can further learn that for Susīma, someone who was liberated must have obtained two apparently connected abilities: (1) various spiritual powers and (2) proficiency in attaining the 'formless liberations'. Since we know Susīma just joined the Buddhist *saṅgha* after being a wanderer for some time, his questions also suggest that these spiritual accomplishments were known to wanderers outside the Buddha's order. This seems to indicate that these attainments were acknowledged in the wanderer's milieu as an indication of complete freedom. What is surprising, however, is that Susīma does not ask the bhikkhus about their attainment of the four *jhānas*. Was it obvious to Susīma that the bhikkhus had attained these states, and therefore, he did not even think to ask them about them? I might hypothesize differently. I would suggest that something to do with Susīma's biography is the reason why he did not ask the bhikkhus about the *jhānas* – or, in other words, why the suttas do not mention such a question. As a newcomer to the Buddhist path, it is plausible to assume that he did not know the *jhānas*, which were the unique discovery of the Buddha,[93] just as Nigaṇṭha Nātaputa was astonished to hear from Citta the householder that there is a *samādhi* without thought and reflection (*atthi avitakko avicāro samādhi*) –[94] a characteristic of the second, third and fourth *jhānas*.

Although the *Susīma Sutta* says nothing about the attainment or non-attainment of the four *jhānas*, the Pāli commentaries interpreted the bhikkhus' answer to imply that one can become an arahant as a dry insight meditator; that is, without the *jhānas* (*nijjhānakā*).[95] This interpretation implies that the commentators identified the attainment of the five *abhiññās* with both the attainment of the *jhānas* and the formless liberations. This assumption is also seen in Nathan Katz's statement that 'we use the term *ubhatobhāgavimutti* to indicate the path that includes the useful but not essential practice of the *jhānas*, along with their resultant *abhiññā*'.[96] However, as Bhikkhu Bodhi has correctly observed in his notes to the *Susīma Sutta*,

> [W]hile Spk seems to be saying that those bhikkhus did not have any *jhāna*, the sutta itself establishes only that they lacked the *abhiññās* and the *āruppas*; nothing is said about whether or not they had achieved the four *jhānas*.[97]

Gombrich has also discussed this sutta in his book *How Buddhism Began*. He has argued that this sutta is an example of a redaction in the Pāli texts for depicting a positive picture of the monks who claimed to be liberated without any meditative accomplishments and the *abhiññā*.[98] Gombrich suggests that some suttas such as the *Susīma Sutta* should be seen as products of historical change in the perception of awakening.[99] By comparing the Chinese version of the *Susīma Sutta* with the Pāli version, Gombrich argues that the bhikkhus in the Pāli version are lying about their attainment of Arahantship.[100] According to Gombrich, the Chinese version describes the outcome of Susīma's cross examination as an exposure: the monk who claims that all of them are liberated is 'shown up: they cannot even claim that they are free of greed and hatred'.[101] According to Gombrich, the redactor of the Pāli texts wanted to change the uncomplimentary image of these monks, perhaps because the notion of *sukha-vipassaka* arahants became predominant in the Theravāda tradition. The redacted version therefore substituted what the monks had not achieved in the Chinese version with something less basic as the elimination of greed and hatred, something such as the five *abhiññā* that were regarded as unnecessary for the attainment of liberation. Gombrich posits that the lack of these powers might allow the assumption that the monks achieved liberation without having meditated.[102] He then argues that the 'redefinition of *paññā-vimutti* to exclude meditation has arisen not as the result of debate but rather as a kind of narrative accident due to saṅgha apologetics'.[103]

Gombrich's hypothesis might be correct but his conclusion misses an important point: both the *Susīma Sutta* and the *Kīṭāgiri Sutta* do not mention the possibility of becoming liberated without the four *jhānas*;[104] rather, they only mention the possibility of becoming an arahant without the formless liberations.[105] In other words, the *Susīma Sutta*, in the Pāli version, does not envision *paññā-vimutti* arahants as attaining liberation without the *jhānas*, namely, without proficiency in meditative attainments.[106]

Another sutta that has been interpreted as demonstrating the notion that one can be liberated without the *jhānas* is AN III.355–6.[107] This sutta has been seen as a text that adheres to the view that there are two valid paths to liberation: with the *jhānas* and without them.[108] AN III.355–6 describes two types of groups: 'those undertaking [the learning] of the Dhamma' (*dhamma-yoga*) and those 'who attained the *jhānas*' (*jhāyin*). The *jhāyins* are depicted as 'those who having touched with the body, abide in the deathless element';[109] in contrast, the *dhamma-yoga* bhikkhus are depicted as 'those who see, having penetrated with wisdom the deep way of the goal'.[110] It is important to note that even though AN III.355–6 uses the phrase *kāyena phūsitvā viharanti* with reference to the *jhāyins*, the 'thing' in which the *jhāyins* abide and have contact with the body is not the formless (*āruppā*) liberations (as stated with regard to *ubhatobhāgavimutta* arahants); rather, it is with the 'deathless element' (*amataṃ dhātuṃ*), namely, *nibbāna*. This is significant also because the attainment of the 'deathless' (*amata*) is associated specifically with the practice of *satipaṭṭhāna* rather than the attainment of the formless states.[111]

Having said that, I believe that Gombrich's suggestion that AN III.355–6 is a later addition to the *Sutta Piṭaka* is reasonable. The main reason for Gombrich's conclusion is the fact that AN III.355–6 has no Chinese parallel.[112] Although in most cases suggesting that a sutta is a later addition is the easiest solution to a problem, in this case, there are a few other factors that support this hypothesis and make this text somewhat extraneous to the Nikāyas. First, a search in the Nikāyas for the terms *dhamma-yoga* and its variations resulted in only one occurrence: AN III.355–6 – the sutta discussed earlier.[113] Further, the term *yoga* in the Pāli Nikāyas usually has a negative connotation, contrary to its use in later Buddhist texts. In the Nikāyas, the term *yoga* appears in two main negative contexts. First, it designates the four 'bonds': (1) the bond of sensuality (*kāmayogo*), (2) the bond of existence (*bhavayogo*), (3) the bond of view (*diṭṭhiyogo*) and (4) the bond of ignorance (*avijjāyogo*).[114] Second, in numerous instances *nibbāna* is referred to as 'peace from bondage' (*yoga-kkhema*).[115] Given all the preceding, it seems that Gombrich's suggestion that this sutta is a later addition is credible. This sutta actually presents a new development in the conception of the path, the idea that there are two valid paths to liberation: one which mainly constitutes learning of the Dhamma, and one which constitutes the intensive practice of meditation. Regarding the narrow interpretation of *paññā-vimutti* that is reflected in the distinction between the *dhammayogins* and the *jhāyin*, Gombrich has further concluded that it required 'a whole turnover of monastic personnel . . . a matter of at least two to three generations'.[116] Following that, it seems justified to argue that the idea of *sukkha-vipassaka* arahants developed after the origination of the early Buddhist schools and reflects later perceptions of the path to liberation as influenced by historical changes in the conditions of the Buddhist saṅgha in Sri Lanka.

The distinction between the 'meditators' and the 'Dhamma-preachers' is significant. Probably as early as the first century BCE, this distinction became predominant in the Theravāda tradition. As Walpola Rahula observes in his book *History of Buddhism in Ceylon*, by the first century BCE the Sri Lankan *saṅgha* had come to understand its calling as one of scriptural study rather than practice. Walpola explains that in the first century BCE there were radical changes in the life of the bhikkhus due to invasions and famine. After the famine, a conference was held at a monastery called Maṇḍalārāma in Kallagāma Janapada, and a new question was raised: what is the basis of the Sāsana – learning or practice?[117] While the Paṃsukūlikas ('those who wear only rag robes') advocated that practice is the basis of the Sāsana; in contrast, the Dhammakathikas ('preacher of the Dhamma') held that learning was the basis. According to Rahula, the 'Paṃsukūlikas were silenced and the Dhammakathikas were victorious'.[118] Rahula cites from the Anguttara Nikāya commentary, which states that 'even if there be a hundred or a thousand bhikkhus practising *vipassanā*, there will be no realization of the Noble path if there is no learning'.[119] This new conceptual formulation and interpretation of the Buddhist path inspired the development of two vocations in the Theravāda tradition: the *gantha-dhura* ('the burden of studying the texts') and *vipassanā-dhura* ('the burden of [practicing] insight [meditation])'.[120] The former denotes the learning of the Dhamma, while the latter refers to the meditators (i.e., the practitioners of meditation as taught in the *Satipaṭṭhāna Sutta*).[121] Rahula explains that

> [O]ut of the two vocations, *gantha-dhura* was regarded as more important than *vipassanā-dhura*. Examples found in the Commentaries show that almost all able and intelligent monks applied themselves to *gantha-dhura* while elderly monks of weak intellect and feeble physique, particularly those who entered the Order in their old age, devoted themselves to *vipassanā-dhura*.[122]

These observations about the nature of spiritual praxis in the early Theravāda community are supported by Reginald Ray in his book *Buddhist Saints in India*. Ray points out that, in the context of Theravāda monasticism, the practice of meditation was less common. According to Ray, the emphasis was on *sīla* as fulfilment of the *vinaya*; in contrast, *prajñā* was defined as knowledge based on learning. Ray further adds that the Theravāda tradition placed considerably less emphasis on *samādhi*. He concludes:

> [A]lthough many classical texts – both Buddha-word and commentaries – recommend meditation as a necessary component of the Buddhist path, in monastic tradition, meditation has often remained a primarily theoretical ideal.[123]

Martin Stuart-Fox also maintains that

> Long before the time of Buddhaghosa, the Buddhist saṅgha had become predominantly a worldly organization, concerned above all with its own preservation, with maintaining its popular appeal and princely patronage. By that time the meditative tradition may well have been reduced to little more than an eccentric group of recluses.[124]

It follows from the preceding studies that, early on in the history of the Theravāda tradition, when most monastics were already living in settled monasteries, the practice of meditation (i.e., the intensive practice of *satipaṭṭhāna*) was rare among monastics (and presumably also lay) *saṅgha* members; this was especially true when the practice of meditation came to be regarded as less important for the preservation of the Dhamma (In the twentieth century, the practice of *vipassanā* enjoyed a revival within the Theravāda tradition). Until that time, we can even speculate that the practice of meditation was the domain of only few monastics, namely, those who joined the order in their old age, and those few who made the effort to leave busy monasteries for a secluded place to practice meditation intensively; this was at the expense of being scorned for engaging in an inferior activity.[125] Sarbacker has offered an interesting observation concerning the historical developments that brought about the preference of scholasticism over meditation practice:

> If we consider the shifting of the śramaṇa traditions from peripheral cults in nature to a central religious tradition or cult, it makes sense that there would be a natural inclination to move towards a scholastic based system of authority, replacing virtuoso practice with scholasticism and ritual. It naturally follows that we would have the development of highly scholastic interpretations of the meditation systems. Particularly represented by attempts to reconcile varied interpretations of such practices and their role in soteriology.[126]

Since the practice of meditation became early on quite rare among monastics in the Theravāda tradition, it ensures that most of the attainments described in the suttas, including the *jhānas*, the formless liberations, the attainment of cessation and *nibbāna*, became no more than a theoretical possibility for most monks, nuns and Buddhist scholastics; rather, meditation practice was mainly a matter for intellectual speculations and analysis. This in turn explains, or so I would suggest, that the Theravāda proclivity to intellectual learning and analysis became a predominant mode of interpretation. This same Theravāda proclivity to intellectual learning and analysis was also directed with respect to terms and doctrinal ideas that were clearly associated in the Nikāyas with the practice of meditation and the attainment of specialized forms of awareness. We have seen that this mode of interpretation was definitely at play when the Pāli commentators interpreted what we might characterize as 'yogic insight' (*paññā*) and consequently their interpretation of the term *paññā-vimutti*.

One might sum this up by saying that finding a rationale for awakening without meditative attainments was a way for the tradition to deal with the reality in which most monastics did not practice meditation. According to Sarbacker, the vision of awakening and the practice leading to it probably changed over time when the Buddhist tradition became more integrated into society and more inclined to theoretical and intellectual learning. The need to reach out to a larger society inspired the development of systems of authority that were gradually based on firmer ground than charismatic virtuosity.[127] In other words, the Theravāda tradition established its authority and hierarchy within the *saṅgha* on scholasticism rather than on proficiency in meditation. Fortunately, the tradition preserved those suttas that affirm the significance of the practice of *satipaṭṭhāna* and the attainment of the *jhānas*. We might also hypothesize that within the monastic *saṅgha* that preserved the teachings, there were always '*jhāyins*' or '*vipassanā-dhuras*' who were influential enough to uphold the teachings that emphasize the intensive practice of meditation and the attainment of the *jhānas* as a necessity for liberation. Yet, the highly scholastic interpretation of meditation practices in the Theravāda tradition and the shift in emphasis from meditative attainments and 'yogic insight' to conceptual learning and wisdom had a potent influence on traditional Theravada's understanding of the nature of the *jhānas*, their role and significance in the spiritual path, and their relationship to other path-factors.

Notes

1 MN I.494: *tena hi tvaṃ vaccha, dve dhamme uttariṃ bhāvehi, samathañca vipassanañca. Ime kho te vaccha dve dhammā uttariṃ bhāvitā, samatho ca vipassanāca. Anekadhātupaṭivedhāya saṃvattissanti.*
2 SN IV.360: *katamo ca bhikkhave asaṅkhatagāmī maggo: samatho ca vipassanā ca. Ayaṃ vuccati bhikkhave asaṅkhatagāmī maggo.*
3 Sarbacker 2005, 33–4. See also Gimello 1978, 185.
4 In chapter 2, I argued that even though the term *jhāna* might have been adopted from the Indian 'pool' of contemplative terms, as far as we know, the fourfold *jhāna* model is uniquely Buddhist.
5 For example, this is claimed in DA II.511 and SA II.127.
6 Alexander Wynne offers an excellent study of the *arūpa samāpattis* in his book, *The Origin of Buddhist Meditation.*
7 See, for example, Snyder and Rasmussen 2009, 99, and also Buddhadāsa and Thepwisutthimethi 1989, 63.
8 See, for example, Vism. X.1ff. See also Gunaratana 1999, 80–1.
9 E.g., Vism III.106. See also comments by Shwe Zan Aung in his introduction to the *Abhidhammatthasaṅgaha* (Shwe Zan 1995, 56).
10 See, for example, Achaan Naeb Mahaniranonda, a Thai meditation master, who explains that the object of the *jhānas* is conventional reality, such as the *kaṣina*, while the object of *vipassanā* is ultimate reality in the four foundation of *satipaṭṭhāna* (Mahaniranonda 1988, 43).
11 See also Cousins 1974, 125; King 1992, 48. Note, however, that Wynne has suggested that the last 'formless attainment', the sphere of 'neither-perception-nor-non-perception', is a state without an object (Wynne 2007, 39). See also Gunaratana 1999, 79.
12 King 1992, 41.
13 E.g., DN II.69 and SN IV 263–8.
14 Sarbacker 2005, 44. He describes this process as 'cathexis', a process of training the mind to do something specific and bringing the mind to specific object.
15 Sarbacker 2005, 44.
16 E.g., MN I 160; I 175; I 205; I 209; III 45; III 28; AN IV 431; IV 438; IV 447; V 209. They also appear together as the 'nine successive abidings' (*anupubbavihāra*) and the 'nine successive cessations' (*anupubbanirodha*): DN III 266.
17 It is beyond the scope of this study to pursue the issue of *saññāvedayitanirodha*. It is also not relevant for the arguments in this study. For a detailed discussion on this special attainment, I refer to my MA dissertation (Arbel 2004).
18 DN II 111–2: *Aṭṭha kho ime ānanda vimokkho. Katame aṭṭha? Rūpī rūpāni passati. Ayaṃ paṭhamo vimokkho. ajjhattaṃ arūpasaññī bahiddhā rūpāni passati. Ayaṃ dutiyo vimokkho. Subhanteva adhimutto hoti. Ayaṃ tatiyo vimokkho. Sabbaso rūpasaññānaṃ samatikkamā paṭighasaññānaṃ atthaṅgamā nānattasaññānaṃ amanasikārā 'ananto ākāso'ti ākāsānañcāyatanaṃ upasampajja viharati. Ayaṃ catuttho vimokkho. Sabbaso ākāsānañcāyatanaṃ samatikkamma 'anantaṃ viññāṇanti' viññāṇañcāyatanaṃ upasampajja viharati. Ayaṃ pañcamo vimokkho. Sabbaso viññāṇañcāyatanaṃ samatikkamma 'natthi kiñcī'ti ākiñcaññāyatanaṃ upasampajja viharati. Ayaṃ chaṭṭho*

vimokkho. Sabbaso ākiñcaññāyatanaṃ samatikkamma nevasaññānāsaññāyatanaṃ upasampajja viharati. Ayaṃ sattamo vimokkho. Sabbaso nevasaññānāsaññāyatanaṃ samatikkamma saññāvedayitanirodhaṃ upasampajja viharati. Ayaṃ aṭṭhamo vimokkho. Ime kho ānanda aṭṭha vimokkhā. See also DN II 70–1; DN III 261; DN III 288; AN IV 306; AN IV 349; MN II 13; MN III 222. The tradition identified the first three with the four *jhānas*. See, for example, Nyanatiloka 1980, 225.

19 Wynne claims that Āḷāra Kālāma and Uddaka Rāmaputta were historical figures, although they do not appear outside early Buddhist literature. He bases his claim on the fact that, besides the early biographies of the Buddha, the two appear in a number of early Buddhist texts (Wynne 2007, 9). Although some scholars such as La Vallée Poussin and more recently Zafiropulo view this account as authentic, some have claimed that the training under the two men is a fabrication (such as Bareau, Bronkhorst and Tilmann. See Wynne 2007, 9–12. However, according to Wynne, Bareau's argument, which is mainly based on the absence of the training of the Bodhisatta under the two teachers in the Mahīśāsaka Vinaya, is not solid enough.

20 MN I 164.

21 MN I 165.

22 See, for example, AN V.60–4 where the Buddha specifically refers to the 'sphere of nothingness' and the 'sphere of neither-perception-nor-non-perception'. In this sutta, before the Buddha mentions these attainments, he describes the *kaṣina* practice and the 'eight stations of mastery' (*aṭṭhimāni abhibhāyatanāni*), which seems close to the first of 'the eight liberations' (*aṭṭha vimokkha*). Although there is no clear reference concerning the connection between these two *arūpa* attainments and the *kaṣina* practice, they seem to be connected. Interestingly, the four *jhānas* do not appear in this sutta at all (although the translator, F.L. Woodward adds in brackets, after the description of the first 'station of mastery', that this is how one enters into the 'musing', which seem to mean the first *jhāna*). See *Anguttara Nikāya*. F.L. Woodward (trans.), *The Book of the Gradual Saying*, vol. 5. (London: The Pāli Text Society, 2003), 42.

23 Wynne 2007, 111.

24 Ibid., 43–4.

25 MN I 166: 'This Dhamma does not lead to disenchantment, to dispassion, to cessation, to peace, to direct knowledge, to awakening, to Nibbāna, but only to reappearance in the base of neither-perception-nor-non-perception.' The same was said by the Bodhisatta with regard to the teaching and attainment of Āḷāra Kālāma (MN I 165).

26 It is important to note that references to the *jhānas* as a way to be reborn in higher cosmological realms are very rare; in contrast, the four *arūpa samāpattis* appear repeatedly as bases for rebirth. Furthermore, the *jhānas* do not appear in the Nikāyas as having a specific corresponding cosmological realm and are not listed as a 'stations of consciousness'. For example, MN III.147 and MN I.289 both describe different attainments that lead to rebirth in different *deva* worlds. Yet, the *jhānas* do not appear in these suttas as a way to certain rebirth; they are also not identified as specific realms of existence. In the *Sankhārupapatti Sutta*, the Buddha enumerates the different 'places' one can re-appear after death; while the four formless attainments do appear as a place of rebirth (MN III.103; DN III.253), the *jhānas* do not. One of the rare associations in which the *jhānas* are associated with rebirth in a specific realm is AN II.126–8. This exceptional occurrence concerns *jhānas* that do lead to 'communication with the *devas*' and rebirth in their world, as the sutta phrases it; I would suggest that this type of *jhāna* is the same type of *jhāna* Ānanda describes in the *Gopakamoggallāna Sutta* as 'unworthy *jhānas*'. In this sutta, Ānanda explains that there is a type of *jhāna* (discussed in chapter 2) that 'the Blessed One did not praise' (*so bhagavā sabbaṃ jhānaṃ na vaṇṇesi*) (MN III.13–14). It would seem plausible to suggest that a *jhāna* that leads to communication with divine beings is a type of *jhāna* that the Buddha did not praise or teach. Perhaps this sutta is referring to a common spiritual goal of other ascetics and contemplatives in early Indian traditions that used the term *jhāna* to

describe spiritual attainments. These two occurrences of the term *jhāna* both appear in unfavourable contexts. It is plausible to suggest that both are examples of the term *jhāna* (*dhyāna*) as describing the quality of vision (*dhī*) that characterized the Vedic *ṛṣis*. The notion of 'special vision' (*dhī*) is the foundation of greater part of Indian religious theory and practice. It is reasonable to surmise, then, that the term *jhāna* was used quite rarely in the Nikāyas as a term referring to practices that aim at certain visions and better rebirth. Yet, we should bear in mind that this type of *jhāna* is inferior to the fourfold *jhāna* model that the Buddha did praise. For a discussion of *dhī,* see Gonda 1963, 18.

27 E.g., DN III.132, SN V.308.

28 MN I.246–7.

29 E.g., SN I.48.

30 MN I 165–6.

31 SN V.308: *Seyyathā'pi bhikkhave, gaṅgā nadī pācīnanintā pācīnapoṇā pācīnapabbhārā, evameva kho bhikkhave bhikkhu cattāro jhāne bhāvento cattāro jhāne bahulīkaronto nibbānaninno hoti nibbānapoṇo nibbānapabbhāro.* Note that the Nikāyas do not offer any evidence that the Buddha taught (or practiced) the complete set of the four *jhānas* before he was awakened. In chapter two, I show that the *jhānas,* in the format of a fourfold model, are uniquely Buddhist – even though the term itself was adopted from the Indian 'pool' of contemplative terms.

32 An interesting reference in this regard is SN IV.298–302. Here, Nigaṇṭha Nātaputta, most probably a Jain teacher and the naked ascetic Kassapa, do not know the experience of the four *jhānas*. They are presented as the unique teaching and domain of the Buddhist path.

33 SN I.48: *sambādhe vata okāsaṃ avindi bhūrimedhaso. Yo jhānambujjhā buddho patilīna nisabho munīti.* See AN II.245, which states that the four *jhānas* are called the Tathāgata's posture.

34 My MA dissertation explores this unusual attainment. Following Schmithausen, I suggest that *saññāvedayitanirodha* is fundamentally different from the formless attainments and is analogous by nature to the state of the *arahant* after death. I demonstrate that this peculiar and unique attainment could only be achieved when the meditator has contemplated, understood and abandoned even the refined 'formless states of mind'. I also suggest that even though the *arūpa samāpattis* are not necessary for liberation, they enable the meditator to realize that even in these subtle and sublime realms, where beings are undefined and formless, the law of *kamma* still operates and there are still fruits and results of good and evil deeds (DN II 327). In other words, the experience of the different realms of existence, which the *arūpa* realms are part of, deepens the attainment of insight into the Buddha's teaching. It broadens one's understanding concerning the cycle of deaths and rebirths, *dukkha* and impermanence. The arahant who attains the *jhānas*, the *arūpa samāpattis* and the 'attainment of cessation' gains insight into the whole spectrum of phenomena, that is, the material (*oḷārika*), the mind-made (*manomaya kāya*) and the formless realms made by ideation (*saññāmaya*). I also suggest that for complete and full liberation (*sammāsambodhi*) (AN IV 447–8), one has to understand all possible experiences in existence; that is, one must not only understand experiences in the *kāmaloka*, *rūpaloka* and *arūpaloka*, but also have attained the state of *saññāvedayitanirodha* where the 'end of the world' has been achieved. As suggested by Schmithausen, in this state, one is beyond *saṃsāric* existence while still alive, meaning one 'experiences' the state of an *arahant* after death while still embodied. I have further suggested that attaining this state is important for the attainment of complete and full Buddhahood. Only by attaining this state we can answer questions such as how can the Buddha profess the knowledge of the nature of '*nibbāna* without a remainder' without attaining a state? What simulates it? Although the attainment of the *arūpa samāpattis* and the 'attainment of cessation' is not necessary for the purification of mind and for the eradication of desire, aversion and

ignorance, attaining these states allows the awakened one to be able to teach the Dhamma in its fullest. See Arbel 2004, 70–2.

35 Note that in MN II 265, the Buddha explains to Ānanda that the sphere of neither-perception-nor-non-perception is the 'best [object of] clinging' and hence, will be an obstacle to *nibbāna*. The Buddha explains that only if a person will not find delight in this state, then his consciousness will not have anything to hold on to and this person will attain *nibbāna* (MN II265). In other words, even in this state some form of mental reactivity occurs, which can produce clinging. This is why Sāriputta includes the *arūpa samāpattis* as attainments in which one should train in non-clinging to any type of experience or attainment.

36 It needs to be noted that *ubhatobhāgavimutti arahants* (*arahants* who are 'liberated in both ways') attain both the four *jhānas* and the four *arūpa samāpattis*. However, as it will become evident, *paññā-vimutti arahants*, although they do not attain the formless attainment, do indeed attain the four *jhānas*.

37 Bronkhorst 1993, 88. For a full discussion, see Bronkhorst 1993, 30–67. Although Bronkhorst argues that it is more likely that Buddhism adopted parts of Jaina meditation that resemble the four *arūpa jhānas* and *saññāvedayitanirodha* (Bronkhorst 1993, 78), this practice cannot be found in this form in Jain texts or in other Indian religious traditions. Gombrich argues that since both arahants who are called 'liberated in both ways' (*ubhatobhāgavimutti*) and 'bodily witness' (*kāyasakkhī*) – who are not fully liberated – reach the formless attainment, the attainment of the formless states does not liberate at all and 'seems to have no function'. See Gombrich 2002, 103.

38 Bronkhorst 1993, 91.

39 For a full discussion see Wynne 2007, 26–37.

40 Wynne 2007, 31, 37, 111.

41 Wynne 2007, 111.

42 Wynne 2007, 107.

43 Vetter 1988, xxiv.

44 Vetter argues that the meditation model in which one goes through the four *rūpa jhānas*, the four *arūpa samāpattis* and finally *saññāvedayitanirodha* was not taught by the Buddha, at least not in the early phase of his teaching career (Vetter 1988, xxi–xxii).

45 Vetter 1988, xxi–xxii. For further discussion on *arūpa samāpattis* see Vetter 1988, 63–71.

46 Stuart 2008, 24–5. Stuart further posits that entering the 'attainment of cessation' after the practice of the four *dhyānas*, was quite possibly one of the earliest Buddhist models of liberation (Stuart 2008, 24–5).

47 See, for example, Sarbacker, who distinguishes between the 'cathexis' (which he associates with both the *jhānas* and the *arūpa samāpattis*) and the *nirodha* aspect of 'catharsis'. According to Sarbacker, the latter is meant to reduce the field of awareness and focus on one object of attention, which he characterizes as a process of conditioning. The former on the other hand, is characterized by the releasing of objects and the de-conditioning of habitual process of awareness (Sarbacker 2005, 43–4). The argument of this study is that some constructed attainments, that is, the four *jhānas*, aid the process of de-conditioning unwholesome tendencies and misconceived perceptions; in contrast, other constructed attainments do not.

48 MN III.252, SN V.9 and SN V.196

49 See, for example, Katz 1982, 69.

50 Griffiths 1999, 19.

51 Gimello 1978, 187.

52 Gimello 1978, 184.

53 Schmithausen 1981, 219.

54 Schmithausen 1981, 214.

55 Schmithausen 1981, 219, 221–2.

56 Schmithausen 1981, 214, 219.
57 Vetter 1988, xxiv. It is interesting to mention Vetter's argument that after the Buddha's awakening, when he continuously taught the five ascetics, he in fact initiated them into the stages of *jhāna* meditation. Vetter 1988, xxix.
58 Vetter 1988, xxxv.
59 Sarbacker 2005, 33–4.
60 E.g., Vism VIII.227.
61 E.g., Vism I.6. Cousins observes that the terms *samatha-bhāvanā* and *vipassanā-bhāvanā*, 'have come to refer specifically to the presence or absence of the *jhānas*' (Cousins 1974, 116).
62 Sue Hamilton points out that 'Buddhaghosa's writings in particular have been so influential as to have become the determinant of the orthodox Theravāda position on virtually every point of religious concern' (Hamilton 1996, 170).
63 See, for example, Snyder and Rasmussen 2009, 3.
64 See Erik Braun's observation that 'Ledi was one of the first teachers in the modern era to offer this approach of pure insight practice as a viable – even preferred – option. What is more, he was the first to do so on a widespread basis in popular writing (Braun 2013, 139).
65 Pa-Auk Sayadaw 2001, 58; Snyder and Rasmussen 2009, 134–5.
66 A good example of the commentarial perspective of this issue is MA I.108–9.
67 Braun 2013, 138. See also Pa-Auk Sayadaw 2003, 89–90. Sayadaw points out that *ānāpāna-sati* is used for developing the *jhānas* before practicing *vipassanā*.
68 Jinavamsa 2003, 19. This type of concentration is not mentioned in the Nikāyas and is described only several times by Buddhaghosa (e.g., Vism IV.32–3). U Nyanuttara Agga Mahā Pṇḍita wrote a rejoinder to a criticism published against Mahāsi Sayadaw's system of meditation. According to Sayadaw, U Nyanuttara Agga Mahā Pṇḍita states that *sukha-vipassaka* has no *lokiya-jhāna* when he practices *vipassanā*, but he does come to possess '*lokuttara jhāna*' at the attainment of the path (Jinavamsa 2003, 22). For a discussion on the terms *lokiya-jhāna* and *lokuttara jhāna* see chapter one.
69 Buddhadāsa and Thepwisutthimethi 1989, 36.
70 Matara 1993, 36.
71 Cousins has pointed out that actually the term *samatha* is also used as a synonym for *nibbāna* (Sn 732, S III 133, M I 235 D III 54). Cousins 1984, 56.
72 Note, that in MN I.33, AN V.131 and Iti. 32, the word *vipassanā* occurs in the same context as one of the qualities a monk possesses. Interestingly, the Nettipakaraṇa states that the Blessed One taught *samatha* for those with sharp aptitude (*tattha bhagavā tikkhindriyassa samathaṃ upadisati*), *samatha* and *vipassanā* for those with medium aptitude (*majjhindriyassa bhagavā samathavipassanaṃ upadisati*) and *vipassanā* for those with weak aptitude (*mudindriyassa bhagavā vipassanaṃ upadisati*). Nettipakaraṇa 101.
73 MN I.294 and AN III.21 (*samatha* and *vipassanā* assist right view); MN I.494, MN III.289 (yoked evenly together); DN I.76 (*vipassanāñāṇaṃ* after the fourth *jhāna*); DN III.213; AN I.100, AN II.92–4, AN II. 247, AN III.373; SN IV.195, SN IV.295 (when attaining cessation), SN IV.360 (the path to the unconditioned), SN V.52, AN V.99. AN II.157 depicts different ways to attain Arahantship. In this sutta, Ānanda declares that the first way is when a monk develops insight preceded by peace (*samathapubbaṅgamaṃ vipassanaṃ bhāveti*); the second way is when a monk develops peace preceded by insight (*vipassanāpubbaṅgamaṃ samathaṃ bhāveti*); the third way is when a monk yokes peace and insight together as a pair (*samathavipassanaṃ yuganaddhaṃ bhāveti*); the fourth way is when a monk is gripped by the excitement of the Dhamma (*dhammuddhaccaviggahītaṃ mānaṃ hoti*). In the last case, the mind attains single-pointedness and abides in concentration. Cousins reiterates the commentary of the Paṭisambhidāmagga on this last point. The Paṭisambhidāmagga explains that while paying attention to the aggregates, elements, bases and so on as impermanence and so

forth, ten *dhammas* arise. This list became of central importance later on, as the ten defilements of insight. Cousins further elaborates, and states that 'states similar to those of Bodhi are reached, but become the cause of excitement. This obstructs the clarity and onward development of insight. The commentary interprets this fourth way as that of the pure insight follower (*sukha-vipassaka*)' [PaṭisA584] (Cousins 1984, 61). Note, however, that the list at A II 157 is given by Ānanda and not the Buddha (or his *arahants* disciples). Also, there is no reference at the end of the *sutta* to the Buddha's consent to this list. Furthermore, it is also not evident that *samatha* refers to the *jhānas* while *vipassanā* does not.

74 The Theravāda commentarial tradition is quite obviously the product of a different generation than that of the Nikāyas. Some of the explanations and interpretations given in the Aṭṭhakathā and Ṭika are idiosyncratic and use terms that do not occur in the Nikāyas at all.

75 See Thanissaro Bhikkhu, who wrote that '*vipassanā* is not a meditation technique. It's a quality of mind – the ability to see events clearly in the present moment.' Thanissaro 1997.

76 Cousins 1974, 116. See also Vism XVIII.5. Cousins also observes that the omission of the *jhānas* from the path to awakening is well established in the Aṭṭhakathā literature (Cousins 1994–6, 48 and 50). Katz also maintains that 'in this context, then, the *ubhatobhāgavimutta* is distinguished from the *paññā-vimutti* by virtue of his mastery of the *jhāna*, although the aim of their method is identical'(Katz 1982, 80).

77 SA II.127. See also the example used in the statement by Shwe Zan Aung in his introduction to the Abhidhammatthasaṅgaha: 'For it must be borne in mind that *jhāna* is not absolutely necessary for Arahantship, as, e.g., in the case of Arahants termed "dry-visioned" (*sukha-vipassakā*) *Abhidhammatthasaṅgaha*' (Shwe Zan 1995, 55). Griffiths also asserts that 'the category of *paññāvimutto*, one who is liberated by means of wisdom, seems to envisage the possibility of the attainment of *nibbāna* without complete mastery over the enstatic practices' (Griffiths 1999, 153–4, n.47).

78 See DA II.511, MA III.188 and PugA 191, which enumerate five types of *paññāvimutta*: one who attains insight without the *jhānas* and four types who attain insight on the basis of anyone of the four *jhānas*. See also Atthasālinī 1976, 307 and Sv II.512. In his article on the *Kīṭāgiri Sutta*, Piya Tan brings in several references of this view in contemporary Theravāda; for example, he refers to Mahasi Sayadaw, *Satipatthana Vipassana*, 3rd ed., 2005, 283 ff. Thai Abhidhamma teacher Sujin Boriharnwanaket speaks of 'two kinds of *ariya-savaka*, namely, the *sukkhavipassaka* and the *cetovimutti*' (Piya Tan 2005, 10 no. 59).

79 The commentaries have distinguished the *cetovimutti* and the *ubhatobhāgavimutti* arahants from the *paññā-vimutti* arahants. According to the commentaries, the former follow *jhāna* practice, while the later follow *vipassanā* practice (Katz 1982, 81). However, De Silva has argued that there are times when *cetovimutti* does not refer to final liberation but to 'temporary and pleasant' (*sāmāyikaṃ kantaṃ*) liberation. However, when it is used in conjunction with *paññā-vimutti*, then it refers to inviolable or permanent liberation (*akuppā cetovimutti*) (De Silva 1978, 120). The terms *cetovimutti* and *paññā-vimutti* were also identified as beneficial for different kinds of obstacles. For the eradication of greed (*rāga*) and hatred (*dosa*), *samatha* should be practiced; in contrast, for the eradication of ignorance/delusion (*moha*/ *āvijjā*), *vipassanā* should be practiced. Gimello, for example, argues that *samatha* meditation conduces 'to the near extinction of the affective obstacles, but it is discernment or doctrinal analysis supported by concentration which completely extinguishes them and which extinguishes also the intellectual barriers' (Gimello 1978, 187). A passage from the Aṅguttara Nikāya is usually used for illustrating that the development of *samatha* leads to the development of *citta*, and to the abandoning of desire (*rāga*) which is *cetovimutti*, whereas the development of *vipassanā* leads to the development of insight (*paññā*) and to the abandonment of ignorance (*āvijjā*), which is *paññā-vimutti* (AN I.61).

However, the distinction between the two is stated quite differently in DN III.270: 'How is a monk well liberated in mind? The mind of a monk is liberated from greed, hatred and delusion. This is how a monk is well liberated in mind. And how is a monk well liberated by wisdom? A monk knows: "for me greed, hatred and delusion are abandoned, cut of at the root, like a palm tree stump, destroyed and incapable of arising again." ' Here it is clear that 'liberation of mind' (*cetovimutti*) refers to the moment in which the mind is liberated from the three 'poisons': *rāga*, *dosa* and *moha*, namely, from both the affective and cognitive obstacles, while 'liberation by wisdom' (*paññā-vimutti*), refers to the reviewing moment after the mind has been liberated – when the arahant knows that the mind is free from greed, hatred and delusion.

80 E.g., SN V.74 where one has 'well liberated' (*suvimuttaṃ*) mind while still practicing the path.

81 See Arbel 2004, 71–2.

82 Note that Sāriputta is said to gain deliverance by wisdom (*paññā-vimutti*) since he gained awakening by listening to the Buddha's discourse (MN I 501). Mahāmoggallāna is said to gain deliverance of mind (*cetovimutti*). Anuruddha was considered to be an arahant who is a meditation master (MN I 209–10). To put it more simply, Sāriputta, who gained deliverance by wisdom, is also described as having proficiency in concentration (SN III 235–8; AN I 41ff; MN III 25ff).

83 MN I 477–9. This list appears also in DN III.253–4 where these seven types of persons are called 'seven persons worthy of offerings'.

84 For a detailed discussion see Gombrich 2002, 96–134.

85 For a fuller discussion see Katz 1982, 83–95.

86 De Silva 1978, 134.

87 MN I 477: *paññāya cassa disvā āsavā parikkhīṇā honti.*

88 It seems that the Buddha was actually an *ubhatobhāgavimutti arahant*. He is described as possessing special powers that are called 'the ten powers of a Tathāgata' (MN I 69–71). These powers emphasize, I would suggest, precisely the difference between an *ubhatobhāgavimutti arahant* and a *paññā-vimutti arahant* who does not possess any of these powers (SN II 121–4). Accordingly, only an *ubhatobhāgavimutti arahant* can teach the Dhamma in its fullest, just as the Tathāgata did, and 'claim the herds-leader's place, roars his lion's roar in the assemblies, and sets rolling the wheel of Brahmā' (MN I 70–1). The difference between an *ubhatobhāgavimutti arahant* and the Buddha is in terms of precedence; the Buddha achieved complete liberation without having an awakened teacher, while *ubhatobhāgavimutti arahants* had the Buddha and his teachings for guidance (Katz 1982, 79, 96). Nyanatiloka explains that *ubhatobhāgavimutta* 'is the name of one class of noble disciples. He is liberated in two ways, namely, by way of all eight absorptions (*jhāna*, q.v.) as well as by the supermundane path (*sotāpatti* etc.) based on insight' (Nyanatiloka 1980, 214). See also Ṭika to MN I.477.

89 MN I.477–8: *idha bhikkhave ekacco puggalo ye te santā vimokkhā atikkamma rūpe āruppā te na kāyena phassitvā viharati, paññāya cassa disvā āsavā parikkhīṇā honti. Ayaṃ vuccati bhikkhave puggalo paññāvimutto.*

90 Although the text does not explicate what kind of liberations we are talking about, it is plausible to assume that his question refers to the last five 'liberations' of the 'eight liberations' (*aṭṭha vimokkha*) mentioned before in this chapter; that is, the four formless attainments and the 'attainment of cessation'.

91 SN II.121–7.

92 SN II.123: *api nu tumhe āyasmanto, evaṃ jānantā evaṃ passantā ye te santā vimokkhā atikkamma rūpe āruppā, te kāyena phusitvā viharathā'ti? No hetaṃ āvuso. Etthadāni āyasmanto, idañca veyyākaraṇaṃ imesañca dhammānaṃ asamāpatti. Idaṃ no āvuso kathanti? Paññāvimuttā kho mayaṃ āvuso susīmā'ti.*

93 E.g., SN I.48.

94 SN IV.298–9.

95 SA II.126–7: *paññāvimuttā kho mayaṃ, āvusoti āvuso, mayaṃ nijjhānakā sukkhavipassakā paññāmetteneva vimuttāti dasseti.*

96 Katz 1982, 83; Sarbacker 2005, 33–4.

97 *Saṃyutta Nikāya*, Bhikkhu Bodhi trans. (2000), 785 no. 210). We should bear in mind that while some arahants (including the Buddha) did possess the five *abhiññās*, only the sixth *abhiññā* – 'the extinction of all taints' (*āsavakkhaya*) – is that which constitutes in the Nikāyas teaching the attainment of complete liberation.

98 Gombrich 2002, 125.

99 Gombrich 2002, 97. Gombrich has maintained that both the *Susīma Sutta* and *Kosambī Sutta* should be seen as presenting a debate within the Theravāda tradition between the 'cognitivists' (those who think that one can be liberated by a process of intellectual analysis) and the 'meditators' (Gombrich 2002, 96, 133).

100 Gombrich 2002, 126.

101 Gombrich 2002, 124.

102 Gombrich 2002, 126.

103 Gombrich 2002, 127.

104 See, for example, AN IV.451–6 where none of the spiritual attainments are envisioned without the attainment of the *jhānas*. These are the attainment of – *kāyasakkhi, paññāvimutta, ubhatobhāgavimutto, sandiṭṭhiko dhammo, sandiṭṭhikaṃ nibbānaṃ, nibbāna, parinibbāna, diṭṭhadhammanibbāna, khemappatto, amata* and so on.

105 *Ye te santā vimokkhā atikkamma rape āruppā, te kayena phusitvā viharathā.* See also AN II.86–7 that a person can attain 'liberation by wisdom', 'liberation of mind' (*cetovimuttiṃ paññāvimuttiṃ*) by eradicated the *āsavas* but without dwelling and touching with the body in the 'eight liberation'.

106 I think that Bodhi's conclusion in his article about the *Kosambī Sutta* is relevant for our discussion as well. Bodhi seems to point out that *paññāvimutta* do indeed attain the *jhānas*. He concludes, 'All arahants arrive at their goal through the same threefold training in virtue, concentration and wisdom. They never bypass the training in concentration but merely differ in the degree to which they pursue this phase of the path. The principle division is between those arahants who gain mastery over the formless attainments (technically called ubhatobhāgavimutta, "both-ways-liberated-arahants") and those settle for a lower degree of concentration (technically called *paññāvimutta*, "liberated-by-wisdom-arahants") . . . regardless of their route of arrival at the goal, all arahants gain access to a meditative state in which they can experience nibbāna with a fullness and immediacy that surpasses the capacity of the *sekha*' (Bhikkhu Bodhi 2003, 64–5).

107 See, for example, Katz 1982, 82–3.

108 Gombrich 2002, 130.

109 AN III.356: *ye amataṃ dhātuṃ kāyena phūsitvā viharanti.*

110 AN III.356: *ye gambhīraṃ atthapadaṃ paññāya ativijjha passantīti.*

111 E.g., SN V.181–2, 184.

112 Gombrich 2002, 130.

113 Contrary to the rarity of the term *dhamma-yoga*, the term *jhāyin* appears in various places in the Nikāyas, such as Sn 719, 1009, 1105.

114 E.g., SN V. 59, AN II.10; DN III.230. The four *yogas* are similar to the four *ogha* (e.g., SN V.59; DN III.230).

115 E.g., DN III.123, 125; MN I.117, 349; SN I.173.

116 Gombrich 2002, 132.

117 *Pariyatti nu kho sāsanassa mūlaṃ udāhu paṭipatti* (AA, 52). Ibid., 158, note 3.

118 AA, 53–3. Rahula Walpola, *History of Buddhism in Ceylon*, 158.

119 Rahula 1956, 158–9 (AA, 53). Rahula cites also from the commentaries to the Majjhima and Dīgha Nikāyas that state, '[T]here may or may not be realization (*paṭivedha*) and practice (*paṭipatti*); learning is enough for the perpetuation of the Sāsana . . . Therefore, the Sāsana (religion) is stabilized when learning endures' (DA, 654; MA, 881).

120 E.g., AA I, 37 and AA III, 379. A search for the two types, i.e., *gantha-dhura* and *vipassanā-dhura* in the VRI CD-ROM (Vipassanā Research Institute, CD-ROM edition), produces references only in the commentaries.

121 It is noteworthy that the differentiation between the *jhāyins* and the *dhamma-yoga* monks in AN III.355–6 was replaced by the differentiation between *ganthadhura* and *vipassanādhura*. In other words, the term *jhāyin* was converted to the term 'practitioners of *vipassanā*'.

122 Rahula 1956, 160. Rahula further points out that initially, '*gantha-dhura* meant only the learning and teaching of the Tripiṭka; as time went on, the connotation of the term widened, and it begun to embrace language, grammar, history, logic, medicine and other field of study as well' (Rahula 1956, 161). A situation in which meditation practice was rare in Sri Lanka is reflected in Buddhaghosa's open remarks in the *Visuddhimagga* in the section on the earth *kaṣina* and the *jhānas*. Buddhaghosa begins with a description of possible disturbances in the monastery for developing concentration (*samādhi*). This is a list of eighteen faults, such as a monastery that is large, new, near a road, disturbance to the fact that people bring flower or fruits, because the monastery is a place of pilgrimage (Vism IV.2). As noted by Ray, it is hard to imagine a settled monastery without any of these faults (Ray 1994, 38, note 20).

123 Ray 1994, 17–18.

124 Stuart-Fox 1989, 103.

125 The anthropologist Martin Southwold found that amongst the Sri Lankan lay people he interviewed, meditation was a euphemism for sleeping, and that many 'village Buddhists, especially men, and including some of the clergy, regard the practice with derision' (Southwold 1984, 102, cited in Shravaski 2001, 52). Dhammika adds his own observation and writes, 'I know that at least some monks in Sri Lanka see meditation as having more a punitive than spiritual value. In one monastery where I used to stay, the abbot would punish the little monks when they misbehaved by making them 'do meditation'. . . Not a few monks have confided to me the embarrassment and discomfort they felt when they first got to the West and were asked to teach meditation' (Shravaski 2001, 52).

126 Sarbacker 2005, 101.

127 Sarbacker 2005, 106.

Final Reflections

> There is no *jhāna* for the one without wisdom,
> no wisdom for the one without *jhāna*;
> the one who has *jhāna* and wisdom
> he indeed is in the presence of *nibbāna*.[1]

This study has tried to look into the question of how the mind can be transformed from ordinary to liberated, according to the Pāli Nikāyas. What is the role of the four *jhānas* in this transformation? Here I wish to reflect briefly on a question that seems to have no definitive answer when reading the Pāli Nikāyas alone but is worthy of reflection nonetheless: does the attainment of the *jhānas* transform one into a 'noble person' (*ariya*) or can one enter and abide in the *jhānas* more than once as an 'ordinary person' (*puthujjana*)? If the four *jhānas* can be attained repeatedly before one attains *nibbāna* (either as an ordinary person or as a 'stream-enterer', 'once-returner' or 'non-returner'), what do they do for the unawakened practitioner and what is their relation to the awakening event? The last question was present in almost every chapter of this book interwoven in the different discussions, so here I wish to summarize my position and research conclusions in this regard.

In the Buddha's own story it is clear that, before he became a Buddha, he attained the first *jhāna* twice and the other three *jhānas* only once.[2] Furthermore, most of the descriptions of the *jhānas* in the context of the Nikāyas' map of spiritual progress give the impression that one might progress through the four *jhānas* once, before one becomes an *ariya* or an *arahant*.[3] The Nikāyas tell us, for example, about Citta, the householder, who was not an arahant but was still able to enter the *jhānas* as he wished.[4] Yet the Nikāyas indicate that Citta was in fact a non-returner and seem to link his 'nobility' with the attainment of the four *jhānas*.[5] Thus, it seems that the *jhānas* are signposts in the spiritual process signalling that one is on the threshold of awakening. If this indeed is the case, we might hypothesize that this experiential event is the jumping point into *nibbāna*.

However, since *nibbāna* is 'unconditioned' (*asaṅkhata*), meaning nothing can 'automatically' condition its unfolding, it will be problematic to uphold that attaining any conditioned state will automatically bring about the 'unconditioned'. From reading the Nikāyas, my overall impression is that the attainment of the four *jhānas* should be regarded as a turning point in the spiritual path. In many suttas it seems that these attainments mark the moment when a practitioner becomes 'noble' (*ariya*), although not necessarily an arahant. Yet, this is only a conjecture that cannot be proven. Still, even if we cannot argue unequivocally that this is indeed the case, the preceding pages have demonstrated that, according to the Nikāyas, the attainment of the *jhānas* is the way to effect wholesome changes in the makeup of the conditioned mind; it facilitates transformation of the mind from ordinary to awakened.[6] We have seen in the course of this book that by going through the *jhānas*, the practitioner becomes intimately familiar with a clarified perception and free mode of being, allowing one to see through the illusory nature of phenomena. The *jhānas*, I argue, exemplify the aim of the Buddhist path: a progression from ordinary mind, filled with many moments of unwholesome states, to a purified mind, wholesome and free. When one progresses from one *jhāna* to the next, insight (*vipassanā*) becomes deeper and one actualizes the aim of Buddhist meditation.[7]

Thus, if the fourth-*jhāna*-awareness is attained repeatedly before one attains awakening (either as an ordinary person or as a stream-enterer, once-returner or non-returner), we might hypothesize that the unawakened practitioner strengthens and establishes what I have called 'wisdom-awareness' – a wholesome and lucid awareness that knows directly the emptiness of all phenomena, knowing that is free from affective and cognitive overlays – thereby weakening the unwholesome tendencies and wrong perceptions of experience, until these mental and cognitive obstructions do not arise any longer. This is a progressive development, although the focus of the awareness is on the immediate present.

If we assume that the 'mind' does not become anything in the process of practice, the early Buddhist spiritual path actually aims at eradicating distorted conceptual structures and unwholesome tendencies and inclinations that obscure the natural wholesomeness and luminosity of awareness.[8] What I wish to suggest here is that the Nikāyas' teaching seems to imply that for this luminosity to be uncovered, the practitioner needs to actualize and stabilize the fourth-*jhāna*-mode-of-awareness, which resembles an awakened cognition. Even though this mode of awareness is temporary and conditioned (as all experiences and insights are), it might reset the mind to complete wholesomeness and, hopefully, awaken the mind.

However, if the mind is not liberated at the first time one attains the fourth *jhāna*, it might allow the practitioner to experience a temporary (albeit prolonged) awakened awareness of reality, not conditioned by desire, aversion and ignorance, thereby enabling one to know directly what it 'feels like' to be without any of the deep rooted habitual conditioning that causes *dukkha*. In other words, though one might attain *nibbāna* the first time the fourth *jhāna* is attained (as in the Buddha's case), if one is not awakened at this point in the spiritual path, it seems that the fourth *jhāna* restores the natural clarity and openness of mind that allows one to gradually release conditioned modes of perception by experiencing a different mode of knowing and being.

It seems plausible to theorize, then, that each time a person experiences the four *jhānas* (either as an ordinary person or as a stream-enterer, once-returner or non-returner') the mind becomes more familiar and grounded in such mode of knowing. This, I wish to emphasize again, is what seems to ameliorate the connection between ordinary mind and awakened mind. It allows one to have a deep sense of ease and freedom in both body and mind, planting and nurturing the seeds for complete liberation. Abiding in such a mode of being, I suggest, merges or intermingles what is usually perceived as mutually exclusive categories: the conditioned and unconditioned.[9]

*

On a more personal note, and in the spirit of the Buddha's teaching, I would like to remind myself and readers that this book contains mere thoughts, thoughts that arose in my mind and passed away (only to arise again and again). Having 'caught' them in these pages as letters, words and sentences, I wish to remember that they are impermanent phenomena, arisen from various causes and conditions. They have no substantiality and independent existence of their own. They do not 'describe' reality. They are only interpretation and conceptual constructions conditioned by my own perceptions, views and predispositions. Thus, these thoughts are offered to the readers with a reminder that they are evanescent events. Hopefully, they will help us understand better the Buddha's teaching but without becoming an object of clinging or aversion. I am completely responsible for these words, ideas and arguments, but I now let them go.

Notes

1 *Natthi jhānaṃ apaññassa, paññā natthi ajhāyato. yamhi jhānañca paññā ca, sa ve nibbānasantike.* (PTS Dhammapada v.372)
2 MN I.247–8. After his awakening he of course attained the *jhānas* many times.
3 In many suttas, after one attains the fourth *jhāna*, the mind is described as 'unshakable purified, bright, unblemished, rid of the imperfections, malleable, wieldy, steady and attained to the imperturbability' (e.g., MN I.247: *evaṃ samāhite citte parisuddhe pariyodāte anaṅgaṇe vigatūpakkilese mudubhūte kammaniye ṭhite āneñjappatte*). When the mind is thus purified, the practitioner attains the three types of knowledge, which means that one achieved complete liberation.
4 SN IV.298–9. This implies that the *jhānas* can be attained before one achieves final liberation, although it might be that attaining the *jhānas* means that one is transformed from ordinary person into one of the three lower noble persons: stream-enterer, once-returner or non-returner.
5 SN IV.301. Note that, although it is not clear if he became a 'noble person', after his attainment of the four *jhānas*, from this sutta, it does seem that this was indeed the case.
6 SN V.308.
7 This means that one abandons the unwholesome (*akusala*) and develops and fulfils wholesome qualities (*kusala*), specifically, the seven factors of awakening.
8 This perspective is apparent in AN I.10. However, I wish to point out that 'luminosity of awareness' does not mean that 'awareness' is a 'thing' but only hints that awareness – as the faculty of knowing – can be free from conditioned psychological setting and deceiving conceptual structures.
9 See Klein 1992, 295.

Bibliography

I have used the Pali Text Society editions for all citations from the Pāli Nikāyas. Quotations from the Aṭṭhakathās are taken from the Chaṭṭha Saṅgāyana CD-ROM Version 3 of the Vipassanā Research Institute.

Primary sources (English translations)

Bodhi, Bhikkhu (trans). *A Comprehensive Manual of Abhidhamma (Abhidhammatthasangaha).* Seattle: BPS Pariyatti Editions, 2000a.
Bodhi, Bhikkhu (trans). *The Connected Discourses of the Buddha: A New Translation of the Saṃyutta Nikāya* (Vols. I & II). Oxford: The Pāli Text Society, 2000b.
Bodhi, Bhikkhu (trans). *The Numerical Discourses of the Buddha: A Translation of the Aṅguttara Nikāya.* Boston: Wisdom Publications, 2012.
Masefield, Peter (trans). *The Udāna.* Oxford: Oxford University Press, 1994.
Ñāṅamoli, Bhikkhu (trans). *The Path of Purification (Visuddhimagga).* Colombo: Singapore Buddhist Meditation Centre, 1956.
Ñāṅamoli, Bhikkhu (trans). *The Path of Discrimination (Paṭisambhidāmagga).* Oxford: The Pāli Text Society, 2002.
Ñāṅamoli, Bhikkhu and Bhikkhu Bodhi (trans). *The Middle Length Discourses of the Buddha.* Boston: Wisdom Publications, 1995.
Nathmal, Tatia (trans). *That Which Is (Tattvārtha Sūtra): With the Combined Commentaries of Umāsvāti/Umāsvāmi, Pūjyapāda and Siddhasenagani.* San Francisco: HarperCollins Publishers, 1994.
Norman, K.R. (trans). *The Group of Discourses (Sutta-Nipāta)*, 2nd edition. Oxford: The Pāli Texts Society, 2001.
Olivelle, Patrick (trans). *Upaniṣads.* Oxford: Oxford University Press, 1996.
Pe Maung Tin, M.A. (trans). Edited and revised by Mrs. Rhys Davids, D.Litt., M.A. *The Expositor* (*Atthasàlinā*: Buddhaghosa's Commentary on the Dhammasangaṇī) (Vols. 1 & 2). London: The Pāli Text Society, 1976.
Radhakrishnan, S. (trans). *Dhammapada.* Oxford: Oxford University Press, 1950.
Radhakrishnan, S. (trans). *The Principle Upaniṣads.* New Delhi: HarperCollins Publishers India, 1994.
Shwe Zan Aung, B.A. (trans). *Compendium of Philosophy.* Oxford: The Pali Text Society, 1995.
Walsh, Maurice (trans). *The Long Discourses of the Buddha: A Translation of the Dīgha Nikāya.* Boston: Wisdom Publication, 1987.

Woodward, F.L. (trans). *The Book of the Gradual Saying (Anguttara Nikāya)* (Vol. 5). London: The Pāli Text Society, 2003.

Secondary sources

Akira, Sadakata. *Buddhist Cosmology: Philosophy and Origin*. Tokyo: Kōsei Publishing Co., 1997.

Anālayo, Bhikkhu. *Satipatthana: The Direct Path to Realization*. Birmingham: Windhorse, 2003.

———. 'Attitudes towards Nuns: A Case Study of the Nandakovāda in Light of Its Parallels', *Journal of Buddhist Ethics* 17 (2010a): 332–400.

———. 'The Scope of Free Inquiry According to the Vīmaṃsaka Sutta and Its Madhyama āgama Parallel', *Rivista Di Studi Sudasiatici* 4 (2010b): 7–20.

Anderson, Carol S. *Pain and Its Ending: The Four Noble Truths in the Theravāda Buddhist Canon*. Delhi: Motilal Banarsidass, 2001.

Arbel, Keren. *The Attainment of Cessation of Perception and Feeling: A Study of Saññāvedayitanirodha in the Pāli Nikāyas*. MA diss., University of Bristol, 2004.

Basham, A.L. *The Wonder That Was India*. New Delhi: Rupa & Co., 1996.

Bechert, Heinz. 'The Importance of Aśoka's So-Called Schism Edict'. In *Indological and Buddhist Studies: Volume in Honour of Professor J. W. de Jong on His Sixtieth Birthday*, edited by Luise A. Hercus, 61–68. Canberra: Faculty of Asian Studies, 1982.

Berkwitz, Stephen C. 'Materiality and Merit in Sri Lankan Buddhist Manuscripts'. In *Buddhist Manuscript Cultures, Knowledge, Ritual, and Art*, edited by Stephen C. Berkwitz, Juliane Schober and Claudia Brown, 35–49. London and New York: Routledge, 2009.

Bhattacharyya, Narendra Nath. *Jain Philosophy: Historical Outline*. Delhi: Munishram Manoharlal Publishers, [1976]1999.

Bodhi, Bhikkhu. 'Musīla and Nārada Revisited: Seeking the Key to Interpretation'. In *Approaching the Dhamma: Buddhist Texts and Practices in South and Southeast Asia*, edited by Anna M. Blackburn and Jeffrey Samuels, 47–68. Seattle: BPS Priyatti Editions, 2003.

———. *Sects & Sectarianism: The Origin of Buddhist Schools*, 2006. Retrieved from http://sectsandsectarianism.googlepages.com

———. 'What Does Mindfulness Really Mean? A Canonical Perspective', *Contemporary Buddhism* 12, no. 1 (2011): 12–39.

Bond, G.D. 'Theravāda Buddhism and the Aims of Buddhist Studies.' In *Studies in History of Buddhism*, edited by A.K. Narain, 43–65. Delhi: B. R. Publishing Corporation, 1980.

Brahmāli, Bhikkhu. 'Jhāna and Lokuttara-jjhāna', *Buddhist Studies Review* 24, no. 1 (2007): 75–90.

Braun, Erik. *The Birth of Insight: Meditation, Modern Buddhism, and the Burmese Monk Ledi Sayadaw*. Chicago: The University of Chicago Press, 2013.

Bronkhorst, Johannes. *The Two Traditions of Meditation in Ancient India*. Delhi: Motilal Banarsidass Publishers, 1993.

———. *Two Sources of Indian Asceticism*. Delhi: Motilal Banarsidass Publishers, 1998.

———. 'The Riddle of the Jainas and the Ājīvikas in Early Buddhist Literature', *Journal of Indian Philosophy* 28, no. 5–6 (2000): 511–529.

Bucknell, Roderick S. 'Reinterpreting the *Jhānas*', *Journal of the International Association of Buddhist Studies* 16, no. 2 (1993): 375–409.

Bucknell, Roderick S. and Chris Kang. *The Meditative Way: Readings in the Theory and Practice of Buddhist Meditation.* Oxon and New York: Routledge, 1997.

Buddhadāsa, Bhikkhu. *Ānāpānasati (Mindfulness of Breathing)*. Translated from the Thai version by Bhikkhu Nāgasena. Bangkok: Sublime Life Mission, 1980.

Buddhadāsa, Bhikkhu and Phra Thepwisutthimethi. *Me and Mine: Selected Essays of Bhikkhu Buddhadāsa.* Albany: State University of New York Press, 1989.

Buswell, Robert E., Jr. 'The "Short-cut" Apparoach of K'an-hua Meditation: The Evolution of a Practicle Subitism in Chinese Ch'an Buddhism'. In *Sudden and Gradual: Approaches to Enlightenment in Chinese Though*, edited by Peter N. Gregory, 321–374. Honolulu: University of Hawai'i Press, 1987.

———. *Tracing Back the Radiance: Chinul's Korean Way of Zen*. Honolulu: A Karoda Institute Book, University of Hawai'i Press, 1991.

Chah, Ajahn. *Collected Teachings of Ajahn Chah: Food for the Heart*. Boston: Wisdom Publication, 2002.

Cho, Francisca. 'Religious Identity and the Study of Buddhism'. In *Identity and the Politics of Scholarship in the Study of Religion*, edited by Ignacio Cabezón José and Sheila Greeve Davaney, 61–76. New York: Routledge, 2004.

Cousins, L.S. 'Buddhist Jhāna: Its Nature and Attainment According to the Pāli Sources', *Religion* 3 (1974): 115–131.

———. 'Samatha-yāna and Vipassanā-yāna'. In *Buddhist Studies in Honour of Hammalava Saddhātissa*, edited by Gatare Dhammapala, R. Gombrich and K.R. Norman, 56–68. Nugegoda, Sri Lanka: Hammalava Saddhātissa Felicitation Volume Committee, 1984.

———. 'Vitakka/vitarka and Vicāra, Stages of Samādhi in Buddhism and Yoga', *Indo-Iranian Journal* 35, no. 2&3 (July, 1992): 137–157.

———. 'The Origin of Insight Meditation', *The Buddhist Forum* IV (1994–6): 35–58.

Crangle, Edward Fitzpatrick. *The Origin and Development of Early Indian Contemplative Practice*. Wiesbaden: Harrassowitz Verlag, 1994.

Dhammika, S. 'The Edicts of King Ashoka', The Wheel Publication (No. 386/387) 1993. Electronic edition is offered for free distribution via DharmaNet by arrangement with the publisher. DharmaNet International. https://www.cs.colostate.edu/~malaiya/ashoka.html

Daniel, E. Valentine. *Fluid Signs: Being a Person the Tamil Way*. Berkeley: University of California Press, 1984.

De Silva, C.L.A. 'Cetovimutti and Paññāvimutti and Ubhatobhāgavimutti', *Pali Buddhist Review* 3, no. 3 (1978): 118–145.

Deussen, Paul. *The Philosophy of the Upaniṣads*. Translated by A.S. Geden. New York: Dovel Publication, 1966.

Dreyfus, George. 'Is Mindfulness Present-centered and Non-judgmental? A Discussion of the Cognitive Dimension of Mindfulness', *Contemporary Buddhism* 12, no. 1 (2011): 41–54.

Dundas, Paul. 'Food and Freedom: The Jaina Secterian Debate on the Nature of the Kevalin', *Religion* 15 (1985): 161–198.

Dutt, Nalinaksha. *Buddhist Sects in India*. Calcutta: Calcutta Oriental Press, 1970.

Edgerton, Franklin. *Buddhist Hybrid Sanskrit Dictionary*. Delhi: Motilal Banarsidass Publishers, 1998.

Flood, Gavin. *An Introduction to Hinduism*. Cambridge: Cambridge University Press, 1998.

Fort, Andrew O. 'Going or Knowing? The Development of the Idea of Living Liberation in the Upaniṣads', *Journal of Indian Philosophy* 22, no. 4 (1994): 379–390.

Gethin, Rupert. *The Foundations of Buddhism*. Oxford: Oxford University Press, 1998.

———. *The Buddhist Path to Awakening*. Oxford: Oneworld Publications, 2001.

Gimello, Robert. 'Mysticism and Meditation'. In *Mysticism and Philosophical Analysis*, edited by Steven Katz, 170–194. London: Sheldon Press, 1978.

Glass, Andrew. *Connected* "Discourse in Gandhāra: A Study, Edition, and Translation of Four Saṃyuktāgama-Type Sūtras from the Senior Collection". PhD diss., University of Washington, 2006.

Gombrich, Richard. *Kindness and Compassion as Means to Nirvana* (1997 Gonda Lecture). Amsterdam: Royal Netherlands Academy of Arts and Sciences, 1998.

———. *How Buddhism Began*. Delhi: Munshiram Manoharlal, 2002.

Gomez, Luis O. 'The Direct and Gradual Approaches of Zen Master Mahayana: Fragments of the Teachings of Mo-ho-yen'. In *Studies in Ch'an and Hua-Yen*, edited by Robert M. Gimello and Peter N. Gregory, 69–167. Honolulu: University of Hawaii Press, 1983.

Gonda, Jan. *The Vision of the Vedic Poets*. The Hague: Mouton & Co, 1963.

Griffiths, Paul. 'Concentration and Insight: The Problematic of Theravāda Meditation Theory', *The Journal of the American Academy of Religion* 49, no. 4 (1981): 605–624.

———. 'Buddhist Jhana: A Form – Critical Study', *Religion* 13 (1983): 55–68.

———. *On Being Mindless*. Delhi: Sri Satguru Publications, 1999.

Gunaratana, H. Mahāthera. 'Place of Jhāna and Samādhi in Theravāda Buddhism'. In *Vipassanā: A Universal Buddhist Technique of Meditation*, edited by D.C. Ahir, 76–91. Delhi: Sri Satguru Publications, 1999.

———. *Should We Come Out of Jhāna to Practice Vipassanā?* Retrieved April 15, 2012 from http://www.bhavanasociety.org/pdfs/Should_we_Come_out_of_Jhana.pdf

Gyatso, Janet. 'Healing Burns with Fire: The Facilitation of Experience in Tibetan Buddhism', *Journal of the American Academy of Religion* 67, no. 1 (March, 1999): 113–147.

Hamilton, Sue. *Identity and Experience: The Constitute of the Human Being According to Early Buddhism*. London: Luzac Oriental, 1996.

———. *Early Buddhism: A New Approach, the I of the Beholder*. Surrey: Curzon, 2000.

Hinṃber, von O. 'Linguistic Observations on the Structure of the Pāli Canon'. In *Selected Papers on Pāli Studies*, edited by O. von Hinüber, 62–75. Oxford: The Pali Text Society, 1994.

Houtman, Gustaaf. "Traditions of Buddhist Practice in Burma". PhD diss., SOAS, London University, 1990.

Jacob, G.A. *A Concordance to the Principle Upaniṣads and Bhagavadgītā*. Delhi: Motilal Banarsidass, 1999.

Jaini, Padmanabh S. *The Jaina Path of Purification*. Delhi: Motilal Banarsidass Publishers, [1979]1990.

Jinavamsa (ed.). *Satipaṭṭhāna Vipassanā Meditation: Criticism and Replies* (Edited and Abridged Version). Malaysia: Majujaya Indah Sdn. Bhd, 2003.

Kaelber, Walter O. *Tapta Mārga: Asceticism and Initiation in Vedic India*. Delhi: Sri Satguru Publications, 1989.

Katz, Nathan. *Buddhist Images of Human Perfection*. Delhi: Motilal Banarsidass Publishers, 1982.

King, Winston L. *Theravāda Meditation: The Buddhist Transformation of Yoga*. Delhi: Motilal Banarsidass, 1992.

Klein, Anne C. 'Mental Concentration and Unconditioned Experience: A Buddhist Case for Unmediated Cognition'. In *Paths to Liberation*, edited by Robert Buswell and Robert Gimello, 269–308. Honolulu: University of Hawai'i Press, 1992.

———. *Knowledge and Liberation: Tibetan Buddhist Epistemology in Support of Transformative Religious Experience*. Ithaca: Snow Lion Publication, 1998.

Kornfield, Jack. *Living Buddhist Masters*. Santa Cruz: Unity Press, 1977.

Kuan, Tse-fu. 'Clarification on Feelings in Buddhist Dhyāna/Jhāna Meditation', *Journal of Indian Philosophy* 33 (2005): 285–319.

———. 'Cognitive Operations in Buddhist Meditation: Interface with Western Psychology', *Contemporary Buddhism: An Interdisciplinary Journal* 13, no. 1 (2012): 35–60.

Laish, Eran. 'The Way of Practice: Principles for the Realization of the Non-Dual View of "The Great Perfection" (Dzogpa Chenpo)', Paper presented at the 11th Annual Conference of Asian Studies in Israel 2012 (May 23), Tel Aviv University.

Lamotte, Étienne. *Histoire du Bouddhisme Indien* (Bibliothèque du Muséon Vol. 43). Louvain: Publ. Universitaires, 1958.

———. *History of Indian Buddhism: From the Origins to the Śaka Era*. Translated by Sara Webb-Boin. Louvain-la-Neuve: Publications De L'institut Orientaliste de Louvain, 1988.

Larson, Gerald J. 'The Trimūrti of Smṛti in Classical Indian Thought', *Philosophy East and West* 43, no. 3 (1993): 373–388.

La Vallée Poussin, Louis de. *The Way to Nirvāṇa: Six Lectures on Ancient Buddhism as a Discipline of Salvation*. Cambridge: The Hibbert Lectures, 1916.

———. 'Le Bouddhisme et le Yoga de Patañjali', *Mélanges Chinois et Bouddhiques* 5 (1936/7): 223–242.

Lindtner, Christian. 'From Brahmanism to Buddhism', *Asian Philosophy: An International Journal of the Philosophical Traditions of the East* 9, no. 1 (March, 1999): 5–37.

Macdonell, Arthur. *A History of Sanskrit Literature*, 2nd Indian edition. Delhi: Motilal Banarsidass, 1971.

Mahaniranonda, Achaan Naeb Achaan. *Vipassana Bhavana (Theory, Practice & Result)*. Chonburi, Thailand: Boonkanjanaram Meditation Center, 1988.

Mahāsi, Sayadaw. *Manual of Insight* (Translated and Edited by the Vipassanā Mettā Foundation Translation Committee). Somerville, MA: Wisdom Publications, 2016.

Matara, Sri Ñāṇārāma. *The Seven Stages of Purification & Insight Knowledge*. Kandy: Buddhist Publication Society, 1993.

McKenzie, Steven L. and Stephen R. Haynes (eds.). *To Each Its Own Meaning: An Introduction to Biblical Criticisms and Their Application*. Louisville: Westminster/John Knox Press, 1999.

Meyer, Karin. 'The Pleasant Way: The *Dhyāna*-s, Insight and the Path According to the *Abhidharmakośa*', Paper from the 2nd International Association of Buddhist Universities Conference: Session on Buddhist Philosophy and Meditation Practices. Retrieved April 15, 2012 from http://www.undv.org/vesak2012/iabudoc/20Karin_MeyersFINAL.pdf

Minh Chau, Thich. *The Chinese Madhyama Āgama and the Pāli Majjhima Nikāya: A Comparative Study*. Delhi: Motilala Banarasidass, 1991.

Ñāṇananda, Bhikkhu. *Concept and Reality in Early Buddhist Thought*. Kandy: Buddhist Publication Society, 1971.

Norman, K.R. 'The Languages of Early Buddhism'. In *Premier colloque Étienne Lamotte*, edited by Publications de l'Institut orientaliste de Louvain 42, 83–99. Louvain-la-Neuve: Publications de l'institut Orientaliste de Louvain, 1993.

Nyanatiloka. *Buddhist Dictionary: Manuel of Buddhist Terms and Doctrine*. Kandy: Buddhist Publication Society, 1980.

Olendzki, Andrew. 'The Construction of Mindfulness', *Contemporary Buddhism* 12, no. 1 (2011): 55–70.

Olivelle, Patrick. *Saṃyāsa Upaniṣads: Hindu Scriptures on Asceticism and Renunciation*. Translated and with an introduction by P. Olivelle. New York: Oxford University Press, 1992.

———. *The Āśrama System: The History and Hermeneutics of a Religious Instituation*. Oxford: Oxford University Press, 1993.

Pagis, Michal. "Cultivating Selves: Vipassanā Meditation and the Microsociology of Experience". PhD diss., University of Chicago, 2008.

Pande, Govind Chandra. *Studies in the Origins of Buddhism*. Allahabad: Department of Ancient History Culture and Archaeology University of Allahabad; Reprint, Delhi: Motilal Banarsidass, [1957]1999.

Peirce, Charles Sanders. *Collected Papers of Charles Sanders Peirce* (Vols. I & II), edited by Charles Hartshorne and Paul Weiss. Cambridge, MA: The Belknap Press of Harvard University Press, 1965.

Pratap, Chandra. 'Was Early Buddhism Influenced by the Upaniṣads?', *Philosophy East and West* 21, no. 3 (1971): 317–325.

Premasiri, P.D. 'The Ultimate Goal of Early Buddhism and the Distinctive Characteristic of Buddhist Meditation'. In *Approaching the Dhamma: Buddhist Texts and Practices in South and Southeast Asia*, edited by Anne M. Blackburn and Jeffrey Samuels, 153–166. Seattle: BPS Priyatti Editions, 2003.

Puri, B.N. *India in the Time of Patañjali*. Delhi: Munshiram Manoharlal Publishers Pvt. Ltd., 1990.

Radhakrishnan Sarvepalli and Moore Charles A. editors, *A Sourcebook in Indian Philosophy*. Princeton, New Jersey: Princeton University Press, 1973.

Rahula, Walpola. *History of Buddhism in Ceylon*. Colombo: M.D. Gunasena & Co. LTD, [1956]1966.

———. *What the Buddha Taught*. London: Gordon Fraser, 1978.

Ray, Reginald A. *Buddhist Saints in India*. New York and Oxford: Oxford University Press, 1994.

Ronkin, Noa. *Early Buddhist Metaphyscis: The Making of a Philosophical Tradition*. London and New York: RoutledgeCurzon, 2005.

Ruegg, D.S. and L. Schmithausen (eds.). *Earliest Buddhism and Madhyamaka*. Leiden: E.J. Brill, 1990.

Sarbacker, Stuart R. *Samādhi: The Numinous and the Cessative in Indo-Tibetan Yoga*. Albany: State University of New York Press, 2005.

Sayadaw, Pa-Auk Tawya. *Knowing and Seeing: Talks and Questions-and-Answers at a Meditation Retreat in Taiwan*, Revised edition. Kuala Lumpur, Malaysia: WAVE Publications, 2003.

Sayalay, Susīlā. *Unravelling the Mysteries of Mind and Body through Abhidamma*. Malaysia: Inward Path Publisher, 2005.

Schmithausen, L. 'On Some Aspects of Descriptions or Theories of "Liberating Insight" and Enlightenment in Early Buddhism'. In *Studien zum Jainismus und Buddhismus (Gedenkschrift für Ludwig Alsdorf)*, herausgegeben von K. Bruhn und A. Wezler, 199–250. Wiesbaden: Franz Steiner, 1981.

Schober, Juliane and Steven Collins. 'The Theravāda Civilizations Project: Future Directions in the Study of Buddhism in Southeast Asia', *Contemporary Buddhism: An Interdisciplinary Journal* 13, no. 1 (2012): 157–166.

Shravaski, Dhammika. *The Broken Buddha: Critical Reflections on Theravada and a Plea for a New Buddhism*, 2001. Retrieved from http://www.buddhistische-gesellschaft-berlin.de/downloads/brokenbuddhanew.pdf

Shulman, Eviatar. 'Mindful Wisdom: The Sati-paṭṭhāna-sutta on Mindfulness, Memory and Liberation', *History of Religions* 49, no. 4 (2010): 393–420.

Silk, Jonathan A. 'What If Anything, Is Mahāyāna Buddhism, Problems of Definitions and Classifications', *Numen* 49, no. 4 (2002): 356–405.

Skilling, Peter. 'Theravāda in History', *Pacific World: Journal of the Institute of Buddhist Studies*, Third Series, no. 11 (Fall, 2009): 61–93.

Snyder, Stephen and Tina Rasmussen. *Practicing the Jhānas: Traditional Concentration Meditation as Presented by the Venerable Pa Auk Sayadaw*. Boston and London: Shambhala, 2009.

Solé-Leris, Amadeo. *Tranquillity and Insight: An Introduction to the Oldest Form of Buddhist Meditation*. Sri Lanka: Buddhist Publication Society, 1999.

Somaratne, G.A. 'Intermediate Existence and the Higher Fetters in the Pāli Nikāyas', *Journal of the Pali Text Society* 25 (1999): 121–154.

Southwold, Martin. *Buddhism in Life: The Anthropological Study of Religion and the Sinhalese Practice of Buddhism*. Manchester: Manchester University Press, 1984.

Staal, Frits. *Exploring Mysticism*. Berkeley: University of California Press, 1975.

———. *Discovering the Vedas: Origins, Mantras, Rituals, Insights*. New Delhi: Penguin Books India, 2008.

Stuart, Daniel Malinowski. 'Thinking about Cessation: A Reading of the *Pṛṣṭhapālasūtra* of the (Mūla-) Sarvāstivādin Dīrghāgama'. In *Wiener Studien Zur Tibetologie Und Buddhismuskunde*. Wien: Arbeitskreis für Tibetische und Buddhistische Studien, Universität Wien, 2008.

———. *Thinking about Cessation: The Pṛṣṭhapālasūtra of the Dīrghāgama in Context*. Wien: Arbeitskreis für Tibetische und Buddhistische Studien, Universität (HEFT 79), 2013.

Stuart-Fox, Martin. 'Jhāna and Buddhist Scholasticism', *The Journal of the International Association of Buddhist Studies* 12, no. 2 (1989): 79–110.

Sujato, Bhikku. *A History of Mindfulness*, 2005. Retrieved from http://santifm.org/santipada/wp-content/uploads/2012/08/A_History_of_Mindfulness_Bhikkhu_Sujato.pdf

Tan, Piya. *Kīṭāgiri Sutta: The Discourse at Kīṭāgiri*, 2005. Retrieved from http://dharmafarer.org/wordpress/wp-content/uploads/2009/12/11.1-Kitagiri-S-m70-piya.pdf

Thanissaro, Bhikkhu. *One Tool among Many: The Place of Vipassanā in Buddhist Practice*, 1997. Retrieved from http://www.accesstoinsight.org/lib/authors/thanissaro/onetool.html

Thapar, Romila. 'Asoka and Buddhism', *Past and Present* 18 (1960): 43–51.

Tieken, Herman. 'Aśoka and the Buddhist "Saṃgha": A Study of Aśoka's Schism Edict and Minor Rock Edict I', *Bulletin of the School of Oriental and African Studies, University of London* 63, no. 1 (2000): 1–30.

U Pandita, Sayadaw. *In This Very Life: The Liberation Teachings of the Buddha*. Boston: Wisdom Publications, 1991.

Vetter, Tilmann. *The Ideas and Meditative Practices of Early Buddhism*. Leiden: E.J. Brill, 1988.

Warnke, Georgia. *Gadamer: Hermeneutics, Tradition, and Reason (Key Contemporary Thinkers)*. Stanford: Stanford University Press, 1987.

Werner, Karel. 'Religious Practice and Yoga in the Vedas, Upaniṣads and Early Buddhism', *Annals of the Bhandarkar Oriental Research Institute* LVI (1975): 179–194.

Whicher, Ian. 'Yoga and Freedom: A Reconsideration of Patañjali's Classical Yoga', *Philosophy East and West* 48, no. 2 (1998): 272–322.

Williams, Paul with Anthony Tribe. *Buddhist Thought*. London: Routledge, 2000.

Winternitz, Maurice. *History of Indian Literature* (Vol. 1). Delhi: Motilal Banarsidass, 1981.

Wynne, Alexander. *How Old Is the Suttapiṭaka? The Relative Value of Textual and Epigraphical Sources for the Study of Early Indian Buddhism*. St John's College, 2003. Retrieved from http://www.scribd.com/doc/106702425/Wynne-Alex-How-Old-is-the-Suttapitaka

———. *The Origin of Buddhist Meditation*. London and New York: Routledge (Taylor and Francis e-Library), 2007.

———. 'The Ātman and Its Negation: A Conceptual and Chronological Analysis of Early Buddhist Thought', *Journal of the International Association of Buddhist Studies* 33, no. 1–2 (2010–2011): 103–171.

Zysk, Kenneth G. 'The Science of Respiration and the Doctrine of the Bodily Winds in Ancient India', *Journal of the American Oriental Society* 113, no. 2 (1993): 198–213.

Index

48049666R00131

Made in the USA
Lexington, KY
14 August 2019